NOTABLE MEN AND WOMEN
OF SPANISH TEXAS

NOTABLE MEN AND WOMEN OF SPANISH TEXAS

~

DONALD E. CHIPMAN
AND HARRIETT DENISE JOSEPH

UNIVERSITY OF TEXAS PRESS
AUSTIN

A portion of this work appeared previously, in different form, as
"Alonso de Leon: Pathfinder in East Texas, 1686–1690," in
East Texas Historical Journal Vol. XXXIII (Spring 1995), pp. 3–17.

First edition, 1999

Requests for permission to reproduce material from this work should be sent to
Permissions, University of Texas Press, P.O. Box 7819, Austin, TX 78713-7819.

⊗ The paper used in this publication meets the minimum requirements of
American National Standard for Information Sciences—Permanence of Paper
for Printed Library Materials, ANSI Z39.48-1984.

Portions of chapter 2 were published previously in the *East Texas Historical Journal* 33
(Spring 1995): 3–17. Reprinted with the permission of the East Texas
Historical Association.

Library of Congress Cataloging-in-Publication Data
Chipman, Donald E.
    Notable men and women of Spanish Texas / Donald E. Chipman and Harriett
Denise Joseph. — 1st ed.
        p.   cm.
    Includes bibliographical references and index.
    ISBN 0-292-71217-0 (cloth : alk. paper). — ISBN 0-292-71218-9 (pbk. : alk. paper)
    1. Texas—Biography.   2. Spaniards—Texas—Biography.   I. Joseph, Harriett
Denise.   II. Title.
CT262.C48   2000
920.0764—dc21   99-19906

For Hillary, Nicole, Alexa, and Lane

CONTENTS

CONTENTS

PREFACE

Had the authors chosen to give *Notable Men and Women of Spanish Texas* a subtitle, it might have been "Biographical Sketches from Near Saints to a Near-Total Sinner." María de Agreda, the legendary "Lady in Blue," and Antonio Margil, renowned Franciscan missionary, have both been designated "Venerable," or worthy of sainthood; and by his actions in early life, Felipe de Rábago earned the second descriptive appellation. As for the title itself, we discussed whether the appropriate preposition should be "of" or "in." We finally resolved the matter by recognizing that we could not prove that María de Agreda ever was *in* Texas.

Our own experience, and that of many others, suggests that only a few readers peruse a preface. But for those who have been diligent enough to read this far and who have the will to continue, we would like to explain why we chose the personalities included in the twelve chapters.

By name alone, Cabeza de Vaca (Cow's Head) evokes interest among today's schoolchildren and adults. But more than half a millennium after his birth, Alvar Núñez Cabeza de Vaca remains the object of scholarly investigation—ranging from speculations that his shamanic powers as a healer among sixteenth-century Native Americans spawned the *curandero* phenomenon in Latino culture to route interpretations of his peregrinations on two American continents.[1] We chose Cabeza de Vaca because his story is inherently interesting and because it demonstrates his essential humanity. Arriving in the New World as an arrogant conquistador, Cabeza de Vaca, himself mistreated as a slave by Indians and forced by his own admission to travel "naked as the day I was born," profoundly altered his view of Native Americans. By ultimately recognizing that "All Mankind Is One," he foreshadowed the great Dominican Protector of Indians, Bartolomé de las Casas.[2]

Alonso de León (the younger) was a pathfinder without peer in late seventeenth-century Texas. The product of a distinguished family in Nuevo León and advantaged by formal education in Spain, León rose to the rank of general and achieved the governorship of his birth province, as well as Coahuila. In leading four overland expeditions in search of René Robert Cavelier, Sieur de La Salle's colony and a fifth to establish the first Spanish mission in East Texas, he wore out his body in the service of his monarch. At the same time, León's penchant for submitting unvarnished but truthful reports to his superiors in Mexico City irritated and provoked those high officials. Those circumstances contributed to his demotion and death at age fifty.

Father Francisco Hidalgo and Louis Juchereau de St. Denis, fueled by differing passions and objectives, interacted in a manner that brought about the permanent Spanish occupation of Texas in 1716, a presence that lasted for 105 years. The interplay of a single-minded Franciscan missionary and a devious French cavalier-entrepreneur profoundly changed the course of history in both colonial Texas and Louisiana.

Father Antonio Margil de Jesús is more famous in Mexico than in the United States, and with good reason. Margil performed signal services for his faith in Central America and New Spain proper before entering Texas late in life. Because of his fame and candidacy for beatification and sainthood, Margil's life has been examined by a number of biographers and admirers. In this instance, we were able to present an essentially "cradle to grave" biographical portrait. His alleged miracles, some of which were performed on Texas soil, and his role as founder of Texas' most beautiful and successful mission, San José in San Antonio, make his story inspiring.

The Marqués de San Miguel de Aguayo, using part of his wife's vast fortune and drawing upon his own considerable energies, ensured a continuing Spanish presence in East Texas after it was abandoned during the Chicken War of 1719. Also among his significant accomplishments was initiating Texas' first big "cattle drive" in the 1720s. Much of his work unraveled in the late 1720s under the aegis of Pedro de Rivera, charged with implementing peso-pinching retrenchment as Spain and France moved toward cementing the Bourbon Family Compact.[3]

Felipe de Rábago y Terán, the near-total sinner, brings the spice of rakish behavior and suspicion of murder to our narrative. But events unfolding in Central Texas at mid-eighteenth century also shed light on the essentially unavoidable conflict that arose between soldiers, separated from their wives and families and stationed on a distant frontier, and missionaries, pledged to extirpate vice and protect the virtue of Indian women. Late in life, however, Rábago attempted redemption of character and sought expiation of sin with some success.

José de Escandón y Elguera ranks among the most remarkable colonizers in Spanish North America. Like Margil, he is more famous in Mexico than in most of Texas, primarily because the great majority of the twenty-three towns and fifteen missions founded by him and his associates were situated south of the Río Grande. But Escandón is also a hero in extreme South Texas. Residents from Laredo to Brownsville properly regard him as the pioneer founder of farming and ranching enterprises along both sides of the lower Río Grande.

Athanase de Mézières was a transitional person between French/Spanish Louisiana and Spanish Texas. Married briefly to a daughter of St. Denis and Manuela Sánchez, this successful Natchitoches officer and landowner became the chief agent of Spanish Indian policy from the late 1760s to the late 1770s. Initially under suspicion as a facile adherent of His Majesty Charles III of Spain, De Mézières soon allayed Spanish distrust and ultimately received appointment as chief executive of Texas—a position that because of ill health and depleted personal finances he never assumed.

The Marqués de Rubí authored sweeping recommendations, which, with the weight of royal mandate behind them, led to profound changes along the northern frontier of New Spain in the early 1770s. Among those modifications were Spain's temporary withdrawal from East Texas and the permanent designation of San Antonio as the official capital. Antonio Gil Ibarvo, through skillful supplication and Machiavellian strategy, countermanded Rubí's influence on viceroy and king, founded modern Nacogdoches, and earned the title "Father of East Texas."

We selected Domingo Cabello y Robles as a notable administrator because of his long tenure as governor (1778–1786), years that overlapped Spain's participation in the American Revolution. Spanish involvement in the war reoriented Texas' cattle industry and brought calumny on the governor; it also tied Cabello's hands with regard to Indian policy and left him chained to an office that he hated from day one. But, importantly, a study of Cabello's administration provides valuable insight into the social and economic life that was San Antonio in the late eighteenth century.

Bernardo Gutiérrez de Lara satisfied our desire to recount the activities of a prominent insurrectionist during the turbulent first two decades of the 1800s. He, more than anyone else, carried Father Miguel Hidalgo's "Grito de Dolores" of September 16, 1810, into the northern reaches of New Spain. Gutiérrez's activities brought down the wrath of

Spain on Texas, and the scythe of vengeance fell into the willing hands of Joaquín de Arredondo. This commandant general of Spain's Eastern Interior Provinces, which included Texas, turned the future Lone Star State into a pathetic wasteland by 1821, paving the way to independence from Spain and assimilation into the new Mexican nation.

Our final chapter, "Colonial Women," presented the most difficult challenge. Aside from such high-profile personalities as María de Agreda, Manuela Sánchez, and Jane Long, hundreds of women in colonial Texas have remained historically "faceless." We know they bore children, washed and mended clothes, swept chapels, and helped their husbands. But this is hardly the stuff of a chapter-length study—not to mention that dwelling on the obvious would constitute nothing less than a gross misrepresentation of women's many contributions. By examining lawsuits, estate settlements, wills, petitions, and other legal instruments, we were able to give names—and faces—to more of these women. We also gained insight into the daily circumstances, privileges, and obligations of colonial Latinas in general. Even illiterate women in colonial Texas demonstrated an "osmotic" sense of Castilian law, a knowledge passed down from grandmother to mother to daughter. And the law granted all women, including those of Indian and mixed ancestry, privileges and rights that were absolutely alien to their gender in contemporaneous Anglo America. That same law, however, made it incumbent on women to conduct themselves responsibly or face serious consequences.

A preface also seems a good place to expound briefly on the pitfalls and benefits of a biographical approach to Spanish colonial personalities. At the considerable risk of alluding to "national character," we believe it accurate to say that Spaniards, as opposed to Anglo Americans, are more inclined to be fatalistic than introspective. Accordingly, Spaniards did not keep personal diaries in which they agonized over matters of conscience, they seldom expressed doubts about their importance as individuals, and they did not often lose sleep over the propriety of their actions.[4]

A biographer is especially at a loss when seeking information on the youth of Hispanic personages. The late Professor France V. Scholes, Chipman's mentor at the University of New Mexico, spent the better part of his adult life studying Fernando Cortés, yet admitted that he could say everything he knew about the Conqueror's early life in two or three pages. Indeed, it was a rare Spaniard of the sixteenth century who even knew his precise age. When deposing in lawsuits, witnesses would typically give their age as "about thirty-five," or "about forty." On other occasions, Spaniards would state a specific year as their age, but usually followed that declaration with the words: *"poco más o menos."* Even in the seventeenth and eighteenth centuries, Franciscans who were experienced historians, notably Father Isidro Félix de Espinosa, failed to say anything of consequence about the birth and youth of his personal friend Francisco Hidalgo. The researcher is thrilled if he or she can find a Spaniard's document of merits and services, and one is ecstatic upon uncovering a will.

Historian and biographer Milton Lomask reminds us that biography essentially falls into three categories. There is narrative biography, using the birth-to-death approach, which we employed with Father Margil; there is topical biography, approaching Cabeza de Vaca as historian, as ethnographer, as geographer, which we did not attempt; and there is the "and" biography, such as looking at Athanase de Mézières *and* Texas, which we chose to do.[5] For the most part, we used the third approach. This permitted us to span almost three centuries of early Texas history.

Covering a broad expanse of time with the lives of notable individuals gave us the opportunity "to humanize history, to make us realize that the past was shaped by individuals with the same strengths and weaknesses that we recognize in ourselves and our leaders today."[6] Placed in the most simple terms, by using the biographical approach we hoped to convince the reader that these people once walked the land and breathed the air that was Texas.

Finally, a word about preparing this book: We shared the research equally but were determined that readers not be forced to guess which one of us composed this or that chapter. For better or worse, the writing style is Chipman's, with substantial (and generally appreciated) editorial suggestions from Joseph. We have tried to the best of our abilities to make the chapters readable. Each begins with a dramatic incident that is later threaded into the narrative. The reader will note, we hope, that the text is fully documented, with scholarly accoutrement contained in extensive endnotes.

Donald E. Chipman
Denton, Texas

Harriett Denise Joseph
Brownsville, Texas

ACKNOWLEDGMENTS

Seven years ago we recorded the first notes relating to this manuscript. From day one, our debt to friends, colleagues, librarians, archivists, university administrators, and fellow historians has mounted. In acknowledging the assistance of those good people, our greatest concern is that we may inadvertently omit someone's name. Should that happen, we apologize in advance for our failed memories.

Our institutions, the University of North Texas (UNT) and the University of Texas at Brownsville (UTB), are at opposite ends of the state, separated by 560 miles. But at both schools individuals have contributed substantially to this publication. At UNT, our friend Randolph B. "Mike" Campbell, who for many years has successfully taught a two-semester course titled "Representative American Leaders," encouraged us to use the biographical approach to breathe life into notable men and women of colonial Texas. Mike's support and advice have helped enormously. A Faculty Research Grant at UNT greatly aided in the preparation of maps and illustrations to accompany the text. At UTB, Research Enhancement Grants (1995, 1996) provided funds for travel and duplication of archival materials. On the Brownsville campus, we especially wish to thank Dean Anthony Zavaleta of the College of Liberal Arts; Robert H. Angell, former chair of the Department of Social Sciences; Philip Kendall, vice president for academic affairs; and Ms. Yolanda González in the Hunter Room of the Arnulfo Oliveira Library.

Three off-campus individuals deserve special consideration for their assistance. Robert S. Weddle of Bonham, Texas, read the entire manuscript before it was submitted to the University of Texas Press. We profited greatly from Bob's "eagle eye." Additionally, Jack Jackson of Austin and Oakah L. Jones Jr. of Albuquerque, manuscript critics for UT Press,

improved the accuracy of the text and offered other valuable sugges-
tions. The following people provided special assistance at various times:
Ralph Elder and his staff at the Barker Texas History Center/Center for
American History in Austin; Kinga Perzynska, archivist at the Catholic
Archives of Texas; Tina Mecham, doctoral student in history at the Uni-
versity of Texas at Austin; Frances E. Abernethy of Stephen F. Austin
State University; Patricia R. Lemée of Austin; F. Todd Smith at UNT;
Betje Klier of Palo Alto, California; Rosalind Z. Rock, park historian at
San Antonio Missions National Historical Park; Anne A. Fox at the Cen-
ter for Archaeological Research, the University of Texas at San Antonio;
Donny L. Hamilton and Helen Dewolf at the Texas A&M University
Conservation Research Lab; Luis López Elizondo, an independent researcher in Múzquiz, Coahuila; Father Barnabas Diekemper, O.F.M., of
Saint Peter's Friary in Chicago; Richard Golden, chair of the UNT Department of History; and Betty Burch, administrative assistant in the
UNT Department of History. We would also like to acknowledge the encouragement of fellow scholars at informal meetings of Spanish Border-
landers, held in conjunction with annual meetings of the Texas State Historical Association.

At the University of Texas Press, we owe a debt of gratitude to the in-
comparable Theresa J. May, assistant director and editor-in-chief, for
her good cheer and constant encouragement. Thanks also to Jan Mc-
Inroy, our copyeditor at the press, and Mandy Woods, manuscript edi-
tor at the press.

Assuredly, those individuals mentioned above have helped make this
a better book, but they should not shoulder any blame for the final product. All omissions, weaknesses, and errors are our responsibility.

ONE

ALVAR NÚÑEZ CABEZA DE VACA

Ragged Castaway

On a bitterly cold morning in November 1528, a small, crudely built boat containing several dozen Spaniards approached the Texas coast near Galveston Island. The men, having departed from northwest Florida some forty days earlier, were weakened by hunger and pounded by the sea. During the previous night, they had begun to pass out and fall one on top of the other in the bottom of the craft until fewer than five remained upright. Two of the strongest, the sailing master and Alvar Núñez Cabeza de Vaca, had accepted the task of steering the boat. At about midnight, Cabeza de Vaca was relieved at the tiller and tried to rest but could not, for in his words "sleep was the furthest thing from my mind." Near dawn the roar of breakers alerted don Alvar and apprised him that land was nearby. Not wishing to come ashore in darkness, Cabeza de Vaca seized an oar and rowed along the coast for a short distance. He then set the bow of the boat toward the shore and awaited landfall. As the craft approached the coast, a great wave caught it and lifted it "out of the water as far as a horseshoe can be tossed." The resulting jolt aroused some of the men "who were almost dead." They and the more healthy ones scrambled overboard and crawled though the surf to the beach. Under such dire circumstances, Cabeza de Vaca, the first European of historic importance to set foot in Texas, reached the soil of the future Lone Star State.[1]

Over the next eight years, Cabeza de Vaca experienced hardships and misfortunes that would have defeated a lesser man. He not only survived incredible odysseys in Texas and Mexico, which he later recorded in his *Relación* (account), but he also entered the annals of colonial Texas as its first merchant, geographer, historian, ethnologist, and physician-surgeon. Additionally, he experienced remarkable personal growth and came to accept Indians on their own terms. In the first book published on portions of the future United States of America, Cabeza de Vaca shaped our earliest impressions of the land that became Texas, and his continuing influence may still be seen in the contemporary Lone Star State, where he reigns as the "patron saint" of the Texas Surgical Society.

Born around 1490 in the small Andalusian town of Jerez de la Frontera, Cabeza de Vaca was the fourth son of alderman Francisco de Vera and Teresa Cabeza de Vaca. Spaniards of that day and age had considerable latitude in naming their offspring. Typically, the choice of surname was patronymic but not infrequently matronymic. For example, Nuño Beltrán de Guzmán, an early administrator and conquistador in Mexico who figures importantly in the story of Cabeza de Vaca, was the full brother of a Spanish diplomat named Gómez Suárez de Figueroa. Similarly, Spaniards at adulthood could select a surname to honor either their mother or their father or both.[2]

Cabeza de Vaca preferred and consistently used the more prestigious maiden name of his mother.[3] During the Spanish Reconquest (ca. 720–1492), Martín Alhaja, a shepherd and distant ancestor of doña Teresa, was credited with helping secure victory for Christian forces at the historic battle of Las Navas de Tolosa in 1212. Alhaja marked a little-known and unguarded pass in the Sierra Morena with the skull of a cow. Using this pass to mount a surprise attack on Muslim forces, King Sancho of Navarre, the Spanish commander, was victorious; and in gratitude he bestowed the name "Cow's Head" on Cabeza de Vaca's matrilineal progenitors.[4]

After spending his youth in a town now famous for its excellent sherry, Cabeza de Vaca entered military service and was sent to Italy. There on April 11, 1512, he fought in the battle of Ravenna. Although the engagement was won by the French, Cabeza de Vaca was promoted to the rank of *alférez* (ensign) for bravery on the battlefield. Back in Spain by 1513, the young soldier served as an aide to the powerful Duke of Medina Sidonia. And he later fought in behalf of King Charles I, soon to be Emperor Charles V, whose authority in Spain had been unsuccessfully challenged in the revolt of the Comuneros (May 1520–April 1521).[5]

Cabeza de Vaca's alignment with factions that remained loyal to Charles no doubt stood him in good stead with the young monarch. Like many royal appointments in the 1520s and 1530s, don Alvar's selection on February 15, 1527, as royal treasurer to the Pánfilo de Narváez expedition may very well have been linked to his record during the Comunero movement.[6]

When selected for service in the Spanish Indies, Cabeza de Vaca was approaching the age of forty. As an intelligent and keenly observant man blessed with an excellent memory, he had learned to read and write, become conversant with passages from the Bible, and familiarized himself with major historical events. He had also acquired a considerable load of "intellectual baggage," which accompanied all Spaniards who emigrated to the Indies.

After the Conquest of Mexico, completed just half a dozen years prior to Cabeza de Vaca's appointment, Bernal Díaz del Castillo commented on why he had accompanied Fernando Cortés in that venture. With remarkable candor, the great chronicler of New Spain remarked that he came to serve God and the king, and also to get rich. This combination of religiosity and ambition was high-octane fuel that drove many Spaniards to risk life and limb as they sought to carve out careers in a New World that offered far more opportunities than did Old Spain.[7]

Spaniards also had wild notions of what they might find in the Americas. In a real sense, they viewed lands across the Atlantic "through medieval spectacles." The great Saint Augustine of Hippo had devoted an entire chapter of *The City of God* to the question of whether descendants of Adam and Noah had produced monstrous and bizarre offspring. Even the most unsophisticated conquistador had seen the facades of medieval churches that sprouted griffins, gargoyles, and a mixture of man and beast. Consequently, for many decades after the Columbian voyages, Spaniards, upon entering unexplored lands, expected to find giants, dwarfs, Amazon women, white-haired boys, human beings with tails, headless folk with an eye in their navel, and trumpet-blowing apes.[8]

Then, as now, literate men such as Cabeza de Vaca often read novels for entertainment, but in the case of Spaniards there was a thin line between fantasy and credulity. The most popular novel of the early sixteenth century was *Amadis of Gaul*. Indeed, *Amadis* was so popular that, like today, it called for a sequel under the title of *Las Sergas de Esplandián* (*The Deeds of Esplandián*). In that work one of the central characters is the queen of the Amazons, named Calafia, who lived on a fabulously rich island called California. So the Golden State owes its name to an early Spanish novel. Later, such legendary figures as Queen Calafia beckoned Spaniards into unknown realms, including Texas. Explorers and conquistadors would look for the Seven Cities of Cíbola, Gran Quivira, the Pearls of the Jumanos, and the Great Kingdom of the Tejas.[9]

Most Spaniards were also imbued with a sense of Christian superiority and a firm conviction that it was their solemn obligation to spread the faith and convert the pagan. With no small amount of pride and arrogance, Cabeza de Vaca, as second in command of a major expedition, would experience a crucible forged in the American wilderness. Over time he shed much of his European frame of reference, especially with regard to Native Americans. For Cabeza de Vaca that transformation was permanent, and it created no end of troubles for him when he returned to the world of Spaniards, which had remained largely unchanged.[10]

With his appointment as royal treasurer in hand and experiences formed solely in Spain and Italy, Cabeza de Vaca entered the service of Pánfilo de Narváez, a red-bearded and one-eyed captain who had been maimed in the conquest of New Spain. Narváez, in command of a sizable army outfitted by Governor Diego de Velázquez of Cuba, had landed on the Mexican coast in early 1520. Don Pánfilo was specifically ordered to pursue and arrest Fernando Cortés, then in control of the Aztec capital, and to bring the Mexican venture under the direction of Governor Velázquez. From San Juan de Ulúa (present-day Veracruz), Narváez marched a short distance to the Indian town of Cempoalla, where he headquartered his army. Because he held a numerical supremacy of four or five to one over Cortés's divided army, about half of which had remained in Tenochtitlán, Narváez ignored all overtures from the Conqueror. But in a brief skirmish, Cortés scored a dramatic victory over his challenger, and in the melee, Narváez took a pike thrust in the face that plucked out his right eye.[11]

Cortés imprisoned Narváez at Villa Rica de la Veracruz, his base of operations throughout the Conquest of Mexico. After being released by Cortés in 1523, don Pánfilo returned to Spain seeking redress from the king for his injury. In 1526 Charles finally awarded a patent to the unfortunate casualty of Cempoalla. Narváez could settle "Florida," which at that time included the peninsula that had claimed the life of Juan Ponce de León in the early 1520s and the entire Gulf Coast region lying between Florida proper and the Pánuco River north of Veracruz.[12]

To carry out the terms of his patent, Narváez assembled five vessels and approximately six hundred men. With Cabeza de Vaca as second in command, the flotilla cleared San Lúcar de Barrameda, the port at the mouth of the Guadalquivir River, on June 17, 1527. The Atlantic crossing to Santo Domingo was uneventful, and upon arrival Narváez remained in port for about forty-five days. During that interval he acquired additional supplies and horses but lost 140 men to desertion.

From Santo Domingo, Narváez sailed to Cuba and arrived there in the early autumn.[13]

Shortly after reaching the port of Santiago, Cabeza de Vaca was sent with two ships to another part of the island to acquire provisions. With the vessels anchored offshore, don Alvar traveled on horseback to a nearby town to arrange for the transfer of merchandise. But even as he left the ships, the weather had begun to turn foul with "swirling winds and . . . heavy rainfall." Upon reaching the settlement, as Cabeza de Vaca noted, "the rain and the storm began to increase so much that it was just as strong in the town as on the sea, for all the houses and churches were blown down, and it became necessary for us to go about in groups of seven or eight men locking our arms together so that we could keep the wind from blowing us away."[14]

After a terrible night in which Cabeza de Vaca and a few companions dared not stay near houses or trees for fear of being crushed beneath them, don Alvar surveyed the damage at first light. The hurricane had passed but left utter devastation in its wake. Both of the ships at anchor had been destroyed, with losses placed by Cabeza de Vaca at sixty Spaniards and twenty horses. One of the ship's boats was found in trees nearly a mile from the coast. In don Alvar's words, "It was pitiful to see the condition the land was left in, with fallen trees, the woods stripped bare, all without leaves or grass."[15]

Narváez used the winter months to re-outfit his expedition, and in April 1528 five ships carried about four hundred men to a bay, perhaps Sarasota, on the west coast of Florida. Shortly after reconnoitering the land, Narváez, despite the vigorous protests of Cabeza de Vaca, decided to take about three hundred men from the ships and go farther inland. At that time, Spanish perceptions of Gulf Coast geography were so faulty that Narváez believed the River of Palms (Río Soto la Marina) to be only a short distance away—but the actual distance via the coast was more than fifteen hundred miles.[16]

Within a matter of hours, the expedition was hopelessly separated from its support vessels and stranded on the Florida coast. By mid-June it had traveled up the inner coast and arrived in northwestern Florida, where it encamped for approximately three months. But food shortages and increasingly hostile Indians convinced the Spaniards that they must exit Florida by sea. Lacking boats, Narváez and his men were forced to improvise. Although Anglo Americans have long prided themselves on possessing a talent for improvisation—sometimes called Yankee ingenuity—Spaniards stranded in the wilderness also coped admirably.

On this occasion, they slaughtered their horses and lived on the meat; they jury-rigged bellows of deerskin and hollow logs to melt metal from stirrups and bridle bits, which they then cast into saws and axes; they flayed and tanned skin from the legs of horses and fashioned it into fresh water bags. Finally, they constructed five boats of rough-sawn planks that were caulked with pine resins and palmetto fibers; they used their shirts and trousers for sails; and they wove hair from the tails and manes of horses into rigging.[17]

Five boats bearing slightly fewer than 250 men set out for the River of Palms on September 22, 1528. The first month at sea went well. But as the small flotilla approached the mouth of the Mississippi River, troubles began. On the thirty-first day, a storm struck and tossed the boats about like driftwood. Several days after passing the mouth of the great river, the situation became desperate. The Spaniards had run out of fresh water, because, in the words of Cabeza de Vaca, "the skins we made from the horses' legs rotted and became useless."[18]

After the first storm had abated, some fresh water was acquired from a stream entering the Gulf; however, a second disturbance began with a strong north wind blowing offshore. It carried the five boats well out to sea, and after two days "each boat had lost sight of the others." On the evening of the third day, the boat carrying Cabeza de Vaca spotted two of the other craft. One of them contained Narváez, and as Cabeza de Vaca's vessel neared, he asked the governor "to throw me a line so I could follow him, but he answered that it would be enough of a struggle for them to reach shore that night themselves." Don Alvar asked what he should do, since it was impossible for him to keep up and carry out the governor's orders. Narváez replied "that it was no longer necessary for any of us to give orders, that each of us should do what seemed best to save his life, since that is what he intended to do."[19]

Rough water whipped up by still another Gulf storm kept the boat carrying Cabeza de Vaca from reaching land for several more days. The voyage ended as described at the outset of this chapter.

Cabeza de Vaca and his companions had landed on an offshore island, which he named Isla de Malhado, or Isle of Misfortune. A second boat containing Andrés Dorantes de Carranza; his African-born slave, Estevanico; Alonso Castillo Maldonado; and perhaps forty-five others had apparently landed on the same island on the previous day. Those named, later known as the Four Ragged Castaways, were the only ones to survive the Texas portion of the Narváez expedition.[20]

Malhado was occupied by Karankawa Indians, who soon appeared near the site of the landing. To Cabeza de Vaca and the other survivors it was an unnerving experience: "We were so scared that they seemed to us to be giants, whether they were or not. . . . We could not even think of defending ourselves, since there were scarcely six men who could even get up from the ground." Fortunately for the Spaniards, the Indians indicated in sign language that they would return in the morning and bring food, for they had none at the time. And the natives were true to their word, providing fish and some edible roots on the following day.[21]

After receiving food and water, Cabeza de Vaca and his crew attempted to relaunch their boat, but their efforts ended in disaster. The craft capsized, drowning three, while the rest of the men were enveloped in waves and cast ashore on the same island. In don Alvar's words, "Those of us who survived were as naked as the day we were born and had lost everything we had." Added to their misery was the cold of early November, which combined with their emaciated state to leave them looking "like the picture of death."[22]

The miserable state of the Spaniards was such that the Indians sat down with them and began to cry, weeping and wailing for more than half an hour. For Cabeza de Vaca, it was a disturbing experience. "Seeing that these crude and untutored people, who were like brutes, grieved so much for us, caused me and the others in my company to suffer more and think more about our misfortune." In short, if the Indians felt sorry for *them*, with their notions of inherent Christian superiority, they were truly in serious trouble.[23]

After joining the survivors of the other boat that landed on Malhado, the Spaniards, certain that after more than a month at sea they were very close to the province of Pánuco, selected four robust men, all good swimmers, and sent them down the coast in the company of an Indian guide. Exposure, hunger, and dysentery had taken their toll of those remaining on Malhado by the spring of 1529, leaving only fourteen or fifteen men alive.[24]

Throughout the winter months, Cabeza de Vaca had become a close observer of the Karankawa Indians, and he later recorded unique ethnographic information about them. He described those Native Americans as tall and well built, with weapons consisting only of bows and arrows. And he credited Karankawas with loving their children more than any other people in the world, for when a child died, parents, relatives, and indeed whole villages would mourn the loss for an entire year. Karankawas also accorded much consideration to everyone except the elderly, whom they regarded as of little use, since they occupied space and consumed food that was needed by children. Cabeza de Vaca also described marriage customs among the Karankawa and the role of in-laws in their society. He wryly commented that these Indians often went hungry, for food and firewood were scarce but mosquitoes were plentiful.[25]

Against his better judgment, Cabeza de Vaca was compelled by the Karankawas to treat their ill. He noted that the Indians "wanted to make us physicians, without testing us or asking for any degrees." "Treatment" consisted of breathing on the patient, making the sign of the cross, and reciting prayers. The fact that these ministrations regularly improved the condition of the sick suggests either the presence of psychoneurotic afflictions among the coastal Karankawas or the salutary benefits of mind over body that can flow from the perception that someone possesses the powers of a great shaman.[26]

During that same first winter, Cabeza de Vaca recorded that five Spaniards had become separated from the larger group and were stranded on the mainland coast in cold and stormy weather. These men, whom he listed by name, became so desperate for food "that they ate one another one by one until there was only one left, who survived because the others were not there to eat him." When the Karankawas learned that those Spaniards had been so disrespectful of their own dead, they threatened to do great harm to the survivors on Malhado. The Karankawas' revulsion to this form of cannibalism stands as a meaningful counterpoint to often repeated but sparsely documented assertions of their appetite for human flesh.[27]

In the late weeks of winter, Cabeza de Vaca crossed over to the mainland, where he became seriously ill. Believing rumors that don Alvar had died, all but two of the survivors decided to travel down the coast toward Mexico. Cabeza de Vaca recovered, although for a variety of reasons he kept Malhado as his home base for nearly four more years. He acknowledged that initially he was unable to follow his companions because of illness, but after his recovery, he was forced to stay with Indians who treated him poorly and worked him hard for more than a year. Don Alvar eventually escaped from captivity and fled to live among other Indians who dwelled farther inland. The new hosts, whom he called the Charruco, treated him well enough, but his primary source of food was roots that grew underwater among canes. In pulling these roots his hands became so sore "that a light brush with a piece of straw would cause them to bleed."[28]

Taking a chance in hopes of finding a better life, Cabeza de Vaca again moved inland, where "he fared a bit better." There he became a merchant and trader, supplying the needs of various Indians groups who themselves could not move from place to place "because of the continuous warfare that goes on." From the coast don Alvar collected seashells and sea snails. The former were especially valued by the inland groups, who lacked tools for cutting mesquite beans. In the interior Cabeza de Vaca collected hides and red ocher, which was used for dye; flints for arrowheads; and canes for the shafts of arrows. He reported that he much enjoyed being a trader, because it gave him the freedom to travel where he wished and it afforded him an opportunity to learn the land and search for a possible route to New Spain.[29]

Cabeza de Vaca recalled that although he enjoyed the freedom, a trader's life was nonetheless filled with peril, for he was frequently hungry, suffered from cold, and faced the wilderness alone. Because of the extremes of temperature, he did not carry out his business ventures in winter. During that season, he regularly returned to Malhado and continued this pattern for three consecutive years. Don Alvaro reluctantly delayed following his former companions down the coast toward Mexico, for to do so would mean the abandonment of the two Spaniards who remained on Malhado.[30]

One of these men eventually died, and the sole survivor, Lope de Oviedo, refused to leave the island. With a note of exasperation, don Alvar remarked: "To get him out of there, I would cross over to the island every year and plead with him for us to leave as best we could in search of Christians. Every year he held me back, saying that we would leave the following year."[31]

In late 1532, Cabeza de Vaca finally convinced the reluctant Spaniard to leave the island and to accompany him down the coast toward Pánuco, following roughly the same course that the larger party had taken four years earlier. Traveling with Oviedo was particularly challenging for Cabeza de Vaca, because don Lope could not swim. But the two men successfully crossed four rivers along the coast, only to be confronted by a wide inlet where Oviedo became increasingly frightened. Across this body of water were Indians who made contact with the two Spaniards. The natives reported that "farther ahead were three men like us and gave us their names." When asked about the other Spaniards who had also departed Malhado, the Indians replied that they were all dead—some having died of cold and starvation, while others had been killed "for sport" or because they had been the subject of bad dreams.[32]

When Cabeza de Vaca asked about the status of the three survivors, the Indians replied that they were badly mistreated because their captors "kicked and slapped them, and beat them with sticks." And, according to don Alvar, to illustrate "that they had told us the truth about the mistreatment of the others, they slapped and beat my companion and gave me my share too." Following this abusive treatment of the Spaniards, the Indians then threw clods of dirt at them and held arrows to their hearts, threatening to kill them in the same manner as they had dispatched their companions. All of this was more than the fainthearted Oviedo could endure. Despite the efforts of Cabeza de Vaca, who "argued with him not to do it," don Lope in the company of some Indian women turned back toward Malhado and disappeared from history.[33]

Two days after the departure of Lope de Oviedo, Cabeza de Vaca was reunited with his former companions, Andrés Dorantes de Carranza, the African Estevanico, and Alonso Castillo Maldonado. The three men were astonished to see don Alvar, for they believed he had died several years earlier. They also were no doubt more than a little embarrassed that they had not verified his death before departing from Malhado. But Cabeza de Vaca bore them no animus, remarking that "we thanked God very much for being together" and that the reunion was one of the happiest days of their lives.[34]

Once reunited, Cabeza de Vaca and Dorantes were in agreement that they should press on toward New Spain at the first opportunity. The other two men had theretofore been reluctant to do so, because they could not swim and greatly feared the rivers and bays they would have to cross. After assuring the nonswimmers that they would be helped en route, the four men agreed on the absolute necessity of keeping secret their plans for escape, for they believed the Indians would surely kill them if their intentions were discovered.[35]

The Four Ragged Castaways decided to wait six months before attempting to flee, because at that time the Indians would gather at another land farther south and strategically closer to New Spain to feast on the fruit of the prickly pear cactus. And at that juncture Cabeza de Vaca became the slave of Indians who also owned Andrés Dorantes. Those natives were a hunting-and-gathering group called the Mariames, while a neighboring group known as the Yguazes claimed Castillo and Estevanico. During their captivity, the four men learned the fate of many of their former companions. Some had died of exposure and hunger; others had been the victims of violence perpetrated by Spaniard on Spaniard. Once again, the last survivors had temporarily kept themselves alive by eating the flesh of their countrymen. But in the end, there were only the Ragged Four—three Europeans and an African.[36]

As a captive, Cabeza de Vaca again revealed the trained eye of an ethnologist by memorizing the things that he saw and asking good questions. For example, he observed that the Mariames regularly killed infant daughters and fed their bodies to dogs. When asked why they would do such an ostensibly cruel and irrational act, the Indians replied that it was "an unseemly thing to marry them to relatives"—an option no doubt proscribed by incest taboos. The alternative was to marry daughters outside the group, but since the Mariames were surrounded by more numerous and powerful tribes with whom they were constantly at war, married daughters would bear children that strengthened their enemies.[37]

Don Alvar also remembered interesting details about the Yguazes. He described them as well-built archers. But their principal food did not come from hunting. Rather, they dug two or three varieties of roots, which were hardly ideal foodstuffs in that they caused severe bloating. Furthermore, the roots were difficult to dig, required two days of roasting, and were bitter to the palate. The Yguazes occasionally supplemented their diet with deer and fish, but they were often so hungry that they ate "spiders, ant eggs, worms, lizards, salamanders, snakes and poisonous vipers." Their diet also included dirt, rotten wood, and even deer dung. Besides these named foods, the Yguazes consumed "other things" that Cabeza de Vaca could not bring himself to record. One may well wonder what these "unmentionables" might have been! Don Alvar added the concluding thought that "my observations lead me to believe that they would eat stones if there were any in that land."[38]

Cabeza de Vaca found the Yguazes to be lacking in character, given as they were to thievery, drunkenness, and prevarication. He also recorded his profound distaste for sodomites in this hunting-and-gathering culture, who were "so abominable that they openly have another man for a wife" and so effeminate that they "do not understand a thing about men but perform every activity pertaining to women." On the other hand, don Alvar marveled at other Yguaze men with astonishing physical stamina, which permitted them to pursue deer on foot, for they could "run from morning to night . . . without resting or becoming tired." In times when food was plentiful, such as during the harvest of prickly pear cactus, he described the Indians as especially merry, "because they are not hungry then and spend all their time dancing." Not surprisingly, these Indians suffered terribly from plagues of mosquitoes, which Cabeza de Vaca, with the eye of a naturalist, discerned as three distinct species. To ward off the insects, the Indians burned damp firewood because it emitted a lot of smoke. The downside to this means of insect repellent, as campers can attest, is eyes that water all night, and the Spaniards and Estevanico also found their sleep interrupted by a sharp kick or beating by an Indian when it was time to gather more firewood. Despite the best efforts of the Yguazes, Cabeza de Vaca described those who suffered the most severe reaction to mosquito bites as resembling lepers or the biblical Lazarus.[39]

During this captivity, Cabeza de Vaca mentioned seeing buffalo, the first account on record of these wild bovines. He called them "cows" and remarked that they were about the same size as Moorish cattle in Spain, although bison had longer hair. Don Alvar observed that the animals had small horns, that their skins were like fine blankets, and that the Yguazes used the hides to make shoes and shields. According to Cabeza de Vaca, buffalo "have more and better meat than cattle . . . in Spain."[40]

At the end of six months, when the Indians had congregated to gather the prickly pears, the Castaways' plans to escape went awry. As they were about to flee, their Indian masters got into a hot dispute over a woman, which ended in blows with sticks and fisticuffs. Their masters became so angry that they marched off in different directions, forcing their slaves to accompany them. Consequently, all plans to flee toward New Spain were placed on hold for another year.[41]

The intervening time was one of great suffering for Cabeza de Vaca. His life was made miserable by constant hunger and mistreatment. On three occasions, he attempted to escape, but each attempt ended with his recapture and threats to kill him. At the end of the year, the Indians again congregated to feast on the fruit of the prickly pear cactus. The Castaways, after some difficulty, were united again and finally made their escape in mid-September of 1534. They attributed their reunion to "God's will," and remarked that it was "their obligation . . . as Christians . . . not to live such a savage life, so far from the service of God."[42]

In South Texas they were accepted as free men by the Avavares, another hunting-and-gathering group. There the Castaways were fed venison, which they had not eaten before and did not recognize. At that juncture, Castillo gained in stature, because he was able to alleviate severe headaches among their Indian hosts by making the sign of the cross and reciting prayers. Although free to move on if they wished, the Castaways were persuaded by the approach of winter to postpone their plans to reach Mexico. But the prickly pear harvest had played out, and food was scarce. While foraging for sustenance, Cabeza de Vaca lost his bearings and nearly died of hypothermia. He saved his life by finding a burning tree, probably ignited by lightning, which he stoked for warmth. Over the next five days he carried firebrands and dry sticks with him, since there was no other relief from the cold for a man traveling "naked as the day I was born."[43]

During his ordeal, Cabeza de Vaca again revealed his deep commitment to God, commending Him for not allowing the north wind to blow, for by his own admission he could not have survived a norther. Upon reaching a riverbank on the fifth day, don Alvar was reunited with friendly Indians and his companions. The natives had several sick persons among them, but once again the ministrations of Castillo worked wonders. He commended the ill to God, and miraculously they were all well on the following morning. Being a "timid physician," Castillo shied away from treating the more seriously afflicted, and at this juncture don Alvar moved to the forefront as a master healer. He allegedly saved one Indian who had no pulse and "showed all the signs of being dead." With his fame spreading, various Indian groups brought their sick children to Cabeza de Vaca, and his ministrations again proved salutary. Nevertheless, he credited God with restoring the health of his patients. The Castaways remained with the Avavares for eight months, tracking time by phases of the moon. During this interval and because the Indians insisted, Dorantes and Estevanico, who had not attempted to treat the ill, joined Castillo and Cabeza de Vaca as healers. But Cabeza de Vaca was "the boldest and the most daring in undertaking any cure."[44]

Aside from his curative powers, don Alvar again took up the mantle of ethnologist. He remembered the legends of the Avavares, noting that they had been terrorized in the past by a creature they called Bad Thing. This demonic being had terrorized the Avavares by pulling arms out of sockets and cutting out portions of their entrails. When asked where "Malacosa" dwelled, the Indians claimed that he lived beneath the ground. This story amused the Spaniards, but they took pains to inform the Indians that if they would worship the Christian God they need no longer fear Mr. "Bad Thing."[45]

Before detailing the Castaways' journey beyond the confines of Texas, Cabeza de Vaca offered a summary of the Indian groups he had come to know. Even though the cultural information contained in his account "quantitatively exceeds that of all his successors [in Texas] combined," readers of the *Relación* always find themselves wishing that he had set down more detail. Nevertheless, Cabeza de Vaca documented universal practices of the Karankawas and various hunting-and-gathering groups that were found from the Galveston area to the lower Río Grande Valley. All males abstained from sleeping with their wives from the first indication of pregnancy until the newborn reached the age of two years old. For those who cling to the idyllic notion of a pre-Columbian Eden in which Native Americans loved all living things, including each other, reading Cabeza de Vaca's *Relación* will be a disturbing experience. Don Alvar stated that "all these people wage war." In his view the Indians were so resourceful in guarding themselves against their enemies that they might well have "been reared in Italy in a time of continuous war." In short, Indians, with their vices and virtues, were like all human beings on this planet. It was a lesson that Cabeza de Vaca never forgot. And later on he himself did a great deal to convince Indians that not all Spaniards were the same.[46]

After leaving the Avavares, the Castaways crossed the lower Río Grande into Mexico. Shortly after they departed Texas, they saw the first mountains they had encountered on the North American continent. Instead of continuing down the coast toward the River of Palms and the province of Pánuco, the wayfarers chose to turn inland toward the sierras that seemed to descend from the North Sea. Their decision was prompted by intelligence obtained from Indian friends that the coastal groups were very bad and that lands to the interior contained friendlier people and more abundant food.[47]

While crossing northern Mexico, Cabeza de Vaca performed the first surgery by a European in what would become the Spanish Southwest. An Indian had been wounded some time before by an arrow that entered the right side of his back. The arrowhead had lodged over the heart, causing great pain and suffering. With a knife don Alvar opened the chest of the native, extracted the projectile, and closed the incision with two stitches. He then stanched the bleeding with hair scraped from the skin of an animal (Figure 1). Although he probably exaggerated the time of recovery, claiming that the stitches were removed on the following day and that the "Indian was healed," it was nonetheless a remarkable piece of surgery that has earned recognition for Cabeza de Vaca in the prestigious *New England Journal of Medicine*.[48]

The Castaways' journey across northern Mexico eventually brought them back to Texas at the junction of the Río Grande and the Río Conchos near present Presidio, Texas, and Ojinaga, Chihuahua. Near La Junta de los Ríos, the four men encountered other Indians, apparently Jumanos, who were labeled Cow People by Cabeza de Vaca, because they left their camps once a year to hunt bison to the north.[49]

From La Junta de los Ríos, the four men ascended the Río Grande on the east or Texas bank for seventeen days. Some seventy-five miles downriver from present El Paso, they struck out overland toward the Pacific Coast, crossing northwestern Chihuahua and northeastern Sonora. On that portion of the journey, the Castaways heard of Indians who lived in a land to the north with populous towns and great houses

FIGURE I

Insignia of the Texas Surgical Society. This is a photograph of an
original drawing by Tom Lea. (Courtesy of the Texas Surgical Society,
Mellick T. Sykes, M.D., Secretary.)

set among lofty mountains. Cabeza de Vaca acquired five green arrowheads, perhaps of malachite rather than turquoise, that the Indians of
northern Mexico had gotten from that distant land and used in ceremonial dances. Although he eventually lost these semiprecious objects, rec-
ollections of them later on would help stir interest in New Spain of
northern lands that lay *más allá*.[50]

In western Sonora, the four men came to a village of friendly Indians
where they were offered six hundred deer hearts as food. From that settlement, appropriately named Corazones by the Spaniards, the Castaways soon reached the Pacific Coast, perhaps to the west of present
Hermosillo. They arrived at the Río Yaqui around Christmas 1535,
about seven months after departing the Avavares in South Texas.[51]

South of the Río Yaqui, Castillo spotted an amulet tied to the neck of
an Indian. The object was a small sword-belt buckle with a horseshoe

nail sewn to it, unmistakable evidence that it had come from a Spaniard. Castillo took the amulet from the Indian, and the Castaways with feigned indifference inquired as to its source. The native replied that it had come from "some bearded men like us." Initially, the wayfarers were concerned that the buckle and nail had come from members of a sea expedition and that they were still in a land uninhabited by Europeans. But as they moved down the coast the four men saw additional evidence of Spaniards, such as tracks of horses and abandoned campsites.[52]

Anxious to make contact with his countrymen, Cabeza de Vaca, in the company of Estevanico, forged ahead of the other Castaways. He soon came upon a slave-raiding party to the north of Culiacán, a Spanish outpost near the Pacific Coast. The mounted slave catchers, adherents of Governor Nuño de Guzmán of New Galicia, were so astonished by the appearance of Cabeza de Vaca "that they were not able to speak or ask me questions." A prominent Texas historian with a flair for the dramatic once described this encounter as a meeting of traditional Spaniards and "a bearded, ragged, nearly unclothed, burned scarecrow . . . [who was] as welcome as an illegitimate child at a family reunion." Humorous but hardly the case. The slavers quickly escorted Cabeza de Vaca to a place nearby, where he met with their captain.[53]

This historic confrontation between Castaways separated from European society for more than seven years and their countrymen was in fact less traumatic for them than for the Native Americans who had accompanied the wayfarers. Those Indians' perception of Cabeza de Vaca and his companions, in contrast to the reputation of Guzmán's slave raiders, underscores the transformation that had occurred in the former. Their native friends protested "that we had come from the East and they had come from the West; that we healed the sick and they killed the healthy; that we were naked and barefoot and they were dressed and on horseback, with lances; that we coveted nothing but instead gave away everything that was given to us and kept none of it, while the sole purpose of the others was to steal everything they found, never giving anything to anybody."[54]

Separated from their Indian associates, the former Ragged Castaways were taken to Culiacán, where they received a warm welcome from its *alcalde mayor*, Melchior Díaz. While resting there, the Christian Castaways summoned rebellious Indians of the region into their presence. Díaz told the Indians that "these Christians came from heaven and had traveled through many lands" and that these same Christians "had come here to tell others not to harm, annoy, nor kill Indians so they could settle in their towns and believe in God and build churches." This encounter may have had a temporary, pacific influence on the Native Americans.[55]

From Culiacán, the Castaways were escorted to the town of Compostela for a meeting with the governor of New Galicia. Nuño de Guzmán was a gracious host, providing the refugees from the wilderness with articles of clothing from his own wardrobe. Newly outfitted, the four men were again sent on their way to Mexico City, where an audience with the recently arrived viceroy of New Spain, Antonio de Mendoza, awaited them (Figure 2). They arrived in the capital on July 24, 1536, and on the following day must have felt at home as they attended a bullfight celebrating the Feast of Saint James, the famed warrior saint Santiago of the Spanish Reconquest.[56]

In the following days and weeks, the four men told and retold stories of their experiences to eager audiences. Against long odds, they had survived nearly eight years of danger from the elements and unfriendly Indians. Cabeza de Vaca and his companions, since fleeing from the Mariames in September 1534, had traversed an estimated twenty-five hundred miles, with most of the journey made on foot. With the possible exception of truth, their stories of lands "*más allá*" lost little in retelling, for they quickly stirred romantic interest in the legendary Seven Cities of Cíbola. Cabeza de Vaca's accounts of seeing evidence of precious metals such as gold and antimony in the mountains of northwestern Mexico also touched off fevered excitement in the capital, and powerful men soon vied to lead follow-up expeditions into the north country.[57]

Despite their glowing accounts of potential wealth in lands they had seen, not one of the three Spaniards was willing to retrace a single step of their odyssey. Estevanico, however, was not given a choice. He was loaned or perhaps sold by Dorantes to Viceroy Mendoza, who prevailed over several competitors in sponsoring a reconnaissance to the north.[58]

The viceroy's interest led to the preliminary expedition of Fray Marcos de Niza in 1539. In early March, with Estevanico serving as his guide, Niza left Culiacán and headed up the Camino Real, as the road to the north was then known. At the Río Mayo on March 21, a fateful decision permitted the African to scout well ahead of the friar and his support party. Soon separated by several days' travel, Estevanico apparently made excessive demands on the Indians he contacted, and he entered towns without the consent of his Franciscan companion. Estevanico was killed at Háwikuh, the southernmost of the Zuñi pueblos in present western New Mexico—known collectively as Cíbola. Shaken by the death of his companion and guide, Fray Marcos beat a hasty retreat

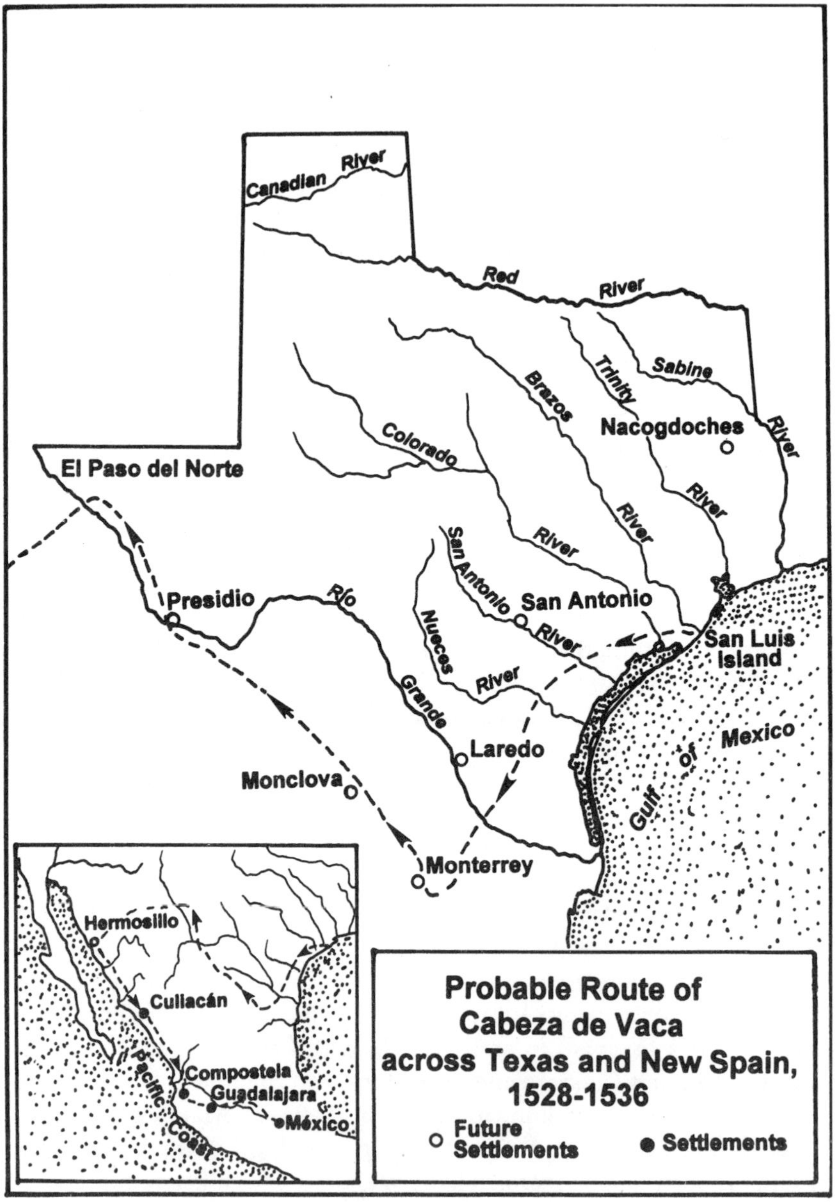

Canadian River
Red River
Brazos
Trinity
Sabine
Nacogdoches
River
Colorado
El Paso del Norte
River
River
River
San Antonio
San Antonio
Presidio
Río
River
San Luis Island
Nueces
River
Grande
Laredo
Gulf of Mexico
Monclova
Monterrey
Hermosillo
Culiacán
Pacific Coast
Compostela
Guadalajara
México
Probable Route of Cabeza de Vaca across Texas and New Spain, 1528-1536
Future Settlements
Settlements

FIGURE 2

Probable route of Cabeza de Vaca across Texas and New Spain, 1528–1536. This map depicts the most likely path of Cabeza de Vaca's trek. (Cartography by Caroline Castillo Crimm.)

to Mexico City, where he reported having seen rich lands that contained seven golden cities, the smallest of which was larger than the colonial capital. Niza's accounts of the north country and hopes of finding the legendary Seven Cities of Cíbola led immediately to the follow-up expedition of Francisco Vázquez de Coronado (1540–1542). When Coronado captured Háwikuh and learned the true nature of it as well as other nearby pueblos, he was easily enticed into a fruitless search for the wealth of Gran Quivira. That undertaking crossed the Texas Panhandle en route to southern Kansas. And when the failed expedition returned to New Spain in the spring of 1542, it temporarily dampened expectations about the riches of the far north country and blunted the impetus for its settlement for half a century.[59]

In the meantime, Cabeza de Vaca returned to Spain in 1537. There he sought reward for his services from Emperor Charles V by requesting a patent to settle Florida. But Charles granted that honor to Hernando de Soto, already rich and famous from his exploits in the land of the Inca. It appears that don Alvar then busied himself composing his historic *Relación*, first published at Zamora in 1542. The manuscript was probably completed by early 1540, for in March of that year Cabeza de Vaca received a consolation appointment from the emperor. He was awarded the titles of *adelantado*, given to early conquistadors in America, and governor and captain general of the Río de la Plata in South America.[60]

In late 1540, Cabeza de Vaca again negotiated the sandbar at San Lúcar de Barrameda, this time as first in command. After a difficult five-month voyage, he and approximately 250 men landed off the coast of Brazil on Santa Catalina Island. His destination, however, was Asunción on the Paraná River in Paraguay. Unwilling to wait several months for an opportunity to board an oceangoing vessel, which would take him to Asunción by way of Buenos Aires, don Alvar elected to lead his men on a one-thousand-mile march through uncharted lands. En route, he became the first European to view the majestic Iguazú Falls; and he again proved to be one of the most remarkable of pedestrians, having crossed substantial portions of both North and South America. On the latter trek, he had lost only two men—one drowned crossing the Paraná River and a second was fatally mauled by a jungle cat.[61]

As governor of Asunción, Cabeza de Vaca gave special attention to Indians under his jurisdiction, decreeing that those who were mistreated by their masters be placed under more gentle hands. He also put restrictions on Spaniards who held Indian women in concubinage and on the illegal purchase of Indian slaves. He could do nothing about the institution of slavery itself, however, for the New Laws of 1542–1543, which abolished Indian servitude, had not as yet been promulgated in the Americas.[62]

Don Alvar's progressive policies, and above all the compassion he demonstrated for his native charges—a sympathy nurtured in the wilds of Texas, where he had himself been enslaved and mistreated—earned him the enmity of many unreconstructed colonists at Asunción. His benign nature also made him a poor judge of character, as evidenced by his selection of unreliable and disloyal subordinates. Those persons and his own retinue soon favored a local strongman, Domingo Martínez de Irala, who had been elected as interim governor before the royal appointment of Cabeza de Vaca.[63]

Continued dissatisfaction with the policies of Governor Cabeza de Vaca, which included the collection of fair and equitable taxes from Spaniards, culminated in a revolt against his authority and his arrest in April 1544. As a recent work notes, "That Cabeza de Vaca was overthrown should surprise no one. His ideas and policies went against the clear self-interest of many of the Spaniards who were attracted to America in the first place." Like Columbus, don Alvar was sent back to Spain in chains, arriving at Seville near the end of August 1545. There he faced long legal proceedings, even by Spanish standards, in which he was accused of various crimes, maladministration, and the enactment of visionary policies. Initial litigation continued for six long years. On March 18, 1551, Cabeza de Vaca, then about sixty years of age, was perpetually banished from the Indies under penalty of death and ordered exiled to Oran in North Africa for a period of five years. Fortunately, the latter part of the sentence was never carried out. At some point don Alvar had married. His wife mounted a determined defense of her husband's reputation, resulting in appeals that expended all her personal property. While he remained at the Spanish court under a legal cloud, Cabeza de Vaca probably worked on a revision of his *Relación*, which was published at Valladolid in 1555. On September 15, 1556, Charles V, in one of his last acts as emperor, authorized a payment of 12,000 *maravedís* to Cabeza de Vaca and named him to the post of chief justice of the Tribunal of Seville. His date of death and place of interment are not known.[64]

Cabeza de Vaca had little direct or lasting influence on the history of colonial Texas. More than 150 years would pass before Alonso de León and Father Damián Massanet attempted the permanent settlement of Spaniards in the future Lone Star State. But Cabeza de Vaca's adventures in Texas and his strength of character remain inspirational, as do the remarkable literary documents he left as his legacy. Professor Rolena Adorno of Yale University, a modern expert on Cabeza de Vaca, sees in him an advocate of kind treatment for American natives that antedates even the great Fray Bartolomé de las Casas by a few years. In don Alvar's own words, that approach was the "only way . . . the road most sure, and no other." But perhaps the best assessment of him in his role as governor of Asunción came from the great naval historian Samuel Eliot Morison, who wrote: "Alvar Núñez Cabeza de Vaca stands out as a truly noble and humane character. Nowhere in the lurid history of the Conquest does one find such integrity and devotion to Christian principles in the face of envy, malice, treachery, cruelty, lechery, and plain greed"—strong words from the "Admiral's" pen about a good Spaniard![65]

TWO

ALONSO DE LEÓN
Military Pathfinder

On April 20, 1689, a Spanish commander stood just east of a river named Our Lady of Guadalupe. He carefully sighted a damaged astrolabe and took a sun shot, which, if accurate, placed him a few miles southeast of present Victoria, Texas. General Alonso de León was close to finding the objective of five sea and six land expeditions, all undertaken during 1686–1689 in search of a seemingly elusive French colony planted somewhere on the northern Gulf Coast by René Robert Cavelier, Sieur de La Salle. Two days later the expedition began a march down Garcitas Creek and, shortly before noon, came upon the ruins of the French outpost Fort St. Louis.[1]

Accompanying León as chaplain was Father Damián Massanet. In respective diary and letter, the two men recorded a scene of utter devastation: "We . . . found six houses, not very large, built with poles plastered with mud, and roofed with buffalo hides, another house where pigs were fattened, and a wooden fort made from the hulk of a wrecked vessel." All of the houses were sacked; chests, bottle cases, and furniture smashed into pieces; more than two hundred books torn apart "with the rotten leaves scattered though the patios—all in French." Among the desolation lay the remains of three bodies, one with a dress clinging to the bones. Also in evidence was French ordnance, consisting of eight pieces of artillery, all of medium bore—four- or five-pounders—some with broken carriages. And lastly, strewn throughout were iron bars, ship's nails, and "casks with their heads knocked in and their contents spilled out." By León's calculation, Fort St. Louis, located 136 leagues from Monclova, contained nothing of value.[2]

As noted in the previous chapter, Alvar Núñez Cabeza de Vaca and his Castaway companions left Texas in September 1534. By 1543 the Coronado and Soto expeditions, which had set off with high hopes of finding "another Mexico" or "another Peru," had ended in bitter disappointment. Those undertakings had discovered no booty in Florida, no riches in Texas, no golden cities at Cíbola in New Mexico, and no wealth at Gran Quivira in Kansas. To the Spanish crown, firsthand information gleaned from several expeditions indicated a landmass of continental proportions to the north of New Spain. Stretching from the Florida peninsula to present-day Arizona and New Mexico, the lands of *más allá* were formidable in size, the inhabitants often inhospitable, and the soil unpromising for treasure-seeking adventurers. As a consequence, future expansion toward Texas over the next century and a third (1543–1680) was more measured and its agents more prosaic than the golden conquistadors.[3]

By the 1560s, an impetus supplied by adventurers, prospectors, friars, ranchers, and soldiers had brought about new towns and mining camps in northern New Spain. Spaniards had reached the upper tributaries of the Río Conchos in the San Bartolomé valley of southern Chihuahua, a locale that became the primary staging area for expeditions to New Mexico and Texas. In 1598 Juan de Oñate brought about the Spanish settlement of New Mexico, and, at roughly the same time, the northeastern frontier of New Spain expanded under the guidance of Luis de Carvajal y de la Cueva. For his efforts, don Luis received the titles of governor and military commander of the Nuevo Reino de León, and he founded a number of settlements, including Villa de Almadén at the site of Monclova.[4]

Carvajal's overweening ambition, combined with his slaving activities and Jewish heritage, landed him in prison, where he died in the early 1590s. Oñate, with much of his personal fortune expended, was removed as governor of New Mexico near the end of the first decade of the seventeenth century, but the province remained under Spanish control until the great Pueblo Revolt of 1680. At that juncture, Spaniards had acquired bits of information about lands that would form parts of the Lone Star State. They had traveled along its extreme southwestern borders en route to New Mexico; they had penetrated its western regions seeking information about the mysterious "Lady in Blue"; they had gained additional information about lands lying north of the Río Grande near present-day Eagle Pass; and they had garnered some knowledge of coastal regions, resulting from shipwrecks and naval expeditions.[5]

But the 1680s ushered in a time of crisis on the northern frontier. The decade began with the Pueblo Revolt, which claimed more than four hundred lives and forced the Spanish to abandon New Mexico. Survivors, numbering about two thousand, retreated down the Río Grande to El Paso del Río del Norte, transforming it overnight into a focus of empire. From El Paso, the first European settlement within the present boundaries of Texas, Corpus Christi de la Isleta, was established in 1682. Also from El Paso, missionary endeavors were undertaken at La Junta de los Ríos. And in 1684 a Spanish captain, Juan Domínguez de Mendoza, founded a camp, perhaps to the south of the upper reaches of the Colorado River, where a few Indians were baptized and large numbers of buffalo were slaughtered. But in the following year, the viceroy of New Spain learned of French designs along the northern Gulf Coast.[6]

The viceroy ordered that all energies be focused on finding the foreign interlopers and extirpating their colony. Response by sea could be carried out most expeditiously, and those efforts were launched in early January 1686 and repeated in December of the same year. To ensure a more thorough search, officials in Mexico City also decided to organize a complementary land expedition. Unable to find a person familiar with lands along the northeastern coast, the search broadened to Nuevo León, where a frontiersman was rumored to have experience in the region of the Río Grande and the Río de las Palmas. That person, Alonso de León the younger, would soon play a significant role as pathfinder in early Texas history.[7]

The younger León was born in Cadereyta, Nuevo León, in 1639 or 1640. He was the third son of Alonso de León the elder, and Josefa González, who had married on September 23, 1635. The elder León had been born in the first decade of the 1600s while his Castilian parents, Lorenzo Pérez and Adriana de León, resided in Mexico City. Growing up in the capital with its well-established schools provided rare educational opportunities for don Alonso, which imbued him with the importance of education. In 1635, the year of his marriage, he entered the frontier province of Nuevo León as a *ganadero* (stockman) but quickly moved into a position of greater influence by accepting an office in the *cabildo* (town council) of Cadereyta.[8]

Over the next twenty years, the senior León participated in nearly three dozen campaigns of pacification and discovery. He had also established himself as a man of letters, having written a brief chronicle of the Spanish discovery, settlement, and control of Nuevo León. In directing his finished work to an official of the Holy Office of the Inquisition in Mexico City, as well as in the first few chapters of his discourse, León reflected his familiarity with Scriptures and deep commitment to God. His unusual devoutness no doubt had great influence on his son of the same name.[9]

In 1653, under orders of the governor of Nuevo León, the senior don Alonso led thirty men eastward toward the Gulf of Mexico. En route, he encountered friendly Indians of differing groups, and he arrived at the coast in the environs of twenty-four degrees north latitude. That position placed León at the mouth of the Río de las Palmas. The goodwill of the natives was in striking contrast to the attitudes of their forebears, who had consistently opposed Spanish presence on the coast and preyed upon shipwreck victims in the sixteenth century.[10]

The expedition of 1653 was intended to discover lands and learn of routes that might benefit the king of Spain. At the time of the entrada, the younger León, a youth of only twelve or thirteen years, was in Spain and perhaps missed an opportunity to tag along with his father. Later, he undoubtedly heard tales of largely unexplored regions toward the rising sun and the Gulf of Mexico.

Because there were no schools on the frontier of New Spain, the younger León, in accord with the wishes of his educated father, journeyed to Spain at age ten. There he enrolled in an academy and prepared for a career in the royal navy as a navigator. While still a cadet, he assisted in the defense of Cádiz when it was attacked by English vessels in 1655. His naval career was brief, however, for don Alonso soon returned to Nuevo León, where he married doña Agustina Cantú.[11]

Over the next twenty years, Alonso de León, by his own admission, led a series of entradas that traversed the northeast coast of New Spain, as well as the banks of the Río de San Juan. Those undertakings resulted in the discovery of salt mines and two promising ports, including one at the mouth of the Río de las Palmas. But claims of his own achievements may well have included those of his more famous father. Blurring a few accomplishments in distant Nuevo León would pad his résumé and improve the prospects of a petition filed with the viceroy in 1682. Don Alonso requested a franchise to work salt deposits along the Río San Juan, open trade with neighboring settlements, and search for new mines.[12]

In any event, León's résumé, whether authentic or perhaps a bit contrived, brought him to the attention of the new governor of Nuevo León, Agustín Echeverz y Subiza, Marqués de San Miguel de Aguayo. The marqués had been handed the responsibility of searching for the forbidden French colony, and he logically turned to León, who had preceded him as governor. While preparations were under way, an Indian brought news to Monterrey of strangers along the Río Grande who were white men from a settlement farther north.[13]

Selected to lead an overland search for the French interlopers, León organized an initial reconnaissance that left Cadereyta on June 27, 1686. His troop consisted of fifty soldiers, an Indian guide, and a chaplain. It followed the Río San Juan north and east toward its confluence with the Río Grande. Upon striking the larger river, don Alonso followed its right bank to the coast. He reached the mouth after "conquering marshes, canebrakes, willow thickets, and dense woods." León then turned southward toward the Río de las Palmas, and along the shoreline found flotsam from a wrecked vessel and a stoppered flask containing a small quantity of spoiled wine. Don Alonso thought the bottle, given its attractive glass and form, to be non-Spanish, but he found no conclusive evidence that Frenchmen had visited the region. León then began the homeward trek to Cadereyta, having spent almost the entire month of July in the field.[14]

Unwilling to accept failure, the Marqués de Aguayo dispatched a second expedition under León's command in February 1687. This effort forded the Río Grande, perhaps at El Cántaro, near the present town of Roma, and followed the left bank to the coast, arriving there on March 20. Ironically, La Salle, the object of León's search, had been murdered in East Texas on the previous day. Don Alonso's troop then marched up the Texas coast until its passage was blocked by a "big salty river," probably Baffin Bay to the southeast of contemporary Kingsville. At that juncture, León turned back, having again found no evidence of Frenchmen or any Indians who could give him information about them.[15]

Although unaware of La Salle's death and the sorry condition of the surviving colonists on Garcitas Creek, Spanish officials were understandably optimistic. Two searches by land, as well as two by sea, had failed to find a single Frenchman. Optimism was further buoyed by a report from Spain, based on pirated French documents acquired by the Spanish ambassador in London. The communiqué suggested that the French colony from the moment of its inception had been racked by disease and dysentery, menaced by Indians, and endangered by lost provisions. However, this hopefulness was soon shattered. Surviving Frenchmen were living among the Indian nations of Texas.[16]

The ominous tidings reached Coahuila via two Indians, one of whom claimed to have been "in the very houses of the French." The informant journeyed to Mission Caldera, situated east of Monclova, and gave the bad news to the resident priest, Father Damián Massanet. At that same time, July 1687, Alonso de León had just been appointed governor of Coahuila and captain of the presidio at Monclova.[17]

Before assuming command of the garrison, León traveled to Mission Caldera. There Father Massanet "made known to him what had passed between the Indians and me." Don Alonso asked for "some unmistakable signs" that the report was true, and the priest summoned the second Indian, named Juan, who professed knowledge of a white man dwelling among Indians at a *ranchería* (temporary settlement) located some sixty leagues distant. The Indian Juan agreed to travel there in an attempt to bring this person to Caldera. Juan found the white man but could not convince him to call at the mission. Massanet then notified León of what had transpired.[18]

In the intervening time, León had turned his attention to Indian affairs in Coahuila. Having previously served as interim governor of Nuevo León, don Alonso was experienced in handling Spanish-Indian relations—a background that had conditioned and hardened his views of all Native Americans. From his first days as governor of Coahuila, León faced bloody Indian insurrections, and he came to distrust even Indians who had accepted mission life. The new governor believed those neophytes to be guilty of "bad faith," for they were in constant communication with unreduced rebels, waiting for an opportunity to join them in a general uprising. In November 1687 his son, another Alonso de León who held the rank of *alférez* (ensign), was wounded by Indians. Indian wars also consumed his energies throughout the early months of 1688. For example, in April he captured a notorious rebel named Geronimillo, whom he charged with raiding missions and new Spanish settlements. On April 11, 1688, León condemned Geronimillo in a brief legal proceeding, placed a rope around the Indian's neck, and hanged him from a tree until he "died naturally." Don Alonso justified the execution by claiming it "served as an example to other Indians of these parts."[19]

Just prior to his third expedition in search of La Salle's colony, León concluded a "campaign that lasted twenty days" against rebellious natives. Again, months of almost incessant Indian wars, coupled with years of experience as a soldier on a dangerous frontier, had created distrust of Native Americans in León's heart and do much to explain his future difficulties with Father Damián Massanet.[20]

When Massanet informed León that the white man living among Indians north of Río Grande could not be persuaded to come to Mission Caldera, the new governor took action. At the head of a detachment of twelve soldiers, he crossed the Great River on May 26, 1688, and after some difficulty found a large settlement of Indians presided over by a naked, aged, and perhaps mentally confused Frenchman, Jean Jarry. The Frenchman, almost certainly a survivor of the La Salle expedition, was apprehended and removed "by diligence" from his encampment on May 30. In custody, he was transported to Coahuila, reaching that destination on June 6. From there he was sent to Mexico City, where his very presence, not necessarily his mendacious testimony, undermined the viceroy's optimism and spurred further efforts by land and sea to find the French colony.[21]

On July 23, 1688, the viceroy commissioned Alonso de León as commander of a fourth entrada and sent Jean Jarry northward to serve as guide. Assembling troops from distant presidios occasioned delays until March 1689. In all, the force totaled 114 men, including Massanet, soldiers, mule drivers, servants, and the Frenchman. León, only recently promoted to the rank of general, was provisioned with eighty-five loads of supplies and presents for Indians. However, at the beginning of the trek, Jarry proved useless as a guide. This forced don Alonso to rely on an Indian known to Father Massanet at Mission Caldera, who joined the expedition at the Río Grande. The native assured León "that he knew the country, and that he would bring us where there were some men like ourselves, in a settlement of six or seven houses; [and] that they had wives and children."[22]

On April 2 don Alonso again forded the Río Grande and began a march eastward toward Matagorda Bay. Although he logged his daily progress, reconstructing his exact path across Texas is not possible, for his latitude sightings were consistently thrown off by a defective astrolabe. Nevertheless, as pathfinder, León established a significant portion of what would become the Camino Real—a road ultimately extending from present-day Guerrero, Coahuila, to beyond the western border of contemporary Louisiana (Figure 3).[23]

León's entry, on Palm Sunday, April 3, 1689, reveals both his educational background and his attention to detail. He noted that his tables for computing the vernal equinox were made "before the so-called Gregorian correction" of 1582. By his computation, April 3 corresponded to March 24 in the pre-Gregorian method of determining Easter. And he added the caveat: "It has been necessary to state these facts in explanation, in case it should appear that a mistake has been made because of our lack of modern tables." Not many field commanders would have felt it necessary to document the rationale for determining religious observances in the wilds of seventeenth-century Texas.[24]

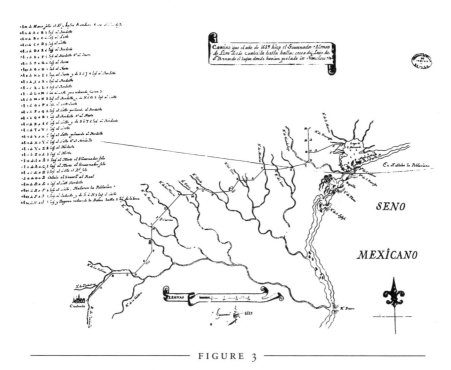

FIGURE 3

*Reconstructed route of the Alonso de León expedition of 1689. This sketch
map approximates the daily progress of Alonso de León from Coahuila to the
sitre of La Salle's colony on Garcitas Creek. (With the permission of the
Archivo General de Indias, Seville, Spain; Mapas y Planos, México 86.)*

En route to Matagorda Bay, León commented on a dense thicket,
forcing his expedition "to cut a passage into it for almost a league with
our cutlasses and axes." He remarked on great stands of prickly pear
cactus and mesquite that impeded progress, and applied names to rivers
that remain to this day: the Nueces, the Frío/Sarco (Leona), Medina
(San Antonio), and Guadalupe. On April 14 León's party encountered
the first buffaloes in one hundred leagues of travel and killed six of them
to supplement their larder.[25] One week later, don Alonso crossed the
Guadalupe River, descended Garcitas Creek, and encountered the awful
scene described in the second paragraph of this chapter. Four years of
searching had finally borne results (Figure 4).[26]

At Fort St. Louis, Father Massanet assumed his priestly responsibilities
by intoning a funeral Mass for the corpses, which were buried in a com-

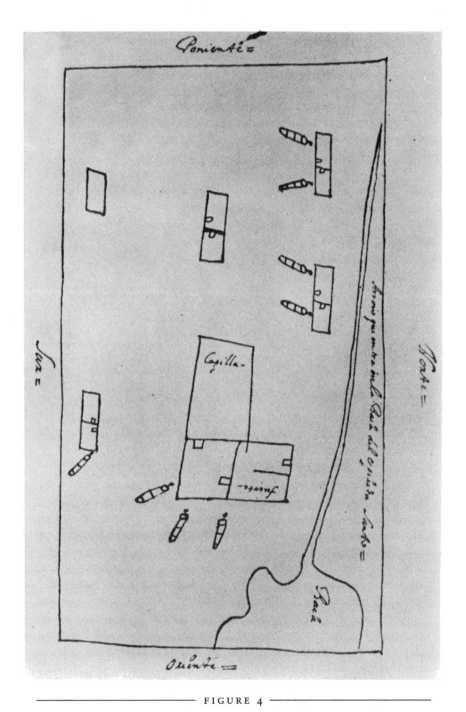

FIGURE 4

Juan Bautista Chapa's sketch of Fort St. Louis and eight cannons.
This sketch was made by Chapa in 1689.

mon grave. And on the next day after the discovery of La Salle's former colony, León, guided by Jean Jarry, who at that juncture demonstrated remarkable familiarity with the Matagorda Bay area, set out to reconnoiter the region. The party viewed the entrance to the bay on April 24 and saw the remains of one of La Salle's wrecked vessels. In a nearby abandoned Indian village the explorers found a book in French and other items, which suggested that the former residents had participated in the final attack on Fort St. Louis. Satisfied that there was nothing further to report, León began the march back to the main camp on Garcitas Creek.[27]

On the outward march to Matagorda Bay, León had routinely questioned Indians about their knowledge of Frenchmen. He learned on April 16 that four white men occupied a nearby *ranchería*, but investigation revealed nothing but an abandoned camp. Indians near the site, however, knew of the Frenchmen and reported that they had gone on horseback to visit Tejas Indians. León ordered his subordinate Francisco Martínez to compose a letter in French and dispatched it to the men by Indian carriers.[28]

The actual letter is not extant, but León summarized its contents in a report. He told the Frenchmen that he had been informed of the death of their fellow Christians at the hands of Indians, and he invited them to return to the world of white men. A postscript was added in Latin in case any of the four might be a religious person. It, too, exhorted the survivors to surrender themselves. In hopes of contacting the men, León promised to wait in the area for several days.[29]

Upon reaching the main camp, León found waiting a reply to his letter, written in thick lines with red ocher. Two Frenchmen, Jean L'Archevêque and Jacques Grollet, agreed to accept his invitation and surrender themselves. Traveling northward for approximately sixty-five miles, a detachment of soldiers followed an Indian guide and encountered the two men on the Colorado River in the Smithville–La Grange area. Also present were eight Tejas Indians and a chieftain. In interrogating the Indians, León and Massanet learned secondhand information about the rich lands of the Hasinai Confederation. This intelligence fired Father Massanet's missionary zeal, and through an interpreter he urged the chieftain and his people to accept Christianity. Massanet also promised to bring priests like himself to their land and "be there in the following year, at the time of sowing corn."[30]

Under questioning, L'Archevêque and Grollet gave an account of the final throes of La Salle's colony at Fort St. Louis. Initially, a smallpox epidemic may have claimed the lives of more than one hundred people. The survivors, finding themselves without a strong leader and divided by internal squabbles, paid little heed to the possibility of Indian treachery. Many of them, in fact, believed that they were on good terms with natives of the region. However, at Christmas time in 1688 five Indians had approached the settlement and entered the most remote house on the pretext of imparting some important news. More Indians then appeared under the same pretext and began to embrace other members of the colony. Those friendly gestures diverted attention from another party of natives, who surreptitiously approached along the bed of a creek. Suddenly, an attack by warriors armed with sharp weapons and clubs killed all of the adults, including three religious persons, and the sacking of houses followed.[31]

An eyewitness account, given a few years later by a youthful survivor, added graphic details. Jean-Baptiste Talon saw his mother slain before his eyes. He reported that Indian women, moved by consideration for the children, had carried several of the youngsters to their village. Unfortunately, they could not save a three-month-old infant—the first European child born in Texas. Its mother died first, and then the baby's life ended at the hands of a Karankawa warrior who "dashed [its head] against a tree while holding it by the foot."[32]

A few men, including L'Archevêque and Grollet, had been off among the Tejas and were spared the general carnage. Later, four of them, having heard news of the attack, returned to Fort St. Louis and buried fourteen of their companions. They also exploded approximately one hundred barrels of powder to prevent its falling into the hands of Indians or foreigners. L'Archevêque and Grollet concluded their testimony by informing León that the settlement had been well supplied with firearms, swords, chalices, and a large collection of books with rare bindings.[33]

León also incorporated comments made by the Tejas chieftain into his report, and those remarks served to heighten interest in East Texas. The Indian leader informed don Alonso that in the past *"una mujer"* had visited his ancestors and imparted religious instruction. In response to her teachings, the Tejas had effected religious accessories, such as a chapel (its interior illuminated by a perpetual flame fed by deer fat), an altar, images of saints, and a cross. These appearances of Christianity would be interpreted in Mexico City as further evidence of miraculous visitations among frontier natives by María Jesús de Agreda, the legendary "Lady in Blue."[34]

Without firsthand observation, León recorded that Indians of the Hasinai Confederation lived in nine settlements of wooden houses and that they had a governmental organization similar to culturally advanced Indians in New Spain. The Tejas chieftain had also reported that his people sowed abundant crops of corn, beans, pumpkins, watermelons, and cantaloupe. Finally, don Alonso noted that the Tejas leader indicated an interest in receiving religious instruction for his followers; and he informed the viceroy that his companion, Father Massanet, as well as brethren of the Franciscan college in Querétaro, would volunteer their services gladly if missions were authorized among the Tejas.[35]

León's diary and a letter to the viceroy, along with L'Archevêque and Grollet, were dispatched to Mexico City in the custody of Francisco Martínez, who had served as interpreter for the Frenchmen. Martínez arrived in the capital in late June or early July, and interrogation of the two captives began immediately. News of La Salle's death, obtained from L'Archevêque, who had been present on the fatal march into East Texas, and the failure of the French colony renewed an air of optimism and quickened religious fervor. Indeed, the viceroy and his advisers viewed the disaster at Fort St. Louis as additional proof of God's "divine aid and favor." [36]

The viceroy submitted Father Massanet's suggestions for missionizing the Tejas to an advisory council, and that body likewise saw the failed La Salle episode as evidence of divine retribution. The junta recommended that Massanet's proposal be accepted, and it ordered León to file a report outlining his suggestions on how to convert the Tejas.

At this juncture, differences between León and Massanet intensified. Their discord was symptomatic of issues that would be played out over and over again on the frontier of New Spain. Over time, the names of military captains and missionary clergy changed, but the fundamental issues dividing them did not. The two parallel agencies, military and religious, were both charged with holding and extending the frontiers of New Spain. But the former stressed Spain's right to rule and backed that claim with military might; the latter, by persuasion, forced confinement, and occasional use of corporal punishment sought to convert the natives and mold them into acceptable, taxpaying Spanish citizens.[37]

Because of his long experience as a military captain, León did not believe that Indians would peaceably accept a Spanish presence in their midst. He was especially dubious, since that very presence was intended to reshape Native American habits and customs into European modes of conduct. Accordingly, León's suggestions for missionizing the Tejas ran counter to the plans of Massanet. Don Alonso urged the construction of a series of presidios to bridge the gap between the Coahuila settlements and the proposed new mission field. Military outposts should be positioned on the Río Grande, the Frío, and the Guadalupe, and a fourth garrison should be located at the mission site itself. This suggestion was ignored, primarily because officials in Mexico City operated on a limited budget and because they and the Franciscan missionaries believed a substantial military presence among the Tejas was not only unnecessary but would actually impede spreading the Gospel.[38]

Still, the matter of French intrusion into Spanish realms could not be ignored, especially in light of the War of the League of Augsburg (1689–1697)—known in the English North American colonies as King William's War—which again pitted France against Spain. Although resisting the notion of converting the natives in an atmosphere of military might, officials in New Spain authorized León to choose a sufficient number of soldiers to prevent further incursions of the French into Spanish possessions. Their objectives, in the words of one crown official, were "to destroy and flatten all vestiges that remained of the French nation and to extend the reach and favorable influence [of Spain] over all Indians from Coahuila to Texas." But the size of León's military contingent, one hundred men, soon became a sore point with Father Massanet, who insisted that the governor was intent on arrogating personal and military ambitions over peaceful missionary goals. This issue in particular sparked strained relations between the two men, and it did not augur well for Alonso de León. He would suffer the unpardonable sin of being right about the absolute necessity of military support for any missionary endeavors. Nonetheless, in the capital "the projected enterprise was viewed almost wholly as religious rather than military in nature."[39]

To implement the conversion of the Tejas, royal officials in New Spain assigned responsibility to the Franciscan college at Querétaro and gave Massanet control over most aspects of the enterprise. In all, the college selected six priests for the Texas mission field. That number included Father Francisco Hidalgo, who would become the greatest champion of missions in East Texas.[40]

Early in 1690, the six friars made final preparations for their trip north toward Texas. Arriving in Coahuila, they experienced a delay, because soldiers assigned to León's command from other provinces had not yet arrived. On March 26 the expedition departed Monclova without waiting longer for the still absent troops. Among the junior officers were Gregorio de Salinas Varona and Francisco Martínez, both fluent in French.[41]

En route the main expedition was overtaken on March 30 by a company of men from Nuevo León, and it crossed the Río Grande on April 6. The combined force forded the Nueces on April 9 and the Frío on the following day. On April 13 León encountered Indians who informed him of a Frenchman visiting among nearby natives. Further investigation led León to a large encampment, where he distributed gifts of tobacco and biscuits in exchange for information. Don Alonso learned that two Frenchmen had been on the far bank of the Guadalupe River, and as proof of their presence, one Indian carried a French musket.[42]

On April 18 a detachment from the company spent part of the day looking for 126 horses that had stampeded during the previous night. That search proved fruitless, for the guide soon lost his way. León, with a full complement of men again intact, crossed the Medina River on the following day and proceeded toward the Guadalupe. On April 25, at the head of twenty men, he again set out to reconnoiter the Matagorda Bay area and inspect the remains of Fort St. Louis. Arriving at the site of the former French colony, and "having ascertained from its form that it was as before," León noted, "we burned the fort."[43]

On that same day, April 26, León made another trek toward the bay of Espíritu Santo, as the Spanish then called Matagorda Bay. From a distance he made an observation that would soon cast doubt on his judgment. Near the mouth of the Lavaca River, in don Alonso's words, "we recognized in the bay what were apparently two buoys . . . indicating the same channel." Lacking a canoe to investigate further and unable to find Indians "from whom to obtain information," León could only report his suspicions to the viceroy. His inability to determine the exact nature of the objects, coupled with mounting friction between himself and Father Massanet, would later serve to damage the commander's reputation.[44]

On the final day of April 1690, additional troops from presidios in Nueva Vizcaya, operating under express orders of the viceroy, overtook León and swelled the ranks of his soldiery. And at that juncture don Alonso bent his efforts toward finding "some Indians who could guide us and inform us whether there were any Frenchmen in these regions."[45]

Using gifts of biscuits, handkerchiefs, tobacco, razors, and knives as inducements, León finally succeeded in luring an Indian into his presence. The man informed the commander that he was a Tejas and that he would be willing to summon the governor of his people, "among whom were some Frenchmen." León gave the Indian a horse and promised to await the result of his mission. Unfortunately, the native soon returned "to inform me that his horse had run away from him."[46]

On the next day, May 6, León cynically noted that this same Indian, "greedy for the gift, told me that if I would give him another horse he would go to summon the governor of the Tejas and that he would leave his wife and a brother-in-law of his to guide us. So I sent him on his way." During the man's absence, don Alonso received word-of-mouth information that there were French youths among the Indian nations.[47]

Choosing eight soldiers and an Indian interpreter, León marched nine leagues and then passed "through a forest of oaks and grape-vines [for] another five leagues." He discovered Pierre Talon, then age fourteen, near the edge of a wood. Two days later, on the morning of May 12, he rescued another French youth of twenty years named Pierre Meunier.[48]

Over the next ten days, León followed a path described as northeast or northeast-by-north but almost certainly along what became the eastern portion of the Camino Real. As he entered the western edge of Tejas settlements, don Alonso remarked on fields of corn and beans and commented that the Indians "had very clean houses and high beds in which to sleep." On May 22 he passed through groves of live oak and pines, passed "hills where there are veins of black and red stone," and finally arrived at "a valley thickly settled with houses of the Texas Indians." Adjoining the houses were bounteous fields of corn, beans, pumpkins, and watermelons.[49]

About half a mile distant from the first valley, León and company came upon a second valley, also thickly populated by Tejas Indians. There he met the Indian governor, who informed the commander that his house was nearby. And to that settlement, in León's words, "we gave the name San Francisco de los Tejas." That afternoon, don Alonso called at the governor's house, where he was initially received by the man's brother, his wife, a daughter, and many other people. The host then brought forth "a bench on which to seat me and . . . [gave] me a luncheon of corn tamales and atole, all very clean."[50]

Over the next several days, León and Father Massanet searched for a site on which to found the first Spanish mission in East Texas. During that interval, don Alonso conferred a staff with a cross and the title of governor on the high Tejas official, whom the Spaniards named "Bernardino." León especially enjoined the Indian chieftain and his people to have respect for the priests, and commanded him to "make all his family attend Christian teaching, in order that they might be instructed in the affairs of the holy Catholic faith so that later they might be baptized and become Christians."[51]

Mission San Francisco de los Tejas and a residence for the padres took shape over a five-day period from May 27 to May 31. Upon completion of the work, León gave possession of the mission to Father Massanet. Mass, with the Indian governor and his people in attendance, was celebrated for the first time on June 1, 1690.[52]

While remaining among the Tejas, León learned that four Frenchmen had recently visited their villages. The Indian governor claimed that he had refused to receive the foreigners, for he professed friendship to the Spaniards, then en route to his lands. The Frenchmen were members of Henri de Tonti's expedition, which had descended from Fort St. Louis on the Illinois River to look for survivors of La Salle's colony. One of the men, described by the Indians as having only one hand, was Tonti himself. Having been rebuffed by the Tejas, the Frenchmen had withdrawn eastward toward the Mississippi River. Don Alonso made no attempt to pursue the retreating Frenchmen, believing that the mission could act as an intelligence-gathering outpost and monitor their activities.[53]

On the day the mission was completed, León began preparations for the return march to Coahuila. He proposed that fifty men be left to guard the new structure, but this suggestion was vehemently opposed by Massanet, who would accept only three soldiers to remain with an equal number of priests. Before leaving the mission, Massanet secured a promise from the Indian leader that he would not mistreat the resident friars. Unfortunately, subsequent events revealed the hollowness of that pledge. For in reality, "the experienced and reasonable Alonso De León knew Indians better than the visionary and impetuous Massanet."[54]

As León's command reached the Guadalupe River, don Alonso learned of additional French children living as captives among the Indians, and he detached a small force to seek them out. The thought of Christian children as captives of the heathen weighed heavily on the commander, and he was determined to rescue them at all costs.

For three days León sought information about the exact location of the children, visiting one *ranchería* after another and distributing presents along the way. On June 21 he came upon Indians who held Marie-Madeleine and Robert Talon—their faces and bodies covered with tattoos and paint in the manner of most Texas tribes. Terms of ransom for the girl, sixteen, and the boy, not yet six, were discussed, agreed upon, and paid. It seems, however, that León miscalculated and was overly eager in his negotiations, for it quickly occurred to the Indians that they had undervalued their human property. To León's disgust, they then came to him "with a thousand impertinencies, begging of us all the horses, and even the clothing which we wore upon our backs." While wrangling continued, León's irritation with the natives apparently rose to a dangerous level. At that juncture, a third child of undetermined age, Lucien Talon, arrived in the possession of other Indians, and in the bargaining León again felt that he was showered with impertinence. Threats of the Indians, brandishing bows and arrows and "begging exorbitant things," soon escalated into shouts that they "would have to shoot and kill us all." In León's words: "Their saying this and beginning to shoot were simultaneous, whereupon we attacked them, and having killed four [Indians] and wounded others, they retreated." The commander's actions, well justified in his own mind and reinforced by his experiences as a frontiersman who traditionally relied on military solutions, drew immediate and harsh criticism from Father Massanet. The priest insisted that the clash of arms had been avoidable, that León's soldiers lacked discipline, and that lives were unnecessarily lost. Once again, the views of soldier and missionary with respect to Spanish-Indian relations set them apart.[55]

After rejoining the main body of his troops at the Guadalupe River, León, with the French children in his custody, marched without incident to the Río Grande. Arriving there on July 4, he found the river at flood stage. For eight days his command waited for the current to subside, and during that time don Alonso drafted his account of the expedition. He again painted a highly favorable portrait of East Texas and its Indian inhabitants. Aside from the Tejas, he noted that to the east and northeast of the settlements were villages of the Kadohadachos, who also raised abundant crops and managed their food supply to last throughout the year. But his report cautioned that Frenchmen were likely to mount challenges to the single Spanish outpost in East Texas. He also noted that intelligence from coastal Indians suggested that a ship, presumably French, had stopped to pick up firewood and fresh water. To avert disaster, León again urged the founding of other Spanish settlements on the Guadalupe River and at Matagorda Bay. He further recommended that additional friars be sent to spread the faith among infidel natives and recounted his recovery of several young survivors from La Salle's colony. When the Río Grande was fordable, Captain Gregorio de Salinas Varona, second in command on the expedition, accompanied by Pierre Meunier, carried the governor's reports to Mexico City. And on July 12, 1690, Alonso de León left Texas for the last time and returned to Monclova.[56]

In September 1690, Father Massanet filed a separate report with the viceroy. The padre requested fourteen priests and seven lay brothers for the Texas mission field, and he supported León's recommendations for additional settlements on the Guadalupe and at Matagorda Bay. As for the Tejas, Massanet requested neither soldiers nor a presidio. Instead, he urged the recruitment of civilian craftsmen to build living quarters and chapels. Finally, Massanet suggested that Hispanicized Indian children from the heartland of New Spain be sent to Texas to grow up there and mingle with the Tejas under the supervision and instruction of priests.[57]

Massanet's proposal was endorsed by the crown agent on October 10 and confirmed by the *Junta de Hacienda* (treasury) on November 16. Officials in the capital, however, deemed a military presence on the Guadalupe to be premature, and in any event an expense that had to be approved in Spain by the king and the Royal Council of the Indies. Unless requested by the padres, no soldiers would be sent to Texas. Viceregal authorities did approve Massanet's request for eight missions in Texas—three among the Tejas, four among the Kadohadachos, and one for tribes along the Guadalupe. The fourteen priests and seven lay brothers proposed by Massanet were likewise approved.[58]

León did not fare so well with his superiors in the capital. The suspected buoys near the mouth of the Lavaca River were of particular concern to the viceroy, who closely questioned Salinas Varona and Pierre Meunier about the suspicious objects. Salinas defended León against charges that he had been remiss in failing to investigate the precise nature of the objects, since the commander did not have access to either boat or canoe. Testimony notwithstanding, the chief executive of New Spain took immediate steps to outfit a sea expedition to Matagorda Bay. The expense of that undertaking, which disclosed that the suspected buoys were nothing more than upended logs embedded in silt, created still another black mark on the record of Alonso de León.[59]

As plans for a new missionizing effort in Texas moved forward, the viceroy and an advisory junta quickly dismissed León from consideration as commander. In the manner of good bureaucrats, it was diplomatically suggested that León's continued presence in Coahuila was essential to the security of that province. In reality, don Alonso had fallen into considerable disfavor. He was blamed for not removing all traces of French occupation at Matagorda Bay; he was criticized for not investigating rumors of French presence to the east of the Hasinai; he was targeted by Father Massanet's bitter complaints; and he was charged with corruption by his former subordinate and French translator, Francisco Martínez. Perhaps most telling of all, his frank and honest nature had offended governmental officials in the distant capital. A new governor for the province of Texas, Domingo Terán de los Ríos, received appointment on January 23, 1691. Within two months, Alonso de León, then just slightly more than fifty years of age, "with his health broken by the rigors of Coahuila Indian wars and long marches into Texas," died at Monclova.[60]

In all, from 1686 to 1690, Alonso de León carried out five land expeditions, four of which entered Texas. His contributions in reconnoitering the land, establishing substantial portions of the Camino Real, giving names to rivers, gathering intelligence on Indian groups north of the Río Grande, and founding the first Spanish mission in East Texas are often not fully appreciated in Texas history. His compassion for the French youths, especially the Talon children, who had witnessed the violent death of their mother and other adults at Fort St. Louis, touched his soul. Although the youngsters were born in a nation that challenged Spain's empire in America, León could not countenance Christian children condemned to spend their lives among pagan people.

Despite a few blemishes on his record, such as perhaps padding his résumé to include some of his father's accomplishments, having a short temper, and being stern in his approach to Native Americans who challenged Spanish authority, one should remember that only in the context of twentieth-century judgments does León's attitude toward and treatment of Indians appear to be "heavy-handed." His approach was in keeping with the times and consistent with what seemed to be called for under the circumstances. With a distinguished record of loyal and dedicated service to his monarch, perhaps León's greatest mistake was to inject unwelcome reality into the euphoria that surrounded the first missionary efforts in East Texas. Long before others would acknowledge it, he, as an experienced frontiersman and a seasoned veteran of Indian campaigns in Nuevo León and Coahuila, recognized that unsecured missions on the frontier that was Texas invited failure and potential disaster. But in voicing that opinion, he committed the unforgivable error of challenging the collective wisdom of his superiors. Warts aside, in our view, Alonso de León the younger stands unchallenged as the most able and dedicated soldier-pathfinder in the early history of Spanish Texas.

~
FRANCISCO HIDALGO/
LOUIS JUCHEREAU DE ST. DENIS
Resolute Missionary/Canadian Cavalier
~

On July 19, 1714, four Frenchmen and an equal number of Tejas Indians forded the Río Grande and traveled a short distance to Presidio San Juan Bautista at present-day Guerrero, Coahuila, where they appeared before Commandant Diego Ramón. The leader of this small party was Louis Juchereau de St. Denis, a Canadian-born cavalier who would soon change the course of Texas history. A popular biographer has depicted this daring French Canadian as dressed in "fresh and beautifully tailored linen" and speaking "forceful Spanish."[1] The facts are otherwise. St. Denis had been in the wilderness of Louisiana and Texas for many months, and in a letter dated July 20, 1714 (one day after his arrival at San Juan Bautista), he described his plight and that of his companions by noting: "[We had] been living on the road by what we could hunt. And up to the present we are devoid of supplies and other things necessary for life."[2] Through an interpreter, St. Denis informed Ramón that he had journeyed from Louisiana to the land of the Tejas seeking Father Francisco Hidalgo. Not finding him there, he had pushed on to the Río Grande, where the Tejas assured him he would find Spaniards. Commandant Ramón, once a lieutenant of Alonso de León, must have remembered two of St. Denis's French companions. They were Pierre and Robert Talon, whose tattooed faces bore witness to their brief experiences among the Karankawas and the Tejas following the assassination of La Salle. The third companion was Médard Jallot, the product of a distinguished Canadian family.[3]

It was no accident that St. Denis justified his intrusion into Spanish territory on the basis of wishing to contact Father Hidalgo. Through a combination of personal ambition and missionary zeal, the lives of two men of widely diverse backgrounds had entwined on the Texas scene at a critically important moment.

Following the death of Alonso de León (1691) and the abandonment of Spanish missions in East Texas (1693), lands of the Hasinai Confederation had slipped to the back of most Spaniards' minds but not that of a stubborn Franciscan—Father Francisco Hidalgo. Hidalgo, surely Texas' most patient and persistent missionary, had never given up on his commitment to refound missions among the Tejas.

The early life of Francisco Hidalgo is little more than speculation, for none of the Franciscan chroniclers of Texas who knew him firsthand includes a detailed discussion of his youth. We know Hidalgo was born in Spain, most likely in 1659, and circumstantial evidence suggests that he was an orphan. He first appears in the historical record at age fifteen, when he accepted the religious habit of the Franciscans. After ordination, Hidalgo joined twenty-three of his religious brethren who crossed the Atlantic in 1683 to help found the missionary college of Santa Cruz de Querétaro. At that time he was a twenty-four-year-old priest.[4]

The two dozen "Brown Robes" sailed aboard vessels in the annual *flota* (fleet) and reached Veracruz after a three-month voyage. Upon arrival at the famed port in late May, they encountered the remains of a pillaged and plundered city. Some two thousand pirates had just completed the rape of Veracruz, carrying off its young women, as well as gold and silver bullion that had been stacked on the docks. Consequently, Hidalgo's first experiences in New Spain were ministering to the maimed and confessing the dying of Veracruz.[5]

Hidalgo remained in Veracruz until the commissary of the Franciscans ordered him and his fellow priests to continue on to their destination. En route to Querétaro, the young clerics stopped at villages to rest and teach the Christian Gospel. Early on, Hidalgo demonstrated a special compassion in his dealings with Native Americans. A fellow priest and later a noted historian, Juan Domingo Arricivita, described him as "a completely artless religious . . . zealous for the conversion of the Indians among whom he passed most of his life." Arricivita also viewed Hidalgo as "incapable of all duplicity, cunning, and malice."[6]

Hidalgo was one of the "founding fathers" of the missionary college of Santa Cruz de Querétaro. Established in 1683 as the first *colegio de propaganda fide* (college to propagate the faith) in North or South America, nine of the college's charter members would serve in Texas.[7] Using Querétaro as his base of operations, Hidalgo earned a reputation in surrounding villages for his passion in preaching against vice. From plazas and streets he importuned sinners to abandon their evil ways, and, indeed—if we may believe Father Arricivita—enjoyed great success. Perhaps fulsome in his praise, Arricivita credited Hidalgo with remarkable accomplishments in 1684 within the Bishopric of Puebla. There he reconciled "ancient enmities," stopped "illicit and dishonest trade," and brought forth "general confessions and public penitences . . . on every hand." [8]

Gifted in his sermons and displaying the natural talents of a teacher, Hidalgo illustrated his homilies with simple examples that were easily understood by congregants. And his preaching and invective became so powerful and moving that those seeking contrition were often reduced to floods of tears.[9]

With two confreres, Hidalgo traveled to Zacatecas in 1686, where their sermons so stirred the populace that they clamored for the establishment of a new missionary college in that city. That request, however, would not be granted for some years.[10]

When the three priests departed Zacatecas to preach in nearby raw mining camps, they were followed by an astonishing crowd of enthusiasts numbering more than three thousand. Again, evidence suggests that Hidalgo had become a gifted and perhaps charismatic preacher, but his near-lifelong calling still lay ahead. In 1688 he and the same two companions took the trail northward toward Saltillo. Their goal, simply stated, was to convert Indians to the Catholic faith. But the rigors of sleeping on the ground wherever darkness found them, combined with a heavy workload at Saltillo, took its toll on one of the priests, forcing him to return to Querétaro. Undaunted, Hidalgo and a single companion, Father Francisco Estévez, continued on to villa Monclova, situated at the very edge of the unsettled frontier.[11]

Hidalgo and Estévez had hoped their superiors at Monclova would welcome them and endorse their plans to carry the Christian Gospel into pagan lands, but such was not the case. Local officials, as well as churchmen, rejected their missionary goals; and when the priests persisted, the authorities declared the road beyond Monclova too dangerous to travel without guides. But at that juncture, three Tlaxcalan Indians, who had joined the padres at Saltillo, offered a solution. They would accompany Hidalgo and Estévez to a place known as Boca de Leones and there recruit potential neophytes from the surrounding countryside.[12]

This arrangement won the priests passage to the north, and at Boca de Leones, located at the present-day site of Villadama, Nuevo León, they built a church and offered religious instruction to the natives. Soon after their arrival at this outpost, the discovery of rich silver ore in nearby mountains turned Boca de Leones into a thriving mining camp. But Hidalgo "sought a different kind of wealth." From his mission church, he ventured into the unsettled mountains and deserts, seeking still more converts. However, the rapid population growth at Boca de Leones soon prompted Spanish authorities to partially secularize the mission in 1690, and the few neophytes remaining there returned to their former way of life.[13]

The disappointment visited on Fathers Hidalgo and Estévez did not last long. For while they labored at Boca de Leones, another founder of the missionary college of Santa Cruz de Querétaro, Father Damián Massanet, had joined them on the frontier and set up Mission San Bernardino de Caldera, located about halfway between Boca de Leones and Monclova. In the previous year, as noted in the chapter on Alonso de León, Massanet had been called from his post to join León in the search for La Salle's Fort St. Louis. That expedition and the subsequent founding of Mission San Francisco de los Tejas in 1690 would make Texas the focal point of Hidalgo's life. And it consumed his energies until the day of his death some thirty-five years later. Although originally recruited as a member of León's 1690 expedition, Hidalgo was not permitted to accompany it. Instead, his superiors assigned him to a new mission in Coahuila, a satellite of Father Massanet's Mission Caldera, and he did not enter Texas until 1691. At that time, he was a member of the Domingo Terán de los Ríos expedition.[14]

Terán, the first governor of Texas, led an expedition that differed from León's earlier entradas of 1689 and 1690. Specifically, don Domingo had to share authority—meaning he headed the military contingent—while Father Damián Massanet exercised control over the religious. To clarify this division of responsibility, Spanish authorities insisted that daily recordings of the expedition reflect the cooperation of all senior officials.[15]

Father Hidalgo's name does not appear in Terán's personal diary, but he was assuredly present on the march to San Francisco de los Tejas. He was one of ten religious listed in the missionaries' separate record of the entrada. The expedition crossed the Río Grande below present-day Guerrero at Paso de Francia and continued on to the future site of San Antonio.[16] However, from the very beginning to the end, this undertaking was troubled. When appointed on January 23, 1691, Terán received detailed instructions: He was to found eight new missions among the Tejas and neighboring tribes; he was to resupply San Francisco de los Tejas; he was to explore the country; and he was to investigate rumors that there were Frenchmen to the east of the Tejas settlements. But in reality, don Domingo would accomplish very few of those objectives. In the field, he grumbled constantly about Father Massanet being placed in full charge of the missions. And even before leaving Coahuila the governor wrote the viceroy protesting that any restriction on his authority was unworthy of his rank. When Terán entered Texas in late May 1691, many of the rivers and creeks, as well as the province itself, had been named by previous expeditions. But don Domingo took it upon himself to rename virtually everything. The Río Grande became the Río del Norte; the Nueces, the Río de San Diego; and so on.[17]

On the march to Mission San Francisco de los Tejas, Terán followed a route, which he is credited with marking, that was a bit off the course of the later Camino Real. On June 13 the expedition stopped at the banks of a small stream with nearby groves of cypress and oaks. Prophetically, Terán remarked that the location, which Father Massanet named San Antonio de Padua, would be an ideal place to found a mission. Traveling north by northeast, the Spaniards recorded seeing great herds of buffalo, but as they passed through the piney woods of East Texas don Domingo began a litany of bitter complaints. It was late July into early August, and the weather was typically hot and dry. Worse, Terán and his company faced an unrelenting assault by mosquitoes, ticks, and chiggers. When they finally reached the Brazos, they found the river so low that what little water still ran was "more salty than the sea."[18]

Problems, unfortunately, had already begun with the vast herd of sheep and goats that accompanied the expedition. As the animals began to die of thirst and exhaustion, Terán slowed the pace to try to save the animals, but this decision infuriated the ten missionaries. Shortly after the Trinity crossing, Hidalgo and his companions left the expedition without permission and hastened on to succor Mission San Francisco de los Tejas.[19] Hidalgo's true calling as missionary to the Indians of East Texas was about to begin.

The priests who had remained at San Francisco de los Tejas in 1690 had founded a second religious outpost, Santísimo Nombre de María, about five miles east of the original mission. However, the natives' response to this mission was mostly negative, and that attitude was also evident among the Tejas at the original site. Camped nearby amid an onslaught of bothersome insects, Terán found his disillusionment with East Texas worsening, and he resolved to leave the province as quickly as possible.[20]

Terán's best hope for a quick exodus lay at Matagorda Bay, where he was to rendezvous with supply ships sent from New Spain. Since the Río Grande crossing, however, the expedition had encountered severe drought, and all of the horses were too weak to ride. Upon reaching his destination in East Texas, don Domingo had intended to let the horses graze and regain their strength, but the drought was so severe that the countryside west of the Brazos had been stripped bare of vegetation by vast herds of buffalo.[21] Accordingly, when Terán set out for the coast, he led a sorry contingent of soldiers riding more-hardy mules with the horses following. On this march, don Domingo followed the trail blazed by Alonso de León to the Guadalupe River, complaining bitterly about its crookedness and remarking that "only a sleepwalker could have opened such a road." From the Guadalupe he descended toward Matagorda Bay.[22] Along the way, don Domingo began to formulate an excuse for withdrawing from Texas. If the ships had not arrived, he intended to follow the coast back to Mexico.

Terán was no doubt disappointed to find a frigate and sloop at anchor. Worse—from his point of view—there were instructions from the viceroy that forced him to remain in Texas for several more months, during which time he was to explore lands toward the Red River. Don Domingo, then in the company of Gregorio de Salinas Varona, who had arrived by ship, began the march back to Mission San Francisco de los Tejas on September 27. The drought persisted for several more days, and then the rains came in torrents. Beyond the Brazos, Terán had to slog through a sea of mud, and he spent days waiting for swollen streams to subside. What had once been dry land had been transformed into newborn marshes.[23]

When he finally arrived at Mission Santísimo Nombre de María, Terán was in a black mood, but he was eager to complete his task and withdraw from Texas. He made immediate preparations for his march to the Red River and Kadohadacho country, which began on November 6. Father Massanet accompanied this expedition and eagerly anticipated founding new missions on the Red. But this march, too, was a troubled one, plagued by freezing rain and more than a foot of snow. Upon finally reaching Kadohadacho villages, even the zealous Massanet became discouraged. He reluctantly agreed that founding even one mission was out of the question. The expedition, marching under extremely difficult circumstances, finally staggered to its return destination on December 30, 1691.[24]

On January 9, 1692, Terán departed on his second march to Matagorda Bay. Six of the ten friars were so disheartened by the East Texas experience that they left with the governor, but Father Francisco Hidalgo remained in East Texas. By early 1692, the ice and snow of the previous December had turned into floods. There followed days of trekking through mud and standing water, while the governor's scouts brought back reports that "the country ahead resembled an immense sea." The Terán entourage then encountered rain so heavy that the men could not build campfires to cook food or warm themselves. In crossing the swollen Navasota River, Terán's raft overturned, dumping him and his baggage in its icy waters. When he finally reached Matagorda Bay, he boarded one of the waiting vessels, which bore him away from Texas, eventually to Veracruz.[25]

Terán's nightmarish experiences in Texas helped form negative impressions of the province that lasted for a lifetime. In his diary he remarked that "no rational person has ever seen a worse one." Twenty-five years later, his lieutenant, Gregorio de Salinas Varona, echoed those sentiments by insisting that the Hasinai country would not support Spanish settlements. Salinas characterized East Texas as a land in which one would suffer a thousand discomforts.[26]

The immediate problem for Spanish officials, however, was to resupply the four priests at San Francisco de los Tejas and further their missionary efforts. That task fell to Salinas Varona, the newly appointed governor of Coahuila. Salinas was an extraordinarily capable and experienced captain, having served under León in 1690 and Terán in late 1691. His journey to East Texas began on May 3, 1693, and essentially followed the route taken by León three years earlier. This path was the only one that Salinas knew, for he had arrived by ship near the end of Terán's stay in Texas.[27]

The Salinas party reached Mission San Francisco on June 8, 1693, and made a quick turnabout. After just six days, don Gregorio headed home along the same road. Two of the four missionaries at San Francisco de los Tejas, discouraged by the indifference of the natives to the Christian message, seized the opportunity to return to New Spain. The departing padres complained that the Tejas would not attend Mass, because they had come to believe that baptismal waters were fatal—a belief rooted in their observation that those accepting the sacrament were invariably at the brink of death. And the natives had absolutely refused to congregate at the mission. With Salinas's departure, the only priests remaining were Father Damián Massanet and Francisco de Hidalgo.[28]

Although Massanet chose to remain among the Tejas, he had to acknowledge the validity of Alonso de León's earlier position with respect to missionizing the Tejas. In a report to the viceroy, the founder of San Francisco de los Tejas stated that unless certain conditions were met, the entire mission project would have to be abandoned. Massanet called for the establishment of a formal presidio with sufficient soldiers to ensure respect for the padres, for the selection of more favorable sites for missions, and for the forced congregation of Indians so that they could be taught the Christian message.[29]

On August 31, 1693, a junta in Mexico City discussed Massanet's ultimatum. It concluded that the threat of French presence in East Texas no longer existed and that there was no reason to maintain a mission for the unresponsive Tejas. Governor Salinas and a small group of soldiers were to proceed to Mission San Francisco and escort the remaining priests and soldiers back to Coahuila.[30]

The rescue effort, however, never reached Texas. It was delayed by the onset of cold weather, while at the same time deteriorating conditions at the mission reached flash point. The Tejas had become more openly insolent and threatened bloody rebellion if the Spaniards did not leave. Secretly, Massanet and Hidalgo began packing their sacred belongings. Large objects such as bells and military cannon were buried. On the night of October 25, 1693, Mission San Francisco de los Tejas was set ablaze by the priests themselves, perhaps to avoid the possibility of desecration by the natives, as the padres and a few companions hurriedly retreated toward the safety of Coahuila. However, the small party became disoriented and lost in the wilds of Texas for forty days. Upon reaching the coast, someone finally reconciled their bearings, but four soldiers turned back, choosing life among the Indians. The battered remains of Spain's first missionary effort in East Texas did not reach Monclova until February 17, 1694. Fathers Massanet and Hidalgo were soon reassigned to their college in Querétaro, and the Texas mission field was abandoned.[31]

The missionaries' experiences and two failed missions in East Texas had dampened the spirits of virtually all except Father Hidalgo. For most Spaniards who had entered Texas, including the vast majority of Franciscan missionaries, the experiences of the early 1690s served to keep them out of Texas for more than twenty years.

After his sojourn in East Texas, Francisco Hidalgo again took up missionary work in small villages near Querétaro and remained there for several years. In 1697 Father Antonio Margil de Jesús, an old associate of Hidalgo and cofounder of Santa Cruz de Querétaro, returned as its guardian. During his thirteen-year absence, the college's field of apostolic work had broadened to include such outlying areas of New Spain as New Mexico. However, Coahuila had received little by way of concerted missionary activity, other than the brief efforts of Fathers Hidalgo, Massanet, and Estévez.[32]

Determined to rekindle conversion efforts in Coahuila, in 1698 Margil dispatched Francisco Hidalgo and Diego de Salazar to the region. For Hidalgo, it was the first step in a long and frustrating journey back to Texas. The two priests eagerly accepted their assignment and began work on Mission Santa María de los Dolores, and they followed those efforts by establishing a second mission to the north of it on the Río Sabinas. The latter mission was the first to be named San Juan Bautista, and it brought Hidalgo even closer to Texas.[33]

Margil encouraged the efforts of his colleagues by assigning two additional Franciscans to the mission field, the more notable of whom was Father Antonio de San Buenaventura y Olivares—future founder of Mission San Antonio de Valero. However, because of the unfortunate accidental death of a Christianized Indian interpreter, related fears of a native rebellion, and the difficulty of acquiring water from the Sabinas for irrigation, the first San Juan Bautista did not survive. It was soon supplanted by a second mission of the same name, located nearer the Río Grande. Aiding in the construction of this gateway mission, which was begun on January 1, 1700, was Diego Ramón. Don Diego would be associated with the San Juan Bautista mission and a soon-to-be-built presidio until his death in 1719.[34] The location of both the mission and the presidio had roots in the Río Grande crossings employed by León, Terán, and Salinas Varona. And the new mission placed Hidalgo at the very threshold of Texas.

Although Texas remained unoccupied for the next sixteen years, it was neither forgotten by Hidalgo nor entirely unvisited by Spaniards. Shortly after the founding of San Juan Bautista, two additional missions were founded in close proximity to it. These religious outposts served the native population of the Río Grande area and ministered to hunting-and-gathering tribes north of the river. Also, an expedition captained by Pedro de Aguirre traveled to the future site of San Antonio in the spring of 1709 and again named the river there San Antonio de Padua, the same designation given to it by Father Massanet and Governor Terán in 1691. This expedition served effectively to dispel a rumor that the Tejas were eager for renewed contact with the Spanish. To the contrary, Fathers Isidro Félix de Espinosa and Olivares, who accompanied Aguirre, as diarist and chaplain, respectively, learned that the old Tejas chieftain whom the Spanish had named Bernardino was still ill-disposed toward their faith. This information apparently dampened the missionary zeal of Espinosa, causing him to return to his college, where he remained for many years, but it prompted Olivares to undertake the long journey to Spain, where he would make special pleading for new and better-funded missions among the Tejas.[35]

It remained for Francisco Hidalgo, still stationed at the Río Grande, to champion the immediate cause of renewed missionary efforts among the Hasinai. After years of frustration with Spanish bureaucratic inertia, Father Hidalgo devised a plan that ultimately brought French adventurers and their Tejas guides to Presidio San Juan Bautista del Río Grande in July 1714.

Although Texas remained unoccupied by Europeans from 1694 to 1715, it was a different story in Louisiana. After the death of La Salle, his faithful friend Henri de Tonti traveled from Canada to Versailles in the 1690s. There Tonti and others urged Louis Phélypeaux, Louis XIV's minister of marine and colonies and count of Pontchartrain, to resurrect La Salle's grand enterprise for a French colony at or near the mouth of the Mississippi River. The count must have listened intently as the strategic advantages of a French outpost on the great river were spelled out for him: It would secure access to the sea for Canada; it would protect against English and Spanish designs in the region; and it could serve as a base for French attacks on the rich silver mines of northern New Spain.[36]

The French minister endorsed the proposal and chose Pierre Le Moyne, Sieur d'Iberville, to lead the colonizing effort. Iberville was a Canadian-born explorer, diplomat, and combatant, and he recruited four of his brothers—the most famous of whom was Jean-Baptiste Le Moyne, Sieur Bienville, the future "Father of Louisiana"—to join him in the enterprise. Sailing by way of French Santo Domingo, Iberville arrived at the Mississippi on March 2, 1699, and in April established a temporary fort near present-day Ocean Springs, Mississippi, before returning to France. By early January 1700, French presence in Louisiana had been strengthened by the arrival of fresh supplies and reinforcements. Accompanying Iberville on his second voyage to the Gulf was a Canadian-born cousin by marriage, Louis Juchereau de St. Denis.[37]

St. Denis was born near Quebec on September 17, 1674. His parents, Nicolas Juchereau and Marie Thérèse Giffard, could afford to send their young son to France for schooling. Late 1699 found him at the port of La Rochelle. There he headed one of two companies of Canadians, and attached to his command were Pierre and Jean-Baptiste Talon, survivors of La Salle's ill-fated colony. Perhaps advantaged by family ties, St. Denis soon gained prominence in the Louisiana colony.[38]

In the first months of 1700, St. Denis, in the company of Bienville, twenty-two Canadians, and seven Indian guides, crossed northern Louisiana under extremely adverse circumstances and ascended country along the Red River toward the Kadohadacho villages. The expedition had a twofold objective: to reestablish French contacts with the Hasinai and to check on the Spanish. Its progress was plagued by incessant rains, swamps with waist-deep water, and impenetrable canebrakes. Of building rafts to protect their packs and pushing them through cold water, Bienville wrote: "Never in all our lives have my men or I been so tired. This is fine business for cooling the fires of youth." [39]

En route, St. Denis and Bienville encountered several Kadohadachos to the east of their villages. From these Indians they learned of mounted Spaniards having reached the Red River, but they failed to comprehend that this visitation—led by Terán in 1691—had occurred more than eight years earlier. The native informants also mentioned Spanish settlements near the Neches River, but again failed to report that Spanish missionary efforts in that locale had been abandoned in 1693. Running short of the time allotted by Iberville for the expedition, St. Denis and Bienville began the descent of the Red by boats on April 23, 1700, and thence the Mississippi. And with them traveled the mistaken impression that Spaniards were then present in Texas. [40]

When Iberville returned to France in late May, he left orders for St. Denis to travel upriver to the Red and then explore to the west as far as possible. The Canadian frontiersman was to gather information on Spanish mines and settlements in New Mexico, reconnoiter trails and rivers, and assess the prospects for French colonization. Evidence suggests that St. Denis and his company ascended the Red in the fall of 1700 but were forced to abort their efforts because of massive illness in the ranks. They tried a second time without positive results, and in their third effort entered the wilderness that separated the French in Louisiana from the Spanish on the Río Grande. Aided by the Talon brothers and Médard Jallot, and prompted by a letter written by Father Francisco Hidalgo in 1711, St. Denis would finally penetrate that vastness, but not until 1713–1714. [41]

The passage of so many years without renewed missionary efforts among the Tejas weighed heavily on Father Hidalgo's conscience, and increasingly he saw the omission as a personal failure. In January 1711 he concocted a plan that reflects his higher commitment to the spiritual welfare of the Hasinai, rather than to imperial considerations. On the seventeenth of the month, Hidalgo put pen to paper, writing in Latin to the governor of Louisiana. He asked if the Río de la Palizada (Mississippi) was settled by French Catholics. If so, would it be possible for the governor to sponsor missions among the Tejas? [42]

Passage of the letter from the Río Grande to the Hasinai was entrusted to an Indian named Lázaro; from there it was carried to a French mission on the Mississippi and was subsequently delivered into the hands of Governor Bienville, reaching him in early May 1713. Shortly thereafter, Bienville received news that he would be replaced by a new governor, Antoine de La Mothe, Sieur de Cadillac. When Cadillac arrived on June 5, he brought important news from Europe. The War of Spanish Succession (Queen Anne's War in the British colonies), in which Spain and France had been allies, had ended. Cadillac immediately sought to take advantage of the friendly relations with Spain that had prevailed during the war. He loaded a ship with merchandise brought from France and dispatched it to Veracruz, but this approach was rebuffed by Spanish officials at the port. Encouraged by Hidalgo's letter, Cadillac used a different approach. He would next try contacts with Spain's remote northern frontier, in the hope of establishing trade there.[43]

The new governor sent for St. Denis, who had on at least three occasions ascended the Red River toward Hasinai country. Cadillac found St. Denis, then thirty-nine years of age and unmarried, eager to accept command in return for a small stipend and trading privileges. Since his forays in 1700, St. Denis had served for a time as a fort commander on the Mississippi and later supported himself as a trader. The young French Canadian was admittedly headstrong but also uniquely qualified for the undertaking.[44]

St. Denis, accompanied by twenty-four Canadians and a number of Indians, left Mobile in the latter part of September 1713. Two members of his entourage were the Talon brothers, Pierre and Robert, who knew the terrain of East Texas and possessed skills as interpreters of native languages and Spanish. Traveling by canoe, St. Denis and his company ascended the Mississippi and Red Rivers to the Natchitoches villages and then set out on foot for Hasinai country. Upon reaching their destination, they inquired about Father Hidalgo's whereabouts.[45]

The tattooed faces of the Talons, indelible reminders of their sojourn among the Karankawas and Tejas, won them ready acceptance among the Indians. Although Father Hidalgo had not been among them for more than twenty years, the Tejas nonetheless agreed to lead St. Denis and three companions to the Río Grande, where they would find Spaniards. The final leg of the journey ended with the events described as the beginning of this chapter.

As it turned out, Father Hidalgo was not to be found at San Juan Bautista, having been recalled to his missionary college at Querétaro, but he would soon hear from both Commandant Diego Ramón and St. Denis.

Ramón wrote: "There are in this presidio four Frenchmen, a captain named Luis de Sn. Dionisio, and another Pedro Talon, and the other Roberto, who were among those rescued by General Alonso de León." The commandant added that St. Denis could not speak Spanish, nor could his companion (Jallot). Hidalgo's heart must have quickened as he read Ramón's urgent warning, a warning that would undoubtedly reach the viceroy's desk: "And I say that if His Majesty (who God protects) does not take warning and the Naquitoises [Natchitoches] villages are not settled, the French will be masters of all this land." Whatever the padre's intent in writing the governor of Louisiana, it could not have played out better for his ambitions.[46]

St. Denis's missive, written two days before Ramón's, acknowledged that Hidalgo's letter of January 1711 had finally reached French missionaries on the banks of the Mississippi. The French leader castigated the Indian Lázaro for not having "the diligence that he should have had because the letter did not fall into to the hands of the Governor General of Louisiana until the second of May of 1713." St. Denis nonetheless remarked that the letter "had given great pleasure to the governor and to all the missionaries who are in the country who look only to the glory of God as does our governor." He recounted his journey to the Hasinai and his disappointment in finding "that your Reverence had established and abandoned residence in different years." Since the cavalier had promised the governor of Louisiana that he would not "return to La Mobila without bringing news of your Reverence," he had pushed on to the Río Grande. St. Denis concluded with the admission that he and his companions were in desperate straits, and he implored "charity and succor" from Hidalgo. He placed himself at the mercy of Captain Ramón, who detained the Frenchman and his party while awaiting instructions from the viceroy. And in the interim, St. Denis directed his attentions toward the ladies of Presidio San Juan Bautista.[47] Quick to catch the roving eye of St. Denis was Commandant Ramón's attractive step-granddaughter, Manuela Sánchez Navarro. The relationship of this young woman, who figures so prominently in the early history of Texas and Louisiana, to the Ramón family has long been in question. Alternately known as Commandant Ramón's "daughter" or "granddaughter," Manuela was neither, nor was her surname Ramón.[48]

As he awaited news of his fate from the viceroy in Mexico City, St. Denis spent pleasant days courting Manuela and engaging in intrigue of his own. In the late winter of 1714–1715, the Talon brothers managed to slip away from San Juan Bautista and cross the Río Grande. With them went a carefully worded letter penned by St. Denis to the governor of Louisiana, a caution dictated by fears that the Talons might be detained and the contents of the letter revealed.

St. Denis wrote that he did not "wish to write you [Cadillac] fully of all that has happened here; the bearers, whom I have sent away in secret, will tell you the better part." He added that he would be detained on the Río Grande, because "the captain dares not allow us to depart without order from the viceroy. As for myself, I do not wish to leave in that manner, seeing a handsome fortune before my eyes for Mobile."[49]

The Talons made good their escape and indeed reported firsthand to the Sieur de Cadillac. They mentioned mines not more than sixty leagues from the Río Grande at Boca de Leones, as well as rich merchants eager to buy French goods with freshly mined and unmarked silver. But there was more. The Talons noted that St. Denis intended to marry Manuela Sánchez, "thus raising Cadillac's suspicions that his wily agent was not tending strictly to business." In writing to Count Pontchartrain, the governor expressed further concerns. He commented on St. Denis's hollow promise to make a quick return to Louisiana, pointing out that "as he must marry a Spanish girl, one may believe his journey will be very long." The governor concluded that St. Denis "has some good qualities but . . . some bad ones also—he loves his comforts, is given to vanity, and is not sufficiently zealous for the king's service."[50]

Under viceregal orders, St. Denis traveled to Mexico City in the spring of 1715, most likely in the company of Domingo Ramón, son of Commandant Diego Ramón. Upon reaching the capital, the French adventurer received exceptionally courteous treatment, for Spanish officials there had much to learn from him. St. Denis obligingly retraced his journey league by league from Louisiana to San Juan Bautista, and his comments about the Tejas Indians especially stirred the interest of the viceroy and his advisors. He reported that the Indians still held the Spaniards in high regard and longed for their return. Significantly, St. Denis also related that the Indians had kept their reverence for the Catholic faith. In this regard, St. Denis and Hidalgo were following the same script but for different reasons. The Canadian adventurer wished to draw the Spanish and French empires closer together, thereby creating the possibility of profitable trade for himself; the Spanish missionary had likely written his letter of 1711 in the hope that the French would respond and that their actions would trigger a reopening of Spanish missions in East Texas—if for no other reason than to lay claim to the area. In St. Denis's case, he either failed to comprehend Spain's stringent mercantile restrictions, which forbade trade with foreigners, or he shrewdly anticipated that illegal trade between the far-flung but tangential outposts of France and Spain in America would become a way of life. In Hidalgo's case, the good padre could relieve his conscience by being the single-minded advocate of new efforts to convert the Tejas.[51]

The *fiscal* (legal officer) in Mexico City quickly demonstrated a firm grasp of the situation. To avoid the widespread introduction of French merchandise into the northern frontier provinces, all Spanish officials there must be alerted. Second, Father Hidalgo and his Franciscan brethren, accompanied by Spanish soldiers, must reestablish missions in Hasinai country.[52]

Domingo Ramón, an experienced frontiersman with family ties at San Juan Bautista, would lead the entrada, and St. Denis, who was soon to marry Commandant Ramón's step-granddaughter, would serve as the expedition's commissary officer. Whatever his personal motives, the Canadian cavalier's cooperation with Spanish officials had the effect of "[quitclaiming] Texas to Spain—a matter that did not pass unnoticed by his employers." Governor Cadillac had expressly admonished St. Denis to communicate with Hidalgo and no other, and he was understandably upset that his agent's "bad qualities" had led him to accept a formal position in Spain's efforts to reoccupy East Texas.[53]

However, St. Denis was too clever to risk the alienation of his own king and countrymen and in the process jeopardize his commercial objectives. Accordingly, he urged his monarch to occupy Matagorda Bay and declare the Río Grande the boundary between Louisiana and New Spain. At the same time, it was not lost on Cadillac that his own agent was aiding and abetting Spanish settlement of a significant portion of the Gulf region, a settlement that was designed to exclude the French. In response, the governor of Louisiana ordered his subjects to occupy Natchitoches villages along the Red River. But this action also fit nicely with St. Denis's master plan of bringing the French and Spanish empires into close proximity.[54]

Meanwhile, Domingo Ramón and St. Denis made preparations for their expedition to the Tejas. Ramón first traveled to Boca de Leones and Saltillo in order to gather soldiers, settlers, and supplies, while St. Denis made haste to San Juan Bautista. Traveling separately were Franciscan religious, including Father Hidalgo, from the missionary colleges of Querétaro and Zacatecas. In late 1715 or early 1716, St. Denis and eighteen-year-old Manuela Sánchez exchanged marriage vows and began a brief honeymoon that was interrupted by the arrival of don Domingo's entourage on April 18, 1716.[55]

St. Denis remained with Manuela for a few more days. He then left his pregnant bride and overtook the caravan, which had already crossed the Río Grande and was en route to its final destination. The entrada included nine priests, three lay brothers, twenty-six soldiers, several dozen settlers, and livestock numbering in the thousands. The size of the Domingo Ramón/St. Denis expedition alone underscores that Spain intended not just to set up new mission outposts but to establish a permanent presence in Texas. As further evidence of that intent, seven of the soldiers were married and brought along their families, making their wives the first recorded Spanish women in Texas. Responsibility for reestablishing Spanish missions in East Texas and beyond into present-day Louisiana was divided equally between friars from the colleges of Querétaro and Zacatecas.[56]

With the assistance of Ramón and St. Denis, Mission San Francisco was reestablished for the Neche Indians and neighboring tribes. Renamed Nuestro Padre San Francisco de los Tejas, its location was apparently east of the original (1690) site. Given his role in returning Spanish presence to East Texas, it was entirely appropriate that Father Francisco Hidalgo received appointment as minister of this first of six religious outposts founded in 1716–1717 (Figure 5).[57]

The new missions were established in the very locale where two had failed in the early 1690s. They were also far removed (more than four hundred miles) from San Juan Bautista. Nonetheless, this combined apostolic and imperial undertaking established a western barrier to French claims in the region. By 1717 the French and Spanish empires faced each other from their respective outposts in western Louisiana— a confrontation that would continue for many more decades. But more immediate events would oblige St. Denis to sever his ties with the Spanish, separate his wife from her family on the Río Grande, and become a persistent thorn in the Spanish side.

After helping the Franciscans establish four missions in East Texas, St. Denis journeyed to Natchitoches island in the Red River. By January 1716, Cadillac had sent a sergeant and a squad of soldiers there to reinforce the site. Reunited with fellow Canadians and Frenchmen, the cavalier then continued on to Mobile. In the heartland of Louisiana, he formed a company composed of Canadian merchants, all of whom saw him, with his strategic marriage into the Ramón family, as the ideal entrée into commercial ventures with the Spanish.[58]

Unfortunately for St. Denis, Spanish officials on the frontier, especially Gregorio de Salinas Varona at Pensacola, warned the viceroy of the Canadian's intent to promote illicit trade in the remote provinces of

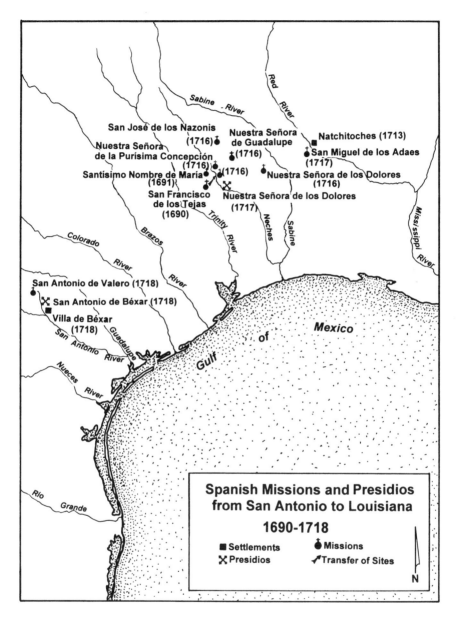

The map contains the following labels:

Sabine - River

Red River

San José de los Nazonis (1716)

Nuestra Señora de Guadalupe (1716)

Natchitoches (1713)

Nuestra Señora de la Purísima Concepción (1716)

San Miguel de los Adaes (1717)

Santísimo Nombre de María (1691)

(1716)

Nuestra Señora de los Dolores (1716)

San Francisco de los Tejas (1690)

Nuestra Señora de los Dolores (1717)

Trinity River

Neches

Sabine

Mississippi River

Colorado River

Brazos River

San Antonio de Valero (1718)

San Antonio de Béxar (1718)

Villa de Béxar (1718)

Guadalupe

San Antonio River

Nueces River

Gulf of Mexico

Rio Grande

Spanish Missions and Presidios from San Antonio to Louisiana 1690-1718

■ Settlements   ● Missions
✗ Presidios   ⚑ Transfer of Sites

N

FIGURE 5

Spanish missions and presidios from San Antonio to Louisiana, 1690–1718.
This map depicts the earliest missions and presidios in Spanish Texas.
(Cartography by Caroline Castillo Crimm.)

northern New Spain. And by extension, the web of suspicion came to include the Ramóns at San Juan Bautista.[59]

When St. Denis returned to East Texas at Christmastime in 1716, he was accompanied by goods from Cadillac's storehouses. Eager to see his wife, the French cavalier selected seven pack mules, loaded them with his personal merchandise, and pushed on to San Juan Bautista. His happy reunion with Manuela and their infant daughter turned sour, however, when Commandant Diego Ramón confiscated all of the goods transported by his step-grandson. Don Diego had been warned by the viceroy to be suspicious of the Frenchman's designs, and he no doubt felt that he must enforce the law against the entry of foreign goods, as well as distance himself from the charge of filial partiality.[60]

For his part, St. Denis reacted angrily, maintaining that he intended to become a Spanish citizen by virtue of his marriage to Manuela and that the goods were not illegal. But it was all to no avail. Commandant Ramón was unmoved, and within days of his arrival at San Juan Bautista, the Canadian adventurer again took the long road to Mexico City.

Two years had passed since St. Denis had charmed the viceroy of New Spain into releasing him and appointing him as commissary officer for the reoccupation of Texas, and in the interim the political climate had changed. The War of Spanish Succession, during which Spain and France were allies, had ended. With the restoration of peace by the Treaty of Utrecht (1713) and the death of Louis XIV (1715), the pro-French attitude of Philip V in Spain and his colonial representatives in Mexico City had changed dramatically. Worse for St. Denis, communication from Martín de Alarcón, the new governor of Coahuila and Texas, cast additional suspicion on his motives. Alarcón had carried out an extended investigation into the affairs of the Ramóns and their French in-law, and in doing so he had compiled damning evidence, suggesting that a sizable contraband operation had been narrowly averted by St. Denis's arrest.[61]

None of this augured well for St. Denis in the capital. Initially, he had been incarcerated but was subsequently released from prison on the recommendation of a friendly and sympathetic official; however, he was forbidden to leave the city. Temporary freedom permitted him to sell a few items of merchandise and pay expenses, but he was strictly enjoined from ever again entering the province of Texas. For more than a year St. Denis languished in Mexico City. During that time his patience wore thin, and he made ill-advised statements. Faced with a second imprisonment, he fled the capital on September 5, 1718, and eventually made his way to Natchitoches. Manuela was later permitted to join him, and at about the same time, St. Denis became commandant of the French outpost on the Red (Figure 6).[62]

Until his death more than twenty years later, St. Denis was never far from the mind of Spanish officials. For reasons that will become apparent in subsequent chapters, they did not trust him, and they feared his persuasive influence over the native population of East Texas and western Louisiana. To one historian who has studied his career, he appears "to have had difficulty in balancing his greed with his devotion to family." It also seems likely that the Spanish were correct in regarding St. Denis warily, for if offered a finger, "he would have taken an arm." First, last, and always, it may be said that St. Denis "was unable to turn his back on the opportunities he saw in contraband trade."[63]

Nevertheless, as he fell victim to advancing age, illness, and the realization of missed opportunities, St. Denis tried to follow the dictates of his heart. On January 10, 1743, just months before his death, St. Denis asked to be relieved of his post as commandant of Fort Saint-Jean-Baptiste at Natchitoches. He also requested permission to retire to New Spain, but that final petition was denied. Louis Juchereau de St. Denis died at Natchitoches in 1744 and was buried there.[64]

Meanwhile, Francisco Hidalgo, much older than his French Canadian counterpart, had died eighteen years earlier. Like St. Denis, Father Hidalgo's declining years had been filled with disappointment and sorrow. Beginning in 1716, Hidalgo served at the second San Francisco de los Tejas in East Texas until the Spanish abandoned the region during the Chicken War of 1719. Reassigned to San Antonio de Valero, the foremost advocate of missions among the Tejas never returned to take up those labors. Instead, Hidalgo's new passion became the establishment of missions in the heart of Apachería, a longing that remained unfulfilled. Discouraged, the good Franciscan left Valero in 1725 and retired to San Juan Bautista, where he died on November 6 of the following year at the age of sixty-seven. In all, Hidalgo had answered a religious calling for more than half a century, having spent forty-three of those years as a missionary. And of those more than four decades of apostolic endeavors, thirty-five years had been spent in Coahuila and Texas.[65]

The scheming of Father Francisco Hidalgo, combined with the failure of Spanish officials to discern Louis Juchereau de St. Denis's true motives—or perhaps because they did read his intentions correctly—meant that both men would play critical roles on the northern frontier of New

FIGURE 6

*Sketch of St. Denis and Manuela Sánchez. St. Denis and his bride stroll
the grounds of Fort Saint-Jean-Baptiste des Natchitoches.
(Commissioned original artwork by Jack Jackson.)*

Spain. With French assistance, Spain reestablished its presence in eastern Texas and western Louisiana, and Hidago continued to pursue his religious goals among the natives. St. Denis, on the other hand, despite an advantageous marriage into the prominent Ramón family, failed to establish his bona fides as a Spanish subject. His Red River outpost came to define the political limits of his entrepreneurial ambition, but not his persistent influence on Spanish Texas. As for Hidalgo, his penned missive of 1711 to Governor Bienville no doubt initiated a series of events that went far beyond what he had envisioned. Nonetheless, the determined Franciscan missionary and the Canadian adventurer set in motion a chain of events that in large measure determined that colonial Texas would be Spanish, not French.

FOUR

ANTONIO MARGIL DE JESÚS

Saintly Franciscan

$\sim$

On a bright afternoon in late April 1697, a Franciscan priest, "burned by the sun, in a habit that was patched considerably," approached the church of Santa Cruz de Querétaro, situated some ninety miles to the northwest of Mexico City. For thirteen years Father Antonio Margil de Jesús had been absent from the missionary college that he and Francisco Hidalgo helped found. Since leaving Querétaro, Margil had invariably walked barefoot through much of Central America, refusing to ride horse or burro. With characteristic humility and a dash of humor, the good padre had labeled himself "God's donkey." But the years had already taken their toll. Margil left Querétaro as a young man; "he returned old and worn out, but his hands were full of good works." After praying on his knees for an extended time, Margil retired to a cubicle reserved for him by his Franciscan brethren. There he allowed a lay brother to wash his feet and shave thick calluses from them with a wood rasp. He had traveled far in his absence from the apostolic college, but ahead for "God's donkey" lay reassignment in Central America, the founding of a missionary college at Zacatecas, the establishment of the most beautiful and successful mission in Texas, and, after death, the prospect of beatification and sainthood.[1]

Born in Valencia, Spain, on August 18, 1657, to Juan Margil Salumaro and Esperanza Ros, Antonio Margil was baptized two days after birth. As a boy the young Antonio displayed talent, humor, and virtue, and his Christian parents sought teachers capable of enhancing his already apparent good qualities. Displaying a "lively and merry disposition," as well as an uncommon youthful predilection for the faith, Margil built miniature replicas of altars at home, said Mass before them to the best of his ability, and prayed at various churches where the Blessed Sacrament was exposed. Worried about his constant fasting and extended absences from home, Margil's mother urged her son to keep a less demanding regimen. But the boy replied that his rapt devotion to the Blessed Sacrament caused time to pass seemingly in an instant and that only the desire of sacristans to lock their churches forced him into the streets of Valencia and sent him toward home.[2]

Given his happy but nonetheless devout nature, it is not surprising that Margil sought and obtained his parents' consent to enter the convent of La Corona de Cristo in Valencia, a training ground for those who wished to join the ranks of the Friars Minor. Official records of the *convento* reveal that "between 5 and 6 o'clock in the afternoon of April 22, 1673, Brother Antonio Margil, a native of Valencia," then nearly sixteen years of age, "asked to be admitted as a choir religious . . . and, in the presence of the community that had assembled for this purpose, received the habit from Fray José Salellas, actual Guardian of said convent."[3]

As a novice, Margil fasted rigorously and displayed unusual penitential zeal by donning a hair shirt. Upon the completion of a probationary year, he made his profession of faith on the afternoon of April 25, 1674. Margil seems to have taken to heart the Gospel text of Saint Luke for the feast of Saint Mark, heard the very morning of his commitment to the faith: "Behold, I send you forth as lambs in the midst of wolves. Carry neither purse, nor wallet, nor sandals." While still a novice he had slipped away to the church, thinking he was unobserved, and opened a tomb containing a corpse that was still decomposing. His supervisor followed him and found Margil with his head thrust into the awful-smelling grave. Asked what he was doing, the novice replied he was "reminding this brute of a body of what it is now and what it will one day become." The young man, who had already labeled himself as "Nothingness Itself," seems early on to have conquered all fears of the transitoriness of life.[4]

At eighteen Margil was sent to study philosophy for three years at a friary in Alicante. Upon the completion of that course, he returned to Valencia to study theology. There he regularly prayed the fourteen Stations of the Cross in the convent garden while weighted under a heavy cross, and on one occasion passively subjected himself to repeated bites from a swarm of mosquitoes. The latter ordeal, a test of will and obedience, was discontinued on the following day when Margil "awoke with his face so swollen and puffed up that he was hardly recognizable."[5]

Margil proved to be an excellent student of theology but no better than good in philosophy. His accomplishments in the former were so profound that he feared appointment as a professor of the discipline in Valencia. That was not his calling, for he would find his life's work among unschooled Indians in the New World, rather than in the company of learned men in the Old.[6]

Several months after Margil had observed his twenty-fifth birthday, he received the sacrament of ordination and was assigned to a friary, where he preached for a brief time. Upon returning to Alicante, Fray Antonio learned that a fellow Franciscan, Antonio Llinás de Jesús María, was intent on recruiting missionaries for service in the Indies. Llinás, a Majorcan, had firsthand experience in New Spain, having served in the Franciscan province of Michoacán for nearly two decades. In Spain to attend a chapter meeting of the Franciscans, Llinás sought missionaries to Christianize Indians of the Sierra Gorda, a mountainous region that lay between Querétaro and present-day Valles.[7]

Initially, Llinás sought permission from Father José Jiménez de Samaniego, the general of the Franciscan order, to recruit twelve friars for the Sierra Gorda enterprise. Jiménez liked the idea but felt that the twelve friars, no matter how intent their efforts, were destined to fail. For, as they died or became incapacitated, there would be no one to sustain their labors. To make missionary efforts more enduring and increase the chances of long-range success, the Franciscan superior suggested the founding of a missionary college of twenty-four religious.[8]

With the backing of Father Jiménez and the king's approval, which came on April 18, 1682, the new missionary college would be founded in the friary of Santa Cruz de Querétaro. As superior of the future apostolic college, Father Llinás set about recruiting his two dozen Brown Robes. He collected his intended followers and was ready to sail for the Indies in June, but the ship's departure was delayed for eight months. In the interim, about three-fourths of the original twenty-four friars returned to their provinces, and a second recruitment had to be undertaken. Among the new enlistees chosen for assignment in the Indies was Father Antonio Margil de Jesús.[9]

Fray Antonio took leave of his fellow Franciscans at Alicante and Valencia and set out on foot for the port of Cádiz. He arrived there shortly before a scheduled departure date on March 4, 1683. On this occasion, ships carrying the religious weighed anchor on time and joined the fleet commanded by Captain General Diego Fernández de Saldívar. Aside from Margil, the assembled Franciscans included many prominent names in the early religious history of Texas.[10]

En route to the Indies, the Franciscan missionaries traveled on various vessels of the *flota* (fleet), with Margil and Llinás aboard Fernández's flagship. In this manner they could preach to the passengers, administer the sacraments, and console the ill. On May 30 the fleet came in view of San Juan de Ulúa, the great fortress built to defend Veracruz, only to learn that pirates had just sacked the city.[11]

Veracruz had been thought to be impregnable to foreign intrusion, for more than one hundred years had passed since the port had last been threatened—at that time by the English sea dog John Hawkins. Of late, the defenders of Veracruz had become complacent, believing that pirates would not be foolhardy enough to mount an attack on the city. But earlier in May, Laurens (Lorencillo) Cornelis Boudewijn de Graaf, Michel de Grammont, and a force of 1,400 struck, knowing that the docks would be laden with silver in anticipation of the fleet's arrival.[12]

When the buccaneer commanders and their cutthroat followers stormed Pólvora Bastion, the great stronghold inside the city, only two of its eleven cannon were functional, and even those could not be used because they lacked appropriate powder and shot. Once in control of the city, the freebooters unleashed an incredible orgy of rape, murder, and plunder on the Veracruzans, leaving more than three hundred dead. In all, De Graaf and Grammont seized 800,000 pesos in specie, 400,000 pesos in wrought silver, and 200,000 pesos in gold chains, jewels, and pearls. Forced to accompany the departing buccaneers were 1,500 blacks and mulattoes who were sold as slaves, as well as attractive young Spanish women sentenced to a brief and brutal life of sexual bondage.[13]

On June 6, 1683, when favorable winds permitted the Spanish fleet to enter the roadstead, the disembarking Franciscans, having spent ninety-three days aboard ship, learned the enormity of De Graaf and Grammont's crimes. The padres' first days in New Spain were spent not among Native Americans in the wilderness but in attending to "the dying and the despoiled . . . picking their way among the putrefying bodies to administer the last rites and give what solace they could." The experience was especially troubling for the compassionate and ascetic Father Margil, who, upon seeing such desolation, was moved to tears.[14]

The missionaries spent several days burying the dead and offering what little consolation they could to the living. But Veracruz was not their final destination. Dividing themselves into groups of two or three and taking different roads, they proceeded to Puebla, where they reconvened for the march to Mexico City. From the capital four of the friars, including Margil, were ordered on to Querétaro, preaching along the way. It seems likely that Margil and the other Brown Robes traveled light, carrying only a staff, crucifix, and breviary, because they were enjoined by the precepts of their order and the Gospel to enter towns and "eat what is set before you." [15]

At Querétaro certain formalities had to be observed. The papal bull of Innocent XI, three royal decrees, and three letters from the minister general and the commissary general of the Indies were presented to the personnel of the major Franciscan friary on August 13, 1683. All communiqués left little doubt that the friary itself and the college of Santa Cruz were to become the home of the apostolic missionaries, although formal acceptance of the inevitable did not come until November 20, 1683. [16]

Father Margil had found a temporary home but not one of comfort by his own choosing. Once again, his asceticism seems extreme to our contemporary world: he prayed the stations bearing a heavy cross and wearing a crown of thorns; and at night, while his brethren slept, he scourged himself. When not in prayer or meditation, Fray Antonio walked the streets of Querétaro, rebuking its revelers for their love of bullfights, feasting, and dancing. [17]

The persistence of Margil appears to have changed the social climate of Querétaro. He visited the slum districts singing hymns, and he admonished frequenters of the wine cask to reform their ways. Slowly but surely, fiestas, gambling, and obscene comedies became less common. One disappointed traveler who was about to leave the city remarked: "Querétaro is no longer Querétaro . . . [for] there are no longer such fandangos as there used to be." [18]

Margil traveled to Mexico City in October 1683, preaching there for about two weeks before returning to Querétaro. He remained at the apostolic college until March of the following year, when he departed for Veracruz and assignment in Yucatán. At Campeche he would join three co-religious from Santa Cruz in forming a friary of the Observants. Margil's constant companion and mentor in this new endeavor was Father Melchor López de Jesús who had known him since the former was a boy in Valencia. [19]

For the next thirteen years, the two men were virtually inseparable. They traversed much of Central America: from Campeche to the province of Tabasco; from Tabasco to the present state of Chiapas— containing then, as now, the poorest of the poor in Mexico. There both men fell gravely ill. Margil, at the threshold of death, received the sacrament of extreme unction but then quickly rallied to regain his health. [20]

Fathers Margil and López next traveled a circuitous route of more than one hundred leagues to the capital of Guatemala, preaching as they went. By 1688 they had entered Nicaragua and from there continued on to Honduras and Costa Rica. Over the next three years, the padres labored among pagan people in the mountains of southern Costa Rica and journeyed to the southern coast. But in late August 1691, the two companions were ordered back to Querétaro. They returned to the Guatemalan capital with emaciated faces, bodies weakened by tumors, and feet covered with sores and insect bites.[21]

Their recall to the college of Santa Cruz was soon rescinded, and the two men were then assigned to the province of Verapaz, the very locale in Guatemala missionized by the great Dominicans Bartolomé de las Casas and Luis Cáncer in the sixteenth century. After six months in the province, Margil and López were ordered from Verapaz to found a hospice in the capital but were unable to accomplish that objective because they lacked the king's permission. This meant a return trip to Verapaz, where they again took up their labors. But the most difficult task lay ahead—so difficult that even the zealous Margil had to admit temporary failure.[22]

The two priests were about to encounter the irrepressible and unconquered Lacandón Maya of present-day Chiapas. En route to their assignment, Fathers Margil and Melchor were twice abandoned by their guides, and after six months had failed to contact a single Lacandón. The experience once again left them at death's door. Margil assessed the condition of his companion by declaring him "a skeleton from hunger." But worse danger lay ahead. The two men were soon pounced upon by Lacandón Indians, who tore their habits into shreds and beat them mercilessly. For five days the men were held without food and readied for sacrifice. Each day the Indians would examine their intended victims by feeling Margil and declaring him "all right," while regarding the aged López as "spoiled."[23]

The equanimity with which the two Franciscans faced death apparently confused the Lacandóns. The priests were spared the knife but still faced danger. Margil reluctantly concluded that "God's hour had not yet arrived for the Lacandóns," and the two priests were permitted to take their leave but soon returned to try anew.[24]

The second visit among the Lacandóns lasted from February 1695 to March 1697. It was occasioned by a desire on the part of Spanish officials to open a road that would link Yucatán with Guatemala, a route that ran through lands of those natives. On that occasion, Margil and López were somewhat more successful. Fray Antonio had learned a number of Lacandón words and was able to translate a good part of the Christian doctrine into that native tongue.[25]

During this two-year sojourn among the fierce Lacandóns, Father Margil's reputation as a saintly man grew steadily. Allegedly, the sick became well by touching his habit; a variant of the "loaves and fishes" miracle of Jesus occurred as Margil distributed a seemingly inexhaustible ration of cornmeal from a small cup; and his borrowed habit proved impervious to rain when used by a companion for protection against a torrential mountain thunderstorm.[26]

Typically, cynics tried to ridicule the curative powers of the increasingly popular and mysterious padre. On one occasion, Margil was "set up" by a group of pranksters who asked him to hear the confession of a "dying laborer" who had supposedly feigned illness. Fray Antonio approached the man and examined him carefully. He then said to those present: "The poor man is dead. May God have mercy on his soul." As it turned out, the man was indeed dead.[27]

While still among the Lacandóns, Margil also gained a reputation for covering great distances in amazingly little time, and he apparently never experienced difficulties in crossing rivers. When asked how he could accomplish such feats without ever being seen on a road or getting wet, he smiled and replied, "I have my short cuts and God also helps me."[28]

In traveling from place to place, Margil almost never walked in silence. He recited the rosary but more commonly sang hymns, especially *El Alabado* to honor the Holy Eucharist and the Virgin Mary. And despite repeated offers of horses or burros to ease his journeys, Fray Antonio with rare exception refused any manner of conveyance. When summoned from Central America to assume the position of guardian at Santa Cruz, "God's donkey" covered the distance between Oaxaca City and Querétaro, the last leg of his return to the apostolic college, in record time. He arrived under circumstances described at the inception of this chapter.[29]

During Margil's absence, the college of Santa Cruz de Querétaro had widened its apostolic work northward to include such outlying areas of New Spain as the province of New Mexico. But little in the way of missionary activity had occurred in Coahuila.[30] The new guardian was determined to correct that omission, and he soon sent forth the determined Father Francisco Hidalgo, as detailed in the previous chapter.

Margil himself was still years away from the twilight of a remarkable career that would be spent in Texas. His college had been strengthened by the arrival of twenty-three priests and four lay brothers in 1692, and Fray Antonio meant to continue that impetus. One of his first acts as guardian was to send Father Francisco Estévez, an old colleague of Hidalgo's, to Madrid and Rome. Estévez was to gain the favor of king and pope so as to recruit even more volunteers for the missionary college.[31]

Margil continued to demonstrate what his fellow religious often regarded as miraculous powers. He seemed at times all-knowing and could ferret out the slightest misdeed committed by his brethren. But he was admired for being much more than a strict disciplinarian filled with rebukes for petty offenders. He built an infirmary in the friary and offered treatment to the lame and the halt, especially a poor ulcerated paralytic whom he came to love dearly. And, of course, his religious observances were second to none.[32]

One of Fray Antonio's favorite activities was to read aloud chapters from Sister María de Agreda's *Mystical City of God*. Writings by the famed "Lady in Blue" of Texas history were especially inspiring to him. Because Margil seems to have needed only about three hours of sleep per night, he could follow a regimen that allowed an inordinate amount of time for hearing the confessions of others and praying on his own. He regularly ate no breakfast and limited his dinner to broth and greens. On rare occasions when Margil allowed himself a sweet, he invariably put salt on it. When asked why he did so, he replied that "very often he had tasted the chalice of bitterness in the sweetest things."[33]

Margil's three-year appointment as guardian of Santa Cruz de Querétaro expired in April 1700. During that time, he received the sad news that Father Melchor López had died in Honduras. And when his term ended, Fray Antonio was once again summoned to Guatemala, where he was to establish a second college for the propagation of the faith. The efforts of Father Francisco Estévez, his advocate in Madrid, had borne fruit.

Margil's leaving occasioned much sadness at the apostolic college. Somewhat later, the brother of his biographer and friend, Father Isidro Félix de Espinosa, commented in a letter to Fray Isidro that "Our Father in Christ left for Guatemala . . . [and] in only ten days he covered the distance to Oaxaca, as though he were a courier. It is the work of God since the impetus and inspiration of the Holy Spirit carries him from town to town and from province to province. Whether Margil will return or not I do not know. He did not leave us much hope."[34]

When intent on reaching a destination, Margil appears to have walked an average of about forty-five miles a day. Accordingly, it is not surprising that he arrived in Guatemala after approximately six weeks on the road. There he supervised and participated in the building of the church and friary for the new apostolic college. In his role as guardian, Margil continued to astound those around him with his mysterious powers. For example, with one hand he lifted a heavy stone that was about to fall and crush a man—a strength that seemed to defy the laws of gravity. And when he was passing through a courtyard, ten oxen appeared to "get down on their knees" to render him homage. Embarrassed that others had observed this, Margil shooed the animals to their feet with his cloak.[35]

Once the new college had begun to function and Margil's duties had diminished, he again took to the mountains in search of souls in need of salvation. Incredibly, he took up the same paths that he had followed years earlier in the company of Father López. Even while away from his college, he followed the strict routine of three hours of sleep at night, one hour for siesta, no breakfast, and broth and herbs for dinner. His travels took him to Nicaragua, where a *corregidor* (regional administrator) described him as coming "like an Apostle, with his habit tied up, his legs muddy to the knees, a skull on his cord, his crucifix clasped in his hand and singing." [36]

In Nicaragua Margil faced a new challenge. One of the provinces contained a coven of witches, who sacrificed human beings and ate their flesh seasoned with chile peppers. Among their satanic rituals was the beheading of adults and young children and the offering of blood to idols. Fray Antonio found and burned some of the witches' diabolical devices but apparently failed to root out the practice of sorcery.[37]

In July 1703 Margil returned to his college, named Cristo Crucificado, in Guatemala. By this time his appearance must have been unusual, to say the least. His ragged and dirty habit had more patches than original cloth, and even fellow clerics were prone to comment on his poor appearance. To those who were openly critical, he replied, "Every one goes to God, some in shoes and others barefoot. There are many ways to heaven." [38]

Margil, in this final assignment in Central America, lost another spiritual bout with witches, and he made still another journey into Costa Rica. While away from New Spain, he had applied for reassignment in far-off Peru, but that request had been denied. In September 1706, having returned to Guatemala, Margil left the province for the last time. He was then forty-nine years of age. Time and asceticism had taken their toll. The saintly Franciscan was bald, had horribly deformed and callused feet, and could no longer walk with an erect bearing.

Margil's return to New Spain was in response to a new challenge. He had been ordered to found an apostolic college at Zacatecas. In amazing time he traversed the distance between Guatemala and Mexico City, where he consulted with Father Francisco Estévez on points pertaining to the new foundation. From the capital he continued on to Querétaro, where he spent Christmas. But in early January 1707 he took five religious from the college and set out for Zacatecas, arriving at the outskirts of the city on January 12.[39]

Since his departure from the wilds of Costa Rica, Margil had traveled some sixteen hundred miles to take up his new assignment, the founding of a third apostolic college, Nuestra Señora de Guadalupe de Zacatecas. For several months, Fray Antonio labored at the legendary silver-rich town fed by the mountain of ore known as La Bufa.

Margil left Zacatecas in early summer and went to preach in Guadalajara at the request of its bishop. He stayed in the capital of Nueva Galicia for a few months, during which he struck up a friendship with nuns of the convent of Santa Teresa de Jesús. From the capital he next journeyed to Jalisco, where he preached for about three months, and from there returned to his college by November.[40]

At the end of 1707, Margil received news that his successor as president of the college of Cristo Crucificado in Guatemala had died. The audiencia of Guatemala requested that he return there and assume control of the college, but it was a petition that he was unable to honor. By Margil's own admission: "My heart is in Guatemala . . . because of the years I spent in those lands."[41] But his Franciscan superiors were unmoved. Margil's destiny lay with his brethren at Zacatecas and their missionary enterprises, and it would remain so for the rest of his life.

From Zacatecas Margil headed north to the city of Durango and thence to San Luis Potosí. Leaving San Luis in the pre-Lenten season, Fray Antonio traveled to Querétaro. En route to his destination, he stopped for a meal at a farmhouse. With unusual appetite, the good padre devoured a plate of food. The woman of the house, who knew something of Margil's reputation, silently thought to herself: "A fine saint this fellow is; look how he eats!" Margil read her mind and in typical good humor remarked, "If we do not feed the burro, he will let us down on the way."[42]

Although Margil had suffered minor setbacks in his apostolic endeavors, such as his initial encounter with the Lacandón Maya, he had not yet experienced total rejection of his Christian message by any native group. But his string of successes was about to end.

By 1710 the western part of the Sierra Madre in New Spain had not yet been Christianized. Especially resistant to all missionary overtures were natives of the Sierra del Nayarit. Those Native Americans who lived among spectacular chasms and mountains kept to their ancient traditions of worshiping pagan gods and ingesting hallucinatory "divine peyote."[43]

Some years earlier, the Nayarit Indians had ambushed a small party of twelve soldiers and a cleric, killing all of them in a narrow mountain pass. That incident in 1701 was followed by subsequent efforts to Christianize the Nayarits, but these, too, failed completely. The audiencia of New Spain then informed the Royal Council of the Indies that the land of the Nayarit was the "center of rebellious and idolatrous practices." On the recommendation of the council, King Philip V issued a decree on July 31, 1709, ordering the governor of Guadalajara to organize a military conquest and spiritual conversion of the region. The latter undertaking was entrusted to Father Margil, "the able and experienced missionary in apostolic excursions."[44]

Margil left Zacatecas for Guadalajara and arrived there in mid-January 1711. He was perhaps naive, or possibly even a bit overconfident, given his unbroken record of successes among the pagan. In any event, he urged an unarmed and peaceful approach to the Nayarit. His admiring biographer, Eduardo Enrique Ríos, thought Fray Antonio, at least in this instance, capable of ignoring the obvious and "of acting against reason in order to avoid abuse of the Indians."[45] Still, like the great Dominican Las Casas, Margil favored peaceful means as the initial approach. That failing, he differed from Las Casas by his willingness to subsequently employ military force, but acceptable spiritual work could not go hand in hand with military conquest. It must come first.

By late March 1711, Margil had set out for the land of the Nayarit. On May 9 he stood at the gateway to their territory and prudently sent ahead two Indian messengers, one of whom spoke a dialect of the Nayarit. The envoys carried a letter containing Margil's heartfelt words: "No human interest brings us to preach the good news in your land but only the desire to snatch your soul from the hands of the devil and from hell . . . and to give our life [sic] if necessary to save your souls."[46]

The messengers were intercepted and did not meet the chieftain for whom Margil's letter was intended. Nonetheless, back came the reply: "The missionary Fathers should not tire themselves out. We are quite happy without any Fathers or Spanish officials. If you want to kill us, go ahead and kill us, but we are not going to give ourselves up so that you can make Christians of us."[47]

Not one to admit defeat easily, Margil pressed forward with a companion and four Indian guides. On May 21 they were confronted by an

Indian covered with black and red paint who asked them if they were armed. When assured that the party did not carry weapons, the native let them continue. But near sundown they were surrounded by more than thirty Indians, all screaming and brandishing arrows and knives. Fray Antonio and his fellow religious fell to their knees, spread their arms, and invited the Nayarit to pierce them with arrows. Although their lives were spared, one of the Nayarit said to the Indian interpreter: "Tell the fathers that they should not tire themselves; we do not want them and they can go no farther, since we were sent and have been ordered by our old chiefs to say the same that was said to the messengers."[48]

Margil and his small retinue then began the return trip by the same route they had followed to the land of the Nayarit. After reaching Zacatecas in July, Margil spent the better part of the remaining year testifying in Mexico City and offering advice as the viceroy prepared a military conquest of the Nayarit. But as sometimes happened, enthusiasm for the entrada waned and attention shifted to other problems in New Spain. Years later, the Jesuits were successful in missionizing these natives, and at that time they paid homage to Father Margil by erecting a monument in his honor. But for the moment, Margil had suffered "the very first outright failure in all his missionary career."[49]

By 1713 Margil turned his attention northward to the provinces of Coahuila and Nuevo León, a new direction for his energies that would at last bring him to the very threshold of Texas. Told by the guardian of his college that he could preach in any part of New Spain, and aware that the Zacatecan friars had not as yet founded a single mission among the infidel, Margil left for the north with a companion in January 1714. As usual, he traveled on foot.[50]

At that juncture, Margil was almost sixty years of age. Although still able to cover great distances in a day, he could no longer do so with grace and ease of movement. His frail body was permanently bent forward, and every step must have been painful. Nonetheless, Father Margil was about to join Francisco Hidalgo, his old friend and cofounder of the first apostolic college at Querétaro, in a Texas missionary venture that would bring him added stature. In that endeavor, Fray Antonio would represent the Zacatecan Brown Robes.

An expedition commanded by Domingo Ramón, with Louis Juchereau de St. Denis serving as commissary officer, took shape in early 1716. Its intent was to bring about the permanent occupation of Texas. At that juncture, Father Margil was a resident at Boca de Leones. He would later be joined at San Juan Bautista by three additional friars from Guadalupe de Zacatecas and two lay brothers. The apostolic college at Querétaro assigned its president, Father Isidro Félix de Espinosa, and five other padres, including, of course, Father Hidalgo, to the Texas enterprise.[51]

Margil was delayed for several weeks in joining his Franciscan brethren at the Río Grande mission. During that time, he assisted Ramón by rounding up goats, oxen, and horses at Boca de Leones, but then he traveled on his own toward San Juan Bautista. Despite being slowed by consideration for eight women and two children riding in oxcarts, as well as the problem of driving more than a thousand head of cattle, Ramón reached the Río Grande settlements well before Margil. The good Franciscan, alone and sick, meanwhile made his way through the desert by following the tracks of the Ramón convoy. En route a fever set in, and Fray Antonio, perhaps for the first time in his life, had trouble crossing a small stream called Juan's Creek.[52]

Stranded without food or assistance, Margil somehow got word of his predicament to the assemblage at San Juan Bautista. Father Espinosa, two missionaries from Zacatecas, and two soldiers hurried to his aid, and with considerable difficulty got him to the mission on April 19, 1716. On the following day, the caravan that would bring about continuous Spanish presence in colonial Texas crossed the Río Grande and waited six days for Margil to recover his strength. Far from getting better, Margil, suffering from a dangerously high fever, slipped from bad to worse. On April 25 a fellow cleric heard his confession and gave him the Last Sacrament; and on April 27 the Domingo Ramón expedition left for the land of the Tejas, leaving behind what all believed to be a dying priest. But once again Margil rallied from the brink of death. His convalescence was slow, but in the company of a few soldiers and companions the padre set out on June 13 for his stay as a missionary in Texas (Figure 7).[53]

When Margil arrived in East Texas, probably in mid-July 1716, four missions, three for the Queretaran and one for the Zacatecan friars, had already been established among the Hasinai Confederation. The Zacatecans set up their lone mission, Nuestra Señora de Guadalupe, near the main village of the Nacogdoche tribe at the approximate site of modern Nacogdoches, Texas.[54]

Throughout the remaining months of 1716, expansion beyond the four mission outposts was out of the question. Although still friendly, the Hasinai tribes refused to congregate or give up their idols and religious temples. Any attempt at forcing the Indians to comply with the wishes of the Franciscans was deemed foolhardy, for the strength of the military escort had been diminished by desertion. To the Brown Robes

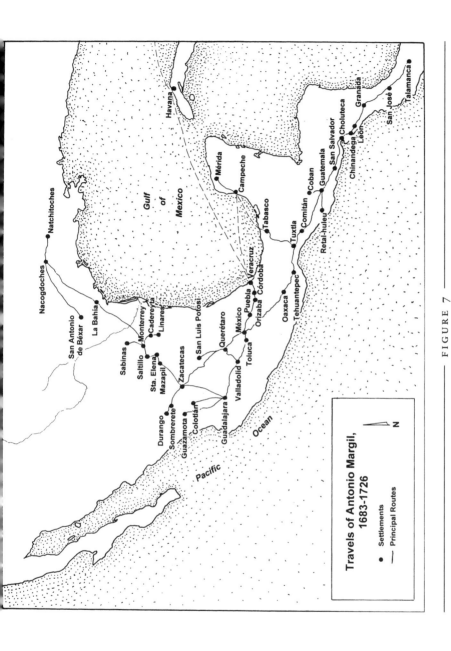

FIGURE 7

Travels of Antonio Margil in New Spain and Texas. This map illustrates the peregrinations of Father Margil from Central America to East Texas. (Cartography by Caroline Castillo Crimm.)

of both apostolic colleges, it became increasingly apparent that unless reinforcements from New Spain were forthcoming, the reoccupation of Texas seemed destined to go the way it had gone in 1693.[55]

Renewed hope came with the return of St. Denis from Mobile in late 1716. The French cavalier brought with him both supplies and cause for renewed optimism. In early 1717, two additional missions were founded by Father Margil and his Zacatecan brethren. Nuestra Señora de los Dolores, Fray Antonio's headquarters, was established for the Ais Indians near contemporary San Augustine, Texas; a sixth mission, San Miguel de los Adaes, intended for the Adais Indians, took form near the site of present Robeline, Louisiana. It seems likely that St. Denis aided in the founding of the these last two missions and helped succor all Spanish settlements by providing maize from the French trading post at Natchitoches.[56]

With the departure of St. Denis for San Juan Bautista on March 22, 1717, matters worsened for Margil and his fellow missionaries. Their second summer in East Texas, marked by unbroken drought, brought crop failures and disappointing harvests of corn and beans; attempts to resupply the friars from New Spain in December 1717 and early 1718 failed because of swollen waters encountered at the Trinity River; floods in the winter and spring, however, were followed by yet another summer of sparse rainfall and meager harvests; hunger drove the Franciscans to eat without salt the "despicable meat of crows," which were shot from their roosts with muskets in the early mornings; and worse, the priests lacked essentials—wine and wax candles—for celebrating Mass on a regular basis.[57]

During the drought of 1717–1718, one of Father Margil's alleged miracles gave birth to an enduring legend in modern Nacogdoches. As creeks dried up and crops failed, Margil received a vision while praying throughout the night. On the following day, the good friar walked to the banks of La Nana Creek and struck a rock twice with his staff. Two natural springs poured forth, appropriately called Los Ojos de Padre Margil, and continued to flow for years, helping to alleviate the drought.[58]

Through all the travails of 1717–1718, Margil apparently suffered less than his compatriots of the cloth and complained not at all. He had faced far worse during his many years in Central America. Indeed, as others voiced their unhappiness over facing a number of hardships, Margil would say: "As gold in the furnace, so God tries his servants. If he is with us . . . in tribulation, it is no longer tribulation but glory." Isolated at Mission Dolores, for there were no resident Indians, Margil appears to have enjoyed living like the hermits of old. "In this way, he spent the days, weeks, and months absorbed in God, growing old gently."[59]

In the meantime, Mission San Antonio de Valero had been founded at Béxar on May 1, 1718, by Father Antonio de San Buenaventura y Olivares. A few days later, Presidio San Antonio de Béxar began its existence, as well as a civilian settlement known as Villa de Béxar. From San Antonio the long-awaited relief expedition for the East Texas settlements, commanded by Martín de Alarcón, next traveled to Matagorda Bay and thence to the land of the Hasinai, arriving there in mid-October.[60]

Alarcón visited the six East Texas missions, completing his assignment on November 21. His assistance, however, was little appreciated by the Franciscans. The Spanish captain distributed a few gifts to the Indians but left behind only six or seven soldiers to replace those who had deserted. And he had failed to bring any new families to help settle East Texas.[61]

Especially of concern to the missionaries was the success of the French in winning the loyalties of the Hasinai tribes. From their settlements in Louisiana, Frenchmen had no compunction about supplying the Indians with firearms in exchange for their goodwill and native products. Father Isidro Espinosa caustically remarked that Indians had fired off more muskets in a salute to Alarcón and his men than all Spaniards combined. In one mission alone, Fray Isidro counted ninety-two guns in the possession of Native Americans.[62]

A damning assessment of the efficacy of Alarcón's relief expedition has been offered by historian Carlos E. Castañeda: "The missions were no better off at the close of 1718 than they had been when founded two years before." Without doubt, the greatest accomplishment of don Martín had been to establish settlements on the San Antonio River. Also, the strategic importance of that way station was soon to be demonstrated.[63]

A brief war between France and Spain, longtime rivals for the control of the North American continent, spilled over into Louisiana and Texas in 1719, where it became known as the Chicken War. The Zacatecan outpost at Los Adaes was easy prey for the French, but they failed to capture a lay brother who escaped and spread word of the attack. Panic seized the remaining five missions and the single presidio in East Texas, commanded by Captain Domingo Ramón. Don Domingo viewed the Spanish positions as untenable, and, significantly, lacked confidence in the local Indians, who had resisted all efforts to congregate them.[64]

Ramón ordered a precipitous retreat of all personnel to San Antonio, bringing an inglorious end to the second effort at establishing Spanish settlements in East Texas. Although panicky at first, the displaced missionaries, soldiers, and civilians camped west of the Trinity River, where they remained for about three months before continuing the march to San Antonio. The ragtag elements, including Father Margil, reached Béxar in October 1719.[65]

The fledgling settlements at San Antonio were understandably strained to accommodate the East Texas exiles. Margil recognized this, and he quickly saw the wisdom of founding a second mission at Béxar. On December 26, 1719, he wrote a congratulatory letter to the newly appointed governor and captain general of Texas, the Marqués de San Miguel de Aguayo. San Antonio de Valero, the single mission at Béxar, belonged to the Queretaran friars, and Margil pointed out the imperative need of the Zacatecans for their own halfway mission between the Río Grande and East Texas. Ever so tactfully, Fray Antonio suggested that the new establishment be named for the governor himself. It was a proposal that Aguayo found hard to refuse, despite the vigorous objections of Father Antonio de San Buenaventura y Olivares.[66]

Having won the approval of Aguayo, Margil chose a site with fertile lands that could be watered by building an irrigation ditch to the San Antonio River. With the aid of Juan Valdez, the military captain at Béxar, Mission San José y San Miguel de Aguayo was officially established on February 23, 1720 (Figure 8).[67] Although it would undergo a number of architectural changes in the course of its long life, San José would become the most beautiful and successful of all Texas missions. And it was another spiritual triumph for Father Margil.

Margil left San Antonio in 1721 and participated in the successful reoccupation of East Texas, carried out by the new governor and captain general. On this occasion, he changed his residence to Mission San Miguel de los Adaes, primarily because this mission and the nearby presidio of Los Adaes formed the capital of Texas. From the refounded mission, Margil frequented the French fort at Natchitoches, where he walked the banks of the Red River.

While ministering to the needs of his flock at Los Adaes, Margil learned that Father Francisco Estévez had died in Querétaro. At that time, Estévez held the post of prefect of the missions of the propagation of faith in the West Indies. In accordance with the apostolic brief issued by Pope Innocent XII, Margil had to assume the interim job of prefect, which he exercised from Texas for a time. But his days in that province were numbered.[68]

Margil soon learned that he had again been elected guardian of his

FIGURE 8

Oil painting by Theodore Gentilz depicting Mission San José in San Antonio in the second half of the nineteenth century. (Photograph used with the permission of the Daughters of the Republic of Texas Library, San Antonio.)

college at Zacatecas for a three-year term, 1722–1725. This appointment ran counter to his wish to stay in Texas and surrender his soul there. He was tired of traveling; he was old and worn out; but he was, however, obedient to the end. Once again, Margil set out on the long road to Zacatecas, on foot. That journey occupied him from January to June of 1722.[69]

After an eight-year absence, Margil was again among his brethren. However, he soon left the college to join his friend and biographer, Father Espinosa, who had also been recalled from Texas to become guardian of the apostolic college at Querétaro. The two men agreed to go to Mexico City, where they made special pleading for their fellow Franciscans in Texas, but it was all to no avail. The viceroy listened politely but refused to authorize one additional peso for the Texas missions. Peace between France and Spain in the 1720s would soon dictate a severe reduction in spending within that province. Of the two veteran priests, Espinosa was much more outspoken than Margil, and he bitterly commented that "since the principal object of the governors and captains [in

Texas], . . . is not to bother themselves about the conversion of the Indians, they want the Fathers to take care of everything and the missions to go on increasing without causing them the least trouble." [70]

From the moment of his unsuccessful meeting with Viceroy Marqués de Valero until his death, Margil never again concerned himself with Texas. Returning from Mexico City to Zacatecas, Fray Antonio preached along the way. At his college Margil again fell seriously ill, apparently from a liver ailment. He ran a high fever and doctors urged that he be given extreme unction. But once again Margil recovered from this near-mortal crisis. He served out his term as guardian and retired from that position in August 1725. [71]

Once out of office, Margil continued his ascetic ways: extreme penance marked by carrying a heavy cross, wearing a crown of thorns, and mortifying his frail body. But Fray Antonio's fame was such that he was in constant demand as a preacher. From Zacatecas he traveled to Guadalajara and Valladolid (now Morelia). In Michoacán, Indians received him in the little towns along the shores of Lake Chapala and expressed their admiration with gifts of flowers, as well as a large wooden cross. [72]

From Michoacán Margil returned once again to Santa Cruz de Querétaro, where he collapsed and lost consciousness. When he recovered his senses, Margil was unusually sad and reduced to tears. His friends asked him if he regretted leaving the temporal world, but it appears that Fray Antonio's remorse stemmed from not having accomplished enough in God's behalf.

Margil's last journey was from Querétaro to Mexico City. By then he suffered from chills, a double hernia, and pneumonia. Warned that he might die en route without a doctor, medicine, or Christian burial, Margil replied: "That is what I deserve; I am not entitled to Christian burial; I ought to die out in the wild, where the beasts can devour me." However, he did reach the church of San Francisco in the capital. There he received the last sacraments and made a general confession. Although untroubled by anything amounting to a sin of consequence, Margil confessed to having been seriously tempted in the past by the devil. And he admitted that an invisible hand had guided him throughout his life, saying, "I have been a brute animal, and if God had not sustained me by His hand, I do not know what would have become of me." [73]

Father Antonio Margil de Jesús died on August 6, 1726, between one and two o'clock in the afternoon at the church of San Francisco. His final words were "It is time now to go and see God." On August 8, 1726, his funeral was attended by the viceroy and his court, as well as other high governmental and ecclesiastical officials. Burial was in a coffin locked with three keys. On it inscribed in Latin were these words, in translation: "Here is buried the Venerable Servant of God, Father Fray Antonio Margil: Missionary, Prefect, and Guardian of the Colleges of the Propagation of Faith, Santa Cruz [of] Querétaro, Cristo Crucificado of Guatemala and Santa María of Guadalupe, erected in New Spain. He was famous for his virtues and illustrious for his miracles. He died in this celebrated convent of Mexico on August 6 in the year of Our Lord, 1726." [74]

After Margil's death, Franciscans of the missionary colleges with which he was associated immediately campaigned for an official investigation into the life and works of their famous co-religious. Such an investigation required support from the king of Spain, as well as from civil and ecclesiastical officials in Mexico and Guatemala. Those authorities were asked to petition the pope, so that after an examination of Margil's remarkable career he might be designated as venerable.

Because Margil's travels and long life had taken him into so many different dioceses, collecting all of the necessary information was a lengthy task. Not until July 19, 1769, forty-three years after Fray Antonio's death, did Pope Clement XIV appoint a commission to head the investigation. Research of this nature had to be assigned to a postulator of the cause of Margil. The first cleric named to the office worked from 1772 to 1790, then was replaced by a second postulator. In all, forty-six letters constituted the case for Margil—letters from the viceroy of New Spain; from the audiencias of New Spain, Guatemala, and Guadalajara; from bishops and archbishops of Mexico and Central America; and from ecclesiastical chapters. [75]

In the wake of these petitions, discussions in Rome continued into the late 1790s. The Napoleonic wars interrupted those proceedings, and they were not resumed for almost forty years. In 1834 a new postulator of the cause, Father José María Guzmán of Margil's apostolic college in Zacatecas, arrived in Rome and became Fray Antonio's energetic advocate. One year later, in the presence of the pope, a general conclave of the Sacred Congregation of Rites discussed Margil in the context of theological virtues (faith, hope, and charity) and cardinal virtues (prudence, justice, fortitude, and temperance). On the crucial issue of whether Margil manifested these qualities to a "heroic degree," the cardinals voted but the pontiff did not. So, again, matters were at an impasse. [76]

In 1836 the theological and cardinal virtues and affiliated virtues of Fray Antonio were judged to be "present in a heroic degree in the servant of God, Antonio Margil." That pronouncement made by the pope and an assembly of cardinals, bishops, and prefects was issued as a papal decree and sent to Mexico at the end of 1836. By then Margil, at last designated as venerable, had been dead for 110 years.[77]

Initially buried at the church of San Francisco in Mexico City, the bones of Margil were twice exhumed and came to rest in 1861 at the Chapel of La Purísima in the metropolitan cathedral of Mexico City. In this resting place could be found the following inscription, in translation: "Here lies the Venerable Servant of God, Fray Antonio de Jesús Margil. He died August 6, in the year of Our Lord, 1726, was exhumed by apostolic authority on February 10, 1778, and transferred from the convent of Saint Francis to this metropolitan church, 1861, anno D."[78] At present, the remains of Antonio Margil are located at the Guadalupe Friary in Zacatecas.

As the 250th anniversary of Margil's death approached, a date that would coincide with the bicentennial year of the United States of America, renewed efforts were launched in this country to advance Margil's status beyond venerable to that of blessed. Those endeavors were spearheaded by two fellow Franciscans, Fathers Benedict Leutenegger and Marion A. Habig, with the former serving as vice-postulator. Unfortunately, the Franciscan postulator general in Rome informed Fray Antonio's advocates that "two new miracles—extraordinary favors obtained from God through the intercession of Venerable Fr. Margil—are required for beatification."[79] More recent attempts to meet those requirements have been made by the Franciscan vice-postulator for Mexico; the Margil House of Studies in Houston, Texas; and the current vice-postulator for the United States, Father Barnabas Diekemper of Saint Peter's Friary in Chicago, Illinois.

Although only a small portion of Father Margil's remarkable life and career was spent in Texas, he nonetheless founded three missions for the Zacatecan friars—two in East Texas and San José in San Antonio. Better known in Mexico than in the United States, Fray Antonio signed himself "*la misma nada*," not out of artificial humility, rather he sought " 'to be not' in order 'to be' in God."[80]

Father Antonio Margil de Jesús was the most famous priest to set foot on the soil of the future Lone Star State. And, at least for the time being, this saintly man has been spared the rancor of Native Americans that has recently surrounded the candidacy for sainthood of a better-known Franciscan, Father Junípero Serra, who later toiled in the California missions. Margil's hand was gentler, and evidence is lacking that he ever accepted corporal punishment as a part of his missionary labors. Throughout his long life, the only suffering he would countenance was his own.

FIVE

MARQUÉS DE SAN MIGUEL DE AGUAYO/PEDRO DE RIVERA Y VILLALÓN

Dedicated Recolonizer/Intransigent Inspector

$\sim$

In mid-June 1719, Mission San Miguel de los Adaes, founded in 1717 by Father Antonio Margil near modern Robeline, Louisiana, was unguarded and unoccupied save for one soldier and a lay brother. During its brief existence, the religious outpost had failed to attract a single resident neophyte, and it was the most remote from San Antonio of the six Spanish missions established by the Domingo Ramón/St. Denis expedition.[1]

Situated only twenty miles from St. Denis's fort at Natchitoches, Los Adaes was a logical target for foreign aggression should war break out between France and Spain. Given the problems of communication between Europe and America in that era, a time lag of two to three months before news of events on the European continent reached the Americas was common. However, more than five months had passed since hostilities had erupted in Europe on January 9, 1719, a conflict that pitted the Quadruple Alliance of England, France, Holland, and Austria against Spain.[2]

Somehow, the Spanish frontier in Texas remained ignorant of those events as the summer season approached. The French at Natchitoches were the first to learn of the far-off war and lost little time in launching an attack. Commander Philippe Blondel gathered up half a dozen soldiers and rode to Los Adaes. There he quickly subdued the unarmed Spanish soldier and gathered up the religious ornaments and meager provisions of the mission. The French captain then directed his attention to the mission chicken house. A few hens were caught; their legs were tied; and the fowl were slung over the back of Blondel's horse. Protesting, the chickens flapped their wings, causing the commander's mount to shy and spill its rider in the dirt. This brief diversion permitted the lay brother to bolt into the woods and make his escape. As for Blondel, he returned a single prisoner to Natchitoches, as well as the appropriated fowl. In the satirical words of Father Juan Domingo Arricivita, one of the missionaries in East Texas, the French commander "doubtless . . . did not spare, according to civilized rules, the lives of the chickens, since they had so treacherously endangered his." [3]

The lay brother reached Father Margil's resident mission at Nuestra Señora de los Dolores on June 22 and imparted the bad news. Fray Antonio, hearing rumors that one hundred French soldiers were marching from Mobile, hastily buried valuable tools and packed his sacred ornaments. He and a small entourage then made their way to Presidio de los Tejas, the sole military garrison in East Texas. [4]

Commander Domingo Ramón faced a serious problem. His soldiers, many of them only boys, were poorly clothed and without arms or mounts. Eight of the soldiers were married, and their wives—no doubt unhappy with life on the East Texas frontier—clamored for a quick withdrawal to San Antonio. All was confusion and panic, a Spanish version of Chicken Little's "The Sky Is Falling" lament. Despite assurances from Father Margil that he could place trusted Indians along the route the French must travel and that these native spies would give advance warning of any troop movements, "nothing could reverse this current of misfortune." [5] What came to be called, derisively, the Chicken War of 1719 would soon bring about the complete withdrawal of Spaniards from East Texas.

Significantly, Spanish fears in large measure stemmed from their lack of confidence in the loyalty of the Hasinai tribes. However, Margil and Father Isidro de Espinosa did not share those concerns. While others began a retreat to Béxar, the two Franciscans and an equal number of soldiers remained for twenty days at Mission Nuestra Señora de la Purísima Concepción. During that time, the two priests penned an appeal for help, which was carried to Béxar and on to San Juan Bautista. However, on July 14 the padres learned that Ramón had retired beyond the Trinity River, whereupon they decided to join the refugees at the western edge of Tejas country. [6]

At the end of July, after a perilous journey across swollen rivers, the two priests reached the Ramón encampment. They remained there throughout August and most of September, "enduring a sojourn like the children of Israel." Specifically, Father Espinosa remembered having to eat unsalted meat and cook with flour befouled by gross impurities. [7]

In late September, Espinosa decided to travel in the company of a few soldiers to the missions at San Antonio and the Río Grande, where he hoped to solicit help for the East Texas exiles. After traveling about fifty miles, the priest and soldiers came upon the fresh tracks of horses, which they followed until they overtook a small relief party sent by the Río Grande missions. The combined groups then returned to the main camp west of the Trinity River. Fresh supplies were welcome; the news, however, was not good, for the caravan also bore letters from Franciscan missionaries, stating that no military force could be raised to help the friars regain their missions.[8]

Shortly after receiving this disheartening information, the entire Spanish contingent continued its retreat toward San Antonio, reaching its destination in the fall of 1719. Conditions were better at Béxar than at the Trinity campsite, but the Zacatecan friars were nonetheless quartered in straw huts. And at that juncture, Father Margil conceived the idea of founding a halfway mission for the brethren of his apostolic college.[9]

In December 1719, Father Espinosa traveled to Mission San Juan Bautista, where he learned of recent political developments that would soon change the course of Texas history. Much to the joy of Espinosa and his fellow missionaries, Martín de Alarcón had resigned as governor of Texas. Since 1718 the Franciscans had held Alarcón personally responsible for bringing neither sufficient supplies nor additional settlers to the East Texas missions. Don Martín's replacement as governor of Texas and Coahuila was an immensely wealthy *hacendado* of Coahuila, the second Marqués de San Miguel de Aguayo.[10]

Since the late 1520s, titles of nobility had been sparingly granted to Spaniards who had performed great deeds for their monarchs in the Indies. The first so honored in New Spain was Fernando Cortés, conqueror of the Aztec Empire. Don Fernando was conceded the title of Marqués del Valle de Oaxaca in 1529. In New Spain the title of marqués was next conferred in 1609 on Luis de Velasco II, son of New Spain's second viceroy, then serving his second term as *virrey*. Others followed into peerage, including a great-grandson of Moctezuma II, who received the title of count.[11]

On November 23, 1682, the title of Marqués de San Miguel de Aguayo was first conferred on Agustín de Echeverz y Subiza, the descendant of a distinguished family that could trace its lineage to notable men of Navarre in northern Spain. Don Agustín, after performing military service in Europe, had emigrated to New Spain in the mid-1660s. By 1666 he held the title of *capitán protector* of Tlaxcalan Indians who had been resettled near villa Saltillo in Coahuila. In subsequent years, the future marqués served as a captain of war on the frontier, where he gained recognition for subduing rebellious Indians at his own expense—a service to the crown that would later be emulated in Texas by his son-in-law.[12]

While earning a military reputation on the frontier, don Agustín had married one of the richest women in New Spain, an heiress named Francisca de Valdés y Urdiñola. Shortly after their marriage, don Agustín drew up a document of merits and services in which witnesses testified on the signal contributions of the houses of Echeverz and Urdiñola. Armed with the sworn statements of his many admirers, don Agustín then crossed the Atlantic, where he gained an audience with the pathetic Spanish king Charles II (the Bewitched). The effort paid handsome dividends. For a price, no doubt, Charles conferred the titles of marqués and viscount on the petitioner. By extension, also included in the royal concession was the title of Marchioness de San Miguel de Aguayo for doña Francisca.[13]

During their marriage, don Agustín and doña Francisca had only one daughter, whom they named Ignacia Xaviera. Following the death of the marqués, his widow imposed a change upon the entail of the house of Aguayo that necessitated the adoption and inclusion of the arms and name of Echeverz.[14]

To broaden her opportunities, doña Ignacia, the second marchioness, was sent abroad, where she married three prominent men in succession. Her third husband was José Ramón de Azlor y Virto de Vera, the second son of an Aragonese nobleman, Count Artal de Azlor, and his wife, Josefa María Virto de Vera. Because of mounting concerns for doña Ignacia's vast estates and entail in northern Mexico, the couple relocated to New Spain in 1712 and took up residency at the hacienda of San Francisco de los Patos in Coahuila.[15]

Don José assumed the title of second Marqués de San Miguel de Aguayo, and from the moment of his arrival, the marqués followed the tradition of his father-in-law, the first Marqués de San Miguel de Aguayo, and his own earlier services to the crown as a military captain on the frontier of Navarre, where he had served with distinction during the War of Spanish Succession (1702–1713). Both men had a history of organizing soldiers at their own expense and financing entire campaigns from family monies.[16]

In northern New Spain, don José recruited a private army of mounted soldiers and Indian allies. He first assumed responsibility for the suppression of Indian revolts and later offered aid to presidios and civilian settlements in Coahuila. After success in those endeavors, the marqués next turned his attention toward Texas and lands beyond the province.[17]

In January 1715, Aguayo corresponded with the viceroy of New Spain, requesting formal authorization to sponsor an expedition of three or four months' duration to Gran Quivira—the name applied to lands along the Arkansas River in present-day Kansas. Then, as before and later, he promised that the undertaking would result in no burden to the royal treasury, but the proposal did not receive a favorable recommendation from the *fiscal* (legal adviser), and it was rejected by the viceroy on July 3. In November of the same year, Aguayo tried a new tack.[18]

The marqués reminded officials in Mexico City that when José de Urrutia lived among the Tejas Indians, the self-imposed exile had met a Native American who had journeyed twenty days from "a land beyond" to the north. The traveler informed Urrutia of Gran Quivira's rich lands and large population of Indians. As before, Aguayo offered to underwrite all expenses for an exploratory entrada and asked only for official sanction. This proposal, however, fared no better than the first, for the *fiscal* counseled the viceroy to reject it "with all brevity."[19]

Unfortunately for Aguayo, the timing of the two proposals was all wrong, for it ran counter to plans then in progress, which resulted in the Domingo Ramón/St. Denis expedition. But Aguayo's third attempt was more propitious. In mid-December 1719 he assumed the office of governor and captain general of Coahuila and Texas, and in that capacity offered to reclaim East Texas for his monarch—with his sword, and, again, at his own expense. It was an offer, in this instance, that Viceroy Marqués de Valero readily accepted.[20]

Aguayo lost little time in preparing for his entrance into Texas. By June 23, 1720, all was ready, but Aguayo's departure was delayed for more than a year by circumstances so troublesome, in his words, that "it seems that all hell" had conspired against him. First, he had to deal with Indian insurrections in Coahuila; then a severe drought killed grass and dried up water sources, causing the death of thirty-five hundred of the four thousand horses he had purchased for the entrada. The prolonged drought was finally broken by heavy rains, but repeated downpours brought preparations to a virtual standstill, as men and animals struggled through a sea of mud.[21]

By late 1720, Aguayo had again assembled thousands of livestock, tons of supplies, and five hundred men, which he divided into eight companies. If his preparedness seems excessive, it must be remembered that France and Spain were at war, that Aguayo had to be ready for any possible contingency, that the missions and presidio in extreme northeastern New Spain had been abandoned earlier in 1719 under threat of French invasion, and that the marqués hoped to act in a forceful manner— thereby discouraging any future aggression by the French.[22]

And then, at least for the marqués, came the worst news of all. Final instructions from the viceroy changed the very nature of the entrada. Aguayo learned that the Quadruple Alliance and Spain were negotiating a truce that would end the war in Europe. Accordingly, he could initiate no offensive action whatsoever. And he could wage a defensive war only if the French encroached on His Majesty's realms. Delays in Coahuila coupled with international considerations had denied him the opportunity to achieve military glory; and, in all likelihood, the intended reconquest of East Texas had been transformed into only a routine reoccupation.[23]

The march to the Río Grande crossing near San Juan Bautista began on November 16, 1720. When the main body of his force arrived on December 20, it found the river swollen with flood waters and more than a musket shot in width. Native Americans familiar with the Río Grande assured Aguayo that it would take a long time for the waters to recede, whereupon the marqués began experiments to determine the best means of transporting bulky goods and thousands of animals across the current. He finally settled on a wooden raft of ten beams, with additional buoyancy provided by empty barrels lashed between the vigas. The heavily laden platform was then pulled across the river by fifty Nadador Indians, who took turns in the water. Not surprisingly, this cold and arduous work soon took its toll on the swimmers. Despite their being plied with brandy and extra rations of hot chocolate and food, all but four of the Native Americans became ill.[24]

In all, six hundred mule loads (*cargas*) of merchandise, more than four thousand horses, six hundred cattle, nine hundred sheep, and eight hundred mules had to be ferried across the Great River. And these numbers did not include livestock already assembled at San Juan Bautista, which also had to be transported across the river. While delayed at San Juan Bautista, Aguayo, fearing that the French in Louisiana would seize the opportunity to occupy Matagorda Bay, sent forty soldiers there under the command of Domingo Ramón. This detachment easily accomplished its mission, for no Frenchmen were present at the site of La Salle's old fort.[25]

Meanwhile, the main expedition marched from the Río Grande to San Antonio. Accompanied by literally thousands of horses, cattle, sheep, and goats, the Marqués de Aguayo deserves credit for successfully inaugurating the first big "cattle" drive in Texas history. When his company reached Béxar on Friday, April 4, it was greeted with much enthusiasm by the former East Texans, many of whom "wished to incorporate themselves with this glorious expedition."[26]

Living under adverse circumstances, the East Texas exiles welcomed Aguayo's stated intent to continue the march on Holy Saturday. However, more reasoned arguments persuaded the marqués to delay his departure for a number of weeks. The horses were exhausted and needed rest, and many members of the expedition wanted to spend the forthcoming Holy Week at San Antonio, rather than camped along the road.[27]

The march toward the land of the Tejas resumed on May 13, 1721. Like many Texans of today, members of the expedition marveled at the beauty and fragrance of spring wildflowers, blooming in such profusion that "they looked like one bouquet or as if placed together in a flowerpot." And at each campsite along a route running northeast from San Antonio to present-day San Marcos and Austin, Father Margil and other Franciscans in the caravan constructed crosses, which symbolized their intent to resume missionary labors in East Texas.[28]

The Aguayo expedition was also more than just a missionary and military entrada. It meant driving thousands of head of livestock, with all the attendant problems of trailing so many animals through unfamiliar terrain. Inevitably, strays wandered away from the herd, and soldiers got lost trying to recover them. Lightning and thunder spooked the horses and made the cattle so uncontrollable "that there was no way of moving them forward."[29]

Between the Guadalupe and San Marcos Rivers, the party encountered its first bison. José Antonio de la Peña, official diarist of the Aguayo expedition, was not impressed with the appearance of a large bull killed for fresh meat: "Its back is humped like the camel's. Its flanks are lean. Its tail, with the exception of the tip, is short and hairless like the pig's. . . . It has a beard like a goat. . . . It has hoofed [sic] feet, and it walks like a bull although its appearance is more ferocious for being more powerful and swifter." After dining on a portion of the carcass, however, Peña remarked that "its meat is as savory as the best beef."[30]

Far less welcome than abundant bison, deer, turkey, prairie chicken, and fish were many annoying insects and dangerous snakes, which were encountered at almost every campsite. In the midst of a beautiful field of flowers, one had to be careful not to step on poisonous "asps"— probably rattlesnakes. And at night the campers were attacked by an onslaught of mosquitoes, ticks, and chiggers.[31]

In the latter part of May, the Aguayo expedition encountered heavy rains that lasted several days. The massive size of the convoy made crossing open meadows and the smallest of streams extremely difficult and time-consuming. Peña added that passage over the soggy landscape, even for Indians "who carried little," was difficult.[32]

After negotiating the Colorado River below today's Austin, Aguayo veered sharply to the north to avoid having to cross major rivers at downstream elevations. On May 31 the expedition encountered a violent thunderstorm with a bolt of lightning that rendered two soldiers unconscious. "One of them regained consciousness immediately; the other took more than an hour." As those familiar with lightning strikes can attest, strange phenomena can happen. The hat of the more severely injured soldier "was riddled as if by a drill."[33]

Aguayo appears to have forded the Brazos near present-day Waco on June 18 and then turned southeastward toward the Camino Real, which he joined east of modern Bryan–College Station. Along the way, continuing rains and time spent hunting buffalo for food and sport slowed progress to no more than eight to ten miles per day. When the caravan reached the Navasota River, it was also delayed by the necessity of building a bridge of more than sixty feet in length and eight feet in width.[34]

After the Navasota crossing, the expedition continued without major delays until it arrived at the Trinity River, possibly between contemporary Madisonville and Crockett. Aguayo, before negotiating the Trinity, journeyed to the south of the Camino Real, where he contacted Native Americans identified as those of the Ranchería Grande. As evidence that the Spaniards were about to enter a domain strongly influenced by the French, Indian warriors of these nations proudly displayed a blue-and-white silk flag with a *fleur de lis*. Aguago, demonstrating good sense, asked only that the flag be lowered to a height below the Spanish standard, and he promised in exchange for professed loyalty of the Ranchería Grande natives to found a mission for them at San Antonio. In the recent past, this Indian group had apparently been pushed by Apaches from their Brazos River homeland into the western edge of Tejas country.[35]

It took two weeks for the convoy to cross the Trinity. The animals could be driven across the current, but the personnel, including families with small children, had to be transported in a large canoe. While the crossing continued, a delegation of friendly Tejas arrived, its members expressing delight that the Spanish were returning.[36]

After traversing the Trinity, the Aguayo expedition followed a road that was familiar to many of the East Texas exiles. It led through stands of pine, hickory, and oak to San Pedro Creek, where the first mission had been founded in 1690 by Father Damián Massanet and General Alonso de León. Near the end of this journey, the Spaniards were well received by other Tejas, who provided them with a fine luncheon of tamales. This hospitality was followed by gifts of flowers, watermelons, and beans. As in the past, a mixture of Spanish and Indian tobacco was passed about and smoked in a ceremonial peace pipe. In response to the Indians' gestures of goodwill, Spanish gifts to them included glass beads, knives, hoes, rings, mirrors, scissors, and blankets.[37]

While camped at San Pedro Creek, Aguayo received Louis Juchereau de St. Denis on July 31, 1721, and treated him with courtesy and respect. Tired by his long trip from Natchitoches, St. Denis spent the night with old friends, the Franciscan missionaries whom he had known since the Domingo Ramón expedition of 1716. On the following day, talks commenced between Aguayo and St. Denis. The French captain assured the marqués that he would willingly accede to the peace accord then in place between the crowns of France and Spain. However, he expressed concerns about the size of the Aguayo contingent and asked for a clarification of its intended goals. The marqués replied that in conformance with his instructions, he, too, would accept the truce, provided that St. Denis would evacuate all former Spanish possessions, including Los Adaes.[38]

St. Denis, in attempting to dissuade the Spaniards, contended that the Los Adaes site was unhealthy and undesirable, because nearby lands were not suitable for farming. But it was a hollow argument. The Spanish had firsthand knowledge of the locale, for they had founded Mission San Miguel there in 1717. And, given the size of Aguayo's command, the Frenchman held no bargaining chip. At the conclusion of their discussion, St. Denis "then took leave promising to retreat without delay with his people to Natchitoches."[39]

The first reestablished missions were San Francisco de los Neches and Nuestra Señora de la Purísima Concepción. At the latter, Mass was sung by Father Antonio Margil, followed by a sermon preached by Father Isidro Félix de Espinosa. Accompanying the religious services was a show of military might, staged for invited guests from the various Hasinai tribes. Ten companies of Spanish soldiers stood at attention, and the panoply of the occasion was further augmented by orchestrated salvos of cannon. Aguayo then spoke to the Indian chieftains, assuring them that on this occasion the Spaniards had come to stay. He stressed that the Indians would not be abandoned in the future and that Spaniards would protect them from their enemies.[40]

A third mission, San José de los Nazonis, was reestablished; the fourth involved Father Margil. Nuestra Señora de Guadalupe de los Nacog-doches had to be reconstructed from scratch, "for not even traces were left of the church or the living quarters of the priests." Once again, Spanish ceremonies and gifts served to emphasize that a sizable commitment in men and money had been made to the East Texas enterprise.[41]

On August 25, 1721, Margil also participated in the refounding of Nuestra Señora de los Dolores, again located near present-day San Augustine, Texas. As in the case of Nuestra Señora de Guadalupe, "there were no traces left" of the old mission. This circumstance was not particularly disturbing to Father Margil, for he "had found a better site along a creek and spring" that was nearby. This new site was "higher and clearer and . . . [had] a large plain for sowing."[42]

With five missions reestablished and in operation, Aguayo next turned his attention to the remaining site, that of San Miguel de los Adaes. Occupying this region, where the Chicken War had begun in 1719, would bring Spanish presence to within only seven leagues of the French fort at Natchitoches. The march to Los Adaes (August 24–29) was again hampered by persistent rains and soggy terrain, which slowed progress to an average of only fourteen miles per day.[43]

Upon reaching Los Adaes, Aguayo could not locate a single Indian. Probing for an explanation, he learned that the nearest encampments of Native Americans were ten to twelve leagues distant. And he soon faced mild resistance from the French. On September 1 a letter arrived from Natchitoches, informing the marqués that St. Denis, upon returning from the meeting with him at San Pedro Creek, had left for Mobile to report the coming of a powerful army of Spaniards. The official left in charge at the French post stated that he did not have authorization to permit the Spanish to settle at Los Adaes; and he asked that the Spanish withdraw from there until the return of St. Denis.[44]

Aguayo immediately convoked a war council. Collectively, it decided to send two officers to Natchitoches to study the strength of the French fort. Once there, the officers assessed the situation and then informed the French captain that Aguayo was firm in his resolve to reestablish Mission San Miguel and found nearby a new presidio.[45]

To anchor Spanish dominions on this remote frontier, Aguayo constructed Presidio Nuestra Señora del Pilar, a short distance from the old mission site of San Miguel de los Adaes, and staffed it with one hundred men (Figure 9). The hexagonal design of the fortress reflected don José's experience in European warfare and his knowledge of fortifications on the Continent—especially those built in France during the long reign of

Louis XIV. As a Spanish officer and gentleman, Aguayo was not only wealthy but also proved to be well educated and well read. He had perhaps studied a work by Sebastien Le Prestre de Vauban on siegecraft and fortification, which existed only in manuscript form until its publication in 1740. Although less sophisticated than Vauban's classic designs, Aguayo's plan was nonetheless impressive, and it employed many of the French military engineer's recommendations for defense.[46] On reflection, it seems more than a little ironic that French innovations in fortifications were adopted by the Spanish as an impediment to any recurrence of French aggression.

The final reestablished mission, San Miguel de los Adaes, was built in close proximity to the new presidio, and it became the new headquarters for Father Margil. Opening ceremonies, with an audience of more than four hundred Indians in attendance, included a sermon by Fray Antonio, as well as gifts of Spanish manufacture.

In the meantime, Aguayo learned that a supply ship, which he had contracted at the expense of thirty-five hundred pesos, had arrived at Matagorda Bay. Its cargo included 350 *cargas* of flour and 150 of maize. Always a careful planner, don José had left mules at San Antonio in anticipation of the ship's arrival at the bay secured by his captain, Domingo Ramón. The pack animals were dispatched to the supply vessel's anchorage, where they picked up the merchandise and transported it to the new missions and presidio—reaching there on October 20. A second shipment arrived in early November, along with three hundred head of beef and four hundred sheep. These supplies, when supplemented by such game as deer and bear, permitted the Spanish outposts to fare nicely through the winter of 1721–1722.[47]

Earlier, while restoring Spanish presence in the northeastern realms of New Spain, Aguayo had refounded Presidio Nuestra Señora de los Dolores. From its location near Mission Concepción, this garrison, commonly called Presidio de los Tejas, guarded the western mission field in East Texas. Its proposed design likewise reflected the marqués's knowledge of French fortifications.[48]

On November 17, 1721, Aguayo began a difficult winter march back to San Antonio, arriving there on January 22, 1722. The trek was especially hard on his horses and mules, forcing him to send to Coahuila for replacements. While awaiting the arrival of animals and provisions for the return trip to Coahuila, Aguayo selected a new site for the Béxar presidio and ordered its construction with adobe brick. He also ordered the founding of an unsuccessful mission to the south of San Antonio de

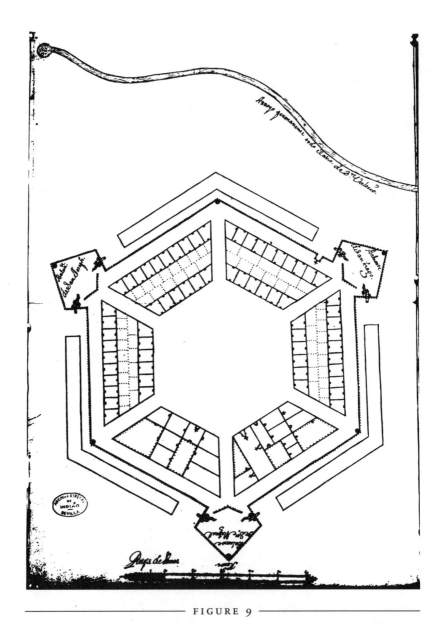

FIGURE 9

Plan of Presidio Nuestra Señora del Pilar de los Adaes. Proposed design of the easternmost presidio founded in 1721 by the Marqués de San Miguel de Aguayo. (With the permission of the Archivo General de Indias, Seville, Spain; Mapas y Planos, México 113.)

Valero. The third mission at Béxar was named San Francisco Xavier de Nájera. It was intended, in part, to honor Aguayo's pledge to Indians of the Ranchería Grande, whom he had contacted in East Texas. Its buildings were never completed.[49]

In early March 1722, Aguayo sent Captain Gabriel Costales to Matagorda Bay with fifty men to augment the forty previously sent there under the command of Domingo Ramón. Aguayo himself followed in mid-March with an additional forty men to ensure the construction of still another presidio that would guard against possible French incursions. The proposed design of Presidio Nuestra Señora de Loreto, founded at the exact site of La Salle's ill-fated Fort St. Louis, was the most elaborate of all (Figure 10). Manned by ninety men, it was to be an octagonal fortress more worthy of the great Sebastien Vauban.[50]

Aguayo also supervised the construction of Mission Espíritu Santo de Zúñiga on the opposite bank of Garcitas Creek. Founded for Coco, Karankawa proper, and Cuján Indians, this mission would later be transferred to two different sites. The new presidio and mission would both be known as La Bahía, after the common Spanish name for San Bernardo/Matagorda Bay.[51]

By the end of April, the Marqués de Aguayo was back in San Antonio, where he was greeted by partisans who had brought a fresh supply of horses from Coahuila. After assigning fifty-four soldiers to the reconstructed presidio at Béxar, he left on May 5, 1722, for the return march to Monclova. Aguayo reached his destination on May 25 and disbanded the remainder of his troops on the last day of the month.[52]

Already suffering from ill health as a result of the rigors of his Texas entrada, the Marqués de San Miguel de Aguayo promptly resigned the governorship of Coahuila and Texas. In recounting his services in Texas to the king, he noted that he had constructed a "barrier of presidios" there; that he had "increased the missions, as the Catholic zeal of Your Majesty desires . . . and left congregated many Indians." His record of accomplishment also included an increase in the military guard from 60 or 70 to 269.[53]

In all, Aguayo expended from his personal fortune, including the salaries of his soldiers, a total amount of 130,000 pesos. He also lent impetus to a plan that would later see the recruitment of Canary Islanders as civilian settlers at Béxar. For his signal contributions and services to the crown, Aguayo requested the rank of lieutenant general but had to settle for a commission as field marshal—equivalent in rank to a major general. This honor was conferred upon him by the Council of the Indies and approved by the king on July 28, 1724.[54]

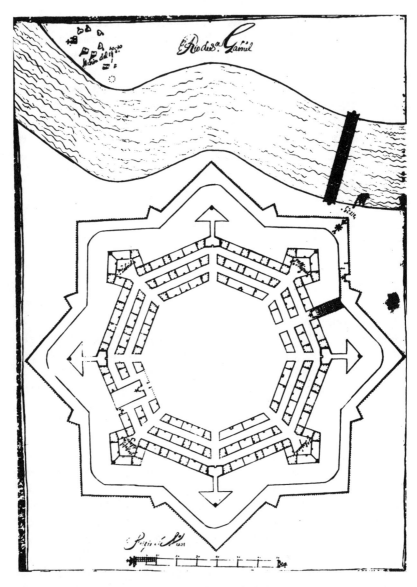

FIGURE 10

Plan of Presidio Nuestra Señora de Loreto. Proposed design of the presidio, commonly called La Bahía, founded in 1722 by the Marqués de San Miguel de Aguayo at the site of La Salle's Fort St. Louis. (With the permission of the Archivo General de Indias, Seville, Spain; Mapas y Planos, México 115.)

It was Aguayo's bad luck that international considerations began to change in the 1720s. The crowns of Spain and France, although both under Bourbon monarchs after 1700, had often been competitors in the Americas and, following the War of Spanish Succession, to a lesser extent in Europe. A cautious rapprochement, coupled with an alliance during the War of Austrian Succession (1740–1748), slowly blossomed over the decades into the renewed Bourbon Family Compact of 1761.

The early progress of those developments would adversely affect arrangements made by the Marqués de Aguayo in Texas. His promises to the Indians, the strength of the four presidios, and the operation of the ten missions would soon be undermined, in large part by peso-pinching retrenchment directed from Madrid. Field Marshal Aguayo died at San Francisco de los Patos on March 9, 1734. He and the Marchioness de Aguayo, who had died a year before her husband, were both laid to rest in the chapel of Santa María de Parras.[55]

Perhaps one of the most painful experiences to this notable man of Texas history came late in life. While suffering from ill health and near death, he saw the dismantling of his accomplishments in Texas and heard his good name besmirched by an uncompromising inspector general, Pedro de Rivera y Villalón.

Operating in the context of peace between Spain and France, Pedro de Rivera could afford to be a "bottom line" administrator. He paid little attention to the circumstances that had prompted the Aguayo expedition of 1721–1722, nor was he impressed that the entrada had been carried out by a man who had offered his sword, his honor, and his fortune in the service of His Majesty the king of Spain. Don Pedro was a man who would sorely vex soldiers, civilians, and clerics who risked their lives on the dangerous frontier of New Spain. Yet his inspection flowed from a very necessary consideration, that of presidial reform.

Who was this new breed of administrator? Rivera was a native of Antequera, a town near Málaga in the south of Spain. Born around 1664, he chose a military career at an early age and rose through the ranks to a position of command. The date of his arrival in New Spain is uncertain, but his first assignment may have been at San Juan de Ulúa in Veracruz harbor. By 1711 Rivera had achieved the rank of colonel in the infantry, and he occupied the office of provisional governor of Tlaxcala for a few years. Leaving that position, he served for a time as second-in-command of the annual fleet.[56]

Back in New Spain by 1715, Rivera next held a number of administrative posts. He again served as governor of Tlaxcala; he was reassigned to Yucatán as its military governor; he then returned to Tlaxcala in his earlier capacity. From that province he answered the call to a new assignment from Viceroy Marqués de Casafuerte. In Mexico City, Rivera received detailed instructions on September 15, 1724, defining an inspection he was to carry out across the north of New Spain.[57]

Shortly after assuming the position of viceroy in 1722, Casafuerte had written to Philip V, suggesting that the king order an inspection of the entire presidio system. The viceroy thought the garrisons to be "costly, inefficient, undermanned, exploited by their officers, and unwieldy." In the same communication, Casafuerte mentioned Pedro de Rivera as the right man for the job of inspector general. However, the viceroy laid down a condition for Rivera's appointment: He must be promoted from colonel to the rank of brigadier general, so that he would outrank any military officer on the frontier.[58]

Philip V accepted Casafuerte's recommendations. On February 19, 1724, the king signed a *cédula* empowering Rivera to make the inspection and conferred upon him the rank of brigadier. Matters then moved quickly. Rivera was given the armament of a powerful Spanish bureaucrat, amounting to an incredible seven thousand pages of documentation, which he was to carry with him at all times! This mountain of paper included copies of all official correspondence; the appointment, salary, and rank of each presidial; the rationale for each garrison's creation, its precise location, its relationship with nearby missions and civilian settlements; and so on. Rivera would also be greatly advantaged by the appointment and presence of an extremely able assistant, Francisco Alvarez Barreiro. Don Francisco, who served the Rivera expedition as engineer and cartographer, had accompanied the Alarcón entrada into Texas in 1717.[59]

Brigadier General Rivera left Mexico City for his tour of inspection in November 1724. With military rank and powers of inquiry that could not be ignored, even by provincial governors, he was ordered to file a report on each presidio, giving its exact location; the nature of the surrounding countryside; the Indian tribes in the vicinity and their general disposition; and the relationship of each outpost to adjoining presidios, settlements, and missions. He began his assignment in the western regions and worked his way eastward across the vast expanse of frontier New Spain. Rivera's commission occupied him for more than three and a half years, during which he traveled some seventy-five hundred miles on horseback. In each of the twenty-four military outposts, stretching from near the Gulf of California to present-day western Louisiana, he compiled a three-stage report: the condition of the garrison when he arrived, its status when he left, and his recommendations for its future.[60]

The inspector general did not reach San Antonio until August 16, 1727, arriving there by way of Monclova and San Juan Bautista, but he rested only one day at Béxar before continuing on toward the provincial capital at Los Adaes. Heading east-northeast, the Rivera expedition encountered its first bison on August 21 and killed two of the animals for fresh meat. On the following day, the party saw more than five hundred of the huge animals and camped at Arroyo de Garrapatas—so named earlier by Father Espinosa for the profusion of ticks along its banks.[61]

Added to the official accounts of the Rivera expedition are the firsthand descriptions of Texas by Francisco Alvarez Barreiro. The engineer and cartographer defined the province's latitude and longitude; he thought Texas generally to have a climate similar to that of Europe; and he commented favorably on the fertility of the land. Don Francisco did find the heat oppressive in the summer season, especially along the Gulf Coast, and to this discomfort was added "the plague of mosquitoes that is experienced greatly at that time." [62]

After leaving Arroyo de Garrapatas (now Onion Creek in Travis County), the outward march to Los Adaes was uneventful, and the inspection tour reached its destination on September 15. Rivera discovered no irregularities in the company of one hundred soldiers. He concluded, however, that the French could bypass the garrison and become masters of the interior lands without losing a man. Accordingly, the inspector general recommended that the size of the guard be reduced from one hundred to sixty, pointing out that if the existing peace were ruptured, replacing the forty soldiers could be accomplished in fifteen days. In any event, "the forty superfluous positions [should] be removed, much to the benefit of the royal treasury." [63]

In contrast, Rivera found appalling conditions at Presidio de los Tejas. Discipline was lacking among the twenty-four soldiers, and the "fort" presented a dismal picture of deficient fabrication. As the inspector general acidly commented, "a collection of huts poorly constructed of sticks and fodder did not merit the honorable name of Presidio de los Tejas." Rivera made a quick judgment that the presidio was not worth preserving, especially since the nearby missions contained not a single resident neophyte. In recommending the garrison's elimination, don Pedro could not have been more blunt: "There is, to my mind, no reason to spend 10,100 pesos—500 for the captain and 400 pesos for each of the 24 soldiers—on such a useless enterprise as the presidio of Texas." [64]

On the other hand, Presidio Nuestra Señora de Loreto received a more favorable review from the inspector general. He nonetheless thought the size of the guard (ninety men) to be excessive, and recommended that it be reduced to forty men—the number at the time the site was occupied by Domingo Ramón. Once again, Rivera revealed his caustic tongue by remarking: "If the forty soldiers are as vigilant as they should be, the Indians [of the area] will cause no problems, since they are known to be cowards and completely lacking in martial spirit." Then, on second thought, because the Indians were "contemptibly docile" and the bay too shallow to accommodate the large ships of a potentially hostile nation, he added: "Although I have said that forty men should be assigned to the presidio, none are really needed."[65]

The fourth presidio at San Antonio impressed even Rivera, for it enjoyed "the best location of any that I have seen." Don Pedro complimented the captain and fifty-three soldiers for their discipline and successful resistance to Apache attacks directed against the San Antonio settlements. Once again, however, Rivera recommended that the size of the Béxar guard be reduced to a total of forty-four, including officers.[66]

Rivera concluded the Texas portion of his inspection on December 12, 1727. While en route to San Juan Bautista, don Pedro offered an interesting firsthand recollection of Texas: "Corn, vegetables, and other crops can be grown everywhere in the province. Even without the benefit of irrigation the land demonstrates its fertility and utility to the pagan Indians who cultivate it." Referring specifically to East Texas, he remarked on the abundance of bears, the fat of which was used to season food, and on the presence of "mice resembling baby rabbits, which serve as food for the pagans."[67]

As mentioned, he found San Antonio, benefiting from ample sources of water and excellent grazing lands, especially to his liking. But his subsequent recommendations for the entire province of Texas and their implementation by the viceroy would negate the accomplishments of the Marqués de Aguayo, place severe pressures on the resources of Béxar, and threaten the security of Spanish Texas.[68]

Rivera completed his report on Texas in March 1728, and it was subsequently included in the Regulations of 1729, published in Mexico City that same year. When enacted, the inspector general's recommendations were unquestionably significant. The garrison at Los Adaes was reduced from 100 to 60 men, at La Bahía from 90 to 40, and at San Antonio from 54 to 44. In accord with don Pedro's assessment that Presidio de los Tejas "ought to be extinguished," it was. The overall troop strength in Texas fell from 269 to only 144, a reduction of 125 presidials.[69]

The friars at Missions Concepción, San Francisco, and San José immediately protested the closing of Presidio de los Tejas, arguing that the military outpost was essential to the survival of those missions. Without it they would be isolated some 60 leagues from Los Adaes and 150 leagues from San Antonio. Indians along the western edge of the missionary field, armed with guns and powder supplied by the French, made it especially risky to operate those religious outposts. However, those arguments failing and the viceroy's decision being irrevocable, the Queretaran padres requested permission to move their missions to a more favorable site or to return to their college.[70]

The protestations and requests of the Franciscans did not evoke the hoped-for response in Mexico City. After completing his massive tour of inspection, Pedro de Rivera assumed a post as counselor to the viceroy, and in that capacity he was able to deflect a flood of special pleading from the frontier. There would be no reprieve for Presidio de los Tejas. However, Rivera did agree that the three Queretaran missions could be moved westward to the Colorado River, provided that this could be accomplished without any cost to the royal treasury.[71]

In July 1730 the three western missions were removed from East Texas and temporarily relocated at the present location of Barton Springs in Austin. From March to May 1731, the missions were again relocated, this time along the San Antonio River, where they became permanent fixtures. Their transfer served to strengthen Spanish presence at San Antonio, but it also brought pressures on the settlers at a time when Apache raids escalated and at the very time they were obliged to integrate civilian settlers from the Canary Islands.[72]

It took more than a decade for San Antonio to absorb the stresses born in the 1730s, created at least in part by enactment of the recommendations made by Pedro de Rivera. For example, until the new religious establishments could become self-sustaining, they had to be supplied with corn and cattle from distant Saltillo, by way of San Juan Bautista. Apaches, themselves pressured by implacable Indian foes (Comanches), began devastating raids on Béxar with its weakened presidio in January 1731—attacks that lasted intermittently until the mid-1740s.

However, many of the problems at San Antonio had little to do with Inspector General Pedro de Rivera. Integrating the Canary Islanders into a community of older Bexareños produced heated discord over water rights and ownership of land. The arrival of Carlos Benites Franquis de Lugo as interim governor in 1736 brought a short-tempered, petulant martinet into the fray. The new chief executive despised the missionaries, allegedly calling them "usurpers of the royal treasury" and "sons of satan." Worse, the padres contended that Franquis de Lugo had defamed them with three nouns strung together—any one of which was horrifying blasphemy. These and other stresses had to be diminished before expansion beyond San Antonio could even be contemplated.[73]

So, to what extent did Pedro de Rivera set back the course of Spanish control over Texas? On this subject historians are simply not in agreement. He unquestionably negated much of the work of Aguayo and weakened the military defenses of colonial Texas. Quite reasonably, the Franciscans from the missionary college at Querétaro were "reluctant to abandon their missions, but the truth is that they had failed to attract many converts from the established villages in the surrounding area." One should also remember that the remaining Zacatecan missions in East Texas and present-day western Louisiana, which continued to operate for several more decades, fared no better. But a less obvious impact of the Rivera inspection was diminished "cooperation between religious and military" personnel, which made the task of all Texas missionaries more difficult. Indians were quick to discern that the padres could no longer count on such assistance as military protection for the missions and the forced return of deserters. On the other hand, the precepts of the Rivera inspection were defined by the necessity of presidial reform, with the attendant budgetary reductions. And in that regard, Rivera certainly succeeded—not just in Texas but throughout northern New Spain.[74]

What of Rivera in his later years? His career continued to ascend after his monumental inspection tour and assignment as counselor to the viceroy. He became governor of Veracruz in 1731 and commandant at San Juan de Ulúa; he advanced to the presidency of the Royal Audiencia of Guatemala in 1732, where he served as governor and captain general; he attained the rank of marshal (major general) before returning to Mexico City in 1743. Don Pedro de Rivera y Villalón died in the capital in the following year. Clearly, he was regarded throughout his life as a loyal and faithful servant of the Spanish crown. But so was Aguayo. That one would wind up undermining the work of the other in Texas can perhaps be best explained in the context of cost-cutting imperatives and international relations that were beyond either man's control.

~

FELIPE DE RÁBAGO Y TERÁN

Sinful Captain

~

At about ten minutes before nine o'clock on the night of May 11, 1752, three men in Central Texas sat at a rustic table eating their evening meal. The night was warm, and the door of a small cell at Mission Nuestra Señora de la Candelaria had been opened to catch a cooling breeze. A single candle lighted the interior of the cubicle. Our Lady of Candelaria was one of three religious outposts known collectively as the San Xavier missions, located approximately nine miles northwest of present-day Rockdale on the San Gabriel River. Seated nearest the door, with his back to the portal, was Juan José Ceballos, a tailor from San Antonio; the other men sharing the evening repast were Franciscan priests—Fathers Miguel Pinilla and José Ganzabal.[1]

The quiet of the late-spring evening was suddenly shattered by the blast of a Spanish blunderbuss, its ball entering Ceballos's chest cavity and killing him instantly. The tailor's body pitched forward and sprawled beside the table. Father Ganzabal seized the candle, rushed to the door of the cell, and peered into the darkness. At that instant, a Coco Indian arrow struck the padre in the left armpit and penetrated his heart. As the mortally wounded priest fell, the extinguished candle pitched the interior of the cubicle into darkness and likely spared the life of Father Pinilla. As the assassins fled into the night, they fired a random shot from a blunderbuss. The investigation into the deaths of Ceballos and Father Ganzabal ultimately cost eight years of "house arrest" for Felipe de Rábago y Terán, the commander of the San Xavier presidio. But in the end, one of the most notorious military captains in Spanish Texas was exonerated and appointed to a second command on the San Saba River in the heart of Apachería.[2]

The early life of Felipe de Rábago is largely shrouded in mystery, although he appears to have acquired a great deal of wealth from mines at Zacatecas. He first appears in the written record at the midpoint of the eighteenth century, having recently arrived in Mexico City with a royal patent dated March 6, 1750. The king, Ferdinand VI, had designated don Felipe as commander of an anticipated presidio for Central Texas.[3]

In the late 1740s, Father Mariano Francisco de los Dolores of the missionary college of Querétaro had spearheaded efforts to found religious outposts some 130 miles northeast of San Antonio on the San Gabriel River. This ambitious undertaking required formal approval by the viceroy of New Spain, as well as from the king and the Royal Council of the Indies. And official sanction was slow in coming. However, the San Xavier project weathered every bureaucratic pitfall, which included repeated inspections of the site and contradictory recommendations of two former governors of Texas. By July 1749, three missions on the San Gabriel sought to address the spiritual needs of Tonkawas, Orcoquizas, Bidais, Deadoses, and Cocos. Still lacking, however, was a presidio that would provide much-needed security for the missionaries of San Xavier and their neophytes. The mission outposts had become the target of daring raids by Apaches, and desertions by the congregated Native Americans were commonplace. As a stopgap measure, a detachment of soldiers under Lieutenant Juan Galván had been assigned to guard the missions.[4]

The actual appointment of don Felipe as commander of Presidio San Francisco Xavier de Gigedo lay in the hands of the viceroy of New Spain. In consultation with the Junta de Guerra, the chief executive, on March 11, 1751, sanctioned the already established missions and approved the founding of a presidio in the immediate vicinity. The viceroy then empowered Rábago as captain of the proposed military garrison and ordered him to recruit a maximum of fifty soldiers, as well as settlers who would live near the missions. At the time of his appointment, Rábago was in his early thirties. He was exceptionally handsome, vain, and pompous. Evidence suggests that Viceroy Revilla Gigedo I regarded Rábago as unworthy of command but had no choice other than to honor the king's directive. In the near future, the Franciscans, who had labored and lobbied so long for a presidio, would see the wisdom of the viceroy's reservations. As Father Agustín Morfi observed in his *History of Texas*, "they were yet to see the work of several years destroyed in . . . [a few] days, their beloved Indians scattered, the missions ruined, their honor stained, and their blood shed by the very persons to whom the king had entrusted their safety." [5]

For the moment, however, the Franciscan padres, who had already proselytized under adverse conditions at the mission sites and had even carried their entreaties for a military garrison across the Atlantic to Spain itself, found victory sweet. Unfortunately, that victory was "short-lived." [6] The good Franciscans were about to take the true measure of Captain Rábago but not before making a serious mistake in judgment.

En route to the San Gabriel River, don Felipe stopped at Querétaro and struck an agreement with the college officials. In the past, disputes arising between missionaries and presidial officers and soldiers had been aired before the viceroy, as well as before the guardian of the missionary college. At San Xavier, things would be different. All points of contention arising between Rábago and the padres would be ironed out locally. It was an agreement that the padres would soon regret, for the handsome young captain proved to be an incredible rake. [7]

As he passed through village after village on his way to San Antonio, don Felipe fed a voracious sexual appetite by seducing Indian and Hispanic women, whether married or single. This conduct scandalized the padres who were traveling in the Rábago entourage. On reaching San Antonio, Rábago, in accord with his instructions, recruited civilian settlers for the San Xavier enterprise—including a Béxar tailor named Juan José Ceballos. Ceballos's attractive wife joined the march to the San Gabriel River, and trouble was not long in coming. [8]

The tailor's wife caught the roving eye of Captain Rábago and soon submitted to his amorous advances, despite angry objections from her husband. As the Rábago party continued onward, the cuckolded Ceballos threatened don Felipe and wound up in chains for defending his honor. On reaching the missions, Rábago placed Ceballos in stocks and later confined him to a cell, even though the tailor had become ill. [9]

Rábago then began a survey of his new post, and he did not like what he found. Only eighteen ragtag soldiers were present, the rest of the guard having deserted or been reassigned to the presidio at Los Adaes in western Louisiana. The missions themselves were in a piteous state of decline, with 109 neophytes at one, 25 at another, and none at the third. Don Felipe was so unimpressed that he urged immediate relocation of the missions to the San Marcos River. But the padres would not hear of moving, and so Rábago chose a site for the new presidio, which was named San Francisco Xavier de Gigedo, in part for the viceroy. [10]

Rábago's relations with the missionaries at San Xavier soon went from bad to worse. He continued adulterous relations with Ceballos's wife, and when the padres tried to intervene by ordering the woman back to San Antonio, the captain's conduct became outrageous. He had Ceballos shackled to a wall, placed a cot within the cell, and then ravished the tailor's wife in full view of her outraged and humiliated husband![11]

During Christmas Eve festivities at the presidio, the unfortunate Ceballos broke free of his fetters and sought sanctuary in the chapel of Mission Candelaria. When Rábago learned that his prisoner had escaped, he violated ecclesiastical sanctuary by riding his horse into the chapel on Christmas Day. There he apprehended Ceballos, returned the tailor to his cell, and cuffed him about the body for good measure.[12]

Father Miguel Pinilla was outraged. On one of the most sacred days of the Christian calendar, Rábago had brazenly defiled the Candelaria chapel. Pinilla demanded a public apology and insisted that Ceballos be returned to the mission. On December 27, don Felipe delivered the mistreated tailor but offered no apology for his actions. It was clear that Father Pinilla and Captain Rábago were locked in a contest of wills.[13]

For his part, Rábago sent a letter to Father Mariano de los Dolores in Béxar, requesting that Pinilla be replaced as chaplain of the presidio with a more compliant cleric. Dolores denied the request, pointing out that he could not accede without just cause for making the change. The founding missionary of the San Xavier enterprise also informed Rábago that he was aware of the captain's secret efforts to prove the site unacceptable, thereby contributing to the poor morale of his command, who were unhappy with their assignment on the San Gabriel River. In mid-January 1752, the padres at San Xavier broke their pledge to settle disputes locally and appealed directly to their superiors at Querétaro. Their letter cataloged a succession of woes endured by the clerics of Texas, as well as a litany of complaints about unsympathetic governors and troublesome civilians of the recent past. But in the final analysis, the priests at San Xavier categorically declared that all "impostures," "craftiness," and "machinations" of past administrators and settlers in all of the provinces had been "outdone by the malice of this man [Rábago]."[14] Lest one view these statements as rank hyperbole, consider don Felipe's overall record on the San Gabriel River.

With their captain as role model, the presidials at San Xavier began an orgy of illicit relations with Indian women. In the words of Father Morfi, "the most lascivious soldier was the most successful; there was no other merit for promotion than to secure new subjects for the satisfaction of the captain. . . . The neophytes saw themselves deprived of their wives and daughters by the soldiers, oppressed by excessive labor, insulted every moment of the day, and denied the right to voice their misfortunes." When some of the Christianized Indian women sought expiation of carnal sins in the confessional, evidence mounted of gross misconduct within the walls of Presidio San Xavier. On February 19, 1752, an astonished Rábago and his entire command found themselves excommunicated by decree of Father Miguel Pinilla, which served to further intensify animosities between priest and presidials.[15]

The garrison soldiers, encouraged by their captain, reacted to the penalty of excommunication with defiance and insolence. First, they tore up the decree and burned it. Next, the soldiers drafted a strongly worded petition in which they demanded immediate absolution. But in the end, Pinilla won this confrontation. Excommunication was not to be taken lightly, and as the soldiers contemplated the fate of their souls, one by one they contritely begged forgiveness. By March 1, 1752, all of the garrison had received the sacrament of penance, delivered by Father José Ganzabal.[16]

In the meantime, Rábago also violated his pledge to settle matters without appeal to higher authorities. On the day following the decree of excommunication, he penned a letter to the viceroy and sent it southward to the capital in the hands of two couriers. Don Felipe leveled charge after charge against the missionaries at San Xavier: They had neglected their sacred obligations; they had been invariably querulous and meddlesome in their relations with soldiers and civilians; and, worst of all, they had actively encouraged the Indians to take up arms against the garrison.[17]

The authorities in Mexico City were sorely vexed. Financial support for the San Xavier enterprise had already cost the royal treasury dearly. Worried that the entire enterprise might be on the verge of collapse, the *auditor de guerra* (military adviser) expressed sympathy for poor ignorant soldiers stationed 430 leagues from the capital, and he argued that their irreverence did not deserve "the awful ban of excommunication—the ultimate knife and penalty of the church." The viceroy's legal advisor *(fiscal)* seconded the opinion of the *auditor* by noting that excommunication carried the certainty of burning in hell, a prospect so horrific that Indians would think "the captain crazy and might kill him." Other crown agents likewise expressed their concern. They criticized Rábago for his arrogance and lack of prudence but also opined that Pinilla had acted too hastily in issuing the decree of excommunication.[18]

Unaware that absolution had already been granted to the presidial soldiers, the *fiscal* requested that an ecclesiastical judge be sent from San Antonio to the frontier missions. The appointed expert in canon law should remove the ban of excommunication immediately. At the same time, the *fiscal* suggested that the viceroy send a directive to Captain

Rábago and the missionaries at San Xavier, urging both parties to exercise more patience and prudence in the future. Finally, in an attempt to further defuse the situation, the college authorities at Querétaro should be asked to remove Father Pinilla from his assignment on the San Gabriel River and replace him with another cleric.[19]

The viceroy accepted these sensible recommendations and took steps to implement them. He sent a letter to the guardian of the missionary college at Querétaro, who quickly complied by directing Father Mariano de los Dolores to look into the matter at San Xavier and follow through on the chief executive's orders. But before any action could be taken, the tragic events described at the beginning of this chapter had occurred.[20]

Surrounding the murders of Father José Ganzabal and Juan José Ceballos were charges and countercharges hurled back and forth for the better part of a decade. Predictably, the legal record as presented by the prosecution and the defense is filled with contradictory testimony and evidence. However, an examination of the case itself lends insights into the social history of the San Xavier missions, as well as life on the Texas frontier.

Given the circumstances that preceded the assassinations, the finger of suspicion pointed quickly at Captain Rábago. His unseemly conduct with Ceballos's wife and rough handling of the unfortunate husband, as well as heated disputes with Father Pinilla, seemed to indicate that don Felipe had ample motive for foul play. Recognizing this, the commander lost little time in deflecting suspicion toward the Coco Indians, whom he blamed for committing the murders.[21]

Ten days before the assassinations, the Cocos had deserted Mission Candelaria en masse. Carlos E. Castañeda, renowned author of *Our Catholic Heritage in Texas*, acknowledged that there had been difficulties between the missionaries at Candelaria and the Indians. He concluded, however, that the defection of the Cocos stemmed primarily from strained relations between the padres and soldiers, which had encouraged impudence on the part of the neophytes. Castañeda further asserted that Rábago's treatment of two Cocos within the walls of the presidio had precipitated the flight of the Indians on that very night.[22]

Whatever the source of their impudent behavior, on May 1, 1752, two Cocos entered Presidio San Xavier armed with bows and arrows. Rábago ordered the Indians seized, disarmed, and beaten. Fearing reprisals, argued Castañeda, the Cocos fled Candelaria in the night, and Rábago's command in the following days proved less than diligent in tracking the Indians and returning them to the mission.[23] The latter assertion has merit, but Castañeda falls short of explaining fully the desertion of the Cocos and circumstances surrounding the double murders.

Before the exodus, Juan José Ceballos, then a resident at Candelaria, had come upon two or three Cocos who had killed a mission cow without permission and were in the process of skinning the animal. Ceballos castigated the Indians and attempted to confiscate the carcass for proper distribution of the meat. The Indians resisted, and in a scuffle Ceballos struck one of them a strong blow with the handle of his knife; whereupon several more Cocos descended on the lone Spaniard. To defend himself, Ceballos fired a blunderbuss at a Coco chieftain, breaking the man's femur. Thus, the Cocos had ample reason for disliking Ceballos. But there was additional bad blood involving another Candelaria resident.[24]

Andrés, a young Hispanicized Indian (*ladino*) of the Sayopín nation, and his Christianized twenty-two-year-old wife, Luisa, had been joined in marriage by Father José Ganzabal at mission Candelaria. Luisa, however, soon caught the lustful eye of Martín Gutiérrez, a soldier at the presidio. Gutiérrez, with the concurrence of Andrés, arranged for sexual favors from Luisa in exchange for the loan of a horse to her husband for "three moons." It seems clear that the details of this unholy arrangement were related by Luisa to Father Ganzabal in the confessional. Whether the priest broke the seal of penitential secrecy is uncertain. Most likely, he strongly rebuked Luisa, who in turn informed her husband and Gutiérrez that Father Ganzabal had been made aware of their arrangement. What is certain, as revealed in the inquest to the murders, is that Gutiérrez was one of five assassins responsible for the double slayings on the night of May 11, 1752. And Andrés later admitted to having fired the arrow that took the life of Father Ganzabal.[25]

Andrés's confession was made at San Antonio, where he had fled with his wife. In relating his account of the murders, the Sayopín Indian initially asserted his innocence but entrapped himself with glaring inconsistencies. He claimed to have left San Xavier two days before the murders, yet knew intimate details of the double slayings. Andrés placed the blame on Martín Gutiérrez and three soldier accomplices. While hunting turkeys on the afternoon of May 11, Andrés encountered four Spaniards along present-day Brushy Creek. Two of the men were armed with blunderbusses; the other two, with bows and arrows. Significantly, the bows and arrows were of Coco manufacture, and they appear to have been the very weapons seized by Captain Rábago at the presidio on May 1.[26]

When Andrés came upon the four soldiers, they lay in ambush, hoping to kill Father Miguel Pinilla as he walked to his favorite fishing hole, but the padre did not appear. The men then decided to wait until nightfall, when the cover of darkness would provide a good opportunity to kill both priests and Ceballos; and they offered a horse to Andrés if he would join them as a bowman. Andrés, who had greater familiarity with bow and arrow and his own reasons for disliking Father Ganzabal, acceded and joined the plot. For their part, the Spaniards, disguised as Indians under skins of buffalo and deer, approached Mission Candelaria at dusk. While four of the men remained hidden in a small creek bottom, Gutiérrez crept forward as scout. Through the opened door of the mission, he observed that the intended victims had just sat down to eat. Gutiérrez returned to the larger party and informed them that the time for action was at hand. According to Andrés, Gutiérrez fired the fatal ball into the chest of Ceballos; and as Father Ganzabal rushed to the door of the mission, the Indian himself let fly the arrow that penetrated Ganzabal's heart. No doubt fearful of disclosure if they took additional time to seek out and kill Father Pinilla in the darkened cell, the five men beat a quick retreat from the mission. The parting shot from the second blunderbuss was fired by Manuel Carrillo. Andrés, now mounted and accompanied by his wife, set out immediately for San Antonio; the soldiers returned to their garrison.[27]

Rábago later testified that on the fateful night of May 11 he was in his house enjoying the company of Diego Ramón, Cristóbal Chirinos, and their wives. Upon hearing the loud reports of blunderbusses, don Felipe mounted a horse and galloped to Mission Candelaria. There he discovered the bodies of Ceballos and Ganzabal. He self-servingly added that the clatter of his horse's hooves had frightened away the craven Coco assassins, who had probably been intent on killing all of the Spaniards in the three missions.[28]

On May 15 Rábago sent a detailed account of the murders to the viceroy of New Spain. Realizing that he would be held responsible if soldiers under his command had committed the murders, don Felipe placed all blame on the perfidious Cocos and begged permission to wage a war of extermination against them. Later, it was incumbent on don Felipe to refute the damning testimony given by Andrés in San Antonio, and he sought to assure Spanish authorities that the Sayopín Indian had lied about the complicity of the presidials. In the resulting investigation into the murders, conducted at San Antonio and San Xavier, pressure, applied in part by don Felipe himself, was brought on Andrés to retract his confession; and in the end he chose to do so. But it was not enough to clear Captain Rábago.[29]

In the final analysis, there were significant contradictions in this double murder case, in which, to repeat, Rábago held the Coco Indians to be solely responsible. Martín Gutiérrez had ample reason to dislike Father Ganzabal, who had uncovered his bargained and illicit relationship with Andrés's wife, Luisa. But what could have been the motive of the other Spanish assassins, if not an intense dislike for Father Miguel Pinilla? That animus had to flow from long-standing disputes—in large measure the fault of Captain Rábago—between presidials and missionaries. It should be remembered also that no one in the military garrison, other than its commander, had any known reason to dislike Ceballos. The fact that Ceballos was likewise the target of assassins again raises questions about the innocence of don Felipe. Additionally, it was widely accepted that the Cocos had little or no experience with firearms. Yet one of the murder weapons was a Spanish blunderbuss. How did Coco Indians acquire this wide-bore musket, learn to load it, and fire it with accuracy? Furthermore, how can one explain the detailed testimony of Andrés? The Native American knew each of the soldier suspects by name. And, finally, one should remember that the Cocos had been absent from Mission Candelaria for ten days. By Rábago's own admission, his soldiers could find no trace of those Indians after they fled the mission on May 1, 1752.[30]

Spanish authorities had to acknowledge overwhelming evidence that pointed to the complicity of Felipe de Rábago y Terán. He was removed from San Xavier and sent to Presidio Santa Rosa del Sacramento in Coahuila, where he languished for eight long years—although he still carried the title of captain. Suspiciously, the Indian Andrés and his wife accompanied Rábago to the presidio and remained under his control for the full eight years. During that interval, the Spanish assassins, the actual perpetrators of Ceballos's murder, disappear from the written record. Manuel Carrillo died while incarcerated; the others, according to testimony given in 1759, somehow managed to escape from jail. Time dimmed the memories of most contemporaries on the scene but not those of the Franciscans who had lost one of their own. And the good padres had not heard the last of Captain Rábago. His eventual reappearance on the Texas scene relates in large measure to the failure of missionary enterprises at San Xavier and to the destruction of a sister mission on the San Saba River.[31]

The desertion of the Coco Indians and the tragic events of May 11,

1752, at Candelaria essentially doomed the San Xavier missions, although contact with Indians in the region continued for some time. However, the ranks of the six Franciscan missionaries had been badly depleted. A second priest died of natural causes; and Miguel Pinilla, accompanied by Francisco Aparicio and a fellow cleric, traveled to San Antonio to report on the deaths of Father Ganzabal and Juan José Ceballos. At that juncture, only one priest remained to minister to the neophytes at San Xavier. The solitary Franciscan was soon reinforced by three companions, including Father Francisco Aparicio, but in the following summer of 1753, a prolonged drought caused the San Gabriel River to recede into stagnant pools. Deprived of potable water and irrigation for their crops, the Franciscans sought another, more favorable site. In that quest, Father Aparicio assumed primary responsibility for closing down operations at San Xavier but lacked permission to do so.[32]

In July 1755, Aparicio joined with soldiers of the presidio in requesting formal permission to move the failed settlements to the San Marcos River. But official sanction never came. Nonetheless, by August 16, 1755, the remaining missions and presidio had been transferred to the banks of the San Marcos. There Father Aparicio and two fellow priests petitioned their new military commander—who, ironically, was the uncle of the infamous don Felipe—for reassignment among the Lipan Apaches on the San Saba River. Pedro de Rábago y Terán denied that request. But in short order the San Marcos venture also failed, and all remaining assets were moved to the Guadalupe River in late 1756. There Mission San Francisco Xavier enjoyed a brief existence. However, events unfolding on the San Saba River near present-day Menard, Texas, finally brought an end to the last vestige of the San Xavier enterprise.[33]

The hope of founding missions among the Lipan Apaches had been a late-life passion of Father Francisco Hidalgo, but events at San Antonio and Hidalgo's death in 1726 had put a temporary end to all thoughts of missionizing those plainsmen. During the last years of the 1720s, the Lipans had been remarkably quiet, but in the 1730s and into the next decade they began devastating raids on the San Antonio community. Two punitive expeditions in 1732 and 1739, as well as a third in 1745, had failed to bring a military resolution to the problem.[34]

To the Franciscans at Béxar, especially Father Mariano de los Dolores, missionizing the Apaches in their own lands seemed to be the best solution to what was then the most serious Indian problem in Texas. By the late 1740s, however, the Apaches themselves had come under relentless pressure from their archenemies, the Comanches, and were finally willing to make peace with the Spaniards. On August 19, 1749, four

Apache chiefs and numerous followers buried a hatchet and other instruments of war in a peace ceremony at San Antonio.[35] To the Lipans, an appearance of willingness to accept Christian conversion seemed a small price to pay in exchange for protection by the Spaniards.

Near the end of the San Xavier enterprise, Father Alonso Giraldo de Terreros established the first mission for the Apaches, but it was situated in Coahuila, west of the presidio at San Juan Bautista. Mission San Lorenzo, established late in 1754, experienced some success until Father Terreros retired from its management and redirected his efforts toward a larger project for the Lipans. Less than a year after its founding, the neophytes at San Lorenzo rebelled, burned the mission, and deserted en masse. Undaunted, the Franciscans insisted that the Apaches had been reluctant to live so far from their native habitat and that success could be assured by locating missions closer to the center of Apachería.[36]

Dovetailing with the Franciscans' missionary impulses were accounts of mineral wealth in the country adjacent to the Pedernales, Llano, and San Saba Rivers, northwest of San Antonio. Those reports had come from scouting expeditions into Apache lands—entradas led by Juan Galván in 1753 and Pedro de Rábago in 1754. Both of these men, as noted, were associated with the San Xavier missions. In early 1756, the governor of Texas ordered still another reconnaissance, this time to the Llano River country in present Llano County. On that expedition, Lieutenant Governor Bernardo Miranda discovered an enormous mound of hematite and contacted Apaches, who assured him that a mountain of silver lay at the end of six days' journey to the north.[37]

Since Spaniards had arrived in the Indies, the lure of wealth, the prospects of converting pagan Indians, and the desire to bolster claims to new lands, as well as the need to secure those acquisitions, had strongly influenced Spanish colonial policy. Those same motives converged in the late 1750s and again served to propel soldiers, missionaries, and civilians toward a disastrous failure on the San Saba River—a failure that would free Felipe de Rábago and provide an opportunity to redeem his reputation.

The primary engineer in the San Sabá enterprise was Father Alonso Giraldo de Terreros. After Mission San Lorenzo's collapse in Coahuila, Terreros traveled to Mexico City in the spring of 1756. While in the capital, Father Terreros learned that his wealthy cousin, Pedro Romero de Terreros, wished to sponsor missionary efforts among the Apaches but only on the condition that Father Alonso Giraldo be placed in charge of the undertaking. By July 1756 the details, hammered out in the presence of the viceroy, appear to have been agreed upon. Pedro Romero would underwrite all mission expenses for three years, after which responsibility fell to the civil government. Military expenses, however, were another matter. From the outset, they were to be borne by the royal treasury. And all personnel associated with the San Sabá project were to report directly to the viceroy, rather than to the governor of Texas.[38]

Responsibility for the proposed missions lay jointly with the college of Querétaro and the newly founded college of San Fernando in Mexico City. The wealthy patron, Pedro Romero, agreed to purchase all assets of the then suppressed San Xavier missions at a fair price. With these details out of the way, Colonel Diego Ortiz Parrilla, who had been appointed by the viceroy to succeed the deceased Pedro de Rábago in May of the same year, assumed military responsibilities for San Sabá.[39]

Ortiz Parrilla was an experienced and capable veteran on the frontier of New Spain, having served as interim governor of Sinaloa and Sonora. But he was arrogant and incapable of accepting advice or admitting mistakes. Though he was anxious to enhance his reputation on the raw frontier of Apachería, it was his misfortune to have "come at the wrong time to the wrong place." Those words, penned by historian Robert S. Weddle, capture perfectly the predicament soon faced by Colonel Ortiz Parrilla.[40]

First, Ortiz Parrilla inspected his "command," the ragtag remnants of Presidio San Francisco Xavier de Gigedo, on the San Marcos River. Appalled by the condition of the presidials, he moved them to San Antonio. Second, he worried about the sincerity of the Apaches, some of whom appeared at San Antonio while preparations were being made for continuing on to San Sabá. He voiced his concerns in a letter to Pedro Romero in Mexico City: "The state in which we have found the Apaches is so different from what I expected that I assure you the method of their pacification is a major concern to me." Third, Father Mariano de los Dolores, instigator of the San Xavier outposts and longtime advocate of missions among the Lipans, was angry. His efforts over the years had apparently gone unrecognized and unappreciated. The assets of his beloved enterprise were to be handed over to a less experienced Franciscan, Father Terreros, who was advantaged by having a rich cousin.[41]

Delays followed by more delays kept Ortiz Parrilla in San Antonio until early April 1757. When the expedition finally got under way, it included tons of supplies, dozens of soldiers and their families, six missionaries, numerous Indian allies, hundreds of horses and mules, fourteen hundred head of cattle, and seven hundred sheep.[42]

The Ortiz Parrilla entourage arrived at the San Saba River on April 17. The commander encamped most of the company, while he

conducted a five-day reconnaisance. At the conclusion of his exploration, the commander's concerns mounted. He had not encountered a
single Apache, and he urged the six Franciscans to abandon the enterprise and return to San Antonio. The padres would not hear of it, and
soon Mission Santa Cruz de San Sabá and Presidio San Luis de las Amarillas took shape near present-day Menard. Mindful of the unsettling
influences of presidial soldiers on mission Indians, the Franciscans insisted that the mission be located well away from the presidio. Separating the two outposts by about three and a half miles reduced the possibility of troublesome fraternization between presidials and neophytes,
but it also made defending the mission more difficult.[43]

During its brief existence of less than a year, Mission Santa Cruz
failed to attract a single resident Lipan Apache. The Apaches did appear
in large numbers on several occasions but were always en route to a
more distant destination. By their general demeanor and periodic appearances, the Lipans nonetheless offered just enough hope to keep the
Spaniards from giving up on the enterprise. But even so, three of the
Franciscans became despondent over the lack of potential converts and
returned to San Antonio, and plans for the second and third missions
were scrapped.[44]

The winter of 1757–1758 was unusually cold, bringing misery to
some four hundred men, women, and children who lived at the presidio.
In the meantime, the Lipans had sowed seeds of anger among the Comanches and their allies by deliberately leaving behind items of Spanish
manufacture, such as shoes and articles of clothing, when they raided
enemy camps to the north. This tactic left the impression that the Lipans
were in close alliance with the Europeans at San Sabá.[45]

As spring approached, the residents at San Sabá anxiously watched
Lipan Apaches scurrying southward with more than an occasional
glance over their shoulders. Unmistakable evidence mounted that trouble for the Spaniards lay ahead, as scouts reported hundreds of Comanches, Bidais, Tejas, and Tonkawas converging on the mission and
presidio. Colonel Ortiz Parrilla felt the safety of 237 women and children to be his primary responsibility and could spare only a few presidials to guard the mission. He requested that the three priests stationed
there move to the presidio until the crisis had passed, but his entreaties
fell on deaf ears. Fathers Terreros, Miguel de Molina, and José de Santiesteban insisted on remaining at the mission.[46]

At about sunrise on the morning of March 16, 1758, Andrés de Villareal, a guard at the mission, "heard an outburst of Indian yells resembling their war cries when going into battle." He then saw "many puffs

of powder smoke and heard a noise of horses toward the northern ford of the river near the Mission, which the enemy immediately began to surround, shooting off their muskets." The Indians gained entry into the stockaded area of the mission by shouting that they did not wish "to fight the Spaniards, but only to maintain friendship with them; that they only wanted to kill Apaches, for whom they were searching." [47]

Inside the mission gate, the Indians were confronted in the courtyard by Fathers Terreros and Molina. The latter provided a chilling description of the intruders: "Filled with amazement and fear . . . I saw nothing but Indians on every hand, armed with guns and arrayed in the most horrible attire. Besides the paint on their faces, red and black, they were adorned with the pelts and tails of wild beasts, wrapped around them or hanging down from their heads, as well as deer horns. . . . All were armed with muskets, swords, and lances . . . , and I noticed also that they had brought with them some youths armed with bows and arrows, doubtless to train . . . them in their cruel and bloody way of life." [48]

Following a dispute over his favorite horse, Father Terreros was shot to death, but Father Molina managed to escape. A second priest, Father Santiesteban, died within the chapel, and at some point his cadaver was decapitated. After looting everything of value and killing a total of eight, the Indians set fire to the buildings and left the ruined mission. [49]

Two days after the attack, Ortiz Parrilla visited the charred mission and surveyed the awful carnage. The Indians had scalped some of the victims, decapitated others, or gouged out eyes. They had even killed the mission cats and oxen, sparing only a few sheep. [50] Mission Santa Cruz was never rebuilt, and it was unique in being the only Texas mission destroyed by outright Indian attack.

The following year, a punitive expedition under the command of Colonel Ortiz Parrilla sought to send a message to the Comanches and their allies that "even in their most remote haunts they would not be secure from the long arm of Spanish vengeance." With a force of more than five hundred men, don Diego advanced from San Sabá to the Red River. On October 7, 1759, he fought a pitched battle with Indians that lasted for several hours. At Spanish Fort, near present-day Nocona, Texas, Spanish forces suffered their most serious defeat in colonial Texas. The colonel's losses, including dead, wounded, and missing, totaled fifty-two. He also lost two cannon, several muskets, saddles, and other equipment. [51]

Ortiz Parrilla retreated to San Sabá and reached his destination on October 25. He placed blame for the failed campaign on the sorry troops he had been forced to lead. As for his own performance, don Diego assured the king that he had served with "zeal, valor, and exemplary conduct . . . in inflicting punishment on the enemy." But with words alone, the colonel could not turn defeat into victory. In 1760 he was ordered to the capital, where the new viceroy removed him from command at San Sabá. His replacement would be the archscoundrel and suspected murderer Felipe de Rábago y Terán, who had languished under house arrest and imprisonment for eight years.[52]

As events unfolded at San Sabá and Spanish Fort, they coincided with a determined effort by Felipe de Rábago to free himself. Despite his impressive title, captain of the Presidio of Santa Rosa del Sacramento, Rábago was in the Monclova public jail when he filed an appeal for his release in 1759. He complained of "grave afflictions and illnesses" that racked his body. "To alleviate his pain and suffering and repair his broken health," he begged the viceroy to reconsider the unjust charge that he had been culpable in the deaths of Father José Ganzabal and Juan José Ceballos. Clearly, argued Rábago, his case should be dismissed because of "nullities and defects" in the judicial proceedings, and he pleaded for release on bail while the appeal went forward to Mexico City.[53]

Once again, Rábago placed full blame for the murders on the Coco Indians. His attorney challenged the testimony of the Indian Andrés, on which the soldiers and, by extension, Rábago himself had been tarred with guilt. The lengthy appeal rehashed the events surrounding the murders and especially targeted the actions of Ceballos, who had struck one Coco with a knife and fired a musket ball into the thigh of another. Clearly, as the argument went, the Cocos had ample reason to seek revenge. Further, reasoned the attorney, since it was no longer possible to punish the four accused presidials—for one was dead and others had escaped from incarceration—charges against Rábago should be dropped.[54]

Rábago's appeal reached Mexico City in the summer of 1760. On June 7, Viceroy Marqués de Cruillas, the newly arrived chief executive of New Spain, ordered don Felipe, the presidials, and Andrés cleared of all charges, and he appointed Rábago commander at San Sabá. On the shaky premises that Rábago had been removed from command in 1753, pending the outcome of charges against him, and that the San Xavier garrison had been moved to San Sabá, the viceroy reasoned that he was simply making just restitution and reappointment. Counterarguments that San Francisco Xavier de Gigedo had been abolished, that San Luis de las Amarillas was a new presidio, and that Rábago had no rights of succession carried little weight with the Marqués de Cruillas.[55]

The viceroy was equally nonplussed by a storm of angry protests from the Franciscans. When Francisco Xavier Ortiz, guardian of the college at Querétaro, learned of Rábago's exoneration, he could scarcely contain his outrage. Father Ortiz pleaded that don Felipe not be sent to Texas because of his "bad conduct in the time he served as commander of San Xavier." He likewise implored the viceroy to select another captain "known to have zeal in the salvation of souls." [56] It was all to no avail. The new commander at San Luis de las Amarillas would be Felipe de Rábago y Terán, and no other. In fairness to the viceroy *and* Rábago, the choice proved to be not that bad.

During Rábago's eight years of house arrest and occasional incarceration, a remarkable transformation appears to have occurred. Even Carlos E. Castañeda, staunch advocate of the cloth, credits don Felipe with seemingly experiencing "a great change of heart," with displaying "the most convincing zeal for the conversion of the natives and their reduction to mission life." [57] Cynics will argue that leopards can never change their spots, but one must give Rábago credit for trying.

Rábago demonstrated both good judgment and sensitivity in avoiding contact with his Franciscan detractors in San Antonio. He also listened to Father Diego Jiménez, president of the missions on the Río Grande, and agreed not to bring Andrés, the confessed killer of Father Ganzabal, back to Texas. As he traveled to his new post on the San Saba River, Rábago blazed a trail through unexplored terrain and arrived at Presidio San Luis de las Amarillas on September 30, 1760. There he found appalling conditions. Don Felipe had inherited a command of one hundred men, made up mostly of disabled veterans, superannuated soldiers, raw recruits left over from Ortiz Parrilla's expedition of the previous year, three tailors, one sacristan, and "boys . . . entirely too young for military service." All, regardless of age or experience, were poorly dressed and had little by way of horses or equipment. Some of the men had no mounts, shirts, or stockings; the majority lacked saddles, bridles, spurs, shields, swords, or leather jackets.[58]

To correct the situation, Rábago petitioned the remarkable José de Escandón, colonizer of Nuevo Santander, for 600 mounts. Don José could spare only 370 horses, but Rábago acquired an additional 260 from Coahuila. To this number, he added 74 brought by himself. Expending his own monies, Rábago ordered tons of supplies, weapons, and ammunition. With his men properly clothed, fed, and equipped, the new captain turned his attention to the presidio itself.[59]

The wooden walls of the stockade were replaced with quarried stone, still visible at the presidio ruins in Menard. The new walls, which incorporated quarters for the presidials, were then encircled with a moat. With justifiable pride, Rábago remarked that the new structure resembled a castle, and he gave it a new name—Real Presidio de San Sabá (Figure 11).[60]

In addition to this flurry of activity, Rábago dispatched expeditions into the plains that separated Texas and New Mexico. Those efforts determined that the distance between the two provinces was greater than generally believed. The entradas also took stock of the Native American population.

In gathering and using ethnographic information, the new commander demonstrated remarkable skills in his dealings with the Lipan Apaches. Several of their most prominent chiefs were regular visitors at the presidio. In those conversations, Rábago stressed his commitment to missionizing the Lipans. His sincerity has puzzled even his harshest critics, including Father Agustín Morfi. In his *History of Texas*, Morfi argues that don Felipe perhaps sought "to eradicate the perverse memory of his conduct, or what is more credible, because he wished to make amends to religion for the damages he had occasioned as a result of his previous scandals."[61]

Whatever his motivation, and evidence supports Rábago's sincerity, his overtures to the Lipans were his undoing. Once again, these Indians had learned how to use Spaniards to achieve their own purposes. The Lipan chieftains shrewdly pointed out that setting up another new mission for them at San Sabá was out of the question. That locale was too close to the range of their enemies' war parties, as evidenced by the devastating attack on Mission Santa Cruz. Even with a fully armed presidio only three to four miles away, the Comanches and their allies had sacked the mission with impunity. What was needed, argued the chiefs, was a mission farther south, in lands where the Lipans felt more secure.[62]

Because the Apaches relied in part on their *rancherías* for food, where crude gardens and small fields were scratched into the soil, they were more vulnerable to attack than were the completely nomadic Comanches. Twice a year, at planting and harvesting times, the Lipans' enemies knew exactly where to find them. If a new mission could be located about halfway between San Sabá and the Río Grande, the Lipans would gladly congregate. This locale, on the upper Nueces River, was a favorite site for their *rancherías*. The Spanish, of course, would have to provide soldiers to defend the mission, and in doing so would also protect Apache crops.[63] Rábago, however, had not been authorized to

—————————— FIGURE 11 ——————————

*Photograph of the ruins of Presidio San Luis de las Amarillas. This photo
shows the main corner bastion, which, like the main buildings, was
reconstructed in 1936 on the original foundations at Menard, Texas.
(Photograph courtesy of Robert S. Weddle.)*

found any missions other than at San Sabá. In acceding to the requests
of the Lipan chiefs, don Felipe entrapped himself like a prehistoric animal in a tar pit.

Recognizing the ill will of the Franciscans at San Antonio, Rábago
had to recruit priests elsewhere for the proposed mission, which would
be situated at the northern edge of present Camp Wood in Real County.
Accordingly, he appealed directly to Father Diego Jiménez at San Juan
Bautista, asking him to supervise the new religious outpost. And the
padre accepted. However, the mission, named San Lorenzo de Santa
Cruz, required a guard of twenty men. This mission had barely been established when Lipan chieftains asked for a second, Nuestra Señora de
la Candelaria del Cañón, to be located about ten miles below San Lorenzo (Figure 12). Rábago again honored the request, which meant si-
phoning off ten additional guards from San Sabá. Those missions did attract Lipan neophytes, mostly women and children, but supplying their

needs further sapped the strength of the San Sabá presidio, for it had to share its men and supplies with the El Cañón outposts.[64]

Worse, the Lipan Apaches, just as they had done before, engaged in perfidious actions that brought down the wrath of the Comanches and their allies on the Spanish. In association with their buffalo hunts, the Apaches raided Comanche camps and intentionally left behind articles of Spanish manufacture. Conversely, the Lipans would acquire the physical accoutrement of their enemies on those same raids and leave them during forays against Spanish settlements. Such double-dealing caused the Comanches to blame the Spanish for being in league with the Apaches, while the Spanish blamed the Comanches for depredations that were in fact carried out by the Lipans. But this duplicity on the part of the Lipans did not go undetected for long. It added to a growing litany of complaints against these plainsmen, which eventually targeted them for extermination or exile to a foreign land.[65]

For the moment, however, it was Rábago and his command who paid a high price for befriending the Lipans. In five years don Felipe spent more than twelve thousand pesos on provisions, clothing, and livestock for the presidio, but the Comanches and their allies intercepted and robbed about half of the supply trains. The Comanches also directed assaults on Presidio de San Sabá itself, which sustained attacks for as long as two months.[66]

Because he had violated his instructions by founding the El Cañón missions, Rábago's pleas for assistance from Mexico City received a cold reception. In the spring of 1769, under almost constant threats by the Comanches, the soldiers and their families dared not plant fresh vegetables and other crops outside the presidio's protective walls. Limited in diet, the residents suffered horribly from scurvy. Rábago, himself, became a Lazarus-like commander, covered with sores and plagued by failing health.[67]

As Rábago's energies flagged, he faced a growing mutinous attitude on the part of his soldiers. In desperation, he abandoned his post and relocated the garrison at the site of Mission San Lorenzo. When the viceroy learned of the unauthorized move, he ordered Rábago back to San Sabá, but don Felipe refused to comply. Leaving the upper Nueces River, Rábago traveled to Coahuila, where he apparently intended to buy supplies for his beleaguered troops and mission residents.

In April 1769, Felipe de Rábago learned that the viceroy had replaced him at San Sabá with Manuel Antonio de Oca. From Coahuila, don Felipe set out for Mexico City. There he hoped to obtain recompense for expenditures of his own money, spent maintaining and defending

——————————————— FIGURE 12 ———————————————

*Sketch of Felipe de Rábago. Captain Rábago orders several runaway
Indians to return to their mission on the upper Nueces River.
(Commissioned original artwork by Jack Jackson.)*

the presidio at San Sabá for nine years. Still in his mid-forties, Rábago never completed the journey. He died in San Luis Potosí, probably in July 1769.[68]

The life of Felipe de Rábago is hardly the tale of a good man. His roguish and wanton conduct at San Xavier created a licentious climate that corrupted his command. That he personally ordered the murders of Ceballos and Ganzabal at Mission Candelaria seems most unlikely. That he was seriously implicated, yes. One can speculate that he openly groused about "meddling priests" and "that damned Ceballos." From Henry II and Saint Thomas à Becket to the present, history is replete with examples of underlings acting out the unspoken yet ardent desires of their superiors. In his command at San Sabá, Rábago demonstrated a good heart but bad judgment. Again, it is worth noting that his most bitter critics, the very Franciscans who had railed against him over the death of a fellow priest, could find little wrong with Rábago's personal sacrifices and devotion to the Lipan Apaches. Perhaps it was in the nature of priests to forgive the penitent? Perhaps in the end, Felipe de Rábago y Terán deserves compassion for trying so hard to make amends for his sins.

SEVEN

JOSÉ DE ESCANDÓN Y ELGUERA

Competent Colonizer

In early September 1770, a seventy-year-old man lay dying in Mexico City. José de Escandón y Elguera faced not only the great mystery of death but also the paradox that was his life. He had been one the ablest and most powerful men on the frontier of northern New Spain, and he had served the Spanish crown for five and a half decades as soldier, pacificator, explorer, colonizer, and administrator. His accomplishments had earned Escandón many rewards, including the titles of Count of Sierra Gorda and Governor of Nuevo Santander. Yet the last years of his life were filled with controversy. His detractors, perhaps envious of his many accomplishments, accused him of crimes ranging from greed to abuse. When formal proceedings were brought against him, Escandón had to defend himself on thirty-eight separate charges. He died in the capital on September 10, while inquiry into his official conduct was still in progress. All that he had accomplished was at stake, because his principal heir, Manuel, could not inherit his father's estate unless don José was exonerated and his honor restored.

Born on May 19, 1700, to Juan de Escandón and Francisca de la Elguera of Soto la Marina, Santander, Spain, José de Escandón was a well-to-do and adventurous young man when he came to the Americas at age fifteen. Initially, he served for six years without salary as a cadet in the Mounted Encomenderos Company of Mérida, Yucatán, a military unit charged with evicting English poachers from the Laguna de Términos. During that time, the young cadet so impressed the local governor that he commended him to the crown.[1]

In 1721 Escandón was reassigned to Querétaro where he served for a number of years, again at his own expense. From there he helped "repel and punish '*indios bárbaros*'" who carried out hostile attacks from the western regions of the Sierra Gorda. When an Indian uprising occurred in the jurisdiction of Celaya in 1727, don José marched there with eighty men to subdue the rebellion, which he accomplished with "promptness, meting out punishment to the aggressors." Viceroy Marqués de Casafuerte rewarded Escandón's efforts by promoting him to the rank of *sargento mayor*, in which capacity he continued to wage war against unreduced Native Americans on the frontier.[2]

Escandón next led troops into an area where Indian depredations had forced the abandonment of a small Spanish settlement (named "Half Moon") and the closing of a royal mine. There he established a town with fifty families; dealt effectively with the natives, who were headed by a chieftain named Lázaro; and succeeded in pacifying the area. In 1732 when still another Indian rebellion created instability in the mining region near Guanajuato, it was don José who responded. Two years later, more than ten thousand natives revolted in the region of San Miguel el Grande. Again, Escandón reacted rapidly with a troop of five cavalry companies from his regiment, which succeeded in "suppressing the uprising, leaving tranquility in the region." At the same time that he pursued aggressive and successful military campaigns, don José became especially renowned for his humane treatment of the hundreds of Indians taken as prisoners.[3]

Escandón's accomplishments in the Sierra Gorda, a rugged mountainous region extending northeastward from Querétaro toward Santiago de los Valles (modern Valles), and beyond into the Costa del Seno Mexicano are particularly noteworthy. Indians of the latter region, which included the present-day Mexican state of Tamaulipas and ultimately Texas south of the Nueces River, "had baffled both missionary and soldier for a century and a half." Those natives had also preyed on the unfortunate victims of shipwrecks since the era of Cabeza de Vaca. Remarkably, Escandón would succeed where others had failed.[4]

In his dealings with Native Americans, Escandón consistently demonstrated a combination of firmness and smooth diplomacy that greatly impressed the viceroy of New Spain. In 1740 the chief executive named him to fill the vacancy of regimental colonel at Querétaro. And in the following year, Escandón earned promotion as lieutenant to the commander general of the Sierra Gorda and adjoining frontiers.[5]

The need for increased attention to the Costa del Seno Mexicano region had been articulated in 1735 by Governor José Antonio Fernández de Jáuregui Urrutia of Nuevo León, who complained of raids on his province from Tamaulipas. Governor Fernández asked the viceroy of New Spain for "blanket permission and financial support" to address the problem. When he received neither permission nor support, he subsequently communicated directly with the crown, but Ferdinand VI also seemed disinclined to take immediate action.[6]

A number of factors ultimately caused the crown to take greater interest in the Costa. Two additional proposals for pacifying the bellicose natives of Tamaulipas were soon to follow. One came from a former provincial official of Santiago de los Valles, who carried his proposal across the Atlantic to the Council of the Indies. Narciso Barquín de Montecuesta asked for appropriate rank, commensurate salary, and sufficient soldiers to complete the task in four years. Barquín pointed out that the crown would be amply rewarded by the working of rich salines, then rendered useless by unpacified Indians. The second proposal came from Antonio Ladrón de Guevara, a resident of Monterrey, who made an attractive offer that required no immediate royal expenditures. Ladrón promised to settle the area between the Río Pánuco and the Río Grande with families from Nuevo León. He, too, made the long trip to Spain, where he likewise presented his plan to the Council of the Indies.[7]

In 1739 the council remanded the matter to New Spain with a stated preference for the Ladrón proposal; however, final resolution was left to a special junta, composed principally of the viceroy and members of the audiencia. The committee's charge was to choose one of the petitioners and provide assistance as needed. Nonetheless, no action was forthcoming, and attention to problems in the Costa languished for four years.[8]

Once again Ladrón appealed to the crown, and once again a new decree, issued on June 13, 1743, called for the junta to stop procrastinating and make a choice. The *auditor de guerra*, legal advisor to the viceroy on military matters, stubbornly refused to approve Ladrón, and the matter continued to drift an additional three years until Viceroy Juan Francisco de Güemes y Horcasitas, Conde de Revilla Gigedo, took office on July 9, 1746.[9]

Meanwhile, José de Escandón's military career had prospered. As lieutenant captain general of the Sierra Gorda and its frontiers, Escandón made four successful entradas into that region. With officers and soldiers of militia companies recruited from the surrounding jurisdictions, he sought to reconnoiter the area and promote "the best means for educating and congregating the gentile apostates, all at his own cost, and without any [expense] to the royal treasury." Also by orders of the captain general, Escandón made an inspection of the few missions then in existence in the Sierra Gorda, repopulated some abandoned sites, and established new ones, again at no cost whatsoever to the royal treasury.[10]

Escandón's services during this same period of indecisiveness by the junta in Mexico City were directed not only to internal problems in the Sierra Gorda but also to external considerations. Spain and England had been at war since 1739, a contest that broadened in 1740 to King George's War in the Americas. In 1742 word reached Mexico of a British plan to attack Veracruz. With remarkable speed, don José recruited a force of five hundred men and marched to defend the famed port. His actions may have persuaded the British to redirect their aggressive actions toward the port of Cartagena rather than the Mexican coast. In any event, a budget-conscious crown became increasingly impressed with Escandón's selfless generosity on its behalf.[11]

While performing notable services for king and country, significant changes had also marked don José's personal life. Returning to Spain in the mid-1720s, Escandón married Dominga de Pedrajo at Soto de la Marina in October 1727. Unfortunately, his first marriage ended with the death of doña Dominga at Querétaro in 1736. After a year as a widower, don José married Josefa de Llera y Bayas, a resident of Querétaro. From this second union would come seven children, including Manuel, his firstborn son. In his professional life, Escandón likewise prospered— as a merchant, owning mills for the production of textiles, and as a rancher, managing thousands of cattle.[12]

Having made significant accomplishments and enjoying financial security by his mid-forties, Escandón might well have rested on his laurels. To the contrary, he was about to embark on even greater service to His Majesty, the king of Spain. Significantly, don José had not actively sought the long-delayed appointment under consideration by the junta in Mexico City, rather his candidacy was promoted by the *auditor de guerra*. The Marqués de Altamira, impressed by Escandón's accomplishments, viewed the lieutenant captain general as "a man well known for his integrity, . . . and particularly for the pacification of La Sierra Gorda, which he had carried out successfully in a very short time at his own expense." The junta concurred with Altamira's assessment, and in September 1746 Viceroy Revilla Gigedo named Escandón as his personal representative and first governor of an entirely new province, Nuevo Santander—a name chosen to honor the appointee's place of birth.[13]

Don José was to reconnoiter the province, establish its northern limit, and compose a map that would facilitate pacification. The viceroy recognized that Escandón's highly successful entradas into the Sierra Gorda and his "clear individual knowledge of those lands" made him particularly well suited for the task at hand. Revilla Gigedo entrusted his appointee with "as much authority as I, if I were to conduct this expedition in person" and ordered the governor of Texas to provide "aid, service, and assistance." [14]

As was his custom, Escandón acted with both efficiency and dispatch, especially considering the length of time other Spaniards of the era often spent in preparing for far less complicated projects. In record time, don José organized a series of seven divisions that ultimately totaled 765 men. Each group was to leave from a different point, to reconnoiter an assigned section of the new province, and to rendezvous in approximately thirty days (Figure 13). The plan had the advantages of limiting the distance that each band had to travel, reducing the overall amount of time in the field, allowing for careful observation and mapping, as well as intimidating the Indians by multiple well-armed entries through their lands. Nonetheless, to ensure protection of the natives, Escandón warned of grave penalties for anyone who separated "an Indian from his lands." [15]

The main body, headed and financed by Escandón himself, included two priests, a captain, two noncommissioned officers, fewer than a dozen soldiers, and servants. It left Querétaro on January 7, 1747. Later, near the end of the same month, coordinated expeditions left the provinces of Texas, Coahuila, and Nuevo León, as well as from the towns of Valles and Tampico in the south. All were to rendezvous at the mouth of the Río Grande in late February. En route, Escandón received dispatches that kept him informed of the progress of his subordinates. [16]

After leaving Querétaro, Escandón proceeded to San Luis Potosí, where he selected forty soldiers from among the many who wished to enlist under his banner. As he marched along the northwest border of the Sierra Gorda, he accepted more eager recruits into the enterprise and acquired an Indian contingent as he skirted the western point of the Sierra de Tamaulipas. The combined force then marched toward the coast along upper tributaries of the Río de las Palmas, known since the late 1740s as the Soto la Marina. After establishing his main camp near salt marshes some twenty-five leagues from the coast, Escandón set out on February 21, 1747, with sixty-five Spaniards and six Indians and marched northeastward toward the Río Grande. Three days later, the Escandón contingent reached the Great River at a point about five miles from the sea. [17]

A Nuevo León contingent led by Captain Blas María de la Garza Falcón had arrived at that location three days earlier. Having followed the

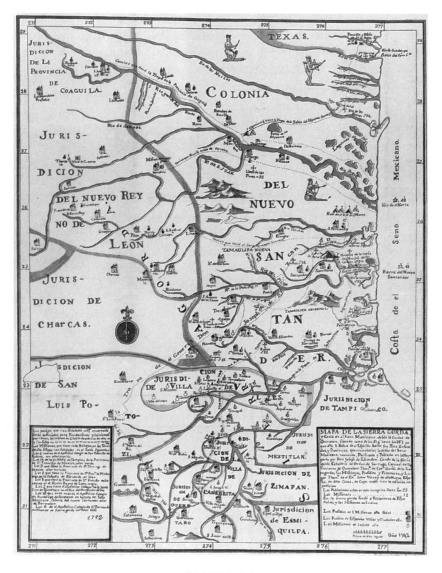

FIGURE 13

Map of the seven Escandón expeditions in New Spain and Texas. This map traces the approximate routes of the exploratory expeditions in early 1747. (With the permission of the Archivo General de la Nación, Mexico.)

course of the Río San Juan to its confluence with the Río Grande and thence downstream toward the Gulf, Garza Falcón provided his superior officer with valuable information about the adjoining terrain. With two dozen men, Escandón then explored regions toward the mouth of the Río Grande. In doing so, he ascertained the breadth and depth of the river. The survey proved disappointing, for the new governor had hoped the Great River's entry into the Gulf would serve as a viable port. Instead, the Río Grande in its final journey to the sea overflowed its low banks, spreading into numerous shallow lakes and sloughs.[18]

Escandón then returned to the main camp on the south bank of the Río Grande, reaching it on March 1. There he found some two hundred Indians from both sides of the river. With the help of interpreters, Escandón acquired more information about the region and its indigenous people. Those natives, some of whom were Comecrudos (raw-meat eaters), had never before had contact with Spaniards. But all of those assembled expressed a willingness to congregate, and since there were no apostates among them, don José viewed the tribes as especially promising neophytes.[19]

Despite Escandón's careful planning, not all of the seven divisions were able to rendezvous as originally planned—a circumstance hardly surprising, given problems of communication across thousands of square miles of unexplored terrain. For example, Blas María's brother, Miguel de la Garza Falcón, had been ordered to march almost due north from Monclova to San Juan Bautista. He then crossed the Río Grande at a nearby ford and explored uncharted lands north of the river and toward its mouth. Hampered first by snow and then by lack of potable water, he failed to make any contact with his commanding officer and returned to Monclova in late March 1747.[20]

The longest trek was that of twenty-five soldiers from Presidio de los Adaes. These men first marched to La Bahía, then located on the Guadalupe River, where they came under the command of Captain Joaquín Orobio Basterra. The Texas contingent, bolstered by an additional twenty-five soldiers from La Bahía, explored along the lower reaches of the San Antonio River, a stream that Escandón hoped to establish as the northern boundary of Nuevo Santander. Don Joaquín next marched to the lower Nueces River and was the first European to discover its mouth.[21]

Traveling south along the inner coast from present-day Corpus Christi, Orobio Basterra skirted Baffin Bay. However, at that juncture his command began to suffer horribly from the lack of drinkable water. The La Bahía commander's situation did not improve as he approached the salty lakes of contemporary Hidalgo and Willacy Counties, and had it not been for small amounts of fresh water found in holes dug by Indian guides, the most northern contingent of the Escandón expedition would almost certainly have perished. But even worse country lay ahead.[22]

Indians warned Orobio Basterra that between the saline lakes and the mouth of the Great River there was no fresh water whatsoever. The expedition then turned southwest and marched to Paso del Cántaro on the Río Grande. On the south bank of the river, don Joaquín met a detachment of soldiers who carried instructions from Escandón. The Texas contingent was to march back to its presidios. On reflection, Orobio Basterra's experiences in extreme South Texas convinced him and others that the trans-Nueces region held "little promise for settlement."[23]

Aside from Escandón's main division, the two Garza Falcón contingents, and the Orobio Basterra expediton, three other detachments explored different parts of the Seno Mexicano. Captain Juan Francisco Barvarena, for example, made a difficult march from Valles, and then near the coast turned northward toward the Río de las Palmas; Antonio Ladrón de Guevara, despite losing out to Escandón in the larger sweepstake, led a second column from Nuevo León; and Francisco de Sosa, who had organized 160 men at Tampico, united with Barvarena on the final leg of the southern approach to the Río de las Palmas.[24]

On March 6, Escandón himself returned to the upper portion of the Río de las Palmas where he had previously encamped. Having been disappointed by the Río Grande, he hoped that the Palmas near its debouchment would offer possibilities for a Gulf port. Upon reaching the area where the river entered a large inland bay, which reminded him of his homeland in northern Spain, don José named the estuary La Ría del Nuevo Santander.[25]

Always thorough, on the return trip to Querétaro, Escandón explored the frontier areas of Nuevo León that bordered on the Sierra Gorda. Then, after dismissing his troops in mid-March, he compiled a map and wrote reports of his multiple explorations. Remarkably, don José and his divisions had not lost a single man during the three-month undertaking. Without doubt, this master planner "had opened the way for pacification and settlement of the Costa del Seno Mexicano, which for so long had been considered virtually impenetrable; his reconnaissance was the step that made the rest possible."[26]

After demonstrating his leadership qualities and organizational abilities—all accomplished without any cost to the royal treasury—Escandón was in a position to formulate recommendations that would lead to the pacification and colonization of Nuevo Santander. His firsthand knowledge of campsites, valleys, arroyos, rivers, lagoons, woods, and salines, as well as Native American inhabitants of the Seno Mexicano, gave him a solid base of information on which to formulate his plans.

Escandón initially proposed the founding of fourteen settlements and accompanying missions at an estimated cost to the crown of 58,000 pesos. Suggested locations took into consideration such factors as the safety of the settlers, the productivity of the area, and the likelihood of converting the natives. The anchor settlement in the south would be on the Las Rusias Plains between eastern Nuevo León and the Huasteca; the proposed northern terminus would be the Santa Dorotea site on the San Antonio River at present-day Goliad.[27]

Influenced by his earlier experiences in the Sierra Gorda, Escandón intended to rely more heavily on civilian rather than military establishments. Initially, he planned to station soldiers in the new towns to provide protection, but only for the first few years. In the long term, civilians would assume responsibility for their own security. To encourage the settlers toward concern for the common welfare, no land would be distributed to individuals until the new settlements were secure.[28]

Escandón suggested that first settlers be given priority at such time when land grants could be issued in fee simple. The *primeros pobladores* would likewise be attracted by one-time cash inducements of one hundred to two hundred pesos, by ten-year remission of taxes, by generous land grants, and by the opportunity to develop a new province. Each settlement would be founded separately and would be economically independent of other frontier units. And each populated area would have two missionaries to minister to the spiritual needs of Native Americans and Spaniards. Finally, a captain general with headquarters at Soto la Marina on the Río de las Palmas would provide general supervision over the province.[29]

A junta in Mexico City considered the proposals to determine their worthiness and whether Escandón as petitioner should be commissioned to implement them. The committee's deliberations ended with a favorable verdict. By decree at the end of May 1748, the Conde de Revilla Gigedo named Colonel José de Escandón to carry out the intended "pacification, reduction, and settlement" of Nuevo Santander. On June 1 don José accepted the charge and expressed appreciation for the viceroy's confidence in him.[30]

Once again, don José lost little time in acting but did not sacrifice effectiveness to haste. Working with his lieutenants to conduct a publicity campaign along the frontier, he and his officers had little difficulty recruiting potential settlers. More than an adequate number of families responded, lured by the opportunity to relocate in Nuevo Santander and acquire productive lands. Many of the enlistees were from Coahuila and Nuevo León, where they had experienced the hazards of frontier life but also knew the potential for rich rewards.

Among those recruited as settlers in the new province were ranchers who already owned large herds of livestock but needed more grazing land. Those stockmen could have expanded on their own at any time, but it was risky to do so, and they would not have received subsidies or remission of taxes. Furthermore, those same ranchers not only had a high regard for Escandón but also recognized that the timing for expansion was right. The central government in Mexico City backed the enterprise, and it would make sure that governors in adjoining frontier provinces provided necessary cooperation.

These considerations made it possible for don José to head one of the largest expeditions ever assembled for the colonization of a frontier province of New Spain. The main company departed Querétaro on December 2, 1748. Escandón's lieutenants and their contingents left from Cerralvo and Linares (both in Nuevo León), Valles, Tampico, and San Juan Bautista with the intent of joining the main group or proceeding directly to specified destinations.[31]

On Christmas Day, Escandón founded Santa María de Llera on the Las Rusias Plains with forty-four Spanish families, several Indians, and eleven soldiers—a total of 257 people. Established nearby was Mission Peña del Castillo. Moving north, the colonizer founded San Fernando de Güemes with forty families in early 1749. Soon thereafter, he peopled San Antonio de Padilla with thirty Spanish families, and the procession continued.[32]

Unfortunately, at this point delays occurred. The governor spent three weeks exploring along the Tamaulipas coast in an attempt to find a suitable port for the province. In the meantime, the main camp suffered serious illnesses, most likely because of contaminated water, which forced a move from the original site named "Hell" to one only slightly better called "Purgatory." And duplicitous natives also complicated matters. Having earlier approached the camp with a show of friendliness, Indians from the Cerrito del Ayre area attacked in the night and killed several horses. Swift retaliation forced the local Indian chief to seek a truce, but problems with the natives were far from over. Despite these difficulties, colonization efforts continued. The "crowning event" in this same region was the founding of the capital, Villa de Nuevo Santander, in February 1749, with more than four hundred people in attendance.[33]

Departing for the Río Grande in late February, Escandón entered the valley of the San Juan River, which he found already occupied. The governor's subordinate, Blas María de la Garza Falcón had come directly from Nuevo León with some forty families, and the settlers had already begun to build houses and irrigation facilities. Consequently, Santa Ana de Camargo was founded on March 5, 1749, again with more than four hundred persons present. Camargo's *pobladores* had also begun the construction of large canoes for crossing the Río Grande. These craft pleased Escandón, for they could be used to transport salt from deposits north of the river, and the canoes would facilitate travel to the Nueces River and beyond to the Santa Dorotea site on the San Antonio River, where La Bahía presidio and mission would soon be relocated.[34]

But even the most competent and conscientious of colonizers could not foresee all eventualities. The realities of distance, difficulties of communication, and dangers on the frontier led to failed plans and loss of lives. For example, efforts to settle the trans-Nueces region in Texas miscarried when Indians killed the missionary and an escort of eight soldiers en route to the proposed location. Accordingly, settlers intended for that part of the province had to wait eight months for Escandón's orders, which eventually sent them to the site of Soto la Marina. Not until September 1750, and then under a new captain, Juan José Vázquez Borrego, were they settled in the town named for Escandón's birthplace.[35]

Meanwhile, a site situated approximately twelve leagues down the Río Grande from Camargo was allotted to Carlos Cantú, who had brought forty families and less than a dozen soldiers from Nuevo León. This villa, then known as Nuestra Señora de Guadalupe de Reynosa, took root across the Great River from contemporary McAllen, Texas. With the founding of present-day Reynosa, Tamaulipas, Escandón headed south to Villa de Nuevo Santander.[36]

In later weeks, don José visited several of the new villas near the capital of the province. Although he deemed their locations suitable, Indian problems posed a continuing threat to lives and property. At that time, Escandón oversaw the founding of Villa Altamira on May 1, 1749, a new settlement named for his advocate, the *auditor de guerra*. But Indian depredations consumed his energies for some time, obliging him to launch punitive campaigns against hostile Huastec apostates.[37]

The colonizer then went to the eastern slope of the Sierra Gorda. There in mid-May he established Villa Santa Bárbara, which already had a few families in residence. With the founding of this settlement, Escandón had "completed the pacification of the southern Sierra Gorda." In a report dated June 13, 1749, he informed Viceroy Revilla Gigedo that this "admirable" accomplishment, long desired by the crown, seemed to have been "reserved by Divine Providence for this propitious time of Your Excellency's administration." [38]

The specific plan submitted by Escandón to the junta in 1748 had called for fourteen settlements in Nuevo Santander, and within six months of his expedition's departure from Querétaro, thirteen had been established with plans for accompanying missions. By the end of 1749, more than eight hundred families of Spaniards and *"gente de razón"* (natives capable of being Europeanized) inhabited these settlements, with ten squadrons of troops assigned for their protection. Some 90,000 pesos had been expended in the first year for aid to the colonists, military functions, and missionary activities. Although this amount exceeded the original estimate of 58,000 pesos, much had been accomplished under don José's leadership, and in remarkably short time.[39]

Recognizing the merits of Escandón's accomplishments, the viceroy commended him to the king. Subsequently, in October 1749, just one year after the colonizer had left Querétaro to embark on his great venture, Ferdinand VI granted don José the titles of Count of Sierra Gorda and Viscount of the House of Escandón (Figure 14). The crown expressly stated that the pacification of hostile Indians in northern Mexico, the exploration of the Costa, and the colonization of Nuevo Santander had earned him those honors.[40]

Despite his many accomplishments—or perhaps because of them—the new Count of Sierra Gorda was not without enemies, both clerical and secular. And he would be plagued throughout the remainder of his life by attempts to discredit him. In fact, complaints from the guardian at the new apostolic college of San Fernando in Mexico City had already surfaced during the first year of Escandón's colonization efforts. Those criticisms, directed at the governor, apparently related to an ongoing power struggle between the friars of San Fernando and those of the older college of Zacatecas over control of the missions in Nuevo Santander.[41]

An anti-Escandón petition, authored by the San Fernando friars, in conjunction with a negative recommendation by the royal *fiscal*, threatened the colonizer's appropriations for the following year. Fortunately, however, the *auditor de guerra* came to his defense. The Marqués de Altamira declared that Escandón's method of colonization "had accomplished more in one year than could have been done in a hundred years following usual procedures." For the moment, at least, the governor remained in good stead and could proceed with his endeavors.[42]

Escandón spent considerable time visiting his existing settlements, as well as establishing new ones, some of which were created for reasons

DESCRIPCION DEL ESCUDO

Escudo cuartelado. Primero: de plata, águila explayada de sable. Segundo: de gules, castillo de plata. Tercero: de sinople, castillo de plata. Cuarto: de azur, caldera de oro con una banda de gules. Entre primero y segundo cuartel cruz de oro. Acolado con la Cruz de Santiago. Soportes: dos rústicos y timbrado con Corona de Conde.

Lema: "Aunque rústicos guardamos con osadía y valor estas armas cuya luz a venido de esta cruz y son de el linaje y casa de Escandón."

NOTA.—La descripción anterior está tomada de la obra de D. Ricardo Ortega y Pérez Gallardo, titulada: "Historia Genealógica de las familias más antiguas de México." Como se observará, dicha descripción presenta algunas variantes con el escudo que reproducimos, en la disposición y color de los cuarteles; pero lo hemos preferido, por ser copia del existente hasta la fecha en Jiménez, Tams., mandado tallar en piedra por el señor de Escandón, circunstancia demostrativa de su autenticidad.

FIGURE 14

Coat of arms of José de Escandón. This escudo honors the lineage and house of Escandón. (With the permission of the Archivo General de la Nación, Mexico.)

related to Indian uprisings. Two of the new outposts were established north of the Río Grande, although several years apart. José Vázquez Borrego of Nuevo León needed more land for his herds and offered to settle his kinsmen and himself across the river from Revilla at no cost to the crown. With the governor's authorization and a generous land grant, Vázquez Borrego established impermanent Nuestra Señora de Dolores in 1750. Dolores, not a true villa but an extensive hacienda, had no mission, requiring the friar from Revilla to serve the religious needs of the residents.[43]

Four additional settlements came about during the years 1751 to 1753, although none was on the north bank of the Río Grande. Not until 1755 was a second settlement placed beyond the Great River. On one of Escandón's inspection tours in 1754, José Vázquez Borrego approached him with a proposed colonization project to be headed by Tomás Sánchez of Nuevo León. Although not as wealthy as some of the other colonizers, Sánchez was willing to bear the cost of populating and defending a settlement at Paso de Jacinto, a ford on the Río Grande. Reacting favorably to the proposal, Escandón conferred military and political authority on Sánchez but ordered him to seek a favorable site on the Nueces River in Texas. After some exploration north of the Río Grande, Sánchez threatened to abandon the project if he could not settle at the originally proposed location. Escandón relented, and on May, 15, 1755, Sánchez established Villa Laredo between the Jacinto and Garza Fords on the Río Grande.[44]

The formal establishment of settlements, however, did not guarantee their success. From the beginning, problems plagued the colonists, who had invariably looked to Escandón for solutions. Experimenting with maize agriculture, the original settlers of 1749 suffered from drought and unrelieved heat, which led to loss of cattle and crops. In 1750 the governor reported to Viceroy Revilla Gigedo that the extraordinary continuation of drought and the related high price of seed corn "threatened imminent total ruin." Predictably, when the drought finally ended, serious flooding hit Güemes and Camargo.[45]

Despite the vagaries of weather, native groups within the Costa provided the greatest internal challenge to the settlers of Nuevo Santander and their leader. Cognizant that "the most benign and gentle reduction" of warring tribes was a major charge of the crown, the governor attempted whenever possible to incorporate natives as neophytes in missions or as laborers for Spanish landowners.[46]

When Escandón and his family moved to Villa de Nuevo Santander, he contended that many Indians congregated there as a result of his presence. Needing a labor force to construct an impressive house, tend herds of livestock, and perform other tasks, the count relocated thirty families of Pames Indians from Río Verde. Each head of a native household received four pesos per month and a ration of maize. Don José also made sure that the transplanted Indians received baptism, Catholic instruction, and the sacrament of marriage. Additionally, he placed five of the Pames families in the nearby mission, where they served as role models for less Hispanicized neophytes.[47]

In 1753 twenty-seven Indians of the Carrizo nation approached Escandón and asked permission to settle in Dolores. The supplicants indicated a willingness to work and promised to encourage other pagans to congregate there. Convinced of their sincerity, the count ordered Vázquez Borrego to admit them under his protection and find "someone who would instruct them in the rudiments of our holy faith."[48]

When visiting Villa de Reynosa in 1753, the count proudly noted that four nations, including the Comecrudos, were congregated there and that the Pintos and Zacatiles were frequent visitors at the missions. A realist, however, he observed that cooperative Indians were probably attracted by gifts of clothing, tobacco, and other merchandise.[49]

Although peaceful conversion was the desired method for dealing with indigenous peoples, Escandón did not hesitate to employ military solutions if he felt that approach necessary. For example, when the Indians of Mission Ygollo in Santa Bárbara rebelled in the early 1750s, he subjugated them by force of arms. In this and similar situations, the count inflicted harsh punishment "to set an example for all others." However, even forceful military reprisals provided no definitive solution to the threat posed by hostile natives in Nuevo Santander. In 1754 don José reported that Janambre Indians had killed Joseph de Escajadilla of Villa de Llera, one of his trusted captains.[50]

Certainly, the demands on Governor Escandón from within his province were daunting. Added to these difficulties was the necessity of dealing with a complex and distant royal bureaucracy. Periodically, don José had to submit voluminous documentation on Nuevo Santander to meet the mandates of the viceroy and to ensure continued support from the crown. Those requirements meant touring the province to gather the necessary information and then compiling it in proper form.

In February and May of 1753, Governor Escandón sent the viceroy "reports on the condition of the twenty new towns in the Colony of the Seno Mexicano." He cited examples of progress, such as the abundance of cattle, horses, and mules, and of congregated Indians at Reynosa, but also acknowledged setbacks, including the necessity of relocating Camargo because of the dangers posed by flooding from the San Juan River. Don José justified the founding of some settlements—Mier, for example—because they safeguarded the route to others, made it possible to establish additional towns on the banks of the Río Grande, and helped control many "pagan Indians." The count also reported that even though the apostolic college of San Fernando had withdrawn its derogatory petition, missionaries in his province from the college of Zacatecas were still "oppressed by want since they have not received even half" of the allotments promised to them by their superiors.[51]

Convinced that his reputation would "speak for him," Escandón did not feel it necessary to provide formal documentation to support information contained in his reports of 1753. However, this omission prompted extreme displeasure on the part of bureaucratic officials in Mexico City. Don José, hardly a novice in matters related to Spanish administration, should have known better.[52]

In response to the February and May reports, the *auditor de guerra* made several recommendations to the viceroy on the conquest of Nuevo Santander, including the following: acknowledge Escandón's report with thanks for his promptness and diligence; approve land grants made to Mier, Revilla, and Dolores, but advise the colonizer in the future to distribute only lands that were "vacant sites" and only in proper conformity with Spanish law; urge the count to promote "the greatest harmony" with and within the church. The *auditor* also directed that a letter be sent to the apostolic college of Zacatecas to ensure that allotments for the support of its missionaries in Nuevo Santander be sent to them and to instruct those religious to work in harmony with Escandón.[53]

The *auditor* reminded the viceroy that "no memoranda or reports" should be made to the crown without "the instruments and documents to prove and verify them especially on matters of so much gravity and on which such heavy expenditures have been made." He also astutely observed that great enterprises inspired great jealousies, which made it even more imperative for don José's information to be fully documented. Finally, the *auditor* suggested that the viceroy order Escandón to prepare a "complete report of the condition of the conquest in question." The account should include the location of the twenty towns, the crops raised by inhabitants, the distribution of land to individual settlers, and census information on troops, settlers, and mission Indians—all with proper authentication.[54]

The viceroy accepted these recommendations, and upon orders to do so, Escandón had compiled a lengthy status report on Nuevo Santander by 1755. However, when he arrived in Mexico City to make his formal presentation, don José learned that the Count of Revilla Gigedo had asked to be replaced as viceroy. Accordingly, the colonizer had to deal with a new royal appointee, Agustín de Ahumada y Villalón, the Marqués de las Amarillas.[55]

As always, Escandón was realistic in his appraisal of conditions within the new province. On the one hand, he praised the fertility of the soil, the abundance of the crops, and the quantity of livestock in Nuevo Santander; on the other, the count elaborated on the many hardships faced by the settlers, ranging from natural disasters to hostile natives. He also acknowledged both successes and failures in congregating the indigenous peoples. Three thousand natives had already been "settled in missions and exposed to Christian doctrine." However, he expressed distress that even more Indians wished to congregate but were prevented from doing so by lack of clergy and necessary provisions.[56]

Among the many topics addressed by Escandón was the difficulty of establishing a viable port near Soto la Marina, owing to the presence of an offshore sand bar. However, by employing smaller craft he had made some progress toward establishing maritime commerce. He also discussed his firm commitment to the communal ownership of land, a practice that had prompted many complaints from the colonists. Granting titles to individuals, explained Escandón, would be a "difficult business" that would cause heated disputes. Furthermore, some of the more recent arrivals in the province were "better and more useful" than certain original *pobladores*, who demanded special status and commensurate consideration. Had the best lands already been granted, argued Escandón, it would have resulted in much disharmony.[57]

In a comprehensive statement on the province, the Count of Sierra Gorda reported that twenty settled areas (*poblaciones*) had been formalized with a population of 1,389 families. Declaring that his only goal in colonizing Nuevo Santander had been to serve the crown, he wrote that "the conquest in essence is concluded."[58]

While informing the viceroy of his successes, don José also insisted that much more remained to be done. The Indians, for example, required "the greatest vigilance to prevent any uprisings." For purposes of security, other strategic sites should be populated.[59] In effect, Escandón sought official recognition for what he had accomplished and royal support to continue that work.

Deliberating at length on Escandón's detailed report, the new viceroy convened a junta in Mexico City to consider the count's proposals. Backed by the committee's recommendations and acting on orders from

Spain, the Marqués de las Amarillas then selected two royal commissioners to substantiate the "progress and present state" of Nuevo Santander. Named judge-inspector, Captain José Tienda de Cuervo received instructions to tour the province. Accompanying him as engineer and lieutenant in the royal army was Agustín López de la Cámara Alta. Armed with an interrogatory of eighteen questions, the commissioners were to formulate a comprehensive overview of Nuevo Santander, based on interviews with the colonists and on their own observations.[60]

Tienda de Cuervo and López de la Cámara Alta spent several months touring Nuevo Santander. They covered the twenty populated areas that Escandón had claimed credit and responsibility for in his 1755 report, as well as three other locations. One of the three was the recently founded settlement at Laredo. As for the other two, the *población* of Jaumave was technically outside the limits of Escandón's colony, and Palmillas was similarly thought to be "independent." However, the judge-inspector ruled that both were in actuality part of Escandón's command and, therefore, should be included in the *visita*.[61]

In the final report, the inspecting officials described Escandón's government in 1757 as being both military and ecclesiastical. Appointed captains in each villa held political and military authority, although missionaries were in charge of converting the natives. Salaries for officers, soldiers, and missionaries totaled about 43,000 pesos annually, an expenditure judged to be excessive. Among suggested remedies were to reorganize or reduce the military and lower the pay of some officers.[62]

Tienda de Cuervo and López de la Cámara Alta acknowledged that many tribes had been congregated but also observed that "in some settlements, the baptismal book of the mission has not registered, during fifteen years, one single baptism." Furthermore, apostates, who deserted the missions, were guilty of committing most of the "hostilities and murders." The religious must shoulder some responsibility for these distressing circumstances, because they chose to reside in the settlements, instead of "living with the Indians in the designated places."[63]

In recommending the reorganization of the province's military forces and the pursuance of aggressive campaigns against troublesome natives, the inspectors concurred with some of Escandón's plans. They also supported the governor's proposal for founding new settlements and accompanying missions at strategic locations. Such approaches would protect mineral regions and roads, while preventing Indians from using mountainous regions of the province as sanctuary.[64]

Directed to inspect harbor facilities along the Gulf Coast, the royal agents declared that the proposed development of port facilities at Soto la Marina was too costly and impractical. They also warned that establishing a port in Nuevo Santander might prove competitively disadvantageous to Veracruz. But they did encourage new efforts to find mineral resources, which would facilitate further settlement of the province and profit the royal treasury. Lastly, the inspectors found the issue of land ownership to be the greatest single cause of dissatisfaction among the colonists. They reached the conclusion that land grants in fee simple should be awarded on the bases of merit and seniority; in implementing this policy, however, consideration must be given to ancestral lands of the Indians.[65]

Compiling detailed statistical information, the commissioners tallied residents and livestock. Those figures were impressive. Like Escandón, they considered some villas and missions well situated and "promising," while observing that others faced serious difficulties, such as unsuitable locations, poor crops, and hostile Indians. Where feasible, the inspectors recommended specific solutions to problems that would ensure continuing progress in an important borderlands province.[66]

Even though Tienda de Cuervo and López de la Cámara Alta criticized certain aspects of the Nuevo Santander enterprise, much of their assessment was favorable. Escandón had successfully colonized a region where earlier efforts by Spaniards had failed for more than two centuries. Nonetheless, prompt attention had to be given to land issues, the establishment of a few more settlements in the interior portions of the province, and other matters of high priority.[67]

From 1757 to 1767, the Count of Sierra Gorda, having cleared a critical inspection, addressed the needs of his growing province. Among his projects were flood control, construction of a road from Tampico to Monterrey, relocation of certain towns, and arrangements for Fray Vicente de Santa María to write a history of Nuevo Santander. Also, during this period don José pursued the controversial initiative of erecting a new bishopric with the seat (mitra) in his provincial capital. According to the governor, this would not only cause "great spiritual consolation and increase in the reduction of the heathens" but also create commercial prosperity.[68]

While Escandón worked with usual dispatch, the royal bureaucracy in Mexico City inched forward. Under still another viceroy, Joaquín de Monserrat, Marqués de Cruillas, Tienda de Cuervo's recommendations were finally given serious attention. In 1763 the crown issued a number of directives, which included instructions for the partition of common lands and the founding of new settlements. Consequently, in the latter half of the decade, three additional villas were set up at strategic sites: Cruillas in 1765, San Carlos in 1766, and Croix in 1770.[69]

Regarding the matter of land distribution, however, don José continued to defend the practice of communal assignment. Land, he insisted, was the main incentive that prompted colonists to settle among the "barbarians" in Nuevo Santander. As governor, he had used that lure so artfully "that they [the colonists] don't cease to come." Escandón insisted that it was still premature to assign individual titles, which would leave the towns deserted as each settler left to reside on his own property. Furthermore, those who complained most vociferously about Escandón's communal approach were only thinking of "selling the land that will be consigned to them."[70]

Other orders by the crown in 1763 concerned the reorganization of the military in Nuevo Santander and the reduction of captains' salaries that Tienda de Cuervo had recommended. In defending the status quo to the viceroy, don José again revealed his adeptness in presenting a coherent and convincing argument. To save money "sounds good," don José conceded. But the reality of hostile, rebellious natives necessitated mounted military troops and "constant vigilance." To jeopardize all that had been accomplished in the conquest of the province by making ill-advised changes based on "bad intelligence" was imprudent. Governor Escandón also warned that there was a real risk "of losing in a few months that which had been achieved in so many years . . . only to save money."[71]

The 1760s were especially difficult times for don José in both his personal and his professional lives. In 1762, Josefa, his wife and the mother of seven children, died. At the same time, the widower found himself increasingly under attack on several fronts. Dissatisfaction among settlers, especially over the issue of land ownership, along with complaints by church officials, threatened everything that Escandón had accomplished.[72]

Early in the 1760s, the dean of the cathedral in Guadalajara protested that don José had offered settlers exemption from payment of tithes and first fruits, along with other incentives, to relocate to his province. Hundreds of families from Nuevo León had taken advantage of the offer, which caused a major loss of revenue to the church. Furthermore, declared the dean, "little harvest has been made of heathens" in Nuevo Santander, and the missions there had not been secularized, even though many years had passed. As a means to remedy this situation, the Guadalajaran official asked the government to determine with "brevity" which diocese had jurisdiction over the new settlements in the Costa del Seno Mexicano.[73]

In 1766 a viceregal advisor briefed the Marqués Carlos Francisco de Croix on the diocesan dispute. With qualifications, the official endorsed Escandón's proposal for creating a bishopric in Nuevo Santander. It was "requisite," however, to have the consent of the archbishop of Mexico, as well as the bishops of Michoacán and Guadalajara, whose dioceses would be adversely affected.[74] Not surprisingly, strong opposition came from Diego, the bishop of Guadalajara, who declared his belief that Escandón's tales of "grand progress, attractive settlements, and reductions [of natives]" were pure "fiction." His excellency stated that he would "happily" execute any orders the viceroy issued, if Escandón's claims of great accomplishments proved to be true.[75]

That same year, 1766, Fray José Joaquín García of the apostolic college in Zacatecas, unhappy with the rate of progress in Christianizing the Indians of Nuevo Santander, placed blame on the governor. Fray García also complained that some of the missionaries had left their posts and moved to the settlements, even though ministering to the spiritual needs of the colonists was not their primary obligation.[76]

Amid swirling controversy, the viceroy ordered Escandón to the capital in 1766. Among the reasons given for this summons was the need to discuss land distribution, but certainly religious issues must also have been a factor. In the following year, Viceroy Croix created a royal commission for Nuevo Santander, headed by Juan Fernando Palacio, then governor of Veracruz. Assisted by Licenciado José de Osorio y Llamas, the commissioner was to conduct an investigation (*pesquisa*) into "the conduct of Escandón" and to determine the actual state of affairs in his province. However, Palacio's primary charge was to appoint surveyors and prepare for the partition of common lands, awarding them on the basis of merit and seniority. The officials carried out this duty with traditional Spanish ceremony and legalistic rituals, first at Laredo on May 15, 1767, and then at other villas as the expedition proceeded through the province.[77]

Because availability of water was a prime consideration, grants along the Río Grande were made in *porciones*, long quadrangles that bordered the river on one side. Settlers receiving a *porción* (grant in fee simple) accepted mandatory responsibilities, which included the obligation of military service. A second group of grants for much larger tracts was to be used exclusively for grazing. These sizable assignments fell within present-day Hidalgo, Cameron, and Willacy Counties. The surveyors also had the task of determining lands that belonged to the respective missions within the province.[78]

Upon their return to Mexico City in 1768, the two officials declared that many of the allegations against the count were unfounded. However, they did criticize Escandón for failing to establish additional settlements. Ironically, a major reason for the colonizer's failure to accomplish that objective was that he had been forced to relocate to the viceregal capital to defend himself against the allegations of critics. And, in his absence, less able interim governors had assumed control over Nuevo Santander.[79]

The cumulative results of numerous complaints over the years, as well as information collected by Juan Fernando Palacio, resulted in a massive inquest into Escandón's tenure as governor of Nuevo Santander. In the late 1760s, a legal proceeding containing thirty-eight separate charges occupied don José's energies for the rest of his life and those of his heirs for years after his death. Specifically, it was charged that the Count of Sierra Gorda had not fulfilled the goals he had promised in settling Nuevo Santander, nor had he remained within budget. Instead, for twenty years he had made excessive expenditures, totaling one million pesos from the royal treasury. In his haste to attract colonists, don José had failed to screen them properly—accepting many delinquents and villainous persons by ignoring their crimes or granting them indulgences. As a result, Nuevo Santander contained such a disreputable population that it "deserved . . . [to be called] the Portugal of New Spain."[80]

Labeled a despot with opulent haciendas and a luxurious palace, Escandón had allegedly used his commissaries and other business enterprises to enrich himself. Through company store and monopolistic practices, the governor had exploited soldiers, defrauded settlers, and abused Indians. And for two decades he had ignored the repeated requests of the colonists for individual allocations of land.[81]

Numerous charges had to do with the mistreatment of Indians. The governor allegedly had not achieved the "commendable objective of pacifying and congregating the Gentile and Apostate Indians." Instead, he killed or imprisoned them. He also failed to punish his captains when they committed atrocities against the natives. Contrary to Spanish law, Escandón had allowed Indians to be transported far from their homelands to tend his livestock or work at building his palatial residence in the capital of the province. Other natives were compelled to labor in *obrajes* (sweatshops), at times exploited to the point of death. Further, the count had caused some missions to be depopulated and then given lands belonging to the natives to friars of the Carmelite Order. Additionally, when Apaches made overtures of peace to the captain at Laredo, don José ordered his subordinate not to deal with them.[82]

Escandón and his family systematically and vehemently refuted each of the charges—arguing that after more than fifty years of service on Spain's behalf, the count had not only fulfilled his original proposals for colonizing Nuevo Santander but had far surpassed them. Instead of fourteen towns with four hundred families, by the time Tienda de Cuervo toured the province in 1757 there were twenty-two settlements with almost thirteen hundred Spanish families. In all, 1,071 pagans had received the sacrament of baptism. Don José had issued indulgences to some settlers, but those were for debts, not crimes. As for his failure to screen colonists, the people of Nuevo Santander were like those elsewhere in New Spain—some good, some bad.[83]

Escandón's defense also maintained that the count had served the crown for twenty years without salary, but "with the sole hope of earning honors." Yes, he had conducted business enterprises within Nuevo Santander, as did others, but Spanish policy did not disallow profitable ventures for colonizers. To the contrary, this was appropriate recompense, because such agents of the crown received no direct salary. Yes, it was also true that his house contained a public store, but operating it was a matter of "honest commerce." Profits from this and his other ventures were only fair compensation for his personal expenditures on exploration and colonization. As for his "palatial" residence, it was built at his own expense, as were many of the public works he had underwritten.[84]

To be sure, continued the defense, Escandón had not awarded individual land titles, because he had been preoccupied with establishing new settlements and fulfilling the mandates of the captain general. However, to have issued titles in fee simple would have caused "disquiet and rivalry." Even worse, by necessity some of the colonists would have received private lands well removed from settled areas, thereby risking their safety. Instead, Escandón had set aside an appropriate amount of land for each settler, soldier, and Indian, with ownership in common.[85]

Apropos of the treatment of Indians, the Escandóns argued that the count had experienced successes in reducing them through "quiet" means and that those accomplishments had been substantiated by the Tienda de Cuervo report. Regarding the natives who had relocated from Río Verde, they did so voluntarily with fair compensation for their labor from Escandón. Furthermore, distinctions had to be made between gentiles (pagans) who were friends and those who had remained enemies. One group of Indians named in the lawsuit had indeed been sentenced to labor in *obrajes*, but those natives had been guilty of waging war and killing ten soldiers. Likewise, it was true that don José had instructed the captain of Laredo to ignore peaceful overtures from the Apaches. But that nation was notorious for its perfidy—offering peace with one hand and double-dealing with the other.[86]

While addressing the thirty-eight specific charges, the defense also aggressively challenged the methods by which the investigation into the count's tenure had been conducted and attempted to discredit his accusers. The Marqués de Croix, having received many complaints, had allegedly used the pretext of wanting information about Nuevo Santander to order the governor to Mexico City and "separate" him from his province. The viceroy's real motive had been to conduct an extensive *pesquisa*, resulting in legal proceedings that effectively ended Escandón's career.[87]

That detractors in Nuevo Santander had spread falsehoods against Escandón was to be expected, continued the defense, because the accomplishments of successful men inevitably arouse envy. For example, not even the great Fernando Cortés had escaped the malice and lies of his enemies in the sixteenth century. But in the litany of complaints against don José, perhaps the most vitriolic were those of María Bárbara Resendi, daughter of Maximiliano Resendi and Catarina de Olvera, as well as the Pisone Indians of Mission Jaumave.[88]

Doña Catarina herself harbored considerable malice for the count, but her daughter's assertions were seemingly outrageous. Doña Bárbara, contended the defense, had presented herself as an "advocate for the Chichimec Indians of the Sierra Gorda." In that guise, she had submitted a formal document to the investigating judges, and in it accused Escandón of committing outrageous crimes against the natives of Jaumave. Not only were the woman's motives suspect, but officials who were paid to defend those very Indians were already in place, and doña Bárbara was not one of them. In any event, the Escandóns asserted, she could not exercise her claims as advocate, "because she was a woman" (*por su sexo*).[89]

Working to solidify his defense and to discredit his accusers, the count undoubtedly hoped for vindication. However, he did not live to see the outcome of this massive *pesquisa*. As mentioned, with legal proceedings still in progress, José de Escandón died in September 1770. His death was doubly tragic. A man who had devoted his entire adult life to the service of the crown—a man who had proved to be one of the most competent royal officials in New Spain—died under a cloud. His children might not inherit anything, for his entire estate had been sequestered.

It fell to Escandón's family to bring the lawsuit to conclusion. Vigorously pursuing the matter, don Manuel not only had to defend the count's name but also had to convince the crown that he, as principal heir, should inherit his father's wealth, titles, and position. Don Manuel's supporters argued that the father's example had taught the son "loyalty" and "love of the king." Since 1756, the younger Escandón "had served in the capacity of lieutenant to the captain of the Villa and Royal Squadron of Nuevo Santander . . . accrediting himself in those capacities by his good conduct, self-abnegation, military skills, and zeal for royal service. [In doing so,] he had contributed with distinguished honor to the . . . peaceful reduction and congregation of the godless Indians." Well qualified in every regard, don Manuel wished to continue his father's work.[90]

Finally justice was served, although posthumously. A royal decree, dated January 1773, completely exonerated José de Escandón. The king also informed Viceroy Antonio María de Bucareli y Ursúa that Manuel de Escandón y Llera should receive title as the Count of Sierra Gorda, with full rights of governance in Nuevo Santander.[91]

Ultimately, José de Escandón y Elguera founded twenty-three settlements in Nuevo Santander. At the same time, Franciscans from the apostolic colleges of San Fernando and Zacatecas established fifteen missions. The Count of Sierra Gorda had hoped to make the Santa Dorotea site on the San Antonio River in Texas the northern limit of his province, and to that end moved the La Bahía presidio and mission to present-day Goliad in 1749. His plans, however, miscarried and both remained under the jurisdiction of Texas. Likewise, proposals for two civilian communities, one on the San Antonio River and one near the mouth of the Nueces River, never became a reality. Consequently, Escandón's Nuevo Santander included a portion of Texas lying south of the Nueces River, as well as the present Mexican state of Tamaulipas.[92]

Only two of the twenty-three settlements, Laredo and Nuestra Señora de los Dolores, were within the confines of the present Lone Star State. However, downstream from Laredo, towns founded to the south of the Río Grande by Escandón and his lieutenants brought hundreds of settlers and their livestock to both banks of the Great River. Belated recognition of Escandón's accomplishments on the Texas side, however, did not come until the centennial of the Texas Republic. In 1936 Rio Grande

City erected a monument with an inscription containing these words: "In memory of the greatest colonizer of Northern Mexico, José de Escandón, who directed exploration from Tampico to the San Antonio River, laid out 23 towns; . . . founded missions, opened roads and established settlers, 1746–1755." More recently, Escandón is remembered in extreme South Texas as the Father of the Lower Río Grande. Descendants of "first families," true pioneers of the region who received land grants along the river in Starr, Hidalgo, and Cameron Counties, have formed the Las Porciones Society, with its headquarters in Edinburg, Texas.[93]

To be sure, Escandón was not always consistent. He claimed vast private lands for himself, while denying that privilege to early settlers in Nuevo Santander. But the fact remains that he accomplished the systematic settlement of the Costa del Seno Mexicano, a goal that had eluded other Spaniards for more than two centuries. And in doing so, José de Escandón laid the foundation for ranching and farming in the modern-day South Texas triangle that lies below the Nueces River.[94]

~

EIGHT

ATHANASE DE MÉZIÈRES
French Indian Agent

~

In October 1770, at a place on the Red River called San Luis de Cadodachos, Athanase de Mézières, a Frenchman by birth but a Spaniard by the vagaries of fate, met with Native American chiefs who represented tribes traditionally hostile to Spain. Engaged in a peacemaking mission for his new sovereign, Charles III, the lieutenant governor of Natchitoches harangued the Indian leaders with news that the transfer of the Louisiana Territory meant "the very name of Frenchman had been erased and forgotten; that [henceforth] we were Spaniards." De Mézières assured the chiefs that despite their past actions, Charles III, the most powerful monarch in the world, would grant them peace if they proved to be invariably deserving. However, if they continued their hostilities, the king's invincible forces would descend upon them. What course would the assembly of chieftains choose to follow?[1]

Near the end of the disastrous Seven Years' War, on November 3, 1762, Louis XV of France ceded the Louisiana Territory that lay west of the Mississippi River to Charles III by the secret Treaty of Fontainebleau. Earlier, Louis had expressed his regrets that Spain had suffered significant losses by entering the war as an ally of France against England. "If New Orleans or Louisiana can be of use in obtaining the restoration of Havana," he wrote to his Spanish kinsman, "or as compensation for what must be given the English for it, I offer them to you." Although Charles reluctantly accepted Louisiana—he and his advisors viewed the province as a financial burden—the transfer remained a secret, even after the Treaty of Paris, which ended the war, was signed on February 10,

1763. Not until 1764 did the French monarch officially notify the director general of Louisiana of the cession and instruct him to surrender the province. But even then Spain did not act in a timely fashion to assume possession. Antonio de Ulloa, the first Spanish governor of the province, finally arrived in New Orleans in March 1766, but he faced so much opposition from local citizenry that the French flag continued to fly over the city.[2]

During his brief stay in Louisiana, Ulloa became impressed with Athanase de Mézières, a retired infantry captain living at Natchitoches. Writing to the Marqués de Grimaldi, Spanish minister of state, the governor suggested that the Frenchman be given command at Natchitoches, with Louis de St. Denis (the younger) as his lieutenant. However, a rebellion by French Creoles led to Ulloa's ouster in 1768, and effective Spanish dominion over Louisiana was not achieved until the following year. On August 18, 1769, Irish-born Alejandro O'Reilly, backed by twenty-one ships and more than two thousand troops, took possession of the territory in the name of Charles III.[3]

Acquisition of the vast and unfamiliar Louisiana Territory and its often hostile populace brought new challenges for Spain. Significantly, Charles III placed the governance of Louisiana under the captaincy-general of Cuba, rather than on the already overburdened officials of New Spain. And although East Texas had become an interior province that was no longer at risk from French attacks, the reality of a strong English presence to—and eventually beyond—the Mississippi River had to be faced. The allegiance or at least neutrality of the native groups, known as Norteños or Nations of the North, who resided on both sides of the Red River, became critical, not only to guard against foreign influence but also in case of an all-out war against the troublesome Apaches. Traditionally, the Norteños had relied on trade with the French and enjoyed gifts from them, while at the same time remaining hostile to the Spanish. If at all possible, they must be brought into the Spanish fold.[4]

Recent experiences in Texas, however, revealed that traditional Spanish missions had not been effective in dealing with these warlike groups, nor were military responses, as confirmed by the Diego Ortiz Parrilla expedition of 1759. Rather, the acquisition of Louisiana opened the possibility of placing "the Red River district in charge of a Frenchman who understood its native inhabitants and . . . [continuing] the French system of control though . . . trade."[5]

As it evolved, Spain's new direction in Indian policy on the Louisiana-Texas frontier aimed at cultivating the friendship of certain tribes, and at the same time making them hostile to foreigners—especially the English. Less cooperative groups would be denied all supplies, except those specifically authorized by the government, and only bonded agents could engage in commerce. Unlicensed persons, whether traders or vagabonds, were to be expelled from Indian lands. Forbidden items of commerce, such as horses, mules, and Indian slaves, which the French had countenanced, must be stopped. Although intertribal hostilities were discouraged among such groups as the Caddoans and the Osages, Spanish officials in the name of expediency had authorization to turn some tribes against each other when it suited their purposes. Significantly, while sanctioning a harsh pragmatism that Spanish officials labeled as perfidy when practiced by the Lipan Apaches, Spain would not abandon its religious commitment to all Indians.[6]

To accomplish these multifaceted goals, Spain intended to utilize the talents of its new citizens of French descent in Louisiana. Accordingly, on September 23, 1769, Alejandro O'Reilly penned a letter to Athanase de Mézières, ordering him to come to New Orleans. In this communication the Spanish official expressed his belief that don Athanase would be "better able than any one else to give me correct information regarding everything relating to your district." As a result of their meeting, O'Reilly named De Mézières lieutenant governor of Natchitoches, with a monthly salary of thirty pesos. Reporting to the Marqués de Grimaldi, don Alejandro remarked that he had been influenced in this decision by "the good reports which I received from the most trustworthy citizens of this country about . . . De Mézières . . . and the good opinion which I have formed of his personal conduct."[7] With this appointment, a newly minted Spanish official began a decade of exceptional, albeit controversial, service to the Spanish crown.

Who was this remarkable Frenchman, often regarded as Spain's "foremost diplomat and Indian agent of the Louisiana-Texas frontier during the second half of the 18th century"? Born in Paris in 1719, Athanase Christophe Fortunat Mauguet de Mézières was the son of Louis Christophe Claude de Mézières and Marie Josephe Ménard de Mauguet.[8]

When Athanase was a youth of about fifteen years of age, his father died, leaving him and an older sister in the custody of Madame de Mézières. The mother, ignoring the customary year of mourning, quickly married the handsome and rich Marquis de la Haye, formerly the lover of the Duchess of Berry. Still young and very attractive, the newly titled Madame de la Haye "took a distaste to her . . . children and proceeded to get rid of them," primarily because they revealed her to be older than she appeared and hindered her lifestyle at the court of King Louis XV. To free herself of unwanted offspring, De Mézières's mother placed the daughter in a convent. She later proclaimed Athanase "an undesirable subject" and had him exiled to Louisiana by royal decree in 1738.[9]

Moving upriver from Louisiana to Canada, young Athanase de Mézières presented himself as an abandoned child and chose to live among unidentified Indians, who accepted him on the condition that he submit to the tattooing of his entire body. Acceding to their demand, Athanase spent approximately four years by his account among the "savages," during which he learned several native languages and remembered French and Latin expressions by scrawling them on bark tablets. Determined not to forget his European education, De Mézières also practiced arithmetic and geometry, likewise committing numbers and symbols to a collection of "bark tablets that he saved with the greatest of care." Athanase's Indian hosts eventually made him a chief, but soon thereafter the young Frenchman left them to join the army. He returned to Louisiana around 1742 and accepted assignment at Natchitoches with the rank of ensign.[10]

With De Mézières's arrival, Louis Juchereau de St. Denis (the elder), who had served as commandant of Natchitoches since 1722, encountered someone with similar abilities and interests—a charismatic and athletic young man who knew Indians, spoke their languages, and traded among them. De Mézières and the St. Denis family acquired even closer ties when don Athanase married Marie Petronille Felicité, daughter of Louis Juchereau and his widow, Manuela Sánchez, on April 18, 1746. The couple had one child, Elizabeth M. Felicité, baptized in September of that same year. Unfortunately, De Mézières became a widower all too suddenly when his wife died on February 1, 1748.[11]

In ensuing years, the young Frenchman became more actively engaged in the Indian trade, and he received promotion to the rank of lieutenant around 1752. By 1756 he had earned the rank of captain and served as lieutenant commander of Natchitoches. Late that same year, Governor Louis Billouart Kerlérec named De Mézières as a joint commissioner to determine whether a recently established Spanish presidio near the mouth of the Trinity River encroached on French soil. However, the assignment proved futile, because Governor Jacinto de Barrios y Jáuregui at Los Adaes adamantly refused to appoint a Spanish counterpart.[12]

The captain's personal life, however, soon proved more productive than his fruitless journey to the capital of Texas. His second wife, Pelagie

Fazende, gave birth to his first son in June 1756. During the next thirteen years, De Mézières spent at least part of every year in Natchitoches, and his wife gave birth to seven additional children.[13]

By 1769, when De Mézières traveled to New Orleans at the request of Alejandro O'Reilly, he was a man of considerable wealth. Even though his principal vocation was that of soldier, he had become a skillful trader and successful planter. A census of Natchitoches in 1766 lists ten thousand pounds of tobacco and thirty-five slaves, four of whom were Indians, among his personal possessions. And in the meantime, De Mézières's linguistic skills and business acumen had brought him intimate knowledge of the Indians of the north.[14]

Perhaps from a sense of pragmatism or opportunism, De Mézières took seriously his new role as a Spanish official. His responsibilities as lieutenant governor included issuing police regulations, enforcing justice in his district, expelling undesirables from the area, making nominations for minor offices, and conducting a census of the district in 1771.[15]

Ironically, don Athanase's superiors often criticized him for doing both too much and too little. O'Reilly, for example, upbraided his appointee for nominating more people than there were positions to fill. On the other hand, technical omissions in the enforcement of justice in the Natchitoches district occasioned numerous complaints, and O'Reilly's successor, Luis de Unzaga, countermanded some of De Mézières's decisions.[16]

In the long run, don Athanase's greatest contributions involved his dealings with Indians on the Louisiana-Texas frontier. O'Reilly instructed the Frenchman to appoint licensed traders to move among the friendly tribes, thereby encouraging them to exchange their furs and surplus crops for necessary supplies. The giving of annual presents in the name of the crown, as practiced by the French, was to continue. But trade in stolen horses and Indian captives must be suppressed, particularly the former, which encouraged the Indians to steal Spanish livestock.[17]

The lieutenant governor selected experienced French traders, whom he provided with exceedingly unambiguous instructions: They could provide goods only to friendly nations, excluding English merchandise and intoxicating liquors; they could not trade with enemy nations, risking punishment as traitors if they did so. Their duties as licensed agents, however, went far beyond the mere exchange of goods with cooperative Native Americans. They must confiscate the effects of any unlicensed agents, arrest any English subjects on Spanish soil, promote harmony among native allies, explain *daily* the advantages of being under the dominion of Spain, and ensure that no Indian died without receiving baptism.[18]

Alejandro O'Reilly approved of De Mézières's appointees "on condition that you [don Athanase] answer for their zeal, intelligence, and good habits." However, these traders did not have exclusive rights of trade, since other "honest men" with governmental permission could also engage in commerce. Don Alejandro did assure his lieutenant governor that he would receive appropriate gifts for placating the Indians of his district, including muskets, powder, shot, blankets, beads, tobacco, and other commodities.[19]

The Natchitoches commander appears to have been enthusiastic in enforcing orders from his Spanish superiors. For example, in January 1770 he confiscated four Indian slaves who had been obtained from enemy tribes; he reclaimed a drove of horses and mules that had been purchased from Indians; and he expelled several people from Natchitoches for engaging in contraband trade. The officer was equally vigorous in arresting "vagabonds" and "outlaws" found living among the various tribes. In May 1770 he reported the detention of twenty-eight such persons.[20]

De Mézières saw as his primary objective "the restoration of peace, so disturbed by the ferocious and numerous gentiles [pagans] who surround us." He also recognized the importance of informing belligerent tribes that Frenchmen and Spaniards were no longer enemies, and that to offend one was to offend the other. Wiser than many of his contemporaries, don Athanase pointed to Diego Ortiz Parrilla's Red River campaign of 1759 as proof that "noise of arms" and excessive expenditures were not the best means for dealing with the Nations of the North. Rather, the influence of astute Spanish officials and the mediation of friendly chiefs, combined with the humbling of warlike groups by cutting off their supplies, were the keys to achieving lasting "love, veneration, and gratitude."[21]

Early in 1770, De Mézières informed Tinhioüen and Cocay, of the Kadohadacho and Yatasi, respectively, that His Spanish Majesty had selected them to be honored as medal chiefs. The lieutenant governor then arranged for the caciques to come to his presidio at Natchitoches. With great ceremony, the Indian leaders each received a medal and a flag.[22]

In an agreement dated April 21, 1770, these chiefs formally ceded proprietorship of their lands to the Spanish monarch and pledged to him the same love, respect, and obedience previously accorded the French crown. They also agreed to help maintain a general peace and refrain from furnishing any military supplies to enemy nations. Furthermore, the chiefs promised to arrest and conduct to Natchitoches any "*coureurs de bois*" and persons "without occupation." For this last service, De Mézières promised rewards of a musket and two ells of broadcloth for each prisoner. Because this arrangement entailed an unauthorized expenditure, the Frenchman offered to "provide it from my pocket, having no other expectation than to extirpate an abuse so contrary to the good of the service of his Majesty." [23]

As De Mézières would soon learn, serving the crown by enforcing its policies was not always conducive to maintaining cordial relations with the Indians. And because he was in almost daily contact with the natives, instructions from his superiors could not cover every contingency. Forced to make pragmatic choices, don Athanase often made decisions that irritated his Spanish superiors.

As a case in point, Tinhioüen seemed sincere in his desire to comply with the agreement of April 21, 1770. Years earlier, a Frenchman named François Morvant had killed an "evil-doer," fled the crime scene, and eventually taken refuge with the Kadohadachos. Morvant lived among those Indians and enjoyed their protection for seven years. However, since De Mézières had expressly ordered all unlicensed traders and vagrants to assemble at Natchitoches, Tinhioüen persuaded Morvant to report there, whereupon De Mézières promptly arrested the fugitive and prepared legal proceedings against him. [24]

Tinhioüen, not recognizing the consequences of his actions, felt that he had unintentionally betrayed Morvant, a longtime friend. Severely distressed, the medal chief begged don Athanase to release his prisoner. In return, Tinhioüen promised to arrest and bring to Natchitoches "each and every delinquent who in the future might . . . take advantage of his aid." [25]

Faced with this turn of events, De Mézières assembled the principal persons of Natchitoches. After deliberations and "with the consent of all the rest," the commander decided that it was not prudent to displease such a distinguished medal chief. Accordingly, the lieutenant governor suspended the legal proceedings, placed Morvant under the protection of the cacique, and advised the fugitive to remain within the district until the governor's "pleasure" could be determined. [26]

Governor Unzaga was not pleased. He angrily asked why De Mézières sought his sanction in a matter that had already been settled. The Spanish official then warned that such conduct was unacceptable. If proper procedures, including a trial in New Orleans, had been followed,

Morvant could have been pardoned on the medal chief's petition. Instead, De Mézières had bypassed Spanish justice to glorify himself and in the process had missed an opportunity to demonstrate the fairness of the Spanish legal system. Unzaga pointedly warned his subordinate that "only your meritorious behavior, good conduct, and honest intentions absolved you from criminality." [27]

In the immediate future, De Mézières worked on "effecting the promised peace with the nations that trouble these provinces [of Louisiana and Texas]." To accomplish this, he devised a plan whereby friendly chiefs, such as Tinhioüen, served as intermediaries and arranged meetings with the leaders of tribes that had been traditional enemies of the Spanish. Don Athanase hoped to coax those caciques into a meeting with Governor Barón de Ripperdá at San Antonio. If peace agreements could be worked out, De Mézières then proposed to accompany the chiefs to their respective villages where he would raise the royal standard. [28]

Don Athanase knew that he needed gifts to promote goodwill among the chiefs and reward them for their lengthy journeys to a preliminary meeting at San Luis de Cadodachos. He provided Governor Unzaga with a list of goods, ranging from flags to muskets to mirrors—with the understanding that he would pay for those items from his own monies. As De Mézières expressed it, he wished to avoid any expense to the royal treasury, because his project might fail. Besides, if the plan succeeded, he would be amply rewarded by having served God and his new king. [29]

Luis de Unzaga's favorable reply did not reach his subordinate in a timely fashion. Writing from New Orleans on September 20, 1770, the governor granted approval for De Mézières's proposed journey into Kadohadacho lands and instructed him to assure the Indians that Spaniards invariably treated their friends in good faith. On the other hand, Spain stood ready to mete out punishments for any "delinquencies." Finally, don Athanase was to make sure that the peace sought by the natives was sincere and not the result of "criminal machinations." [30]

Late in September, before Unzaga's reply reached Natchitoches, three chiefs with large entourages arrived at that post to take the lieutenant governor to San Luis de Cadodachos, where representatives of the enemy nations were waiting. This opportunity caused De Mézières considerable consternation, for he had just recently been castigated for acting on his own initiative. But if he refused the moment, the natives would think him fickle or cowardly. Worse, in their anger the Indians might launch new attacks on Spanish settlements. Therefore, don Athanase decided that he must undertake the expedition without formal authorization. He would, of course, send a detailed report to Governor Unzaga on his return.[31]

Accompanying De Mézières on this journey were men from the presidios at Natchitoches and Los Adaes, presumably because don Athanase and Lieutenant José González, commander at the latter garrison, wanted the Indians to witness the close union between the Louisiana and Texas jurisdictions. Despite ill health, Father Miguel de Santa María y Silva, president of the Los Adaes mission, accompanied the expedition so that he might deliver a religious message to the natives. En route, the party traversed the lands of the Adaes, Yatasis, and Petit Caddos. At San Luis, seven chiefs of the previously hostile Taovayas, Tawakonis, Yscanis, and Kichais awaited the group's arrival.[32]

After De Mézières delivered the powerful message recounted at the beginning of this chapter, the chiefs responded that they had not been hostile toward Spaniards until the latter had aided their mortal enemies, the Lipan Apaches, at San Sabá, followed by the military expedition of Diego Ortiz Parrilla. Having learned, however, of the abandonment of the San Sabá presidio, the Indian leaders now desired peace. Unfortunately, the Comanches, former allies of the assembled tribes, had been angered by the tribes' pacific intentions and had waged war against them. When the beleaguered Indians sought help from the French, their old protectors, don Athanase told them that he and his fellow citizens had become subjects of Spain. De Mézières patiently informed the chiefs that because of the many outrages they had committed against Texas settlements and because they resided in that jurisdiction, the caciques should go with him to San Antonio and humble themselves before Governor Ripperdá, who must ratify any agreements made with them.[33]

Despite their protestations of friendship, the Indian leaders refused to accompany the lieutenant governor, even when he modified his request by asking them to go to Los Adaes. The Frenchman concluded that the chiefs' reluctance was based on fear of retribution for past hostilities, because to the Indians "vengeance is not a defect, but a virtue." Insisting that he had told them the truth, De Mézières could only say that time would prove his words. Meanwhile, he refused to distribute the gifts he had brought from Natchitoches; rather, he would keep them on deposit until the natives agreed to his just demands.[34]

On October 29, De Mézières sent Governor Unzaga a detailed report of the events at San Luis. Admitting that his methods for peace had not succeeded, he emphasized that the Indians had agreed to assemble again in the spring. Don Athanase also addressed other issues of concern. With respect to the Comanches, he predicted that "their reduction will be one of the most costly and difficult that may be planned in this America." In that same report, he described those plainsmen as "a people so numerous and so haughty that when asked their number, they make no difficulty in comparing it to that of the stars. They are so skillful in horsemanship that they have no equal; so daring that they never ask for or grant truces." Accordingly, De Mézières planned to create discord between the Comanches and other nations "from which . . . this heathendom may . . . pay for its past insolence and pride." [35]

In reply, Unzaga stated that in his opinion De Mézières's "harangue" had not convinced suspicious Indians of Spain's sincerity. Nevertheless, if the lieutenant governor believed the caciques would receive him in good faith, he should provide the reasoning behind his convictions. On this basis, don Luis would make his decision, because granting the Spanish flag to Indians could not be done without strong proof of their fidelity and merit. [36]

Meanwhile, disgruntled persons in Louisiana and Texas leveled serious charges against don Athanase. Lieutenant José González, perhaps questioning De Mézières's facile allegiance to his new monarch, took depositions on his own initiative from members of the October expedition. Sergeant Domingo Chirino, for example, claimed to have identified unauthorized French traders among the Kadohadachos who were ignored by the lieutenant governor. Worse, Chirino opined that relations with the Norteños would actually worsen rather than improve, because the Indians were angry at not receiving the gifts brought by don Athanase. González also sought damaging testimony from Father Santa María y Silva. The padre concurred that the October expedition would likely result in "graver insults" but hedged his comments, claiming he could not speak openly about state matters without the permission of his religious superiors. [37]

In correspondence with Unzaga, De Mézières expressed deep anguish over "unworthy" charges filed against him by critics, including the preferential treatment of his sons who were military cadets at Natchitoches. He noted that far from profiting from his service to the Spanish crown, as also alleged by González, he had suffered a deteriorating financial situation that had forced him to sell his plantation and slaves to satisfy creditors. [38]

With regard to the Indians' behavior, the lieutenant governor commented on the "marked quiet" of the past few months. He again declared himself ready to meet with the chiefs, if authorized to do so. If not, he dreaded what Unzaga feared most—a worsening of hostilities. [39]

Unzaga tried to lessen the concerns of his subordinate by noting that ill-founded rumors should not strike fear in a man of honor. He also offered assurance that the stationing of De Mézières's sons at Natchitoches was appropriate. However, when Alejandro O'Reilly had assigned them to that post, it was not a guarantee that they would remain there throughout their father's tenure. Reflecting on his own training, don Luis remarked that "boys under the protection of their parents and not subject to the discipline and rigor of the army become effeminate and useless for military service."[40]

Rather than make an independent decision on the French commander's request to revisit Kadohadacho country, Governor Unzaga referred the matter to his counterpart in Texas. As it turned out, Barón de Ripperdá had already taken initiatives by sending emissaries and gifts to Bigotes of the Hasinai Confederation, who agreed to act as an intermediary among the "enemies." Through this cacique's intervention, four chiefs of the Nations of the North made offerings of peace.[41]

Buoyed by this success, Bigotes traveled to Natchitoches during the summer of 1771. There he hoped to promote the accord sought by De Mézières in the previous year. The lieutenant governor quickly organized an "embassy," which included Father Francisco Sedano, a Frenchman versed in native languages, two Spaniards, and Bigotes, to invite the chiefs of the Nations of the North to Natchitoches. The heads of the Yscanis, Tawakonis, Kichais, and Cahinnios accepted the invitation and treaties were drafted. The contracting parties, both native and European, wrapped themselves in the same Spanish flag as a sign of unity, and De Mézières presented numerous gifts to the four chiefs.[42]

Acting for the other caciques, Bigotes and a few Bidais then traveled to San Antonio, where the treaties were ratified by Governor Ripperdá. The Hasinai leader promised that representatives of the tribes in question would themselves travel to San Antonio in the following year during the "good" season. The governor bestowed gifts on the natives, with special honors reserved for Bigotes, who received a medal and a new name, Sauto.[43]

Despite earlier reservations about De Mézières, both Unzaga and Ripperdá had become increasingly impressed with the Frenchman's skills in dealing with Native Americans. For example, Ripperdá wrote his New Orleans counterpart that whenever there was anything to arrange between the interior nations of Texas, Louisiana, or New Mexico, De Mézières "will know the best method of bringing this about suitably."[44]

Meanwhile, the lieutenant governor continued to demonstrate his extraordinary abilities. At Natchitoches in late October, he signed a treaty with the Taovayas, who also presented themselves "as deputies and intermediaries for their ally, the Comanche tribe." With Tinhioüen again participating as intermediary and witness, these Indians promised to cease their attacks on Spanish presidios and return the two cannon abandoned by Colonel Ortiz Parrilla. The Taovayas likewise agreed to accept responsibility "for the good behavior of the Comanche[s]." De Mézières and José González signed this treaty as representatives, respectively, of the governors of Louisiana and Texas. The following April, at San Antonio, the chief of the Taovayas in a public ceremony before Governor Ripperdá buried a hatchet with the understanding that anyone who used it again would die. By the end of 1771, don Athanase also achieved an agreement with Gorgoritos, medal chief of the Bidais, who pledged to help stop coastal Karankawas from committing further outrages against shipwrecked mariners.[45]

Despite the new alliances, the situation remained unstable. Royal officials placed little confidence in the sincerity of peaceful pledges by their former enemies. Persistent rumors also indicated that the warlike Apaches were trying to undermine Spanish relations with the Tejas, while at the same time seeking an alliance with the Bidais. Other reports indicated that one or two of the treaty nations had been in indirect communication with the English.[46]

Once again, De Mézières was commissioned to visit the villages of the new allies, gather crucial information about them, strengthen their commitment to Spain, and investigate rumors of English infiltration. However, when the Frenchman suggested the possibility of using the Bidais to achieve a reconciliation between the interior tribes and the Apaches, Governor Ripperdá vetoed the idea. Believing that such an arrangement would "result in the ruin of the province," he instructed don Athanase to strengthen the hatred that the Nations of the North had for the Apaches. The Frenchman should also approach the Comanches, the other major enemy of the Spaniards, and seek an accord with them.[47]

De Mézières, accompanied by interpreters and a small troop of soldiers, left Natchitoches in March 1772. During a trek lasting almost ninety days, he crossed the Sabine, Angelina, and Neches Rivers to contact the Kichai, Yscani, Tawakoni, and Tonkawa Indians. Next came a trek to the upper Brazos, west of present-day Fort Worth, where don Athanase received Taovaya Indians and sought information from them on the Comanches.[48]

The Frenchman accurately reported that the Comanches were a large nation divided into bands that "have no fixed habitation, neither do they plant crops, but live in continual motion." With uncharacteristic naïveté, the experienced Indian agent opined that those natives would by choice cultivate the soil in fixed settlements if provided tools in exchange for their peltry.[49]

Crossing difficult terrain to reach San Antonio, De Mézières arrived there on June 10 with seventy natives from the villages he had visited who wished to ratify their promises. At a formal ceremony, the chiefs did a feather dance as a sign of peace and wrapped the governor in buffalo skins.[50]

While in San Antonio, don Athanase offered to lead a campaign in the spring against the Apaches, who were committing depredations on Spanish settlements. Promising to do the greatest possible damage, he proposed to invite the Nations of the North to participate and supply them with weapons at his own expense. Ripperdá approved of the plan and forwarded it to the viceroy. The governor also asked that he be allowed to take a force of about two hundred men and strike the Apaches simultaneously with De Mézières's attack.[51]

In his reply, Viceroy Bucareli instructed Governor Ripperdá to use all suitable methods in persuading natives to settle in villages, become "semi-civilized," and subject themselves to the authority of the Spanish crown. Noting the insults of the Apaches, which consisted primarily of stealing horses, Bucareli was hesitant to disturb the relative "tranquility" in Texas by launching an offensive campaign against them. That decision should be determined by a council of war. In the meantime, De Mézières should retire to Natchitoches.[52]

While in Natchitoches, De Mézières received a communication from Ripperdá indicating that several Apache chiefs were en route to the Bidais and Hasinai to make a treaty. Ruthlessly, don Athanase sent Alexis Grappe with orders for Chief Sauto. Under the guise of friendship, Sauto was to massacre the perfidious emissaries. The medal chief not only followed those brutal instructions to the letter but murdered three Apache leaders who had accepted the hospitality of his own dwelling![53]

Meanwhile, Luis de Unzaga had again entertained grave concerns about De Mézières's effectiveness as an Indian agent, and he secretly employed an informant to spy on his subordinate. The informer, José de la Peña, viewed the lieutenant governor's claims of his "great doings" as pure deceit. He also reported that Chief Sauto suspiciously saw De Mézières as a "man of two words," which the spy interpreted as one who would say one thing but do another. Finally, Peña charged don Athanase with trying to prevent unfavorable comments about his performance from reaching the governor.[54]

In the midst of increasing controversy, De Mézières requested permission from the Spanish crown to visit Europe on matters of business.

One suspects that he may also have deemed it advisable to remove himself from the turbulent colonial scene, perhaps to cultivate more powerful connections in France and Spain. The king granted the request in November 1772, and Unzaga issued the passport in April of the following year.[55]

Don Athanase spent nearly a year in Europe, during which he acquired the rank of lieutenant colonel from the Spanish crown. While visiting France, most likely in 1773, De Mézières astonished the Paris elite at the Palais Royal with his entirely tattooed body, displaying flowers on his chest and arms and snakes that could be seen through his silk stockings.[56]

In February 1774, don Athanase returned to New Orleans and in March reached Natchitoches, where he relieved his temporary replacement. During De Mézières's absence, the interim official had attempted sporadic but largely unsuccessful efforts at peacemaking among Native American tribes. Accordingly, don Athanase once again assumed primary responsibility as diplomat to the Nations of the North, and criticisms of his actions began anew.[57]

At that juncture, Commandant Inspector Hugo Oconor leveled damning charges that don Athanase's treaties with the Nations of the North were deceitful. Specifically, Oconor pointed to allegedly pacified Indians who stole horses under the guise of friendship and to supposedly loyal French traders, secretly headed by De Mézières, who profited by acquiring these animals. Worse, the irascible commandant inspector accused Governor Barón de Ripperdá of being in league with don Athanase. And it appears that Viceroy Bucareli accepted those charges at face value.[58]

Despite Oconor's allegations and the viceroy's suspicions, Lieutenant Colonel De Mézières enjoyed the confidence of the Spanish monarch, whom he had only recently visited. Charles III voiced concern over reports of trade between the "savage" nations and the English but also expressed confidence in don Athanase's experience and "practical knowledge" as the best hope for terminating this illicit traffic. The treaty chiefs also continued to regard don Athanase as the man with whom they should deal. Upon his return from Europe, they visited the French commandant and assured him of their continuing commitment to peace and harmony.[59]

Although De Mézières's efforts centered on the Red River region, his attention was momentarily diverted to the coast by stories gleaned from Orcoquiza Indians. In September 1774, don Athanase informed his superior at New Orleans that the Orcoquizas had reported a previously unknown island, unfortunately occupied by hostile Karankawas, that contained abundant timber and lush pasturage. Reportedly, a channel between this island and the mainland formed one of the best ports to be found on the coast. The lieutenant governor suggested that the area, near La Bahía, be explored by launch. Unzaga responded favorably, but three years would pass before exploration got under way.[60]

Meanwhile, in March 1775, Unzaga, acting in conjunction with Viceroy Bucareli, reiterated an earlier order for the Natchitoches commander to "abandon" immediately any contact with the governor of Texas. And in July of the same year, the viceroy reminded Ripperdá that he must cease correspondence not only with De Mézières but also with all Frenchmen and citizens of New Orleans.[61]

Prohibitions on any form of communication between Louisiana, which was attached to Cuba, and Texas, a province of New Spain, hampered De Mézières in his role as Indian agent. Although the boundaries between the two jurisdictions were real to the royal bureaucracy, they were irrelevant to the movements of Native Americans.

Ripperdá's effectiveness was adversely affected, not only by orders to cease communication with De Mézières but also by his inability to conduct legal trade with the natives, which was permitted from Louisiana. For example, in May 1776 Viceroy Bucareli reprimanded the baron for allowing Indians to obtain weapons in San Antonio.[62]

For the remainder of 1776, De Mézières occupied himself with routine events. The following year was particularly traumatic for him and his family, for a severe epidemic struck the Natchitoches district, and fatalities included his wife and one child. Don Athanase was again a widower, this time left a single parent with several children of varying ages; he never remarried. The epidemic, perhaps smallpox, took a heavy toll on the Native American population as well.[63]

Ironically, at a time of great personal loss, De Mézières was soon restored to favor and professional prominence. Profound changes in jurisdictions and administrative personnel occurred in 1776–1777. Young Bernardo de Gálvez, nephew of former inspector general José de Gálvez, became provisional governor of Louisiana. During don Bernardo's tenure, more liberal trade policies were instituted, which stimulated the Louisiana economy and gave don Athanase a freer hand in Indian matters.[64]

The change from Luis de Unzaga to Bernardo de Gálvez proved important for De Mézières, but more critical to his future was the reorganization of the northern provinces of New Spain under a commandant general who was largely independent of the viceroy in Mexico City.

Teodoro de Croix became head of the newly created Interior Provinces, and the restrictive policies of both Bucareli and Oconor were removed.[65]

In April 1777, Governor Ripperdá of Texas sent a detailed report on his province to Croix. The baron included information on the Nuestra Señora del Pilar de Bucareli settlement, established in August of 1774 by Adaesanos, and expressed his confidence in Antonio Gil Ibarvo as a suitable leader of the Trinity River outpost. Ripperdá also made pointed reference to the Comanches as the most troublesome Indians in Texas, while at the same time excoriating the Lipan Apaches for their perfidious conduct. On the other hand, Barón de Ripperdá heaped praise on De Mézières and by extension on himself for existing treaties with the Nations of the North.[66]

Accordingly, the commandant general had received some information on various Native American groups in his Texas jurisdiction, and on the recommendation of the Marqués de Rubí identified the Lipan Apaches as the likely target of new imperatives in Indian policy. To remove any lingering uncertainty, Croix summoned a council of war at Monclova. Present in December 1777 were "officers of [the] highest rank, longest experience, and greatest knowledge" of Indian affairs. In brutally frank discussions, Croix poised a pragmatic question. Was it better to ally with the Lipan Apaches and make war against the Comanches and Nations of the North or vice versa?[67]

The recommendations of the Monclova council were unequivocal. No real progress had been ever been made with the Lipans, for their treaty commitments had proved invariably deceitful. On the other hand, the Comanches and Northern tribes were staunch enemies of the Apaches. The participants unanimously agreed that an alliance with the Nations of the North could lead to the general pacification of the country, especially if the Apaches were sufficiently intimidated. The latter could be accomplished, in part, by an increase of six hundred soldiers assigned to the frontier.[68]

However, almost all of the conferees admitted to having no personal knowledge of the Nations of the North, and they recommended convening a second council at San Antonio. That gathering should be followed by a third council in Chihuahua, where a final decision, based on cumulative input, could be made.[69]

At San Antonio, the second war council convened early in 1778, with Governor Ripperdá in attendance. Delegates concurred that peace agreements with the Lipans had proved fruitless. They also informed Croix that the Comanches and Norteños had not committed depredations against the Spanish until the Lipans had been promised shelter at San

Sabá. Following the abandonment of Mission San Lorenzo on the upper Nueces River and the treaties negotiated by De Mézières, there had been no trouble with the Nations of the North. However, the peace accords did not include the Comanches. The San Antonio group agreed that the number of additional troops recommended at Monclova would be sufficient to deal with the Lipans but emphasized that the involvement of Athanase de Mézières was crucial to any future treaty arrangement with the Indians.[70]

The council members further recommended that Bernardo de Gálvez allow don Athanase to come to San Antonio without delay. Once present, the experienced lieutenant colonel could offer the best methods for securing an alliance with the Nations of the North against the Lipans. After proper briefing, De Mézières should forward to Croix his detailed recommendations on how to strike the Apaches with maximum chances for success.[71]

Athanase de Mézières, bearing a passport from Bernardo de Gálvez, arrived in San Antonio by February 1778. After reviewing the sealed papers of the war council, the French officer compiled a detailed report for the commandant general. Not surprisingly, don Athanase stressed the importance of trade conducted from Louisiana in binding these natives to Spain. A Spanish merchant of Natchitoches, versed in appropriate Indian languages, already resided in each village to indoctrinate the natives and report to the king. Addressing the hostility of the Comanches, the lieutenant governor suggested that trade items might stabilize them, but if that approach failed, force of arms would be necessary. Defending his recommendation for approaching theretofore hostile Comanches, De Mézières noted their prolonged enmity for the Apaches. Successful recruitment of the Comanches would also send a strong message to the Lipans. The arms of Spain had been joined by those of their most hated enemies.[72]

Stressing the need for secrecy in organizing the campaign against the Apaches, the most suitable place for the native troops to meet by prearrangement would be the villages of the Taovayas on the Red River. And because assistance by carefully selected treaty nations was considered crucial to the successful military offensive, De Mézières listed the number of warriors that should be recruited from each specific group, with the total amounting to more than a thousand. However, he cautioned against making the natives cognizant of Spain's dependence upon them. For this reason, he advised that Indian forces be accompanied by about three hundred soldiers. Further, don Athanase stressed the importance of a combined force from the Interior Provinces and Louisiana, which would underscore the unity and cooperation of the two dominions.[73]

Don Athanase recommended September as the optimum time for a campaign, for the agricultural Nations of the North would have completed their harvests by then. Strategic plans called for troops from the Interior Provinces to wait between the Colorado and San Saba Rivers, where they would be joined by those from Louisiana.[74]

After completing his report, De Mézières journeyed to Villa Bucareli, preparatory to visiting tribes along the upper reaches of the Trinity, Brazos, and Red Rivers. At Bucareli he recruited Captain Gil Ibarvo, Father José Francisco de la Garza, and thirteen militiamen. While present at the villa, don Athanase expressed strong support for the location of the settlement at Paso Tomás.[75]

Heading west, De Mézières visited a number of tribes and penned detailed accounts for Commandant General Croix. Illness, however, thinned the ranks of his militiamen, forcing several of them to drop out of the expedition and return to Bucareli. On reaching his destination, the lieutenant governor described the Taovayas as sedentary Native Americans living in two villages on opposite banks of the Red River. These Wichitas were an industrious and largely agricultural people who feared the Osages and the Apaches.[76]

While among the Taovayas, De Mézières scheduled a general gathering, during which he distributed gifts in Croix's name and assured the Indians they were under the protection of the "chiefs" of the Interior Provinces and Louisiana. The natives responded by expressing their desire for Spaniards to settle among them, which don Athanase thought to be essential to his charge. In his view the Taovayas region was the "master-key" of the north, for through it friendly Indians could be influenced through mediation. Equally important, the clergy would find many souls to harvest (Figure 15).[77]

De Mézières learned from the Taovayas that two Englishmen had come to their lands in the previous winter to engage in trade and declare friendship. Insisting that they had followed don Athanase's instructions, imparted during his earlier visit, the natives seized the English goods, and the foreigners retreated. Although the French commander praised the natives for their loyalty, he nonetheless chastised them for failing to arrest and detain the Englishmen.[78]

On this occasion, don Athanase acquired the two bronze cannon abandoned by Colonel Ortiz Parrilla in 1759. Significantly, when he asked the chiefs to surrender the armament, they willingly did so, actions

FIGURE 15

Sketch of Athanase de Mézières. Don Athanase harangues Taovaya Indians
in 1778, urging their alliance with Spaniards against Lipan Apaches.
(Commissioned original artwork by Jack Jackson.)

that De Mézières interpreted as evidence of sincere friendship. The expedition also discovered ten Spanish captives from New Mexico, whom the Taovayas had purchased from the Comanches. Those unfortunates, both men and women, remarked that their present captivity was an improvement over their previous situation, but they understandably begged for freedom nevertheless. Whatever his private feelings, don Athanase did not offer to negotiate their release. Pragmatic as always, he noted that paying ransom would only encourage further traffic in Spanish captives, and his primary goal of bringing the Taovayas into an alliance against the Apaches overrode all other considerations.[79]

While camped on the Red River, De Mézières encountered eight Comanches who boasted of a deadly raid directed against Spaniards on the road from Béxar to the Río Grande. That information and details of other Comanche depredations prompted him to declare that he would not negotiate directly with any natives who had stained their hands with Spanish blood. He did agree, however, to send an emissary among those plainsmen with a message that they must stop all attacks on Spaniards. If the Comanche chieftains complied and genuinely desired peace with the arms of Spain, he would parlay with them at another time and place.[80]

Ironically, after De Mézières returned to Villa Bucareli, his presence there may have triggered a chain of events that eventually ended with the abandonment of the settlement. In May 1778 a small band of Comanches came into that vicinity. Later, De Mézières would assert that those natives had presented themselves in good faith, but settlers at Bucareli insisted that they were scouts for a planned attack on the community. Whatever their intentions, the Comanches created panic among the settlers, who hurriedly gathered livestock and raised a squadron of armed men. According to De Mézières, the Indians quickly withdrew but were overtaken by the militia, which overreacted, opened fire, and inflicted several casualties on the Indians.[81]

The lieutenant governor expressed regret over this incident, because Indian informants told him that the Comanches had come to Bucareli as a result of the emissary he had sent among them. Through a grave mistake made by the Bucareli colonists, don Athanase feared that "affairs [would] return to a worse condition than before." He could not have been more prescient.[82]

In the meantime, De Mézières had sent report after report to the commandant general, informing him of his trip among the Nations of the North, advising him of Spanish captives among the Taovayas, and apprising him of his unsuccessful contacts with the Comanches. For his part, Croix finally responded after the conclusion of the third war council in Chihuahua.

Croix praised De Mézières for his clearly written communications, zealous efforts, good judgment, and excellent arrangements. Importantly, the council had recommended that don Athanase should return immediately to San Antonio to relieve Governor Barón de Ripperdá until the arrival of the new gubernatorial appointee, Domingo Cabello y Robles. However, should the Frenchman arrive to find Cabello already in possession of the government at Béxar, he was to await further instructions from Croix.[83]

The commandant general also sent Bernardo de Gálvez copies of his war councils' proceedings and the reports of De Mézières. Croix noted that the king had denied his request for the participation of a corps of Louisiana hunters and Indians in the proposed campaign against the Apaches. However, the king had authorized Croix to correspond directly with Gálvez, who was to offer aid in other ways. Such assistance, suggested don Teodoro, could best be accomplished by allowing De Mézières to serve as interim governor of Texas. The Frenchman's "knowledge, practical experience, zeal, and conduct might contribute much to the success" of the commandant's overall Indian policy.[84]

Two weeks later, on September 23, 1778, Croix notified José de Gálvez, then minister of the Indies, of don Athanase's successful journey among the northern Indian nations. Don Teodoro noted that the Frenchman had fulfilled his mission with "zeal, tact, prudence, aptitude, and efficiency." His skillful diplomacy would facilitate peace in Coahuila and Texas by bringing the Lipans and other Eastern Apaches under control. If those natives were subdued, Croix conceptualized an advancing Spanish frontier that would reach Taovaya settlements along the Red River.[85]

Croix further advised the minister of the Indies that commerce in firearms between Louisiana and the Nations of the North was not desirable. When traded among the natives, such weapons often fell into the hands of the Lipans and Comanches. However, don Teodoro, a realist like De Mézières, acknowledged that attempts at stopping the trade would likely be counterproductive, not only because the Indians of the North would retaliate by making war on the Spanish but also because such an interdict would open the way for the English to provide muskets, "since for no Indian of the North is there any jewel more precious than firearms." [86]

In the interim, De Mézières had received Croix's orders to proceed immediately to San Antonio. Even though those instructions carried Bernardo de Gálvez's endorsement, don Athanase chose not to obey them, arguing that he would have to cross many rivers at flood stage. But, in reality, there seems little doubt that De Mézières was hesitant to leave his children, his French associates, and his sole source of material well-being. Seeking to stay his orders, he set out for New Orleans to discuss his new assignment and other important matters with Governor Bernardo de Gálvez. En route, however, the lieutenant governor suffered an accident, forcing him to return to Natchitoches. From there he wrote don Bernardo, stating his strong desire to remain under the governor's command rather than to accept a transfer to Texas. If, however, he must serve under the commandant general of the Interior Provinces, he asked Gálvez to intercede with Croix on his behalf, so that his sons might accompany him.[87]

Because Cabello had arrived in San Antonio (October 29, 1778) to assume his executive duties, in March 1779 don Athanase asked Bernardo de Gálvez to approve another visit to the Norteños. Among his reasons was a desire to contact the Comanches, who, because of the misunderstanding at Villa Bucareli, impeded trade between Spaniards and peaceful Indians in Louisiana and Texas.[88]

If the visit was approved, don Athanase asked Gálvez for goods that could be secured only in New Orleans, which would be used as gifts for the Indians. The Louisiana governor gave his full endorsement to the expedition, with funds to be paid from monies set aside for keeping friendly relations with the Indians. Among the merchandise delivered to De Mézières were muskets, powder, shot, hatchets, glass beads, and tobacco. The Frenchman also requested 3,200 reales in equipment and supplies for the mounted militia that would accompany him. That request was likewise granted.[89]

Despite the cooperation of Governor Gálvez, weather conditions and swollen rivers delayed don Athanase's expedition. In May De Mézières wrote Commandant General Croix from Los Adaes, reporting that the rivers were passable and that he could commence his march to San Antonio. Shortly after visiting an Ais village near the Sabine River, De Mézières learned that Villa Bucareli had been abandoned in the early months of 1779. Settlers in the new town of Nacogdoches, which was poorly defended, worried about the fidelity of the treaty Indians and the intentions of the Comanches. Asked to lend his assistance, don Athanase set out immediately for Nacogdoches. Near the Attoyac River, he fell victim to another accident when his horse shied and pitched him down the side of a steep hill. In the fall, he suffered "such a shock . . . that fever, delirium, and other symptoms resulted." His retinue carried the severely injured man to the banks of the river, where it camped for five days. Don Athanase's condition became so grave that servants bore him back to Natchitoches on a stretcher. He had thus suffered two serious accidents in a matter of months, and one can speculate that years of exposure to the elements and the infirmities of advancing age had made him more prone to misfortune.[90]

After two months in bed, De Mézières's condition improved somewhat, and he was able to complete the journey to Nacogdoches. While there he disparaged the settlers' fear of the Comanches and pointedly accused them of cowardice. And he unequivocally asserted that the new location was no better than the one abandoned at Bucareli. Its lands were attractive to ranching but lacked open meadows for agriculture.[91]

Continuing on to San Antonio, De Mézières distributed many of the gifts supplied by Bernardo de Gálvez to Kichai, Tonkawa, and Tawakoni Indians. The remaining presents, intended for the Taovayas, were placed on deposit at Béxar (Figure 16).[92]

In San Antonio, Governor Cabello expressed displeasure to Croix at having to expend funds and shower flattery on De Mézières and his entourage. He also informed the commandant general that don Athanase's version of how the settlers at Bucareli had created their own troubles by attacking the Comanches was erroneous. According to the governor's sources, the Comanches had not approached the settlement with good intentions.[93]

Governor Cabello nevertheless offered hospitality to don Athanase, as he had been instructed to do, albeit reluctantly. With difficulty, he found suitable lodging for the Frenchman and provided a gift of sheep as well. At church services, don Domingo placed a chair next to his for De Mézières. He also provided "medicaments" from his personal apothecary, because, in his view, don Athanase was seriously afflicted with diarrhea and gonorrhea.[94]

Despite ill health, De Mézières attempted to carry out his responsibilities. He placed on deposit at Béxar the merchandise remaining from his visit to the Indian nations and asked for a receipt from the governor. Although without official authorization to accept the goods, which included rifles, axes, knives, combs, and tobacco, Cabello did so, pending orders from Commandant General Croix.[95]

Shortly after his arrival at Béxar, De Mézières penned two forceful communiqués to Teodoro de Croix. This time he did not, as usual, couch his words in diplomatic parlance but rather made forceful pronouncements on a number of topics. The tone of these reports suggests a sense of urgency, most likely brought on by his declining physical fitness. De Mézières wrote of the vastness and fertility of Texas' lands, depicting the

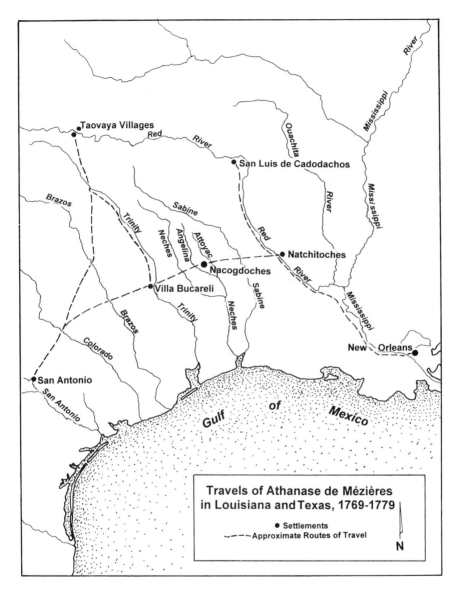

Map labels:
River
Mississippi
Taovaya Villages
Red River
Ouachita River
San Luis de Cadodachos
Brazos
Sabine
Trinity
Neches
Angelina
Attoyac
Red River
Natchitoches
Mississippi
Nacogdoches
Villa Bucareli
Sabine
Trinity
Neches
Brazos
Colorado
San Antonio
San Antonio
New Orleans
Gulf of Mexico

**Travels of Athanase de Mézières
in Louisiana and Texas, 1769-1779**

● Settlements
‒ ‒ ‒ Approximate Routes of Travel

N

──── FIGURE 16 ────

*Map of Athanase de Mézières's travels in Louisiana and Texas. This map
depicts the extensive journeys of don Athanase as Spanish Indian agent from
1769 to 1779. (Cartography by Caroline Castillo Crimm.)*

province as conducive to robust rather than decrepit health. Why, then, he asked, had so little progress been made there? The answer to his own question lay in the indolence of the Texas settlers. For example, trade had not been developed, although the sea was nearby, and livestock, although plentiful, had been neglected.[96]

De Mézières wrote at length about the threat posed by the English, who were increasing their influence among the Texas nations. Anglo foreigners came by land, and others might well arrive by sea. Who would defend against them? The troops from Béxar were always engaged in other duties, and those at La Bahía were preoccupied with their own defense. Certainly, one could not count on mission Indians, who were hostile or indifferent. Declaring that the enemy was near, don Athanase predicted that the English would soon arrive with arms and with them be able to lure away the treaty nations. "Hear and believe!" he exclaimed. The English had not been stopped by mountains, rivers, or forests. In Louisiana they had encouraged native uprisings and paid bounties for French scalps. The skilled diplomat warned the commandant general not to be complacent, even though the English were then involved in a war with their North American colonists. Whatever the outcome of that conflict, Spain's interests would be jeopardized.[97]

The lieutenant governor asked Croix to relax trade restrictions, so that hides, salt, and other goods plentiful in Texas could be exported to improve the province's economy. Also, Matagorda Bay should be used to import merchandise from Tampico, Campeche, and Louisiana. The commandant general should consider the adoption of policies that would persuade the treaty nations to assemble and trade their meat and hides to the Spanish. His desire, as don Athanase expressed it, was for the whole of Texas to be prosperous and happy.[98]

The second of the missives related specifically to the Karankawas, whom the Frenchman labeled as treacherous. He outlined plans for a massive attack on these coastal natives, with combined land and sea forces from Texas and Louisiana. Every warrior who resisted should be killed in retaliation for outrages committed against helpless shipwreck victims. Women, children, and male captives should be removed to distant lands to perform labor for Spaniards, thereby guaranteeing that they could not return to their perverse life styles.[99]

On October 12, 1779, don Athanase received word through Domingo Cabello that he had been appointed governor of Texas. On the following day, he wrote Croix and begged to be excused—arguing that he was unfit for such high office, he was inexperienced in matters of law, he was hampered by precarious health, and he was simply too poor. He also observed that as governor he might have to treat the Lipan Apaches with friendship, which would anger the Nations of the North and undermine his diplomacy of the past decade. His knowledge and expertise, suggested don Athanase, could best be used in Louisiana to prevent the enemy—the English—from advancing. Above all, he stated his desire to return to his family in Natchitoches, because he could not countenance separation from them. But, if Croix insisted, De Mézières would "sacrifice his own views and his personal comfort to comply with his duty." However, in that event, his family should be brought to him at San Antonio under safe conduct. Regarding his sons, the youngest of whom was only twelve, don Athanase beseeched Croix's protection for them.[100]

As his health continued to decline, De Mézières, in Domingo Cabello's words, "was overcome with . . . a strong melancholy, knowing that he was dying, that the illness could not be restrained." He begged Cabello to send all papers relating to the council of war at Chihuahua to the commandant general, so that they would not be found among his effects. Significantly, those documents, which had been secured under lock and key, contained deceitful considerations of the most expeditious manner of manipulating all Indian nations to the benefit of Spaniards.[101]

The Frenchman made out his testament and named don Joseph María Armant, a merchant and citizen of Natchitoches who had accompanied the expedition to San Antonio, as his executor. Apologizing for his inability to write in Spanish, he penned a letter in his native French to Teodoro de Croix. In it don Athanase asked the commandant general to "make my two daughters participants of the Monte Pío [military pension fund]. They are in want, and I leave them only debts[,] which my journies [sic] of last year and this have compelled me to contract. I die confident of your Lordship's protection of my family."[102]

After receiving the sacrament of penance, the viaticum, and Extreme Unction, Athanase de Mézières died at 1:00 p.m. on November 2, 1779. Interment on the following day for the burial fee of five dollars was in the parish church of Villa San Fernando. Father Pedro Fuentes y Fernández conducted services, with such "military honors as the small number of troops comprising this garrison permitted."[103]

Saddened by the death of a trusted subordinate, Croix in January 1780 expressed his concerns to Bernardo de Gálvez: "I realize how much I shall miss him unless you replace him in Natchitoches with another of equal qualities—and those of the deceased were very excellent." He noted that don Athanase had acquired the love of the Nations of the North, who played a key role in the commandant general's plans concerning the Apaches. Don Teodoro provided for a "gratification" of three thousand pesos for De Mézières's family, which, in effect, amounted to reimbursement for expenses incurred during his final journeys. Croix ordered Governor Cabello to see that the lieutenant governor's heirs "receive this aid with proper security." He also commanded the chief executive of Texas to write Joseph María Armant and inform him "that to the extent possible I [Croix] shall attend to [the interests of] the sons of the above-mentioned deceased." In letters to José de Gálvez, Croix expressed his confidence that the king would "designate the two legitimate daughters [of De Mézières] as recipients of a pension that would assure them a decent life." The commandant general also asked the minister of the Indies to comply with don Athanase's wishes by placing his three sons as cadets or as officials in frontier presidios.[104]

The passing of Athanase de Mézières, in the view of historian Elizabeth A. H. John, deprived Spain of a talented and skillful agent, for "no Indian diplomatist of comparable ability existed in Texas, or even in Louisiana."[105] However, because he was French-born and a longtime native of Louisiana, De Mézières's commitment to his new king and country was often called into question. Initially, he seems to have incurred the suspicious wrath of Alejandro O'Reilly and Luis de Unzaga, although both officials later expressed confidence in his abilities. Don Athanase also appears to have inspired both envy and distrust among Spaniards assigned to his command. Those impressions of his leadership, however, did not change over time.

A transitional person between French Louisiana and Spanish Texas, De Mézières regularly found himself caught in an administrative conundrum. He took orders from the governor of Louisiana, who answered to the captain general of Cuba in Havana; he frequently operated in Spanish Texas, which until 1777 was under the viceroy of New Spain; he then received orders from Teodoro de Croix, who as commandant general of the Interior Provinces reported to the minister of the Indies in Madrid but had to ask Bernardo de Gálvez, the governor of Louisiana, to release De Mézières so that he might perform duties in Texas!

In the final analysis, Athanase de Mézières was driven by pragmatism—perhaps his natural inclination. He did not shy away from ordering cold-blooded assassinations, as in the case of the Apache emissaries murdered at the hand of Chief Sauto. He did not risk upsetting delicate negotiations with the Taovayas by insisting on the release of Spanish captives—despite their pleas. And because he had larger stakes in mind, he may have given the Comanches too much credit for their allegedly benign intentions at Villa Bucareli. Nonetheless, his remarkable service to

Spain over the last decade of life apparently left De Mézières impecunious and unable to provide for his young children. This was quite a sacrifice for a man who had acquired substantial material possessions, as evidenced by the Natchitoches census of 1766.

The death of Athanase de Mézières also meant that alliances with the treaty nations were more tenuous, and it increased the difficulty of achieving Spanish goals with respect to the Lipan Apaches, Comanches, and other uncooperative groups. Years later, Commandant Louis de Blanc at Natchitoches expressed those very concerns. In September 1790, Blanc reported that Indians, including Taovayas and Tawakonis, told him that "when don Athanase de Mézières died he had carried with him all the promises of peace which he had made with them, and that for this reason they were abandoned, without traders . . . and that they were not obliged to keep the peace." [106] More immediately, in the 1780s Indian matters remained prime concerns for Commandant General Teodoro de Croix and Governor Domingo Cabello y Robles.

NINE

MARQUÉS DE RUBÍ/
ANTONIO GIL IBARVO

Imperious Inspector/Father of East Texas

O n September 11, 1767, a saddle-weary Spanish nobleman and his entourage crossed Arroyo Hondo and proceeded through "forested glens, hills, and dales" before arriving at Presidio de Nuestra Señora del Pilar de los Adaes near present-day Robeline, Louisiana. Since its founding under the aegis of the Marqués de San Miguel de Aguayo in 1721, Los Adaes had served as the provincial capital of Texas, although San Fernando de Béxar would soon surpass it in population and importance. In the aftermath of the Chicken War of 1719, one marqués had secured Spanish presence in East Texas and western Louisiana. Another marqués would contribute to the depopulation of the area and the removal of the capital to San Antonio. Who was this powerful visitor with seven names—not counting his impressive titles of nobility—and how does one explain his devastating impact on Spanish settlers in this region of the future Lone Star State? [1]

Cayetano María Pignatelli Rubí Corbera y San Climent, Marqués de Rubí, knight commander in the Order of Alcántara, and Barón de Llinas, also held the high rank of field marshal in the royal army when he arrived at Los Adaes in late summer 1767. Rubí was most likely born in Barcelona around 1725. His father, Francisco de Pignatelli y de Aymerich, was a lieutenant general in His Majesty's armies, captain general of the Kingdom of Granada, commandant general of the Kingdom of Aragón, and onetime ambassador to France. Don Cayetano's mother, María Francisca Rubí Corbera y San Climent, was an even more impressive Spanish blueblood, for she held the titles of second Marquesa de Rubí and Baroness of Llinas. [2]

The early life of don Cayetano is largely a mystery, primarily because neither his military record in Spain nor his document of merits and services has as yet come to light. Rubí likely entered a select military academy as a cadet and achieved knighthood in the prestigious military Order of Alcántara while still in his twenties. His intellectual inclinations suggest a strong bent for mathematics and the sciences. In any event, his nearly lifelong career was as military tactician and crown advisor. With distinguished lineage from his mother, impressive accomplishments by his father, and significant achievements on his own, the Marqués de Rubí was not to be trifled with. His imperious nature and lack of diplomacy made don Cayetano more feared than loved. Indeed, as those with whom he came in contact would discover, Rubí's "own integrity was above reproach, [and] he could not abide dishonesty in others." [3]

The Marqués de Rubí was about forty-two years of age when he took shelter at the Los Adaes presidio. He had been chosen as inspector of presidios on the northern frontier of New Spain by Charles III (1759–1788), perhaps the most able monarch in Spain's long history. Charles's reign began shortly before his country's ill-advised entry (1762) into the Seven Years' War as an ally of France. That conflict, which went badly for the French and Spanish, and the resultant Treaty of Paris of 1763 cost Spain control of Florida for twenty years. More important, however, near the end of the war, France transferred its Louisiana territory west of the Mississippi River to Spain. It was an acquisition viewed with mixed emotions by Spaniards in the Old World and the New.[4]

Spanish officials knew that Louisiana had been a drain on the French treasury and that it would be no less burdensome for Spain. They also recognized that gaining possession of Louisiana profoundly changed the status of Texas, transforming it from a buffer province against French aggression to an interior one. In reality, however, the Spanish had little choice but to accept the French offer. Rejecting Louisiana would have brought aggressive Englishmen to the borders of Texas and New Mexico. The threat of Anglo influence over the northern Indian nations was unacceptably dangerous, and the Spanish worried about the security of their silver mines in northern New Spain.[5]

As an enlightened monarch, Charles III ordered sweeping reforms and energetic measures to protect Spain's empire in America. Central to that effort was the appointment in 1764–1765 of powerful and distinguished officers for service in New Spain. The list included Lieutenant General Juan de Villalba, who organized regular army units and colonial militia patterned on the European model; the Marqués de Rubí, who sailed from Spain with Villalba; and José de Gálvez, who as visitor general assumed responsibility for revamping the entire financial and administrative affairs of New Spain.[6]

Rubí's charge was limited to a careful inspection of presidios and, in a related sense, to missions and settlements on New Spain's northern frontier. Although he was commissioned separately from Gálvez, his findings were expected to assist the visitor general's goal of recommending major reforms that addressed the radically changed situation in America. In the recently concluded Seven Years' War, French possessions on the North American continent had been eliminated, leaving England and Spain as principal rivals.[7]

In many respects, the Rubí visitation was a reprise of the Pedro de Rivera inspection of the 1720s. Both began in the western regions and moved eastward to present-day Louisiana. Both were designed to bring about cost-saving changes that would benefit the royal treasury. Both were to look into abuses associated with the operation of frontier presidios. Both inspectors concerned themselves with defense against Indian nations along the Spanish frontier. And both drafted reports—Rivera's *proyecto* and Rubí's *dictamen*.[8]

Already in New Spain, Rubí was commissioned by Charles III on August 7, 1765. In assessing his assignment, don Cayetano quickly realized that the northern fringes of Spain's empire in America were most vulnerable to attack. New problems included how to defend Louisiana and what should be done about Texas since it had become an interior province. Old problems were more serious. From the Gulf of California to Texas, Indian raiders launched devastating raids on Spanish settlements, killing civilians and stealing livestock. And despite the near doubling of crown expenditures on defense over the course of the eighteenth century, Spain's military garrisons seemed more ineffectual than ever. Central to those concerns were long-standing abuses committed by presidial commanders, whereby they charged excessive prices for commodities supplied to their soldiers. Such practices had contributed substantially to inefficiency and poor morale. Particularly vexing was the conduct of the various Apache nations, most notably the Lipans, who were regarded as unparalleled in duplicity.[9]

Shortly after his arrival in Mexico City in 1764, Rubí's superior, Juan de Villalba, had launched inquiries into the condition of frontier presidios. Although the garrison commanders were notorious for their mismanagement and dishonesty, Villalba leveled a far more serious charge. He contended that Viceroy Marqués de Cruillas not only failed to demonstrate interest in reforming presidial abuses but also was guilty of embezzling funds earmarked for the garrisons themselves. When informed of those suspicions, the crown moved quickly to commission the Marqués de Rubí as a special inspector of presidios. Accordingly, it is not surprising that don Cayetano ran into trouble with the viceroy, who proved to be less than cooperative.[10]

Although Rubí was to report directly to the king through Julián de Arriaga, the minister of the Indies, his specific instructions were issued by Viceroy Cruillas, and delays occurred. Cruillas explained that it took time to collect relevant documents from scattered archives and that the expedition's cartographer, Joseph de Urrutia, needed time to assemble the instruments and equipment that were needed for the trip.[11]

Also assigned to the Rubí inspection team was Nicolás de Lafora, a sharp-eyed, twenty-year army veteran and member of the Royal Corps of Engineers. In his diary, Lafora logged firsthand observations on the expedition's travels. He began by explaining that the purpose of the inspection was to find out why the Indians "are so audacious" and why Spanish soldiers are "of so little use." More important, Rubí also kept a diary or itinerary, which has only recently come to light. Combined, these original sources provide wonderfully fresh insights into the land that was Texas in the late 1760s.[12]

After delays of more than two months, during which he waited in the capital, Rubí received his instructions from Viceroy Cruillas on March 10, 1766. Two days later, don Cayetano set out on his mission with a skeleton crew, going first to Querétaro and then on to Zacatecas. On March 18 Lafora left Mexico City and joined Rubí at Durango on April 14.[13]

At each garrison, the inspection team spent a number of days, during which it ascertained the post's geographic coordinates, drew maps of the locale, secured provisions for the presidials, and rested the expedition's tired mounts. As Rubí explained, his primary objectives throughout a twenty-three-month reconnaissance were "to inspect the presidios, their condition, their forces, and [to determine] their compliance with . . . [pertinent] ordinances or the culpable results against the governors and captains," and to assess "the advantage or disadvantage of the present location of the presidios in order to propose . . . the means most suitable for the defense of the dominions of His Majesty, protecting them from the hostilities of the barbarous [Indians]."[14]

After three months in Nueva Vizcaya, Rubí's command moved on to the province of New Mexico, which it reached at El Paso del Río del Norte. The presidio there contained approximately fifty men on active duty, although the troopers spent most of their time protecting livestock, pursuing Apache thieves, and guarding those who passed along the Camino Real. Nevertheless, Rubí found no reason to maintain the El Paso garrison, arguing that the nearby community was large enough to form militia units and assume responsibility for its own defense.[15]

After six months in the field and some 1,800 miles of travel, Rubí had completed the inspection of the Santa Fe presidio and then retraced his route through New Mexico to Nueva Vizcaya. From there he journeyed westward to Sonora. After reviewing the northern portion of the province, don Cayetano returned to the east by a different route across Nueva Vizcaya. He recrossed the Sierra Madre Occidental and struck the Camino Real below Chihuahua. By then it was April 1767, and Rubí had been on reconnaissance for more than a year. But the final leg of his monumental journey still lay ahead. The province of Texas would be subjected to the inspector's close examination, and it would not fare well.[16]

As Rubí prepared for his entrance into Texas, he was well aware that the province, like the others he had visited, had not undergone a comprehensive visitation since the Rivera inspection of the late 1720s. On that occasion, Rivera had failed to find abuses in Texas that were commonplace in other presidios on the frontier—most likely because the Texas garrisons were relatively new, having been founded only five or six years earlier. However, as Rubí would discover, by the 1760s presidial malpractices were as common in Texas as elsewhere. Those abuses included payment to soldiers in goods only, for which they were charged excessive and unauthorized prices; as well as enlistment practices whereby a recruit entering duty was relieved of service only by death, desertion, or his commander's permission. For the most part, a soldier's tour of duty meant unrelenting poverty, poor nutrition, and compulsory labor on the private lands of his commander.[17]

The Marqués de Rubí, en route to San Sabá, completed his crossing of the Río Grande on July 17, 1767. Before entering Texas, the inspector had traveled mostly by carriage, but the lack of roads and rough terrain of Texas made it prudent to switch to horseback. As he waited three days for his baggage and equipment to be ferried across the Great River by canoe, Rubí remarked unfavorably on a nearby encampment of Lipan Apaches, observing that once the Indians learned of his ample guard, "they left because of their natural distrust and fear of . . . their well-deserved punishment."[18] As it turned out, don Cayetano's views of the Lipans did not improve by his coming to know them better.

Rubí first inspected the missions at El Cañón on the upper Nueces River—religious outposts founded by Felipe de Rábago y Terán. The inspector noted their beggarly condition, specifically remarking that Mission San Lorenzo de la Santa Cruz "was found to be without a single Indian." He credited Comanches, the Lipans' "implacable enemies," for having driven the Apaches from their encampments in January 1766.[19]

When the Marqués de Rubí reached the San Sabá presidio, he unleashed a torrent of bitter criticism. Overall, the garrison was "badly constructed"; its two bastions were "ill-aligned." Its efficacy as a fortification was "as barbarous as the enemy who attacks it." He would later declare that San Sabá served no useful purpose whatsoever "to the interests of His Majesty in New Spain," because it provided no more protection for San Antonio or any Spanish outpost than "a ship anchored in mid-Atlantic would afford in preventing foreign trade with America."[20]

Compared to San Sabá, Rubí was favorably impressed by Presidio San Antonio de Béxar, Villa San Fernando de Béxar, and the nearby missions administered by Franciscan friars. He commented on the impressive number of Indians "from several nations" who were congregated at the five religious establishments. His stay at Béxar lasted from August 8 to August 24, 1767.[21]

Leaving the San Antonio River, Rubí's party remarked on farms and several small ranches encountered along the banks of the Río de Cíbolo in present-day Karnes County. Those settlements belonged to residents of San Antonio who risked their lives for the opportunity of acquiring fertile lands for grazing and farming. Based on the inspector's recommendation, in the 1770s a permanent military post was officially authorized for their protection.[22]

Making good time, the Marqués de Rubí arrived at Mission Nuestra Señora de Guadalupe at present-day Nacogdoches on September 7. His observations on this largely failed mission were devastatingly sarcastic. Commenting on the then resident missionary, he wrote: "For forty-six years in this area he has [had] little more to do than baptize a few of the dying, whose catechism, in that condition, has been somewhat difficult to practice." He further noted that Indian children who survived beyond the sacrament of baptism had often "reverted to the category of apostates." Nicolás de Lafora echoed those same sentiments, remarking that there was not "one Indian to whom he [the priest] could minister," nor had there ever been one.[23]

Father Margil's old mission for the Ais Indians at modern San Augustine received equally bad reviews. It was dismissed with a single sentence: "This mission, dedicated to the conversion of these Indians, is as ineffective as the Nacodoches [sic] mission." Its two resident missionaries, in Rubí's words, "hid themselves upon our arrival" and avoided any contact with the inspector. Lafora remarked that matters were actually worse at Mission Dolores, because the king had to pay the salaries of two priests, not just one.[24]

One day later, in following the Camino Real, Rubí crossed the Sabine River and later commented on thick woods containing cypresses (*sabinas*), from which the river took its name. As the inspector approached the Arroyo Hondo, he also remarked on thick stands of pines and small clearings containing "plantings of corn and vegetables." On that same day, September 11, the Marqués de Rubí arrived at Los Adaes.[25]

While encamped at the provincial capital of Texas, Rubí recorded its mean condition. The presidio's hexagonal enclosure contained three bastions made of pine poles, all of which were "badly constructed and in worse condition." The structure included sixteen crude houses that provided shelter for the presidials, a guardhouse for prisoners, and a small chapel dedicated to Our Lady of Pilar. The civilian population consisted of twenty-five families, sustained by "little ranches on meager plains, cleared of trees and brush for that purpose." The inspector, perhaps moved uncharacteristically by sympathy, noted that crops grown in the area were so sparse that they could not even supply the needs of the presidio. There was no potable surface water, and existing wells often provided only enough volume for drinking.[26]

Rubí concluded his inspection in this region by traveling to the former French outpost at Natchitoches, still occupied by "a garrison of troops of that nation." Don Cayetano ascertained that the French soldiers devoted themselves at vespers to the Spanish king, as well as to the Spanish captain general of the province. Upon returning to Los Adaes, he assessed its nearby mission as absolutely worthless. The two Franciscan friars there had achieved "as little results as those two previously cited, for there is not one single Indian in the mission."[27]

Two additional presidios in Texas awaited inspection by the Marqués de Rubí. Reaching the first, Presidio San Agustín de Ahumada, which was situated on the lower Trinity in contemporary Chambers County, occupied the Rubí party for approximately two weeks. The trek traversed exceptionally difficult terrain, with passage further hindered by almost incessant rain showers. Near the end, don Cayetano encountered lowlands that had been transformed into virtual "lakes and bogs, in which the horses sank up to their chests."[28]

Swampy conditions surrounded the presidio in all directions, producing the most unhealthful environment in all of Texas. The garrison itself contained wretched human beings who were constantly "at death's doorstep," for heat and humidity made it impossible to store foodstuffs and supplies without their spoilage in a matter of days, if not hours. Nevertheless, Rubí reported that the garrison's thirty-one men had decent uniforms and arms in good condition. Civilians, however, consisted of three or four discharged soldiers who, driven by hunger, "fruitlessly plant[ed] some plots of corn." The nearby mission, Nuestra Señora de la Luz, contained not a single Indian.[29]

From the lower Trinity, Rubí and his entourage began the trek to La Bahía on October 16. Crossing the swollen river with baggage and mules caused "no small difficulties," and the march continued with frequent delays occasioned by floods, which hampered fording the Colorado and Guadalupe Rivers. On the last day of October, the marqués arrived at the Santa Dorotea site on the San Antonio River and began his inspection on the same day. For a change, he liked the location of Presidio La Bahía del Espíritu Santo, which he described as "free, unhampered, and commanding." At Mission Nuestra Señora del Espíritu Santo, Rubí found the first resident Indians since leaving San Antonio—Cocos, Cujanes, Karankawas, and Aranamas.[30]

From La Bahía the Rubí party set out for Laredo. Reaching that site on November 18, after a perilous crossing of the Nueces River on rafts and hide boats that nearly cost the lives of three personal servants (his *familia*), don Cayetano once again made a caustic observation. The town, founded twelve years earlier by Tomás Sánchez, carried the designation of "villa," despite the fact that it consisted of "only twelve huts made of branches and leaves." Without comment about their status, Rubí also mentioned the settlements of Revilla, Camargo, and Mier, likewise founded by José de Escandón or his lieutenants.[31]

Crossing the Río Grande at Laredo, the Rubí party proceeded up the right bank of the Great River to San Juan Bautista. After inspecting the gateway presidio, the marqués, then reunited with his refurbished carriage, moved south to Monterrey and Saltillo. Via Zacatecas and Nayarit, he returned to Mexico City on February 23, 1768. In all, Rubí's inspection of twenty-three presidios on the northern frontier of New Spain occupied him for twenty-three months, during which he traveled an estimated 7,600 miles.[32]

In the capital, Rubí immediately set to work. His *dictamen*, or report, addressed the thorny problems of frontier defense. The marqués saw the portion of New Spain stretching from the Gulf of California to the Gulf of Mexico as mostly a fraudulent operation. In the words of a Spanish Borderlands historian, "with rare exceptions, the northern frontier presidios were military mockeries: crumbling structures, incompetently and corruptly managed; garrisons of untrained soldiers short of basic equipment, skills, and morale; each outpost so entangled in the mechanics of its own survival as to be nearly useless against the swift-moving *indios bárbaros*." [33]

In a similar vein, many of the frontier missions were also not viable. Rubí asked why those religious establishments should be maintained at no small cost to the crown when after years of operation they contained not a single resident Indian. Furthermore, because the garrisons were so poorly managed and commanders so abusive in their practices, those outposts did not serve their intended purpose. As a case in point, the destruction of the San Sabá mission within three to four miles of a fully armed and manned garrison had demonstrated the ineffectiveness of the presidial system as then structured.[34]

To be sure, Rubí's suggested remedies were radical, for the northern frontier of New Spain had expanded in spurts since the mid-1500s. That approach, carried out by miners, missionaries, entrepreneurs, and stockmen, had much to recommend it. Expansion discovered potentially rich new lands; it brought pagan people under the mantle of Christian instruction; and it claimed new domains that might otherwise fall under the control of foreign competitors. Nonetheless, in Rubí's judgment, extension of empire must cease. A "real" frontier should be established along a line running from the Gulf of California to El Paso del Norte. At that juncture, the cordon would follow roughly the course of the Río Grande to the Gulf of Mexico. Apaches and other hostile Indians must be kept north of that line—on lands the marqués deemed to be an "imaginary" part of the Spanish empire.[35]

South of the proposed line, which would be defended by fifteen presidios spaced at regular intervals (each about one hundred miles apart), lay Spain's "real" empire. Despite his penchant for rigidly inflexible patterns, Rubí recognized that two long-established communities did not fall within his master plan. Santa Fe and San Antonio lay north of the cordon but could not be abandoned. Both entailed irrevocable responsibilities to those citizens and their property, not to mention converted Indians therein.[36]

The new arrangement of presidios included only two within the confines of Texas. As mentioned, Rubí found the garrison at La Bahía somewhat to his liking, and he made it the eastern terminus of his proposed reorganization. San Antonio de Béxar had to be maintained to protect the five missions there, as well as the civilian settlement. More important, the marqués recommended the total abandonment of East Texas and the removal of its citizens to Béxar, which was to become the new capital of Texas. Accordingly, the presidio at San Antonio assumed even greater significance.[37]

Most controversial were Rubí's recommendations regarding the Apaches. Never one to mince words, the marqués assessed those Native Americans with comments that are the very essence of political incorrectness. In his view, not even once had the various Apache nations honored their obligations as vassals of the king. But the inspector singled out the Lipan Apaches as the worst offenders of all. They were "perfidious" and belonged to a "vile nation." Their behavior most resembled the "profession of thieves"; their conduct resembled "housebreakers"; their "deceitful friendship" was unequaled in the annals of Spanish-Indian relations; and their "sagacity, rapacity, and industry" stood as impediments "to the progress of the arms of the King and to the tranquility of his possessions."[38]

As an important corollary, Rubí endorsed a policy that did not originate with him but now carried the weight of his high office. The Spanish must abandon all attempts at cooperation with the Apaches and make common cause with the Comanches and the Nations of the North. Particularly conducive to that approach was the recommended closure of the San Sabá presidio and the missions at El Cañón, for this would eliminate prime irritants that had fueled the anger of both Comanches and Norteños.[39]

Once implemented, this new direction in Spanish Indian policy would place the Apaches in the jaws of a huge vise. They would be driven south by their ancient enemies in the north and eventually pressed against the newly constructed line of presidios. At that juncture, the marqués thought it probable that the Lipans "will seek asylum in our missions and presidios; but this should not be conceded to them except at the cost of moving them far to the interior and dividing them, extinguishing or confusing them."[40]

Rubí's *dictamen* makes it clear that the marqués was stern in his recommendations, but he did not advocate genocide. True, the Lipans must cease their marauding ways and adapt themselves to the Spanish system wherein they were to become productive tax-paying citizens. But don Cayetano was not unqualifiedly committed to their extinction. For example, he recommended humane treatment for Lipan captives taken in warfare, as well as an option for those who faced certain death at the hands of their Native American enemies. Refugees should be relocated in missions distant from the frontier, where they would be less tempted to take up their old ways and where they would be unlikely to anger the Nations of the North, whose friendship was vital to the security of Texas.[41]

More than four years passed before the crown acted upon the Marqués de Rubí's recommendations. The New Regulations for Presidios, issued on September 10, 1772, called for the abandonment of all missions and presidios in Texas except for those at San Antonio and La Bahía; the strengthening of San Antonio by designating it the new capital of Texas; the establishment of a fort on the Arroyo de Cíbolo; the removal of soldiers and settlers in East Texas and at El Orcoquisac; and the implementation of a new Indian policy aimed at establishing good relations with the Comanches and the Northern Nations at the expense of the Apaches (Figure 17).[42]

Rubí had sailed from Veracruz in July 1768. The remainder of his life, like the years before he arrived in New Spain, is largely obscure. He was summoned to the Spanish court in 1769 to explain and defend his proposals, and he was in Barcelona in April 1772. When Charles III died in 1788, the marqués held the rank of lieutenant general, served as counselor of war, and occupied the office of commanding general and governor of the military district of Madrid. Unfortunately, he was then at odds with the Conde de Floridablanca, the king's first minister, who was retained in the same capacity for a time by Charles IV. Caught on the wrong side in a power struggle, Rubí may have accepted involuntary retirement at about the age of sixty-three.[43]

One must read between the lines of Rubí's diary and *dictamen* to flesh out his character and personality. He apparently lacked "people skills," but his imperious nature was consistent with the nature of his mission. Because he rebuked both presidial commanders and missionaries for dishonesty or incompetence, his unpopularity with those individuals was assured. Rubí also appears to have been humorless, unless one interprets as mordant wit his remarks about the dead not being able to practice catechism.

It should also be remembered that Charles III, a reform-minded monarch at the height of the Spanish Enlightenment, placed enormous confidence in Rubí. With very few exceptions, his recommendations for improvements in frontier policies were implemented as written. Those policies were costly, in real terms, because only three presidios in "the Line," as he called it, remained where they were located, while twelve had to be moved, and in human terms, because settlements and missions

INSTRUCCION

PARA FORMAR UNA LINEA Ó CORDON

DE QUINCE PRESIDIOS

Sobre las Fronteras de las Provincias Internas de este
Reino de Nueva-España,

Y

NUEVO REGLAMENTO

Del número y calidad de Oficiales y Soldados que estos
y los demas han de tener, Sueldos que gozarán desde el
dia primero de Enero del año próximo de mil sete-
cientos setenta y dos, y servicio que deben hacer
sus Guarniciones.

Año de   1 7 7 1 .

DE ORDEN DE SU EXCELENCIA
En Mexico en la Imprenta del Br. D. Joseph Antonio de Hogal,
Calle de Tiburcio.

FIGURE 17

*Title page of the New Regulations, which largely implemented
recommendations of the Marqués de Rubí, called for the reorganization of
frontier defenses from the Gulf of California to Texas. (With the permission
of the Archivo General de Indias, Seville, Spain; Guadalajara 274.)*

built near existing presidios were left unprotected or forced to move—as was the case with the settlers of East Texas.[44]

Not surprisingly, Rubí's perception of the Spanish empire in North America and the consequences of his radical recommendations still stir historical debate. Without doubt, Texas was weakened, especially in East Texas and at San Sabá, to the benefit of more populous settlements in Coahuila. But the marqués appears to have been correct in recognizing that "Spain had spread itself too thin on the vast frontier" of New Spain. Establishing a line marking a "real" empire that could be adequately defended made sense. Spain would subsequently expand beyond the Rubí line into California but not through the Apache barrier. It is also worth noting that the international border separating Mexico from the United States, established primarily by the Treaty of Guadalupe Hidalgo in 1848, closely resembles the Rubí line of repositioned presidios.[45]

The Marqués de Rubí's recommendations for a profoundly different direction in Indian policy, coupled with Spain's acquisition of Louisiana, brought into play the extraordinary talents of Athanase de Mézières as an agent of that new approach. Although not intended by Rubí, removal of the Adaesanos to San Antonio soon led to the systematic reoccupation of East Texas and the founding of modern Nacogdoches in 1779. The latter circumstance tapped the leadership qualities of Antonio Gil Ibarvo, the remarkable pioneer and important founder of modern East Texas.

As mentioned earlier, José de Gálvez in his capacity as visitor general arrived in New Spain in the aftermath of the Seven Years' War. In all, Gálvez spent six years in New Spain. About halfway through his stay, he set out for an extended tour of the northern frontier—his departure, in April 1768, coming at the very time Rubí worked on his *dictamen* in the capital. Gálvez's overarching powers authorized him to recommend changes that affected the entire administrative system in New Spain. Overall, the visitor general concluded that the Interior Provinces, so named because one had to go inland from the heartland of New Spain to reach them, were too distant from Mexico City. And when he returned to Spain in 1772, Gálvez lobbied for the appointment of a commandant general, an officer at brigadier rank stationed on the northern frontier who had separate administrative and military powers that approximated those of the viceroy in Mexico City.[46]

The suggested changes were vigorously opposed by the chief executive of New Spain, who saw the proposed reorganization as a significant diminution of his powers. Sensitive to the arguments of the viceroy,

Charles III was not at that time receptive to such drastic measures. Accordingly, when the New Regulations for Presidios were issued in September 1772, the king placed the Interior Provinces under a commandant inspector who answered to the viceroy, rather than to an independent commandant general. The officer chosen as first commandant inspector was Hugo Oconor, a redheaded Irishman long in the service of Spain.[47]

The New Regulations for Presidios, as issued by the king in September 1772, could not have been more explicit with regard to Texas. Upon its extinction, the garrison at San Sabá would be moved to the Río Grande; El Orcoquisac and Los Adaes were deemed "to be useless in actuality" and the troops there were to be removed "at once." Missions at Nacogdoches and "others that are maintained without any Indians in the shadow of the said presidios" were to be eliminated. The "few settlers who live around them" were to be removed to the "villa of San Antonio de Béjar or its vicinity, where I order land to be distributed to them for their settlement and subsistence."[48]

In January 1773, Viceroy Antonio María de Bucareli y Ursúa informed Juan María Vicencio, Barón de Ripperdá, then Governor of Texas, of Oconor's appointment as commandant inspector with the new rank of colonel. Ripperdá had been in office since 1770, and although Los Adaes was technically the provincial capital, the de facto seat of government had become San Antonio where the governor resided. The viceroy's communiqué informed the baron that Oconor was occupied with the relocation of presidios in Nueva Vizcaya and Coahuila, to be followed soon by the same task in Sonora. Accordingly, changes in Texas, as provided in the New Regulations, would have to be implemented by the governor of the province. Ripperdá was especially enjoined to remove the civilian population from East Texas—an obligation he viewed with great reluctance. Moreover, all changes in the province were subject to the final approval of Oconor, who was to be kept informed of the governor's every action.[49]

At the same time, Viceroy Bucareli sent detailed instructions to Oconor. The new commandant inspector was expressly ordered to bring about the immediate closure of the presidio and missions in East Texas and the prompt removal of those settlers. So Oconor likewise sent instructions to Governor Ripperdá, directives that provided no leeway whatsoever.[50]

Governor Ripperdá had to close the three Zacatecan missions in East Texas and the one at El Orcoquisac. He was also to destroy the presidios at Los Adaes and El Orcoquisac, transferring their ammunition and cannon to San Antonio. All families associated with the four suppressed missions and two presidios must be moved to San Antonio, although property belonging to the five missions there, as well as to Bexareño settlers, could not be compromised.[51]

Unfortunately, in recent years the Barón de Ripperdá and Hugo Oconor had developed "a jealous hatred for each other," which made cooperation between them exceedingly difficult. Ripperdá resented having to take orders from a younger man only recently promoted to colonel, a rank held by the governor for more than ten years. Oconor, on the other hand, reveled in his position of power, often issuing detailed orders with excruciating pedantry.[52]

Nonetheless, Ripperdá was a "good soldier" and faithful servant of the king. Following orders, in May 1773 he sent explicit injunctions to East Texas. The settlers, preparatory to their removal, were to stop planting crops and round up their livestock. In his directives, the baron mentioned by name one Antonio Gil Ibarvo, a successful rancher living at a place called El Lobanillo (the Wart) near present-day San Augustine, Texas.[53]

Gil Ibarvo, a hero in East Texas history, provides a compelling sequel to changes wrought by the Rubí visitation. He was born at Los Adaes in 1729 to Mathieu Antonio and Juana Hernández Ibarvo. Both parents were natives of Andalucía in the south of Spain. By way of New Orleans, the married couple had come to Los Adaes and settled there a few years after the Marqués de Aguayo reclaimed the region. Their son, Antonio, grew up among the French, Spanish, and Indian population of the region, learning firsthand how to traffic in merchandise—both legal and illegal—in this polyglot atmosphere.[54]

Arriving with the Gil Ibarvos in the 1720s were the Padillas, who settled a few miles north of the Nacogdoches mission. As a young man, Antonio sought and won the hand of María Padilla, daughter of the family's patriarch, Pedro Padilla. During what would become a troubled marriage, the couple built a ranch in present-day Sabine County, to the east of Father Antonio Margil de Jesús's old mission for the Ais Indians. Known as El Lobanillo, there is speculation that the Gil Ibarvo ranch, because it was an excrescence or "wart" in the world of contraband trade, received its appellation from a military commander at Los Adaes.[55]

For the most part, trade between Spanish realms and foreign colonies in the Americas was absolutely forbidden by His Majesty's mercantilistic restrictions. Similarly, Spanish colonists were not to trade on their own with Indian nations. Such restrictive policies were intended to preserve the royal prerogative and, importantly, force Native Americans into missions where they would receive the king's largess in exchange for their commitment to the Roman Catholic Faith. But both policies failed miserably in East Texas, and the "wart" ranch apparently served as an important conduit for much illicit trafficking.[56]

Gil Ibarvo, however, became so accomplished as a trader that even a governor of Texas used him to obtain supplies in a region where smuggling had become "a way of life." In such capacity, he won the confidence of Barón de Ripperdá but not that of his predecessor—Hugo Oconor, who had served as ad interim governor from 1767 to 1770.[57]

As always, Oconor was a stickler for rules and regulations. During his tenure as governor, he was determined to rid Spain's eastern provinces of illicit trade, and he soon clashed with Gil Ibarvo. On Oconor's orders, don Antonio was arrested in New Orleans. In his possession were horses allegedly stolen from the Spanish by Indians at various missions and presidios, including San Sabá, La Bahía, and Béxar. For his complicity, Gil Ibarvo was imprisoned and fettered for seven months until released on orders of Barón de Ripperdá, Oconor's successor and archenemy.[58]

Unlike Oconor, Ripperdá had always been friendly to the East Texas settlers. He liked Gil Ibarvo by reputation, and he knew that hundreds of East Texans had been born and reared in homes and ranches nestled among the piney woods. Many of the Adaesanos had made improvements on their ranches and cleared lands for farming. But it was the baron's sad obligation to tell those people in person that they must give up their homes and move to a strange land where they would be outsiders.

It speaks volumes about the Spanish system of colonization that a king in far-off Spain could tell his subjects where they could live and where they could not. In the Anglo-American world, the Proclamation Line of 1763 limited where settlers could go, but after 1783 frontiersmen were free to live where they wished in United States territory between the Appalachians and the Mississippi River.

The settlers in East Texas were given only five days to prepare for the long march to San Antonio. Since the order to evacuate their homes came in mid-June, the Adaesanos were unable to gather spring crops, and there was little time to round up scattered livestock. For many, the thought of abandoning their homes for an uncertain future was too traumatic. Perhaps thirty-five persons at Los Adaes fled into the forests or were harbored by Indian friends. An equal number near Nacogdoches probably did the same thing. Those persons later reappeared at their old homes and continued their lives on the frontier. So East Texas was not entirely "combed out." For the most part, however, it was a Texas exodus.[59]

Because affairs at San Antonio demanded the governor's attention, Ripperdá did not remain to oversee the evacuation. Left in charge was Lieutenant José González, a forty-year veteran at the Los Adaes presidio. González compassionately granted the settlers a few more days of grace before demanding that they fall out of their homes and join the procession to Béxar, which began on June 25, 1773.[60]

By the time the Adaesanos reached El Lobanillo, about two dozen of them had fallen ill, and they, along with Gil Ibarvo's mother, sister, and sister-in-law, remained at the ranch. With González's permission, an able-bodied son of don Antonio was also left to care for those persons. These events certainly suggest that Gil Ibarvo intended to keep his roots in East Texas and that he viewed the forced evacuation as little more than a temporary setback.[61]

After the approximately four hundred men, women, and children departed from Nacogdoches, their suffering intensified. The emigrants' initial leader, Lieutenant González, had died at the mission, and command passed to a sergeant. Hasty preparations for the journey meant poor supplies and inadequate mounts; drought plagued the first half of the trip; and torrential rains and floods mired the second portion. Ten children died en route, and most of the adults had to travel on foot until they reached the Brazos River. At that juncture, fresh mounts and supplies sent by Ripperdá bolstered spirits.[62]

Nonetheless, it was a footsore, health-broken group of refugees who finally reached Béxar on September 26. In all, more than thirty had lost their lives on the three-month trek, and thirty more would soon die of related illnesses. Although the king's instructions had mandated that new lands be given to the exiles, the lack of suitable tracts brought a petition from them, signed by seventy-eight men, within eight days. First on the list and likely author of the petition, Gil Ibarvo spoke of "the lamentable miseries with which we traveled so long a road," experiencing on it "thirst . . . lack of beasts of burden, death of some children and parents [and] . . . the abandonment of the greater part of our small goods." The petitioners asked Governor Ripperdá for nothing less than permission to return to their homes in East Texas.[63]

The governor was again sympathetic, but his hands were tied by directives from both the viceroy and commandant inspector. Ripperdá did agree to support an appeal to Viceroy Bucareli, asking for a reversal of crown policy. At that juncture, Gil Ibarvo and Gil Flores, another prominent East Texan, volunteered to carry the petition to Mexico City. They left Béxar in December 1773, bearing with them a letter of endorsement from Barón de Ripperdá. Accompanying the two Spaniards was Texita, a prominent Hainai chieftain who desired their return to his land.[64]

En route, Gil Ibarvo prepared a second appeal, dated January 8, 1774, addressed to Hugo Oconor. Reaching the capital in February, the two delegates won an audience with Viceroy Bucareli. The chief executive then convened a Junta of War and Treasury, and that advisory body recommended acceptance of the petition, pointing to the advantages of reestablishing settlements among the Indians of East Texas. Bucareli concurred. On March 17 he granted the East Texas exiles the right of settlement between the Trinity and Sabine Rivers and forwarded his recommendation to Madrid. Gil Ibarvo and Flores were understandably ecstatic. But Hugo Oconor again entered the scene.[65]

Oconor reminded the viceroy of his determined efforts as interim governor to end contraband trade among East Texas settlers, Indians, and French agents at Natchitoches. And he almost certainly pointed to Gil Ibarvo, whom he had incarcerated in New Orleans, as the primary agent of that illegal commerce. The commandant inspector was absolutely adamant. The Royal Ordinances of 1772, which he was specifically charged with implementing, must be enforced.[66]

At that juncture, Viceroy Bucareli suggested a compromise. He informed Governor Ripperdá by letter that any settlements reestablished by Gil Ibarvo and his followers must be no closer than one hundred leagues (about 260 miles) from Natchitoches. In the meantime, an appeal would be made to Charles III, in hopes that the king would give his royal blessing to the plan.[67]

Gil Ibarvo recognized that a tiny crack had formed in the central government's bureaucracy—just enough for a man of his talents to slip through. He thanked the viceroy for providing Flores and him with a daily allowance of two reales, for they had found themselves "entirely destitute" in the capital. The two men then hurried back to San Antonio, and plans for the reoccupation of East Texas were put in place. The displaced East Texas refugees were, of course, delighted, calling Gil Ibarvo "the restorer of his country, the lover of the common good, and the father of the *adaesanos*." Fortunately, the implacable Oconor found himself so involved with more pressing matters elsewhere in New Spain that he agreed to let Ripperdá handle the details of resettlement.[68]

Always a shrewd businessman with natural leadership qualities, Gil Ibarvo suggested El Lobanillo as his preferred residence. But that location was too close to Natchitoches, and Ripperdá would not disobey the viceroy's explicit directive on this point. Instead, the governor selected a site on the Trinity River, known as Paso Tomás. To honor the viceroy who had made the reoccupation of East Texas possible, the new villa built there would be named Nuestra Señora de Pilar de Bucareli.[69]

The trials and distresses of this town and its inhabitants, as well as the subsequent founding of Nacogdoches in 1779, are discussed in the chapters on Athanase de Mézières and Domingo Cabello. Of particular concern here is the continuing role of Antonio Gil Ibarvo as a leader in East Texas history.

In 1777 an earlier recommendation by Visitor General José de Gálvez came to fruition. Charles III created the office of commandant general of the Interior Provinces, the post going first to Teodoro de Croix (1777–1783) on January 1. Significantly, this administrative change made Texas essentially independent of the viceroy of New Spain. In the following year, Texas also came under a new governor, Domingo Cabello y Robles (1778–1786). Accordingly, Gil Ibarvo for the next several years dealt with changed circumstances and new officials.

After the establishment of Nacogdoches, toward the end of April 1779, Gil Ibarvo filed a claim against the government for reimbursement of funds expended from his private fortune. Don Antonio contended that he and his son had spent thousand of pesos on the aid and protection of East Texas settlers, and he further requested arms to defend Nacogdoches, which did not have a presidio. His petition brought limited results. On October 15, 1779, Croix granted Gil Ibarvo an annual salary of five hundred pesos and gave him the titles of lieutenant governor and chief justice of Nacogdoches and captain of militia. In the following year, don Antonio also received appointment as judge of contraband seizures.[70]

The new settlers at Nacogdoches, however, faced hard times. Unable to get a crop in the ground until May, they experienced meager or failed harvests and much privation during that first year. After nearly six years of abandonment, few of the old buildings were habitable, but structures still standing were patched and jammed with people desperate to have a roof over their heads. The newcomers' spiritual needs, however, were attended to by Father José Francisco Mariano de la Garza, who took up residence in the old mission.[71]

Gil Ibarvo assumed leadership in establishing good relations with the Indians. To that purpose, he asked permission from Governor Cabello to establish a commissary, and the governor granted his request. Indelible memories of food shortages during the first year and the necessity of trade with nearby Indians apparently combined to bring about the construction of a large stone house, now referred to as the Old Stone Fort—

one of only a few buildings from the Spanish era that remain standing in Texas (Figure 18).[72]

Don Antonio also established an informal system of verbal land grants. Because there was no machinery by which the king's sovereignty over land could be divested, these grants rested on shaky legal foundations. In a litigious society, Gil Ibarvo was eventually censured for granting without authority enormous tracts of real estate, some in excess of fifty thousand acres! Furthermore, in his capacity as lieutenant governor of Nacogdoches, Gil Ibarvo fell into old habits. Although specifically charged with eliminating smuggling, he apparently engaged in clandestine trade with French agents, who in turn traded with Americans east of the Mississippi River. In late December 1791, the commandant general ordered the arrest of Gil Ibarvo and his transfer to San Antonio.[73]

During his twelve-year tenure as lieutenant governor of Nacogdoches, don Antonio recorded incidents that provide unique insights into the social history of the town, a raw frontier community in Texas. Of particular interest is a criminal code for the community and district of Nacogdoches, drafted by Gil Ibarvo in 1783. From the preamble, it is clear that the governor thought Draconian measures for "the preservation of good order" to be essential.[74]

Don Antonio noted that "vices and crimes of every description" were progressing rapidly; that "notwithstanding repeated public injunctions, disorders of all kinds are spreading torrentlike amongst persons of both sexes." In order that "the ignorant as well as the evil disposed" should be apprised of impending punishments for their transgressions, Gil Ibarvo laid down fifty-four statutes. These laws addressed such offenses as blasphemy, defamation of the king, arson, and murder. Punishment for the latter would be "quartered alive, previous to being hanged." Other acts of criminality included practicing sorcery, dueling, ravishing a maiden, committing adultery or incest, cohabiting outside matrimony, engaging in bestiality (which called for burning the offender and "said beast"), pimping, breaking and entering houses, robbing one's neighbor of livestock, jail breaking, resisting arrest, singing with indecent language in streets or plazas, drinking and gambling, harboring deserters or criminals, uttering pejorative appellations, conducting illegal lotteries, failing to clean the soot out of chimneys once every fifteen days ("to prevent the sad effects of . . . conflagration"), and the selling of "spirituous liquors to Indians."[75]

That lawlessness among the settlers of Nacogdoches remained a problem, despite seemingly all-inclusive injunctions and penalties for miscreancy, is illustrated, for example, by a case recorded by Gil Ibarvo

FIGURE 18

Drawing of Antonio Gil Ibarvo. This original artwork by Charles Shaw depicts Gil Ibarvo and the Old Stone Fort in Nacogdoches. (Courtesy of the East Texas Historical Association Exhibit, Ralph Steen Library, Stephen F. Austin State University.)

several years after the codes of 1783. The offender was Juan José Peña, an incredible braggart, bold highwayman, and Houdini-like escape artist.[76]

Peña (it is best not to dignify him with "don Juan") entered the annals of criminal behavior in 1789 by robbing a trader and stealing six horses from different owners. Caught by hunters, he was brought before Gil Ibarvo, who placed him in irons. Peña broke loose, stole a gun and another horse, and then killed a milk cow. While in hiding, the fugitive tried to force his attentions on an Indian woman and beat her unmercifully when she resisted. Indian males who had come to the assistance of the abused woman helped capture Peña, bringing him once again before Gil Ibarvo and the bar of justice.[77]

On this occasion, don Antonio placed the culprit in stocks, secured him additionally with ball and chains, and then confined him within the jail! In Gil Ibarvo's words, "by some miraculous way he escaped again." Free to commit further mischief, Peña broke into a house, took "much clothing," and stole three more horses. "After using all the means possible. . . I managed to capture him again with all the stolen properties, which I returned to the owners. I punished this evil-doer and gave him what he deserved. . . . Several days after his confinement, and by the same miracles that freed him before, he once more evaded the law."[78]

Bent on revenge, for he had made public threats against the lieutenant governor, Peña broke into Gil Ibarvo's sleeping quarters but unexpectedly found the magistrate awake and ready to defend himself. Again, the fugitive avoided capture. On the following morning, "he stripped the town of all the clothing he found hanging in the sun to dry" and fled into the country. Once again, don Antonio, with the help of several citizens, caught the outlaw, and on this occasion "took particular care that the thief was securely detained." Incredibly, Peña escaped yet again and stole three horses before he was apprehended.[79]

More than a little irritated, Gil Ibarvo "took the greatest precaution of placing the evil-doer in double handcuffs and double ankle-chains." Still Peña escaped, taking the handcuffs and ankle-chains with him! There followed four months of "further depredations"—offenses that included stealing horses, breaking and entering houses, and pilfering personal effects.[80]

At last Peña was apprehended and again brought before Gil Ibarvo. "This time and with rigor, I took all the means of precaution in my power to guard against his escape, and I my own self took charge of the jail and guarded him." Don Antonio finally rid the Nacogdoches community of this arch criminal by transporting him with armed guards, supplemented by six militiamen, to San Antonio and there Peña disappeared from the written record.[81]

As the years passed, Gil Ibarvo began to tire of his duties as lieutenant governor of Nacogdoches, captain of militia, judge of contraband seizures, and chief justice. In a letter to Governor Manuel Muñoz, dated March 22, 1791, he described himself as "now worn out by my advanced age, which exceeds sixty years." Despite his desire "of dying in the royal service," don Antonio also included a petition to the viceroy, likewise dated March 22. In it he briefly recounted his services since August 7, 1774, and asked for a pension of one-half his annual salary of five hundred pesos. It was not granted.[82]

Under suspicion as a contrabandist, Gil Ibarvo was removed from Nacogdoches in January 1792 and incarcerated in San Antonio. Although eventually cleared of charges (September 15, 1796) and given a small pension, he was nonetheless banished from Nacogdoches, where his presence was deemed "contrary to the union and best harmony of its inhabitants." While he was defending himself in legal proceedings at Béxar, his wife had died at Nacogdoches on January 21, 1794. At that time, the Gil Ibarvo estate was placed in the hands of the eldest daughter, María Antonia. While still in the capital, on January 25, 1796, don Antonio sought and won permission to marry a second time. His bride was María Guadalupe de Herrera.[83]

On October 3, 1799, Gil Ibarvo left Nacogdoches with his reclaimed possessions. A long line of carts and wagons containing every transportable item from his houses and ranch rumbled by under the watchful eye of the military commander at Nacogdoches. Looking for contraband, José Miguel del Moral had inspected every piece of merchandise and examined every brand on the cattle, horses, and mules that were part of the procession.[84]

Unfortunately, the last years of Gil Ibarvo's life were marred by lawsuits between the children of his two marriages, as well as litigation between himself and former business partners. Those legal proceedings, combined with the default of a friend for whom he was surety, deprived this pioneer in East Texas of most material possessions. He appears to have lived for a time in Louisiana before Spanish officials lifted banishment and permitted him to return to the Nacogdoches area. At the age of eighty, Gil Ibarvo died at his home on the west bank of the Attoyac River in 1809. His descendants still live in East Texas.[85]

Antonio Gil Ibarvo more than qualifies as a notable leader in Texas history. He was a skillful but not always legal trader. Taking advantage of new market opportunities in Spanish Louisiana, he became a successful entrepreneurial rancher at El Lobanillo for many years. And he was the prime founder of modern Nacogdoches. This East Texas official stands in dramatic contrast to the straitlaced and imperious Marqués de Rubí. As a frontiersman, don Antonio learned how to bend the law. For example, when he discovered a slight chink in the armor of Spanish bureaucracy—differences between Viceroy Bucareli and Commandant Inspector Oconor—he worked it to perfection. Gil Ibarvo, more than anyone else, found a way to reoccupy East Texas after the implementation of Rubí's recommendations in 1773. His legacies include a fine city in East Texas and a commendable tradition of helping fellow settlers on a remote frontier. Indeed, Father José de la Garza, longtime missionary at Nacogdoches, offered a stirring tribute to don Antonio in 1787. In his view, the settlers in East Texas regarded Gil Ibarvo as "the father, protector, and comforter of their recovered homeland."[86]

TEN

DOMINGO CABELLO Y ROBLES

Reluctant Governor

On August 4, 1777, Teodoro de Croix, newly appointed commandant general of the Interior Provinces of New Spain, left Mexico City to carry out an inspection of his jurisdiction. By way of Querétaro and Monclova, where he encountered extended delays, Croix and his entourage crossed the Río Grande near San Juan Bautista on Christmas Eve and reached San Antonio de Béxar on December 31, 1777. Remarking on his first visit to Texas, the commandant general voiced decidedly negative impressions of the province and its capital: "A villa without order, two presidios, seven missions, and an errant population of scarcely 4,000 persons of both sexes and all ages that occupies an immense desert country, stretching from the abandoned presidio of Los Adaes to San Antonio, . . . [that] does not deserve the name of the Province of Texas . . . nor the concern entailed in its preservation." [1]

Appointed as governor of this unimpressive province but not yet in office was a fifty-three-year-old army colonel who would exercise gubernatorial powers for eight years. His relatively long tenure as chief executive of Texas (1778–1786) spanned critical years—years that witnessed consideration of a dramatically altered Indian policy toward the Karankawas; the abandonment of Villa Bucareli and the founding of modern Nacogdoches; the conclusion of a successful treaty with the Comanches and its impact on the Indians of East Texas; the establishment of direct contact between San Antonio and Santa Fe; and the entry of Spain into the American Revolutionary War (1779). A central figure in those important events was Texas' nineteenth governor—Domingo Cabello y Robles.

Born around 1725 in León, Spain, Domingo Cabello joined an infantry regiment in March 1741 as a teenage second lieutenant. Within seven months, he was promoted to first lieutenant, a rank that he held for ten years. His promotion to *sargento mayor* came in October 1751, and he stayed at that rank for more than twenty-two years before becoming a lieutenant colonel on March 13, 1774. Cabello's lengthy military service earned him recognition from the Spanish crown and consideration for several important administrative posts in the Americas.[2]

Entering the infantry regiment of Portugal in 1741 as a youth of fifteen or sixteen years, Lieutenant Cabello experienced his first combat in the War of Austrian Succession (1740–1748). His regiment sailed from Spain in 1742 to reinforce the garrison at Santiago de Cuba, but the frigate, loaded with military hardware, was challenged by an English vessel. In a running battle lasting for more than four hours, young don Domingo was wounded in the right thigh.[3]

On April 9, 1748, near the end of the war, Cabello again saw action in defending Castillo del Morro, the great bastion overlooking the harbor of Havana, Cuba. On this occasion, the port was challenged by a squadron of seven English vessels, but a battery of cannon mounted near the entrance to the harbor unleashed "intensive firepower," which repelled the attackers. While in Cuba, don Domingo also carried out military campaigns against English corsairs who launched damaging raids on coastal haciendas.[4]

With the achievement of peace by the Treaty of Aix-la-Chapelle (1748), the Regiment of Portugal was recalled to Spain and reorganized, and Lieutenant Cabello accepted reassignment at Toledo. There he applied for and received command of four battalions of fixed regiment, charged with defending Cuba and coastal presidios in Florida. While stationed at Havana, Cabello helped defend the port against an assault by British land forces, lasting from June 6 to August 11, 1762, during the Seven Years' War (1756–1763). Overrun by superior forces, Major Cabello became a prisoner of war at the conclusion of the siege, and in that capacity the English returned him to Spain in 1763.[5]

In the following year, Cabello received appointment as the governor of Nicaragua. He assumed that post on December 12 and held it until July 20, 1776. During his tenure in Central America, he served as commandant general of its four administrative districts (*corregimientos*) and boasted of augmenting Indian tribute payments by 3,800 pesos per year. In his military capacity, don Domingo carried out campaigns that punished a number of Indian misdeeds, especially those perpetrated by Mosquitos and Caribs. Those nations had captured fellow Native Americans, burned their villages, and sold the captives as slaves to English wood-cutters on the coast of Honduras.[6]

While governor, don Domingo worked at Christianizing some three hundred families of Caribs by placing them in specially created settle-ments (*reducciones*). And he counted the conversion of Chief Yarrinzen, who accepted the name don Carlos Yarrinzen, among his signal accom-plishments for the faith. In recognition of the chief's commitment to His Catholic Majesty, Governor Cabello bestowed on him the honorary rank of captain, carrying a monthly salary of twenty pesos, and gave him a gold medal bearing the likeness of Charles III. By his own assessment, when he departed Nicaragua for Texas, Cabello left behind a province that enjoyed both peace and security.[7]

On October 31, 1777, almost a year before he assumed duties as chief executive of Texas, Domingo Cabello earned the rank of colonel. He was then a man in his early fifties who described himself as "robust" in health. Colonel Cabello had felt the sting of battle and bore its scars; he had suffered the indignity of capture and life as a prisoner of war; and he had served his king honorably in Spain, Cuba, and Nicaragua. As we shall see, Cabello considered his office in Texas to be the absolute nadir of a promising career. He objected to the assignment, took his time in getting there, and tried every means possible to gain a better post. After several near misses, don Domingo finally achieved promotion and reas-signment, but it took eight years.[8]

This candid statement of Domingo Cabello's ambitions, however, should not be interpreted as a damning and unequivocal assessment of the man. He approached his responsibilities as governor of Texas profes-sionally, although reluctantly, and, despite a few "warts" on his conduct, he deserves consideration as a notable man in Texas history.

When Cabello assumed his duties at Béxar in late October 1778, events played out on the Gulf Coast over the previous year resulted in the first serious problems that confronted him. Governor Bernardo de Gálvez of Louisiana, acting on instructions from his uncle, who was minister of the Indies, had dispatched the schooner *El Señor de la Yedra*, commanded by Luis Antonio Andry, from New Orleans on Decem-ber 13, 1777. Andry, a French engineer, carried orders to explore and map the coast westward to Matagorda Bay.[9]

Serving on the *Yedra* were Andry's cadet son of twelve years and a dozen crewmen. Among that number was Cristóbal Gómez, who as a former soldier stationed at Presidio La Bahía claimed familiarity with the Texas coast and its native inhabitants. Another crew member was

Tomás de la Cruz, a young Maya Indian from the Yucatán Peninsula. The schooner's sponsors and all those aboard were aware of the inherent dangers associated with this voyage, and when the vessel did not return in a timely manner concern mounted.[10]

On October 24, 1778, just four days before Domingo Cabello took the oath of office in San Antonio, Bernardo de Gálvez had written his uncle, expressing fears that Captain Andry had suffered much worse than the "misfortune of having been lost, in view of the long time which has elapsed since his departure from this post." Don Bernardo's fears were confirmed in January 1779 when Athanase de Mézières reported that the remains of the *Yedra* had been found in the vicinity of Matagorda Bay. Through Indian contacts, the French commandant learned that the vessel carried a crew of fourteen. Virtually certain that Andry and his men were victims of foul play, Governor Gálvez urged the minister of the Indies to "turn the merciful heart of our sovereign to the relief of [Andry's] afflicted family." [11]

The fate of Captain Andry, his son, and a dozen others aboard the *Yedra* was not learned until almost a year after the schooner had arrived at Matagorda Bay. Details came from Tomás de la Cruz, who had been freed from Karankawa slavery through the intercession of a missionary. By way of La Bahía, where he was initially interrogated, the young Maya arrived at San Antonio on orders of Governor Cabello. There don Domingo took Cruz's statement and forwarded it to Teodoro de Croix, his superior in Sonora. The commandant general did not reply promptly, and Cabello, concerned that no official word of the tragic events recounted by Cruz had as yet reached Governor Bernardo de Gálvez, sent the Yucatán native and an accompanying letter to New Orleans.[12]

Through the testimony of Cruz, Cabello learned of the last days of *El Señor de la Yedra*'s crew and the incredible duplicity and cruelty of two apostate Karankawa brothers, Joseph María and Mateo, runaways from Mission Rosario. The schooner had arrived at Matagorda Bay in early March 1778, and exploring and mapping of the region had gone smoothly. Unfortunately, the ship was short of provisions, and Cristóbal Gómez assured Captain Andry that he could go ashore with a few men and acquire what was needed from Indians who were familiar to him. Andry consented, and a party of five disappeared into the wilderness in the company of coastal Indians, who soon set upon the unsuspecting Spaniards and murdered them.[13]

As time passed, Andry became increasingly concerned. He fired a swivel gun and raised a flag, hoping the five men would soon respond. Instead, Joseph María and Mateo answered the salvo by appearing on shore. The Karankawas were brought to the schooner by boat, and once on board explained in Spanish that they were intelligence-gathering soldiers from the presidio at La Bahía. Naively, Captain Andry permitted the two apostates to familiarize themselves with the ship and its weaponry. After a brief conversation, Joseph María and Mateo persuaded the captain to let three sailors accompany them back to shore, promising to return with fresh meat. Once out of view, the apostates and their Karankawa confederates fell on the three men and murdered them, too.[14]

When Joseph María and Mateo returned to the *Yedra*, they came bearing meat and explained that the three missing sailors had remained on shore to feast on a recent game kill. As the famished captain and skeleton crew relaxed their guard and sat down to eat, Karankawa reinforcements quietly slipped aboard the vessel. On signal, they seized the sailors' guns and murdered them with their own weapons, sparing only the Maya Indian whom Joseph María claimed as a slave. Afterward, the Karankawas threw the slain Spaniards into the bay, stripped the ship of its six swivel guns, muskets, powder, and balls, and burned the vessel.[15]

Buoyed by their bloody successes, Joseph María and Mateo soon encouraged the Indians of Mission Rosario to take flight and join them in conducting raids along the Río Grande that eventually extended as far as Camargo. However, when the war party was slowed by Joseph María's aged mother, who could not keep pace with the Rosario fugitives, the Karankawa thrust a lance through the unfortunate woman and left her body along a trail! Although initially well armed with weapons stolen from the *Yedra*, the Karankawas' lack of familiarity with Spanish swivel guns and muskets soon rendered the weapons useless. Nonetheless, the successful raids of some sixty warriors, most of whom were Karankawas, presented a serious problem for the new governor of Texas.[16]

Except for extraordinarily bad luck and circumstances beyond his control, Domingo Cabello would never have had to face the problems created by Joseph María and Mateo. By the narrowest of margins, he had missed assignment to a much more prestigious post. En route to San Antonio, don Domingo learned in May 1778 that José Rubio, an assistant to Teodoro de Croix and commandant inspector of presidios for the Interior Provinces, had died suddenly. Croix intended to replace Rubio with Cabello, but the appointment was contingent on De Mézières's willingness to serve as governor of Texas. As noted in an earlier chapter, don Athanase begged off the assignment, primarily because of failing health, and Cabello was stuck with a governorship he had hoped to avoid.[17]

During his final days at San Antonio, Athanase de Mézières had unleashed a torrent of hatred for the "treacherous" Karankawas. He lamented that even Matagorda Bay remained in the hands of the same vile Indians who had butchered the colonists of the great "Don Roberto de la Salle." Don Athanase was especially moved by the disaster that had befallen his fellow Frenchmen, Luis Andry and his young son. With great eloquence, he penned anguished words: "O, sad event! O, deplorable adventure, in which a sad father saw assassinated his beloved son whom he clasped in his pious arms; in which a tender and helpless child saw the paternal breast, to which he was clinging, laid open by dagger thrusts." As for the matricidal Joseph María, De Mézières fumed that he should be given the most severe punishment, "if it is possible to administer it in proportion to his atrocious deeds." [18]

Cabello needed little encouragement to wage a war of extermination against the Karankawas. But plans for such a campaign, which would have combined Texas presidials with Louisiana "boat people," had to be placed on hold. The Comanche problem, worsened by the loss of De Mézières's skilled intercession and diplomacy, momentarily diverted the governor's attention from the Gulf Coast. [19]

In the meantime, however, the arch renegade Joseph María continued his marauding ways, leading raids that penetrated to the outskirts of San Antonio. By late 1782 Cabello viewed the Karankawa problem as intolerable. Unable to deal with it in direct military terms, don Domingo took a page from Barón de Ripperdá, his immediate predecessor in Texas. He employed Nicolás de La Mathe, another French Indian agent and longtime trading partner of Antonio Gil Ibarvo. La Mathe proposed a campaign whereby one hundred hunters and oarsmen in canoes would drive the Karankawas from their island strongholds onto the coast, where soldiers from Béxar and La Bahía would "put them to the sword." For a variety of reasons, however, that plan also languished for the remainder of Cabello's tenure as governor. [20]

Maurading Karankawas were only one of several problems that demanded the governor's attention. Within a few months after his arrival at Béxar, Domingo Cabello faced an administrative problem involving fellow Spaniards who had without authorization abandoned Villa Bucareli, the community founded on the Trinity River in 1774 by Gil Ibarvo and displaced Adaesanos. To the end of his life, Athanase de Mézières had condemned the villa's demise, branded its inhabitants as foolhardy or cowardly, and committed himself to extirpating the new settlement of Nacogdoches. Cabello, however, did not have a similar mind-set.

A practical man, the new governor was appalled by the military weaknesses of his jurisdiction, and he recognized the necessity of seeking where possible the temporary cooperation of Native Americans. For example, on January 20, 1779, a party of four hundred friendly but fully armed Indians appeared at San Antonio. Cabello, by his own admission, had only one gunsmith and two sick soldiers at the Béxar presidio. All other presidials were either on assignment or performing duties elsewhere: ten were on reconnaissance; twenty had escorted Barón de Ripperdá as he left Texas; another twenty manned the new outpost at Santa Cruz del Cíbolo, and twenty-four guarded a distant horse herd numbering 1,232 animals.[21]

On this occasion, Cabello's extensive military experience stood him in good stead. He boldly confronted the Indians and ordered them to leave their arms outside the villa. On this condition, they would be welcomed and treated as guests. Don Domingo's stratagem worked. The Native Americans filed into the square "without a bow or arrow, a gun or rifle, a tomahawk or scalping knife." There they were plied with food, candy, and cigarettes, and they departed Béxar without incident.[22]

This experience convinced Cabello that certain exemptions from royal taxes then accorded frontier settlers ought to be revoked immediately, with the resulting additional revenues earmarked for beefing up military garrisons throughout Texas. The province must be militarized to the point that every Indian be either subjugated or exterminated. In communications with his superior, Teodoro de Croix, Cabello insisted that the notion of a "friendly Indian" was a farce. Not even missionized Indians could be trusted, and the various Nations of the North with whom the Spanish had alliances were not much better than the hated Apaches. In the final analysis, don Domingo argued that goodwill on the part of Indians could be relied on only to the proportional extent of the goods provided them and in accord with their perception of the attendant benefits of amicable relations with Spaniards. Given his military perspective and dim view of all Native Americans, it is little wonder that Cabello felt sympathy for the Adaesanos who pulled stakes at Bucareli after the Comanches had threatened them. Without a single soldier to defend the villa, the residents had to go where they felt the greater degree of security.[23]

Indeed, security figured importantly in the minds of the Adaesanos. By moving to Nacogdoches, they would be living among friendly Tejas and their allies. Contrariwise, at Paso Tomás on the Trinity River, the settlers faced a serious dilemma. In the words of Father José Francisco de la Garza, "these miserable inhabitants are left in such deplorable state that they have no way even to hunt for food . . . for they cannot go out to hunt except in large numbers and well armed, nor yet can they go out together and with their weapons, lest they should leave the settlement helpless." Worse, the settlers panicked over persistent rumors that the dreaded Comanches were forging alliances that would result in razing Bucareli and selling its inhabitants into slavery.[24]

Faced with numerous petitions to relocate, Antonio Gil Ibarvo essentially told the Adaesanos that they could settle where they wished. However, he could not give them official sanction to do so. Don Antonio then took the precautionary measure of informing the viceroy that he had been unable to stop the exodus: "I am giving you notice of the decision taken as well as of the fact that all of the men have left with their families. My people, too, have gone. . . . Today the Reverend Father Garza set out on foot, accompanying the sick. With him I have sent the ornaments and sacred vessels belonging to the church. I beg your lordship to give his approval to this measure, which I have also communicated to the *Commandante General*." [25]

Actually, a few men and their families had remained at Bucareli, primarily to guard property left scattered in the fields by the fleeing Adaesanos. One of the exiles had departed in such haste that he failed to extinguish a fire burning in the hearth. The log cabin caught fire, and flames spread to adjoining structures, destroying more than half of the town's residences. The conflagration was soon followed by a ruinous flood that hit the community on February 14, 1779. Except for thirty-eight head, all of the cattle drowned. To add misery to misfortune, a band of Comanches then attacked the devastated villa and succeeded in driving off all of the surviving livestock.[26]

The majority of the Adaesanos had left Villa Bucareli by January 25, 1779. Father Garza and the sick departed two days later. By Gil Ibarvo's account, the distance between Paso Tomás on the Trinity River and the abandoned mission of Nuestra Señora de Guadalupe de los Nacogdoches could be covered in a two-day trek. However, the exiles' transit to safety amid the Tejas was undoubtedly slowed by consideration for women with small children and the infirm. It seems likely that modern Nacogdoches was occupied by mid-February 1779, but the first formal report from the community is dated April 30.[27]

The question of whether the displaced Adaesanos would be permitted to remain at Nacogdoches or compelled to return to the Trinity site, as recommended by Athanase de Mézières, hung in the balance for the better part of a year. The major policymakers in that decision were Governor Cabello and Commandant General Croix. Don Teodoro, aware of the hardships and sufferings endured by the settlers at Villa Bucareli, left East Texas matters squarely in the hands of don Domingo.[28]

In a lengthy report, dated May 31, 1779, Cabello recapped the determined opposition of Hugo Oconor to the reoccupation of East Texas, as well as the establishment of the hasty and unauthorized community at Paso Tomás on the Trinity. He defended the Bucareli settlement on grounds that Father Garza had scored successes among forty families of Aranama Indians, who had reverted to apostasy, and of the beneficial coastal expeditions carried out by Gil Ibarvo, which had discouraged incursions by foreigners. But don Domingo also recounted the many travails of the Adaesanos at Villa Bucareli.[29]

The new location at the abandoned site of Mission Guadalupe de los Nacogdoches was admittedly farther from San Antonio and the coast, but it had advantages that offset those adverse considerations. The settlers were living among the friendly Indians of East Texas, they could still carry out reconnaissance of the coast, and they enjoyed a healthier climate at Nacogdoches. Unfortunately, the new town was inadequately defended.[30]

In part because of the death of De Mézières, with the attendant loss of his diplomatic skills, and partially because nontreaty Indians resented their exclusion from Spanish gift giving, Cabello observed that growing Indian discontent called for the placement of a garrison at Nacogdoches. His proposal suggested a command that included an officer, a sergeant, two corporals, and twenty soldiers. The governor's request received serious consideration, but no garrison was authorized at that time.[31]

Commandant General Croix referred the question of Nacogdoches's continuation to Pedro Galindo Navarro, a trusted adviser. Acknowledging that in accord with the New Regulations of 1772 the forced return of the East Texas settlers to San Antonio had not proved viable, don Pedro recommended an inspection of the Bucareli and Nacogdoches sites by the governor of Texas. Then a final decision would be made, based on the inspector's report.[32]

Croix accepted Galindo Navarro's recommendation. However, when Cabello received orders to conduct the inspections, he was recovering from a dislocated arm caused by a fall from a horse. Postponing the journey because of his injury and depleted personal finances, the governor suggested that Croix send a trained engineer and cartographer to accompany the expedition. The commandant general replied that he could neither spare an engineer nor provide financial assistance. As it turned out, Cabello continued to delay the inspection tour, because he had already concluded that Nacogdoches was the better site.[33]

As noted earlier, Antonio Gil Ibarvo received official appointment as captain of militia and lieutenant governor of Nacogdoches in October 1779, and in the following month Athanase de Mézières died at San Antonio. Those unrelated events not only ended all serious consideration of eliminating Nacogdoches but also permitted Domingo Cabello to turn his attention to other matters.[34]

On July 21, 1779, while the fate of Nacogdoches and its settlers occupied officials in Texas, Chihuahua, and Mexico City, Spain joined the war for American independence as an ally of France. Entry into the war meant that Spanish resources would increasingly be funneled into attacks on British settlements in the lower Mississippi Valley and defense of the Gulf Coast, rather than into the Interior Provinces. Significantly, the military campaign against the Apaches, recommended by the three councils of war in 1778–1779, could not be implemented. For Domingo Cabello, Spain's new priorities and limited finances meant that he could not pursue an aggressive Indian policy in Texas. Thus, despite the passionate urging of Athanase de Mézières and the atrocities of Joseph María and his gang of apostates, the Karankawas also went unpunished.[35]

Even worse, in late summer 1779, Governor Juan Bautista de Anza of New Mexico, in alliance with Utes and Jicarilla Apaches, delivered a crushing blow to the Western Comanches. Ironically, Anza's victory persuaded the Comanches, in the words of Teodoro de Croix, to concentrate their activities on "the province of Texas where they find less resistance, greater helplessness, and cowardice in some settlers who become accustomed to living in the bosom of peace." By August 1780, Cabello reported that his jurisdiction was beset by Comanche attacks. He informed the commandant general that the bold plainsmen had stolen so many horses and mules from the Béxar presidio that he could not mount retaliatory campaigns. The governor likewise complained that he felt powerless to deal with renewed hostilities on the part of the Lipan Apaches, who were also taking advantage of Spanish weakness.[36]

Recognizing the seriousness of the situation in Texas, Croix remarked to the viceroy that the reports of Cabello on the "incessant attacks of the Comanche[s] [are] so horrible and bloody that, if they continue with the same steadfastness, the desolation of the province will be constant, irremediable, and immediate." In communications with Cabello, however, the commandant general could offer little but sympathy and advice. He recommended that both Apaches and Comanches be shown the benefits of peace by bestowing presents on them and by overlooking their depredations. For a hard-nosed military man like Cabello, peace by purchase must have been especially galling.[37]

Peace by persuasion, although far less than satisfactory to Domingo Cabello, eventually worked, but it was initially a failure. And it took four years of intermittent fighting between Spaniards and Comanches, punctuated by sporadic diplomacy, to bring about a treaty that was acceptable to both parties. For most of the remainder of his tenure as governor of Texas, don Domingo concentrated on the "Comanche problem."

Throughout 1781 Comanche raids on Spanish settlements in Texas continued. In the last month of the year, Governor Cabello received intelligence of a Comanche village on the Medina River northwest of San Antonio. He sent a small detachment of soldiers to attack the *ranchería*, believed to contain about eighty men, women, and children. A firefight ensued, resulting in the death of eighteen Comanche warriors, including their chief, "who wore a horned headdress and a scalp-ornamented shirt." The abandoned camp contained clothing and jewelry that were identified as belonging to settlers in the vicinity of Béxar.[38]

Fearing retaliation, Bexareños remained vigilant over the next several months. Although there were signs of nearby Comanches, such as smoke signals and tracks, there are no recorded contacts between Spaniards and these plainsmen for about fifteen months. The hiatus can perhaps be explained by an epidemic of smallpox known to have afflicted Comanche tribes at this time.[39]

The quiet of 1782 was broken in the spring of the following year. Governor Cabello learned that a sizable Comanche encampment had been spotted on the Guadalupe River. He raised an armed party and ordered an attack on the *ranchería*. Forewarned by their scouts, the Comanches fled, leaving behind the frames of forty tipis. Fearing revenge, don Domingo again placed the Béxar community on alert, and again there were ominous signs of Comanche presence but no direct contact with them.[40]

Another fifteen months passed without incident, but in the early summer of 1784, violence again erupted between Spaniards and Comanches. In pursuit of a Wichita raiding party, a company of presidials came upon forty mounted Comanches on the Guadalupe River, and a clash of arms occurred. When the smoke of an eight-hour battle cleared, ten Comanches lay dead and an equal number had been made captive. Cabello, worried that retaliation might descend on Bexareños, ordered increased vigilance, but, just as before, there were no clashes with the plainsmen.[41]

Handicapped by Spain's participation in the American Revolution and bound by Croix's orders to overlook the natives' depredations, don Domingo had begun sending emissaries among the Comanches and Norteños as early as 1780. Those efforts, however, had enjoyed little success until the late summer of 1784. But from that juncture onward, events moved rapidly toward peaceful accommodation with the Comanches.

The first of Cabello's agents to achieve success was Juan Bautista Bousquet, a trader from Louisiana. Sent among the Wichitas, Taovayas, and Tawakonis, Bousquet carried news that the Spaniards desired peace with them. His persuasiveness delivered four Wichita and Taovaya chiefs before Governor Cabello at San Antonio, where don Domingo bestowed modest gifts on all of them and a medal on one of the Taovaya chiefs. Also accompanying Bousquet were three non-Indians who had established successful enterprises among the Norteños.[42]

The most important of the trio was French-born Pedro Vial, destined later on to serve as pathfinder between San Antonio and Santa Fe. Vial spoke halting Spanish and knew little about the Comanches, yet he was soon to become the most successful intermediary with these plainsmen. Under orders of Domingo Cabello and laden with gifts, Vial and a companion, Francisco Xavier Chávez, headed back north in the spring of 1785. Their experiences resulted in an extraordinary document on the Comanches.[43]

Guided by Guersec, newly appointed medal chief of the Taovayas, Vial and Chávez were led to an enormous Comanche *ranchería*. This impressive settlement, containing a large meeting tent of tanned buffalo hides and more than two hundred warriors, was but a hint of what was about to transpire. Asked to remain encamped until two principal chiefs could be summoned, the Spaniards launched themselves into a week-long crash course on Comanche culture. At the conclusion of their sojourn, two high chiefs, whom Vial dubbed Captain Iron Shirt (*capitán de camisa de hierro*) and Captain Shaved Head (*capitán de cabeza rapada*), rode into the *ranchería* in the company of about a dozen "little captains."[44]

Vial drew on his recently acquired knowledge of Comanche customs to reward each chief with presents of tobacco, knives, vermilion, and other items in strict proportion to his rank. Impressed, the high Comanches then led Vial and Chávez to an encounter where the Spaniards stood at the center of a circle ringed by "an infinity of young men, women, and children." Vial addressed the throng in the Taovaya language, which the Comanches understood. He reminded his audience that he and his companion were not strangers to them. Years ago Chávez had been taken captive by the Comanches and sold to the Taovayas. After the death of his Indian masters, the Spaniard had only recently passed to San Antonio to be with his own people. Vial, on the other hand, had visited Comanche *rancherías* as a longtime trader.[45]

In his harangue, Vial reminded the Comanches that he and Chávez were good and honest people who had dealt fairly with them. While living among Indians, the two Spaniards had first learned of the "*capitán grande de San Antonio*" (Cabello), who was a valiant and just man. On their recent visit to Béxar, Chávez and Vial had met the great captain and learned that he had assembled an array of presents to bestow on the chiefs of friendly nations and their people. Contrariwise, the Spanish captain had also assembled many soldiers, horses, muskets, powder, and ball in order to launch an "incessant war" on the Comanches.[46]

At that juncture, Vial became melodramatic. He recalled that tears had welled in his eyes and in those of Chávez as they thought about the injustice of Spaniards' making war on Indians who had treated the two of them so kindly, as well as the tragic circumstances of Comanches and Taovayas' not being among those Native Americans who would receive "*regalos*" (presents). The Spanish emissary reminded the Comanches of the "many times [that] you do not have a knife to cut meat, a pot with which to cook in, nor a grain of powder with which to kill deer and buffalo for your sustenance."[47]

Overcome with remorse for their Native American friends, the two Spaniards had begged the "*capitán grande*" to include Comanches and Taovayas in his gift giving. At first, their efforts were to no avail, for the Spanish governor became angry. He recounted the many times that Comanche warriors had killed unarmed and hungry Spaniards who were merely foraging for food on the plains. Anyone who would commit such base murder, insisted Capitán Cabello, was "without a good heart, without valor." However, the persistent and earnest entreaties of Vial and Chávez had gradually softened the governor's stance toward their Indian friends. Finally, they had persuaded the great captain to think of the Comanches as "good people, very generous, and very friendly to their friends." Still somewhat wary, Cabello had asked, "Is this certain?" Both men were quick to reply that their words were "extremely true."[48]

Convinced, the great captain had authorized Vial and Chávez to carry his own words among the Comanches: "If they want to be my friends, and friends of the Spaniards, I will promise not to kill them, and to stop sending my soldiers, those who make war on them. And if they want to come to San Antonio to talk to me, I will give them my hand in advance, like friends, as also they would be to the other nations who are my friends, except the Lipans and Apaches, with whom I do not want anyone to be friends, but to make continual war against them." If they would do that, then Cabello "would forget the many deaths which they had caused among my people, as they must forget those which my people did to them." To formalize a pact, the Comanches must send two or three chiefs to San Antonio in the company of the Spaniards.[49]

When Vial finished his speech, he and Chávez retired to a tent. Guersec, the Taovaya medal chief, then asserted that everything the Spaniards had said about the great captain in San Antonio was true. Throughout the rest of the day and continuing into the night, the Comanches parleyed with much noise and excitement—so loud that the two Spaniards could not sleep—and the natives intently watched for certain "signs" that would speak to the truthfulness of what they had heard about the *capitán grande*: there had been no wind, no cloud had cast a shadow across the sun, and the smoke from their pipe had not twisted. All were favorable omens. On the following day, the Comanches vowed to "forget the deaths of our fathers, sons, and brothers caused by the Spaniards . . . and from now on the war with our brothers the Spaniards is finished, we will not kill, nor make any raids, nor rob. And there will be three little captains from our nation named to go with you to hear what the Capit[á]n Grande says about the mode of establishing the peace." [50]

In October 1785 the small delegation of "little captains," after first dismounting and embracing an astonished Cabello "with the most peculiar demonstrations one can imagine," signed an accord at Béxar with the "big captain" (Figure 19). It was a remarkable treaty, for the most part adhered to by Spaniards and Comanches for the remainder of Texas' days as a Spanish province: Both parties would cease hostilities and henceforth meet as brothers; the agreement extended beyond Texas to include all subjects of the Spanish monarch; the Comanches would not admit any foreigners to their *rancherías*, for Spaniards would provide goods in exchange for their hides; the friends and enemies of one party were the friends and enemies of the other; the Lipan Apaches were the declared enemies of both signatories; the Comanches would seek permission of the governor of Texas before passing through the province to make war on the Apaches in Coahuila; and Spaniards would provide annual gifts to the Comanches' chiefs and smaller captains as a gesture of their continuing goodwill. [51]

The October 1785 accord with the Comanches was a tremendous accomplishment for Governor Domingo Cabello, and there is little doubt that he believed it to be the apogee of his service in Texas. Springing from the treaty was a quiet that settled over Béxar for more than three decades. Year in and year out, Spaniards through their trading posts supplied the Comanches with "staffs of command, medals, flags, daggers, clasp knives, razors, scissors, iron kettles, mirrors, combs, glass beads, bells, tobacco, shoes, frock coats, stockings, and cloth of various kinds"—much of this in exchange for peltry. In time, relations improved to the extent that items of European manufacture even came to include

──────────────── FIGURE 19 ────────────────

*Sketch of Colonel Domingo Cabello. Governor Cabello greets the Comanche
chiefs brought to San Antonio in 1785 by peace emissary Pedro Vial.
(Commissioned original artwork by Jack Jackson.)*

guns, shot, powder, and flint. Peace by purchase, diplomacy, and trade between former enemies undoubtedly saved lives and property, and gift giving in the long run was far less expensive than military campaigns. Like most enduring treaties, this one lasted because it worked to the benefit of both parties.[52]

Less dramatic were Domingo Cabello's determined efforts to alienate the Lipan Apaches from the Hasinais and Kadohadachos of East Texas, accomplishments that coincided chronologically with his successful overtures to the Comanches. With the death of De Mézières in November 1779, concern mounted that a possible alliance of Caddos, Bidais, Tonkawas, and Lipans would come to fruition. Cabello, who had narrowly averted a meeting of Hainais and Lipans in 1779, faced a new crisis in August of the following year.[53]

In late summer of 1780, a small Hainai delegation that had come to San Antonio to parley with the governor was persuaded to accompany don Domingo on a journey to Presidio La Bahía. While at the garrison on the lower San Antonio River and under strict orders to accommodate all Native Americans, Cabello was confronted by a large group of Apaches who wished to speak directly with his Hainai guests. Cabello refused and kept the Lipans outside the presidio compound. But his ruse backfired when the Apaches "shouted over the walls that they would give the Hainais horses, guns, and even women in exchange for an alliance." [54]

For the moment, Cabello headed off an impending accord by supplying the Hainais with gifts, including horses, but in late 1782 the Apaches, secured a trade alliance with the tribes of East Texas, including the Hasinais, that lasted for four years. Don Domingo, however, was not one to give up easily. When the American Revolutionary War ended in 1783, thereby concluding Spain's role as a combatant against Great Britain, don Domingo was free to pursue a more aggressive policy in Texas. In the summer of 1784, with at least the tacit concurrence of Governor Cabello, Spaniards evidently arranged the assassination of El Mocho, the pro-Lipan high Tonkawa chief, when he was an invited guest at La Bahía. In his report of the incident, Cabello stated that the death of El Mocho "has been accomplished," and "with this good fortune we shall free ourselves from the evils of this traitor." Having robbed the natives of their powerful leader, Spaniards succeeded in turning the Tonkawas against the Lipans by 1786, leaving only the Hasinais and Kadohadachos as friends of the Apaches. But the East Texas natives rather quickly succumbed to Cabello's Machiavellian negotiations.[55]

Once he had secured an alliance with the powerful Comanches in

1785, Cabello turned up the heat on the two Caddo confederations. First, recognizing that their "forces are so few," don Domingo cut off gift giving to them; then he reminded them that their close friends and co-linguists, the Wichitas, had close ties with the Comanches, who had become recent allies of the Spaniards; and, finally, he threatened to inform the Comanches that for four years the Hasinais and Kadohadachos had aided and abetted their despised enemies—the Lipan Apaches.[56] By a combination of murder and Realpolitik, Cabello had succeeded in isolating the Lipans, and that objective, articulated at the three war councils held by Croix in Monclova, San Antonio, and Chihuahua, had been accomplished.

Because relations among Spaniards, Hasinais, Comanches, and the Norteños were much improved after late 1785, Domingo Cabello again called upon Pedro Vial—this time as pathfinder between San Antonio and Santa Fe. Travel between the two provincial capitals had traditionally been long, dangerous, and circuitous. From Santa Fe one had to detour southward along the Río Grande by way of El Paso to reach Nueva Vizcaya. From there travelers journeyed eastward to San Juan Bautista before turning northward to San Antonio.[57]

Vial's passage over the first, more direct overland trail between the ill-defined provinces of Texas and New Mexico began almost one year after treaty-signing ceremonies were concluded at Béxar. Commissioned by Cabello near the end of his Texas governorship, the French-born Indian agent left San Antonio on October 4, 1786, in the company of a single companion, Cristóbal de los Santos.[58]

Vial appears to have become sick and disoriented during early stages of the trek. In any event, his path was hardly on a direct line with Santa Fe. He and Santos traveled by way of Tawakoni villages near present Waco and then continued on to the Red River. From there, the two men turned westward and eventually reached Santa Fe on May 26, 1787. By then Domingo Cabello was no longer governor of Texas.[59]

In early January 1787, Domingo Cabello departed San Antonio for the last time. It must have been a joyous occasion—one that he had yearned for throughout his eight-year term as governor of Texas. Indeed, even in his first year on the job, he had complained bitterly about the mean circumstance that was life on the Texas frontier. Writing to Commandant General Teodoro de Croix in June 1779, Cabello described his quarters as a "pigsty." Referring to an impending visit by Athanase de Mézières, he protested that he could not house an official of don Athanase's rank "in such a miserable place." Warming to the art of complaining, he whined "that, on account of my coming here, a cook who [sic] I had in my service for fourteen years preferred to stay in Mexico." As a consequence, his daily fare was nothing "but tortillas and jerked beef." [60]

In this same missive, Domingo Cabello complained of a nearly empty supply room and the growing number of Indians who came to Béxar. Specifically, he lacked "the merchandise with which my predecessor used to flatter them." Taking a mean-spirited swipe at Barón de Ripperdá, whom he replaced as chief executive, don Domingo accused him of having "much left over from his former businesses" so that he could afford large expenditures on merchandise. [61]

Writing to Commandant General Croix in October 1779, Governor Cabello had also expressed irritation over having to provide accommodations for Indians traveling in the retinue of De Mézières: "Considering what an unhappy place this presidio is, it cost me drops of blood to procure these arrangements." He reported that one head of cattle each day had to be provided for their fare. The animal's meat, garnished with squash and tender ears of corn, was boiled in two large pots that don Domingo had to rent, since the governor's quarters did not have such cookware. Worse, in the words of Cabello, the Native Americans kept him from performing his duties as governor "for they wish to spend all day talking with me . . . and I must attend to their requests and a thousand other kinds of [inconveniences] which the mind of these peoples devises." [62]

In Cabello's view, the quality of life at San Antonio did not improve over the years. For example, he complained about the incessant barking and howling of dogs at night, which disturbed his sleep and caused him to observe sarcastically that "there is no reason for making serenades." To quiet the cacophony, don Domingo ordered that stray canines be shot, and he imposed fines on those who would not restrain their animals at night. He also fulminated against Béxar's street gangs (*bandadas*)— youths not under the proper control of their parents who went about "giving cries and disturbing the tranquility at all hours of the day and night." [63]

On other occasions, Cabello objected to the raucous dances (*fandangos*) and insolent songs that served as frontier amusements. Such activities, in the governor's view, contributed to moral degeneracy and affairs that were "grave offenses to God." More serious, when fueled by alcohol, hurled expletives and insults between Latino males often provoked bloodletting or bodily injury. Calling someone a "bastard" (*cabrón*) or a "snot-nosed dog" (*perro mocoso*) was almost certain to cause trouble for don Domingo in his capacity as chief magistrate of the villa. [64]

Disaffected with his appointment as governor of Texas, Cabello never ceased his determined efforts to acquire a better assignment. In May 1779 he accepted appointment as interim governor of Coahuila, but obligations in Texas kept him from assuming that post; in April 1785 he received appointment as interim governor of Nueva Vizcaya and begged to be immediately relieved of his duties at Béxar, but reassignment was again delayed until a new governor could be chosen for Texas. Finally, in December 1785 Cabello fared better. He received a prestigious appointment as lieutenant to the king and subinspector of troops in Cuba, where his military career had initially blossomed. But even then, don Domingo had to wait a year before he could transfer the office of governor to his successor, Rafael Martínez Pacheco.[65]

Martínez Pacheco, the new chief executive of Texas, was an old hand on the Texas scene, and a controversial one as well. In 1764, as commander of Presidio del Orcoquisac on the lower Trinity River, don Rafael had clashed with Texas governor Angel de Martos. As garrison commander, Martínez Pacheco was repeatedly charged with abusive conduct, actions that had caused most of his presidials to desert. To correct the situation, Martos sent Lieutenant Marcos Ruiz to forcibly remove Martínez Pacheco from command, but the officer and two servants barricaded themselves within the walls of El Orcoquisac. In the confrontation, Martínez Pacheco fired a cannon, killing a corporal, and he wounded two of Ruiz's soldiers in a firefight. The lieutenant finally drove the presidial captain from his stronghold by burning the garrison to the ground! Martínez Pacheco, however, escaped the inferno through an underground passage and later stood trial in Mexico City, where he was exonerated. Ironically, a military officer with such a checkered record was enthusiastically accepted as Domingo Cabello's replacement at Béxar. This strange circumstance relates in part to don Domingo's handling of livestock exported from Texas, and it arguably constitutes the most controversial aspect of his governorship.[66]

While visiting San Antonio in early 1778, Commandant General Teodoro de Croix had noted the large number of unbranded cattle that grazed the surrounding prairies. On January 11 don Teodoro posted a decree that gave the owners of livestock precisely four months to corral and brand their animals (Figure 20). After May 12 all unmarked livestock, as well as the semi-feral offspring of branded animals, would automatically become crown property. Cattlemen must design different brands and register them with the governor, who was then Barón de Ripperdá. Rustlers, according to the Croix decree, were to be punished in accord with the damage caused by their actions. And, finally, all settlers, irrespective of their position and rank, were subject to all provisions and penalties.[67]

Because the unpopular decree required the approval of the king before it became permanently operative, it raised a continuing storm of protest among civilians and missionaries alike. Through petitions and letters, they decried to the king in far-off Spain the unfairness of Croix's mandates, but in the interim the commandant general's edicts went into effect in late spring 1778.[68]

Implementation of don Teodoro's pronouncements coincided almost exactly with the governorship of Domingo Cabello, for royal revocation of Croix's initial order and all subsequent modifications of it did not reach Texas until early 1786. And during that interval, don Domingo's actions stirred up a hornet's nest of hatred among Texas stockmen.[69]

In July 1779, as mentioned earlier, Spain joined the war for American independence as an ally of France, which had entered the conflict in the previous year. Accordingly, Spanish possessions in Louisiana were especially vulnerable to English attacks. Trade between Louisiana and the Commandancy General of the Interior Provinces was expressly forbidden by royal decree, but out of expediency Teodoro de Croix deliberately bent the law. He justified illegal commerce on the grounds that the Gulf of Mexico was likely to become a war theater and because Governor Bernardo de Gálvez of Louisiana needed beef. This new market provided incentives for Texas cattle drives through the piney woods of East Texas, and it opened Domingo Cabello to charges of profiteering under the pretext of defending imperial interests.[70]

Initially, Gálvez dispatched Francisco García to Texas with a commission to buy fifteen hundred to two thousand head of cattle. Commandant General Croix ordered Cabello not only to supply the beeves but also to provide a military escort for the drovers who trailed the livestock eastward. Thus began a series of organized cattle drives, the first in Texas history. Cabello, however, by implementing Croix's unpopular decree of January 1778, was later charged with outright theft and moral laxity.[71]

After he left Texas in January 1779, and it was safe to "lay bare the former governor's black heart," a litany of complaints descended upon Cabello. His refusal to take communion and confess once a year set a bad precedent; his unexplained failure to attend Mass and his shocking use of profanity appalled the citizenry; his insistence that God did not have the power to alter things—by pointing out that accidents had happened to him—served to undermine the faith; his sexual insinuations toward Bexareñas created endless gossip; and so it went.[72]

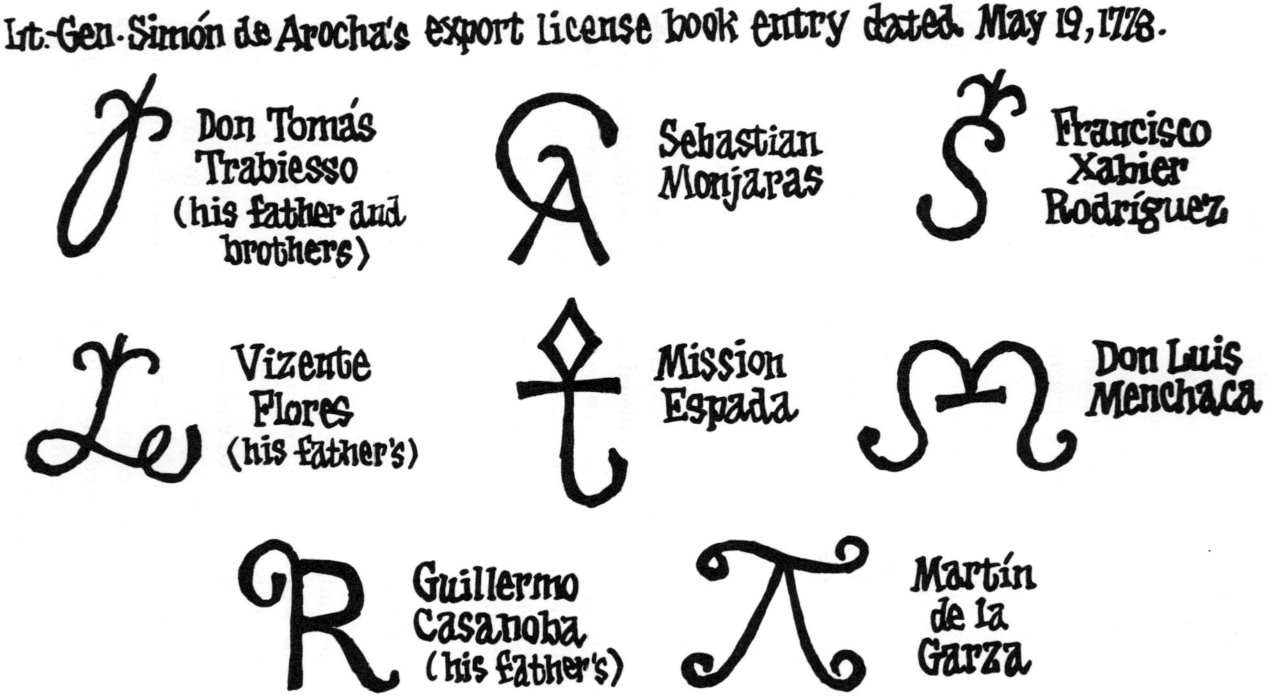

Lt.-Gen. Simón de Arocha's export license book entry dated May 19, 1778.

Don Tomás
Trabiesso
(his father and
brothers)

Sebastián
Monjaras

Francisco
Xavier
Rodriguez

Vizente
Flore
(his father's)

Mission
Espada

Don Luis
Menchaca

Guillermo
Casanoba
(his father's)

Martín
de la
Garza

FIGURE 20

Cattle brands used in Spanish Texas. These brands were in use during the governorship of
Domingo Cabello, 1778–1786. (Artwork by Jack Jackson.)

But the greatest controversy stirred by don Domingo was his alleged profiteering at the expense of the king and the blatant defrauding of civilian and missionary stockmen. Specifically, it was charged that Cabello's accounting of cattle exports from Texas to Louisiana was both erroneous and incomplete. For example, some herds contained far more livestock than recorded, with the clear implication that the governor had pocketed the difference. In other instances, entire herds were missing from the ledger books. When faced with a shortage of animals for export, Cabello routinely rounded up privately owned cattle, even those bearing brands, and declared them royal property.[73]

In the latter category, ranchers insisted that they had been defrauded of 10,901 head of cattle, amounting to 27,254 pesos. Additional "unrecorded sales" brought Cabello's indebtedness to a total of 32,508 pesos. Since he had deposited only 13,096 pesos in the royal treasure chest, don Domingo additionally owed more than 19,000 pesos. To this sum stockmen added the cost of litigation against their corrupt governor, bringing the grand total to 34,468 pesos. On a lesser scale, without paying the owner a fair price, Cabello had seized two pet buffaloes raised from calves by Juan Andrés Travieso and sent the animals to Spain to please his monarch, Charles III. Worse, instead of defending the ranchers' herds from various thieves who preyed upon them, don Domingo had ordered his soldiers to shoot the stockmen's dogs if they wandered into San Antonio. Being charged as a *mataperros* (killer of dogs), meant, as historian Jack Jackson has noted, that in the minds of Texas ranchers Cabello had sunk to about the lowest level of humanity.[74]

But there was more. When Commandant General Croix had visited San Antonio in early 1778, he badly needed additional sources of revenue to finance a war against the Lipans and provide gifts for the Comanches and Norteños, whom he wished to recruit as allies. Again, it did not take Croix long to observe that a potentially rich source of new funds lay in Texas's thousands of head of *mesteños* (feral and semi-wild livestock). These animals, according to don Teodoro, had no known owner; they were born and raised on untitled lands; therefore, they belonged to the king.[75]

In the past, unclaimed cattle and horses had been killed with impunity by Indians or vagabonds. Oftentimes only the choicest parts of cattle were harvested, while the rest of the carcass became fare for coyotes and buzzards. Henceforth, decreed Croix, no one in the entire province could round up or kill these animals. Fines for initial offenses, plus increased fines and hard labor for subsequent misdeeds, were also set forth by the commandant general. However, since roundups on mission and private lands were a regular part of working range stock, feral and semi-wild horses and cattle sometimes wound up among legitimately claimed animals. Such rodeos in the future must be licensed and attended by a commissioner who would assess six reales for each horse and four reales for each cow.[76]

In this manner, the Fondo de Mesteñas (Mustang Fund) was created, and alleged improprieties in the handling of such monies became still another charge leveled at Domingo Cabello—one that would dog him for more than a decade. Typical of Spanish security in colonial times, royal funds were stored in an *arca de tres llaves* (chest with three keys) that could be opened only when three officials were present with keys in hand. Despite attempts to ensure "honesty by committee," persons with access to the Mustang Fund, which was also collected at Nacogdoches and La Bahía but kept at Béxar, were almost always charged with malfeasance, with most of the complaints coming from those taxed.[77]

Initially, Croix's creation of the Mustang Fund did produce some new revenue that helped finance efforts to pacify Indians or purchase gifts for them, but in the long run it turned into such a headache that it hardly justified the revenues collected. It did solve the question of who owned *mesteño* stock, but the rate of taxation varied over time, and stockmen in the 1780s and 1790s reacted about as favorably to new taxes as Texas ranchers in the 1980s and 1990s.

As Domingo Cabello left for a coveted and well-deserved reassignment in Cuba, he did not, as implied, leave behind his Texas troubles. Protests against him from the cabildo of San Fernando de Béxar plagued him year after year until he was finally exonerated in 1797. In the mid-1790s from Havana, where the British had made him a prisoner of war in 1762, he lashed out at his accusers in San Antonio, labeling their charges "absurd, unfounded, and unjust." Don Domingo consistently maintained that Rafael Martínez Pacheco, his successor as governor of Texas, refused to release papers that were crucial to his defense. On February 16, 1797, resulting from a decision of the royal *fiscal* in Mexico City, Cabello was declared "free and absolved of the unjust charges" relating to his mismanagement of the Mustang Fund. That decision was acknowledged at Béxar in the following month.[78]

The last years of Domingo Cabello y Robles remain unknown to us. Perhaps he died in Cuba, or perhaps he returned to Spain to die there, as did so many Spanish administrators sent to the Americas. He was certainly an energetic and effective governor of Texas. Despite his lack of enthusiasm for his post at Béxar, he nonetheless performed well in most regards. Like Cabello himself, we view the peaceful accord with the Comanches in 1785 as his most notable accomplishment. Given the penury associated with his office as governor of Texas, and his complaining remarks about life at San Antonio, he may well have skimmed funds from the cattle export business. On the other hand, repeated and lengthy inquiries into Cabello's management of the Mustang Fund did not find him culpable.

It should also be noted that Domingo Cabello's contemporary administrators and superiors were extremely generous in their praise of him. Commandant General Teodoro de Croix, commenting at the beginning of don Domingo's governorship, wrote: "The notice that you have taken possession of that government has given me particular pleasure because of your zeal, devotion to duty, your self-effacing, talented ability to produce results, and your prudent manner assure me of the happiness of the province that you command." [79]

Athanase de Mézières, having declined to replace Cabello in Texas, spoke of the diligence with which the incumbent governor served and lauded him as "an officer in whom are united the qualities most adaptable to the critical circumstances of this government." This was high praise from a Frenchman not accustomed to showering compliments on anyone. [80]

Finally, José de Gálvez, who as minister of the Indies held a post second only to that of the king in matters relating to Spain in America, wrote in 1783 that he had reviewed reports from Texas for the last six months of 1779. The minister concluded that he had derived "much satisfaction from the good state of arrangements and government in which these things find themselves [under Governor Domingo Cabello]." [81]

ELEVEN

JOSÉ BERNARDO GUTIÉRREZ DE LARA / JOAQUÍN DE ARREDONDO

Ill-Fated Insurgent / Vengeful Royalist

August 18, 1813, like all too many days in Texas summers, dawned with the promise of unrelenting heat. By early afternoon, with temperatures soaring, two opposing armies, the republican forces of the Gutiérrez-Magee expedition and a Spanish royalist army under Commandant General Joaquín de Arredondo, had maneuvered themselves into a battle that would become the bloodiest in Texas history. The self-styled Republican Army of the North, made up of Anglo-American volunteers, Tejano settlers, Indian allies, and former royalists, numbered about 1,400 men. Arredondo's forces contained 1,830 soldiers and officers, one of whom was a then obscure lieutenant named Antonio López de Santa Anna, who would receive a commendation for conducting himself "with great bravery." [1]

On the day before the battle, republican forces under General José Alvarez de Toledo had camped south of the Medina River at the edge of a sandy oak forest, some twenty miles from San Antonio. Toledo planned to ambush Arredondo's forces as they marched through a defile on the road from Laredo, but one of his junior officers, Miguel Menchaca, committed a strategic error on the following morning, August 18. Ignoring his commander's orders, Menchaca followed the tracks of royalist scouts and a large cavalry unit into the dense oak forest where General Arredondo had thrown up hastily constructed breastworks. Trudging through loose sand that at times mired cannon "half-wheel deep" and suffering from thirst and heat throughout most of the morning, the republican army advanced to within forty paces of Arredondo's defenses before it faced withering artillery fire, followed by a fusillade of musket balls and a cavalry charge. The republicans kept their ranks and fought bravely for three and a half hours, and then the survivors broke and ran—making themselves easy targets for royalist swords and lances. An estimated 1,300 republicans were either killed at the battle of the Medina River or executed later as prisoners of war. Commandant General Arredondo had lost only fifty-five men. San Antonio, twenty-five miles north, stood undefended and would soon experience the "tender mercies" of Joaquín "the Butcher" Arredondo.[2]

Following the governorship of Domingo Cabello y Robles (1778–1786), Spanish Texas had faced a disastrous void in leadership under two ineffectual governors, a bewildering litany of changes in the Commandancy General of the Interior Provinces, a fatal decline of missions, and a brand-new United States of America as its increasingly aggressive neighbor.

As mentioned in the previous chapter, Rafael Martínez Pacheco succeeded Domingo Cabello, much to the delight of Texas ranchers. The new governor, however, has been described by one scholar as an "impulsive and erratic individual, whose past behavior suggested mental problems." Historian Elizabeth A. H. John is in agreement, insisting that don Rafael "had gone berserk" while serving as commander of Presidio El Orcoquisac on the lower Trinity River. That Martínez was allowed to return to Texas in any capacity, in John's view, "underlines the appalling shortage of leadership material in the Comandancia General as the century waned." But things got worse instead of better. Manuel Muñoz, who governed Texas from 1790 to 1799, has been described as "old, ill, and almost criminally ineffectual."[3]

Governor Muñoz was followed by the more enlightened Juan Bautista Elguézabal, but he died in office at San Antonio in 1805. Antonio Cordero y Bustamante, Elguézabal's successor, was an extremely able military man but had to divide his energies between his duties as acting governor of both Texas and Coahuila. Not until 1808 did Texas receive a talented and courageous resident governor in the person of Manuel María de Salcedo, who remains Texas's youngest chief executive.[4]

The last year of Domingo Cabello's governorship also coincided with the start of rapid changes in the Commandancy General of the Interior Provinces. In 1786 the viceroy of New Spain regained control over the northern provinces, whereupon the single administrative unit that had prevailed in the days of Teodoro de Croix was carved into three military regions. Texas logically fell into the eastern unit, along with Coahuila, Nuevo León, and Nuevo Santander. But that arrangement lasted for only one year before the three divisions were consolidated into eastern and western provinces. In 1792 King Charles IV of Spain combined the two regions into one and removed them from the control of the viceroy. Twelve years later, in 1804, Charles reversed his position and again ordered the division of the Commandancy General into eastern and western provinces, but the ambitions of Napoleon Bonaparte in Spain delayed implementation of the king's decision until 1813. In June of that year, the eastern provinces fell under the heavy hand of Joaquín de Arredondo and remained there until Texas joined the Mexican nation in 1821.[5]

The slow decline and eventual secularization of the San Antonio missions in the 1790s is too familiar to repeat here. But San Antonio de Valero had been completely secularized by 1793, and at the same time the remaining four missions at Béxar had become moribund. This phenomenon has been called the Passing of the Missions, and it signaled with certainty that henceforth Spain would rely almost exclusively on treaties and military solutions as its approach to the "Indian problem" in Texas.[6]

The 1790s also witnessed the first serious penetration of Anglo Americans into Texas. That phenomenon is best exemplified by the exploits of Irish-born Philip Nolan and his Anglo-American followers, dating from 1791 to 1801. As it turned out, Nolan's fourth expedition proved fatal to its leader. On March 21, 1801, quite likely near present-day Blum in Central Texas, Philip Nolan died when attacked by royalist forces and struck in the head by a cannonball.[7]

Between the death of Philip Nolan and the independence of Mexico in 1821, the events played out in Spanish Texas over the next two decades became an important thread woven into the fabric of Mexican, Spanish, and United States history. Related to those developments, although not immediately, were the lives of José Bernardo Gutiérrez de Lara and Joaquín de Arredondo.

Following the French and Indian War (1754–1763), when Spain acquired the Louisiana Territory from France, Texas had been transformed from a frontier to an interior province. But that circumstance changed in 1800 when Louisiana again passed under French control, and it was altered substantially in 1803 when the United States purchased the territory. The eastern and northern borders of Spanish Texas then adjoined a nation that had doubled in size in just fourteen years. However, it was not U.S. expansion or subversion that would end three hundred years of Spanish claims to Texas. The real problem, although few could discern it in 1803, lay in Spain and in the heartland of New Spain itself.[8]

In 1808 Napoleon Bonaparte forced Charles IV to renounce the Spanish throne, while at the same time capturing his son and heir, Ferdinand VII. Charles retired to the Italian peninsula; Ferdinand spent the next six years under house arrest at the country estate of Charles Maurice de Talleyrand. By imperial decree, Napoleon's brother, Joseph Bonaparte, became monarch of Spain. On May 2, 1808, Spanish patriots in Madrid, angered at the French and the loss of the genuinely popular Ferdinand, launched the first stage of the Spanish War for Independence.[9]

Spanish resistance to Napoleon's armies in the name of Ferdinand, *El Deseado*, came from local guerrilla units, who were soon joined by British forces under the command of the Duke of Wellington. In the Americas, actions taken in behalf of the "Desired One" complicated political events from 1808 to 1814, and they often masked the underlying motives of revolutionaries from Texas to Argentina and Chile.

News of Charles IV's retirement, the capture and imprisonment of Ferdinand VII, and the outbreak of war on the Iberian Peninsula reached New Spain in the summer of 1808 and produced a flurry of activity there. With few exceptions, *peninsulares*, Spaniards born in Spain, had traditionally monopolized the most important positions in colonial government. Predictably, those Spaniards insisted that control of New Spain remain with them—in the name of Ferdinand VII. On the other hand, Mexican-born *criollos* countered with the contention that the viceroyalty should be governed by revolutionary committees—again, in the name of Ferdinand—which they intended to dominate.[10]

Viceroy José de Iturrigaray, himself a *peninsular* but also a corrupt and scheming chief executive, shrewdly assessed the situation and concluded that "if he played his cards right he might see a Mexican crown on his head." Driven by ambition, the viceroy shifted his support to the *criollos*, who outnumbered the *peninsulares* by a ratio of roughly ten to one.[11]

Unfortunately for Iturrigaray, a small group of *peninsulares* apprehended his plot. On the evening of September 15, 1808, they attacked the viceregal palace, arrested the turncoat viceroy, and dispatched him to Veracruz to await passage to Spain. The *peninsulares* then chose Pedro Garibay, a senile but compliant octogenarian, as the new viceroy. With their puppet in place, the *peninsulares* launched a witch-hunt, arresting *criollos* and handing out drumhead justice.[12]

However, the preemptive strike of September 1808 had set a dangerous precedent, with implications that extended as far as Texas. Although Iturrigaray was probably guilty of treasonous plotting, a royal official had been removed from office by force of arms. And the repressive actions of *peninsulares* in the fall of 1808 drove many *criollo* elements underground and led to the formation of secret organizations that demanded better government for New Spain.

The most important of those movements, headed by Father Miguel

Hidalgo y Costilla, raised the banner of revolution on September 16, 1810. The details of that insurrection, although vitally important in Mexican history, are only tangentially significant to our treatment of Texas in this era. In this same vein, we must look briefly at related developments in the United States.

The interest of Anglo-American adventurers in Texas had not ended with the death of Philip Nolan in 1801. Left unsettled in the Louisiana Purchase was a determination of the western and southern boundaries of that territory, prompting President Thomas Jefferson's claim of the Río Grande as the legitimate southern limit. U.S. claims to that effect had persuaded Charles IV to issue a royal directive on May 20, 1805, calling for the compilation of data and maps pertinent to determining the true boundary between Louisiana and Texas. With the appointment of José Antonio Pichardo in 1808, that commission became finalized. Until his death in 1812, Pichardo worked night and day to complete his massive assignment.[13]

Without waiting for the conclusion of scholarly disputation, Thomas Jefferson aggressively pursued U.S. claims to western lands. In rapid succession, he sponsored the Lewis and Clark expedition (1804–1806), the William Dunbar and John Hunter effort of 1804, and the Thomas Freeman and Peter Custis undertaking of 1806.[14]

Spain was no less determined to protect its interests. Repeated threats short-circuited the Dunbar/Hunter exploration, and Spanish soldiers turned back the Freeman/Custis party in the upper reaches of the Red River. More ominous were the actions of Commandant General Nemesio Salcedo y Salcedo, who ordered Spanish troops to take up a position east of the Sabine River near the abandoned site of Presidio Los Adaes. By June 1806, Spanish troop strength in Texas had reached an unprecedented 1,368 men, with nearly two-thirds of that number (883) posted at Nacogdoches and its environs. War seemed imminent.[15]

By the fall of 1806, however, caution began to replace saber rattling. Commandant General Salcedo ordered Governor Antonio Cordero y Bustamante, then in Texas, and Governor Simón de Herrera of Nuevo León, who had been transferred to Texas, "not [to] begin the action or attack the Americans without an entire and absolute certainty of evicting them from the disputed territory." A communiqué from Charles IV likewise commanded that every effort be made to settle differences peaceably with the Americans, but at the same time the king authorized no concession on the contested territory.[16]

The United States also began to soften its stance. General James Wilkinson, commander of U.S. forces in Louisiana, offered a compromise on

October 6, 1806. He would withdraw American troops stationed east of the Arroyo Hondo if Spanish forces would pull back to the west of the Sabine River. The resulting Neutral Ground Agreement preserved the peace, but it nevertheless created a corridor that soon filled with an incredible assortment of thieves, fugitive slaves, and smugglers—"the refuse of both Texas and Louisiana."[17]

Following the Neutral Ground Agreement, Texas received its own resident governor, the intelligent and vigorous Manuel de Salcedo, a nephew of Commandant General Nemesio Salcedo. Don Manuel had proceeded to Texas by way of the United States, passing through Philadelphia, Natchez, and Natchitoches. He reached Béxar on November 7, 1808, and assumed his post. In the following year, the new governor offered an eye-opening assessment of his jurisdiction. Salcedo praised the province for "its prodigious space and beautiful lands," but he pointed to the existence of only two fixed presidial companies and the absence of aides to the governor, such as legal advisor, secretary, or scribe, as injurious to the interests of good government.[18]

Governor Salcedo's report on Texas clearly expresses his amazement that there were only 353 veteran soldiers and a civilian population of just 3,122 persons. The mean condition of the settlers meant that they farmed without necessary tools, suffered from heat and cold, and lived in houses made of sticks and straw. The new chief executive seemed especially distressed that the populace could not even dress themselves decently.[19]

In a different vein, Salcedo waxed eloquent about the land, describing it as blessed with immensely rich soil that was "capable of producing anything that is planted, particularly cotton, indigo, tobacco, cochineal, wheat, corn, etc." He also named the major rivers of Texas and alluded to lesser streams that held the potential for irrigation.[20]

Don Manuel next turned his attention to the United States and its people, some of whom he had met firsthand en route to Texas. He assessed U.S. citizens as greatly advantaged by being "owners of the Nile of North America (thus they call the Mississippi)." Salcedo also branded as ridiculous "the idea that some have that we ought to hold the Americans in contempt," and he warned that "they are not to be underestimated as enemies." In his view, "the Anglo-Americans are naturally industrious. If this were not true, they would not love to live in deserts, where their sustenance depends on their industry. This very kind of life hardens them and necessarily makes soldiers of them; that is to have the traits of robustness, agility, sobriety, and valor."[21]

Manuel de Salcedo drafted his report, dated August 8, 1809, just thirteen months before Father Miguel Hidalgo proclaimed his revolutionary "Grito de Dolores." Tragically for Texas' youthful governor, from 1811 onward his tenure would be consumed with defending his monarch from enemies outside and within Texas, and in the end devotion to duty would cost his life.

Before revolution from the south swept over Béxar, in March 1810 Governor Salcedo began an inspection tour of East Texas. Once there, he found that unsavory characters of every description had filtered into the Neutral Ground. Other transients of questionable loyalty had claimed lands in Texas without a hint of legal title to them. In the past, Commandant General Nemesio Salcedo had opposed all alien encroachments beyond the Sabine. However, at the time of don Manuel's inspection, don Nemesio had begun to alter his stance. In effect, the commandant general gave wider discretionary powers to the governor of Texas and the deputy commandant general, who was then stationed in the province. Those officials and Hispanic residents would be allowed to make "a sharp distinction between alien settlers who engaged in peaceful pursuits of the soil and chronic trespassers who entered for illicit purposes." At Nacogdoches, Manuel de Salcedo tried to determine the true intentions of squatters, granting some of them titles to lands, farms, and ranches, while extending amnesty to others.[22]

On his return to San Antonio, following a three-month inspection of East Texas, Governor Salcedo found himself confronted with the extended impact of the Hidalgo revolt. In the early stages of insurrection, Hidalgo and his *criollo* officers had recognized the necessity of obtaining foreign assistance. To that purpose, they assigned Mariano Jiménez the responsibility of overturning royalist control of Coahuila and Texas. Of the two provinces, Texas was more important because of its proximity to the United States, where the rebels hoped to enlist aid.[23]

As the Hidalgo-led rebels looked to the United States as the logical conduit to aid and arms, so did the royalists. Nemesio Salcedo, although long wary of the United States, authorized his nephew Manuel to acquire guns and equipment from that nation and shipped twenty thousand pesos into the province to underwrite the purchase. Unfortunately for don Manuel, his uncle later rescinded the plan to buy firearms in Louisiana, suggesting instead that they be obtained in Nuevo León or Nuevo Santander. This lack of constancy essentially resulted in no additional armaments for Texas throughout the remainder of 1810.[24]

Shortly after Christmas, Governor Salcedo made a decision that weakened Texas' defenses. Recognizing that Coahuila was more exposed than Texas to insurrectionist activities in the south, don Manuel decided to return one hundred men to Saltillo. Those troops had originally been under the command of Antonio Cordero, his predecessor in Texas. In early 1811, Salcedo reflected concerns for the security of his immediate family by secretly moving his wife and daughter from Béxar to East Texas. When their absence became apparent, rumors ran rampant in San Antonio. Those fears were greatly intensified when Salcedo announced on January 2 that the entire three-hundred-man garrison stationed at Béxar would be moved to the Río Grande, where it could more effectively defend the province.[25]

At that juncture, word arrived that Antonio Cordero's command in Coahuila, without mounting so much as token resistance, had defected to the insurrectionists and that Cordero himself had become a prisoner of war. Salcedo reacted by canceling the marching orders of the Béxar command, arguing that San Antonio itself rather than the Río Grande barrier had more need for protection. The crucial question, however, was whether royalist troops in Texas would remain loyal to the king and far-off Spain.[26]

The answer was not long in coming. On the night of January 21, 1811, Juan Bautista de las Casas, a retired militia captain from Nuevo Santander, orchestrated a strike against royalists in San Antonio. Las Casas and a number of adherents, mostly enlisted personnel from the barracks complex in La Villita, seized Governor Salcedo and his entire military staff on the following morning. Elsewhere, co-conspirators soon took control of Nacogdoches and other settlements in Texas.[27]

In February, after confiscating the property of loyal supporters of Ferdinand VII, Las Casas sent Manuel de Salcedo, Simón de Herrera, and twelve officers under heavy guard to Monclova, where they were incarcerated at a nearby hacienda that was partially owned by Ignacio Elizondo. The ordeal must have been especially painful for Herrera, a lieutenant colonel and former governor of Nuevo León who had compiled a splendid military record in behalf of his monarch.[28]

Intoxicated by his own importance, Las Casas failed to build a solid base of support in San Antonio. He especially erred in not courting old-line descendants of *isleños* (Canary Island settlers) and in not taking friends into his confidence. Clandestine opposition to Las Casas and his upstart followers found a nucleus in Juan Manuel Zambrano, a subdeacon of Villa San Fernando and an ardent royalist. On March 2, 1811, counterrevolutionists swept a surprised Juan Bautista de las Casas from power. His absolutist regime had lasted for only thirty-nine days.[29]

Royalists at Béxar quickly dispatched two trusted couriers to the Elizondo hacienda, where they imparted news of the successful countercoup against Las Casas. Don Ignacio, a former defender of the king who had defected to the Hidalgo cause, again switched allegiance. Elizondo released Manuel de Salcedo, Simón Herrera, and the other officers, and then joined them in laying an ambush for Hidalgo. Previously, Father Hidalgo and his ragged followers had suffered irreversible losses in a huge battle fought near Guadalajara, and they were in full flight toward Texas. As the insurrectionists approached Monclova from the south, they were apprehended near the Wells of Baján on March 21, 1811.[30]

As an indelible lesson to would-be revolutionaries in Texas, Las Casas underwent trial by victorious royalists in Monclova. Found guilty of high treason, the Béxar insurrectionist died from shots fired into his back. His executioners severed his head, then salted and boxed it for shipment to San Antonio, where soldiers placed it on a pole and displayed it in the military plaza.[31]

The trial and execution of Juan Bautista de las Casas, however, had failed to quash revolutionary sentiment throughout the northern provinces, and the mantle of leadership next fell on the shoulders of José Bernardo Maximiliano Gutiérrez de Lara. Don Bernardo's family had been among the pioneer founders of Revilla (modern Nuevo Guerrero, Tamaulipas) during the colonizing efforts of José de Escandón. Don Bernardo, himself, the son of Santiago Gutiérrez de Lara and María Rosa de Uribe, was born in Revilla on August 20, 1774. Shortly before the turn of the century, he married a widowed cousin, María Josefa de Uribe, who bore him five sons and a daughter. A blacksmith/businessman by trade, Bernardo de Gutiérrez quickly heeded Father Hidalgo's *grito* for better government.[32]

By his own account, Gutiérrez's first act as an insurrectionist involved the recruitment of his brother, Father José Antonio, to the cause. He then learned that Hidalgo had sent Lieutenant General Mariano Jiménez into the northern provinces to enlist aid, a development that prompted him to become an active propagandist for the insurgent movement in Nuevo Santander. Don Bernardo's actions included the sending of agents throughout much of the province with well-worded appeals to rebels who were willing to throw off the royalist yoke. The success of these efforts may be measured by the hundreds of loyalists who fled into Coahuila, where they sought refuge under Governor Antonio Cordero.[33]

Encouraged by their successes, the Gutiérrez brothers next directed their attention toward Coahuila and Nuevo León. As mentioned, those efforts bore fruit when insurrectionists succeeded in undermining troops commanded by Antonio Cordero, resulting in the governor's capture.

Nuevo León likewise came into the fold, meaning that revolutionists, with few exceptions, controlled northern New Spain from San Luis Potosí to Monterrey.[34]

Father Antonio Gutiérrez then accepted a commission from Mariano Jiménez. The cleric was to seek out and nurture insurrectionists in five towns along the lower Río Grande—Laredo, Revilla, Mier, Camargo, and Reynosa. Those efforts were enormously successful, prompting the exiled governor of Nuevo Santander to remark in February 1811 that "revolution and terror raged in the settlements along the Río Grande." And, by that juncture, the impetus for revolution had already swept beyond the Río Grande into Texas and produced the briefly successful rebellion of Juan Bautista de las Casas. These triumphs, however, represented nothing more than a momentary high tide of insurrection.[35]

Following the restoration of royal authority in Texas and the capture of Hidalgo and his followers at the Wells of Baján, affairs of government at Béxar temporarily fell into the hands of Juan Manuel Zambrano and a royalist junta. Zambrano and his associates exercised authority from March 2, 1811, to July 22, 1811, when they were replaced by Interim Governor Simón de Herrera. This ad hoc arrangement was necessary because Governor Manuel de Salcedo was detained at Villa Chihuahua, where he conducted the trial of Father Hidalgo and the courts-martial of the priest's major lieutenants, a responsibility that kept don Manuel away from San Antonio until September 11, 1811.[36]

Meanwhile, the faint hopes of insurrectionists in northern New Spain lay in the hands of Bernardo Gutiérrez de Lara, who had been authorized to seek aid in the United States. To elude his numerous enemies, don Bernardo hid at his house for a time "like the miserable mole under the leaves, expecting death if I was discovered, but life, if things took on a more favorable aspect." In the company of José Menchaca, another rebel partisan, Gutiérrez decided to leave his family in Revilla and undertake a perilous journey across royalist-controlled Texas. The two men arrived safely on U.S. soil at Natchitoches, but while crossing the Neutral Ground they had been attacked by presumed adherents of the king. In don Bernardo's words, we lost "everything we carried, and most important of all, the papers and dispatches which proved my commission in a positive manner." After a month's stay in Louisiana, don Bernardo traveled overland to Washington. En route, he suffered greatly from cold and exposure before reaching the U.S. capital on December 11, 1811. There he enjoyed a favorable reception from United States officials in both the Departments of War and State, as well as from President James Madison. But, to the dismay of Gutiérrez, "the first unofficial representative from the Mexican people to the United States," he could garner little more than the unofficial blessing of Secretary of State James Monroe.[37]

Spanish agents in Washington and Philadelphia were soon aware of don Bernardo's activities and kept him under close scrutiny. On January 1, 1812, Luis de Onís, longtime Spanish minister to the United States, penned a letter to the viceroy of New Spain. In it Onís noted that his informants were aware of "hostile movements" in Philadelphia that had been initiated by an insurgent Colonel Menchaca and "another named Bernardo." Onís also reported "various secret discussions" between Bernardo Gutiérrez and members of the U.S. government, as well as news that the Mexican insurgent would soon depart for Natchitoches.[38]

Although U.S. officials had been cautious in their dealings with Gutiérrez, they did provide him with a letter of introduction to Governor William C. C. Claiborne in New Orleans. Sailing from Philadelphia on January 12, 1812, don Bernardo on March 23 reached New Orleans, where Claiborne introduced the former blacksmith to William Shaler, a special agent for the United States who was to monitor Gutiérrez's activities and accompany him to Natchitoches. In late April 1812, the two men arrived at their destination, and Gutiérrez began immediate preparations for an invasion of Texas. As it turned out, don Bernardo found no shortage of volunteers, one of whom was Augustus William Magee, a West Point graduate and former artillery officer in the United States army.[39]

Shaler's support influenced other Americans to join the banner of the Mexican revolutionary. Gutiérrez also enlisted the support of Samuel Davenport, an experienced Indian trader in Spanish Texas and successful merchant of Nacogdoches. The involvement of Americans in the rapidly organized Bernardo Gutiérrez–Augustus Magee expedition also represented the not-so-unofficial goals of the United States in Texas.[40]

Operating under the name of the "Republican Army of the North," Gutiérrez and Magee crossed the Sabine River on August 8, 1812. Although Anglo Americans had joined the enterprise "for reasons of land, loot, and adventure," the primary goal of don Bernardo was to bring Texas into the fold of Mexican revolutionaries, then under the banner of Hidalgo's successor, Father José María Morelos y Pavón.[41]

The successful invasion of Spanish Texas, which William Shaler had helped organize, caused him to exult in a letter dated October 5, 1812, to Secretary of State James Monroe: This "volunteer expedition from the most insignificant beginning is growing into an irresistible torrent, that will Sweep the crazy remains of Spanish Government from the Internal Provinces, and open Mexico to the political influence of the U.S. and to the talents and enterprize [*sic*] of our citizens." [42]

Initially, Shaler's optimism seemed well founded. The republicans had scored an easy success at Nacogdoches, where not a single Tejano citizen answered the Spanish commander's appeal for volunteers to help defend the town. And at that juncture, an army of perhaps 130 men swelled to about 300, whereupon Gutiérrez and Magee headed inland in mid-September 1812. Learning that La Bahía was poorly defended, the commanders changed course and marched directly there. The presidio's few defenders fled, allowing the Republican Army to occupy a stone fort and capture two or three cannons. Three days later, a royalist army under Manuel de Salcedo and Simón de Herrera arrived at La Bahía and opened a four-month siege. During the investment, Gutiérrez momentarily wavered in his commitment to make Texas a part of an independent Mexico. He wrote William Shaler, offering the province to the U.S. in return for military aid and protection from Spanish vengeance. However, nothing came of the offer, and in all clashes of arms the republicans were victorious. [43]

Leadership of the republicans changed in February 1813 when Augustus Magee died under circumstances that remain uncertain, with explanations ranging from death by consumption to murder or suicide. The republicans, then under the command of Gutiérrez, nevertheless continued to attract new volunteers, some of whom were deserters from the Spanish army that engaged them. Republican Indian agents also managed to recruit Lipan and Tonkawa allies. [44]

On February 19, 1813, Governor Salcedo and Simón de Herrera lifted the fruitless siege that had seen the ranks of their opponents grow almost daily and retreated to San Antonio. Two days later, the republicans marched on Béxar. To defend the capital, Herrera made a stand at Salado Creek, about eight miles southeast of San Antonio. But in the ensuing battle, a combination of Anglo Americans, Mexicans, and Indian auxiliaries soundly defeated the royalists in a contest that lasted no more than twenty minutes. Herrera had suffered 330 killed and 60 captured, while the republicans had only 6 killed and 26 wounded. [45]

The defeated royalists left the battlefield littered with baggage, cannon, and supplies, all of which fell into the hands of Gutiérrez and his military officers. Approaching San Antonio without opposition, don Bernardo set up his headquarters at Mission Concepción and prepared to besiege the capital. Several hundred men in San Antonio then defected to the insurgents, leaving Manuel de Salcedo and Simón de Herrera with little choice other than surrender. The two officials asked for conditional guarantees, including respect for the lives and property of noncombatants and protection of church property—all to no avail. The reply came in a document with the heading "Don José Bernardo Gutiérrez, Commander in Chief of the Mexican Republican Army of the North, and Don Samuel Kemper, Lieutenant Colonel, Commander of the American volunteers in this army, to the Governor and Commander of the forces in San Antonio." The text warned Salcedo and Herrera that only unconditional surrender would avert the capture of San Antonio by force. However, the two Spanish officials were assured that the laws of warfare governing the treatment of the vanquished would be observed.[46]

On April 2, 1813, the governor and town council of Béxar surrendered the capital to the republicans. Royalist soldiers had the option of enlisting in the Republican Army of the North or becoming prisoners of war, but that choice did not include Spanish officers and noncoms. In great triumph, an insurgent honor guard raised the green flag of the first Republic of Texas over the military plaza of San Antonio.[47]

Governor Manuel de Salcedo and Simón de Herrera had no reason to expect clemency. Their surrender had been unconditional, and a hostile mob coursing through the streets of the provincial capital demanded bloody vengeance. On the following day, April 3, 1813, a hasty trial brought charges that the two men had bribed Ignacio Elizondo to betray Father Hidalgo and that they had authorized flagrant and punishable actions against insurrectionists in Béxar. The sentence of death for Salcedo and Herrera and fifteen of their officers was as certain as night follows day.[48]

Bernardo de Gutiérrez may have tried to spare the condemned Spaniards by granting them pardons, but this assertion has never been documented. More certain are the objections raised by American military officers who protested the impending executions, arguing instead for confinement of the royalists well away from Texas, perhaps on American soil in New Orleans. Aides of Gutiérrez appeared to concur, and under this guise the seventeen prisoners left Béxar on the night of April 3. The captives, with hands tied behind their backs, were in the company of sixty Mexican soldiers, commanded by the rebel Captain Antonio Delgado. Arriving at the site of the recent battle of Rosillo, the defenseless Spaniards were unhorsed, humiliated, and set upon with knives. Governor Salcedo, Colonel Herrera, and fifteen Spanish officers and noncoms died of stab wounds and slit throats; their mutilated bodies were left where they fell and denied decent burial.[49]

With the capture of San Antonio, Gutiérrez was in a position to determine the destiny of Texas, and at this juncture he began to assert an independent attitude that would soon alienate his American collaborators. Don Bernardo made it clear that he would no longer countenance any plans to annex Texas to the United States. Although he insisted that he did not hold grievances against the Anglo Americans, he made it clear that he was committed to making Texas a part of a new and independent Mexican nation. Not surprisingly, Gutiérrez's theretofore good relations with William Shaler in Natchitoches and General William C. C. Claiborne in New Orleans quickly deteriorated.[50]

In San Antonio on April 6, 1813, Gutiérrez proclaimed a declaration of independence. His break with king and country began with the announcement that "the bonds that kept us bound to the dominion of Spain have been severed forever; we are free and independent and have the right to establish our own government. In the future, all legitimate authority emanates from the people where it rightly resides." Don Bernardo asserted that the United States had declared its independence from Great Britain with far less cause than that of the people of Texas and Mexico. In a province blessed with rich natural resources and fertile soil, it was a travesty that human beings should have to go about half naked and half starved.[51]

Gutiérrez gave no credit to Anglo Americans for their role in the triumph of the republicans—thereby ignoring the military contributions of Augustus Magee and such officers as Samuel Kemper and Reuben Ross, as well as the assistance of Shaler and Claiborne. Instead, the new government in San Antonio had been solely created by the "Illustrious Liberator, Don Bernardo Gutiérrez, Commander in Chief of the Mexican Republican Army of the North." Out of concern for his emancipated subjects, Gutiérrez designated himself as president-protector, to be joined by a provisional junta of six members, whose primary responsibility was to assist don Bernardo in drafting a constitution.[52]

Lest there be any doubt that Gutiérrez intended for the province of Tejas to be free of all ties to the United States, the initial article of Texas' first constitution states that the new political entity was "inviolably joined" to the Mexican nation. The framers of the constitution, however, did give credit to American volunteers who had joined the Gutiérrez-Magee expedition. Those who had served for a minimum of six months were entitled to one square league of land (4,428 acres). A draft of the constitution of 1813, completed on April 17, was sent to Shaler and Claiborne, Gutiérrez's erstwhile friends.[53]

Five days later in an emotional appeal to faithful *criollos*, Gutiérrez called upon them to recognize that for too long they had groaned under the weight of a European yoke. He implored his American-born compatriots to "open their eyes and know" that their cause, independence, was just, and that the oppression they had endured was against all natural law. In a formal proclamation, he also exhorted Bexareños to "cast off the weight of slavery under which they had suffered" and raise their voices against the evil *peninsulares* who were the cause of a bloody internecine war that pitted brothers against brothers.[54]

Gutiérrez and the junta, although obviously committed to the Mexican nation, quickly demonstrated that "they could not push out beyond the boundary of their political experience into the new frontier of republicanism." With only minor modifications, Texas's first constitution was an endorsement of Spanish political heritage. The president-protector and his advisory council controlled all matters of state, war, and foreign affairs. They also chose magistrates, as well as delegates to future Mexican congresses and foreign nations, and they could dismiss any government official without cause or appeal. However, in the final analysis, even the junta, like the Béxar cabildo that had preceded it, was subject to the will of don Bernardo, president-protector of Texas.[55]

Gutiérrez was not so drunk with power that he could afford to ignore the possibility of enlisting support in Mexico. And to this end, he sought to recruit Ignacio Elizondo, reminding him that he had once been an admirer and follower of Father Hidalgo. But don Ignacio remained faithful to his newfound royalist commitment. In a written reply, he rejected Gutiérrez's "repulsive" proposal and heaped scorn upon the president-protector. The Spanish officer insisted that even if Gutiérrez were to hide in "hell itself as the last refuge," he would seek him out, burn his body, and cast his "remains to the four winds."[56]

But much worse lay ahead for Gutiérrez and his absolutist regime than being excoriated by a former royalist turned insurgent turned royalist. The brutal murders of Manuel de Salcedo, Simón de Herrera, and a cadre of fifteen officers and sergeants had cut royalist pride to the quick. Observing what he saw as less than a valorous defense of king and country was a no-nonsense military officer in New Spain who would profoundly alter the course of Texas history.

Born in Barcelona in 1778, Joaquín de Arredondo was the son of Nicolás de Arredondo y Palegrí, a prominent Spanish official who would later serve as governor of Cuba and viceroy of the Río de la Plata (Buenos Aires), and Josefa Roso de Mioño. Entering the military as a cadet in the mid- to late 1780s, young Joaquín must have earned rapid promotions, for he had achieved the rank of colonel by 1810. In the following year, he received appointment as military commander of the Huasteca (headquartered at modern Tampico) and as governor of Nuevo Santander. He had also been knighted in the prestigious Order of Calatrava. Don Joaquín's Mexican-born wife, Guadalupe del Moral, hailed from Tehuacán in the present state of Puebla.[57]

Joaquín de Arredondo first demonstrated his commitment to the loyalist cause by suppressing all pro-Hidalgo elements in the Tampico area, and he chafed under restraints imposed by Viceroy Francisco Xavier Venegas, which specifically ordered him to stay out of Nemesio de Salcedo's jurisdiction in the Commandancy General of the Interior Provinces. However, as mentioned earlier, the unified Commandancy General was effectively divided into eastern and western provinces in 1813. And with the death of the superbly credentialed Simón de Herrera on April 3, don Joaquín was a logical choice to replace him as commandant general of the eastern jurisdiction. That was especially the view of Félix María Calleja, who succeeded Francisco Javier de Venegas as viceroy in early 1813. Calleja was an inordinately capable and tough general, who saw matters much as Arredondo did. On April 28 of that same year, the new chief executive appointed Joaquín de Arredondo as commandant general of the eastern provinces.[58]

Meanwhile, Arredondo had been quick to congratulate Viceroy Calleja on his accession to office and to suggest that he, don Joaquín, was just the man to take immediate action against the insurrectionist "rabble" in the north. Arredondo also leveled a tactful but critical barb against José Ramón Díaz de Bustamante, a recent appointee as governor of Nuevo León and acting governor of Nuevo Santander. In effect, Arredondo suggested that Díaz de Bustamante was a "do-nothing" administrator. And he said as much to Bustamante himself.[59]

In March 1813, Arredondo informed Bustamante that he had decided to enter the governor's jurisdiction in Nuevo Santander and deliver it from the hands of rebels. This missive drew an immediate and heated response from Bustamante. Don José Ramón informed Arredondo: "I am the legitimate governor of and the only one responsible for Nuevo Santander." Furthermore, raged Bustamante, "I have not solicited from you in any manner the need to augment my forces." Governor Bustamante then reminded Arredondo that New Spain was beset by rebels in the north *and* the south and that he should stay where he was and defend San Luis Potosí. Finally, don José Ramón fumed that for "thirty-three years I have had the honor of serving our Catholic majesty in all tasks entrusted to me."[60]

But Bustamante was soon to "whistle a different tune." Shortly after this clash of monumental egos, don José Ramón learned that San Antonio had fallen, as well as details of the horrible murders at Salado Creek.

The panicky governor sent a letter by courier, urging Arredondo to "fly to his rescue." In a flurry of activity, Arredondo gathered supplies and armaments and sent a detachment of mounted troops to Revilla to arrest the family of Gutiérrez. Anticipating that move, don Bernardo had already moved his relatives to San Antonio, thereby delivering them from the clutches of Arredondo's dragoons. However, the Gutiérrez family soon suffered the loss of its house, library, and more than 4,200 pesos— all seized by soldiers of the "cruel and renowned brigadier, Joaquín de Arredondo."[61]

Arredondo also prevailed upon Calleja to lend him all the experienced soldiers the viceroy could spare. Those entreaties brought results, and as don Joaquín approached Laredo he learned that a thousand Spanish veterans, recently arrived from Spain, had been dispatched from Veracruz to join his command. He also received intelligence that hundreds of American volunteers in Texas, sickened by the executions at Salado Creek and disaffected with the pretensions of Gutiérrez, had left San Antonio for Natchitoches. At that same juncture, additional good news informed Arredondo of his selection as commandant general of the four eastern provinces (Figure 21).[62]

In a sobering vein, Viceroy Calleja issued a stern warning to his new commandant general. He must not take action without the absolute certainty of victory. Don Joaquín offered quick assurances to his superior that no offensive would be initiated until he was thoroughly prepared. But things went momentarily awry for the royalists.

When Arredondo reached Laredo, he learned to his satisfaction that Ignacio Elizondo had recruited some seven hundred men from Nueva Vizcaya and Coahuila. Don Ignacio was apparently anxious to demonstrate his trustworthiness as a recent convert to royalism, and he eagerly lobbied for an opportunity to establish an advanced base in Texas. Arredondo agreed to Elizondo's proposal but placed him under strict orders. His subordinate could advance to the Río Frío but not one step beyond. However, don Ignacio did not halt his march until he reached San Antonio. When Arredondo learned of his officer's failure to follow orders, he flew into a black rage. Should Elizondo capture Béxar, it would rob the commandant general of a victory that was to have been his; if, on the other hand, don Ignacio should fail, it would undo months of careful preparation.[63]

But Arredondo's concerns that he might be denied victory were without foundation. Conditions were indeed bad among the insurgents in San Antonio, but they put aside their differences when confronted by a large loyalist army at the very outskirts of the town. Gutiérrez and

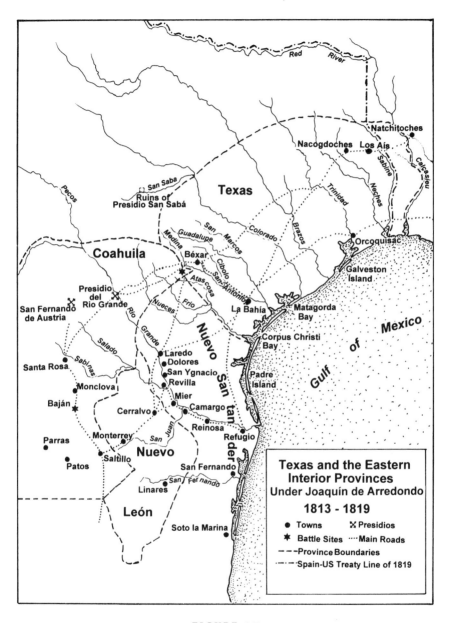

Map of Texas and the Eastern Interior Provinces under Joaquín de Arredondo.
This map depicts the jurisdiction of Commandant General Arredondo from
1813 to 1819. (Cartography by Caroline Castillo Crimm.)

Major Henry Perry threw together an effective fighting force and quietly surrounded the troops of Elizondo on the night of June 19, 1813. On the following morning, as Elizondo's men knelt for Mass, they faced attack from all sides. In the chaotic battle of Alazán, lasting for about two hours, the forces of Elizondo were soundly defeated and scattered in all directions. Don Ignacio himself was lucky to escape with his life, having had two horses shot from under him.[64]

Left on the battlefield was a treasure trove of spoils—including four thousand pounds of biscuits, forty mule loads of flour, two thousand horses and mules, three hundred muskets, five thousand pounds of powder, goods and clothing amounting to $28,000, $7,000 in specie, and hundreds of saddles and other tack. But victory at Alazán marked the apogee of Bernardo Gutiérrez de Lara's leadership in Texas, and from this point onward, he fades quickly from our narrative.[65]

Gutiérrez, thanks in large part to the intrigues of Shaler and Claiborne, was soon obliged to surrender power as president-protector in San Antonio. His successor, José Alvarez de Toledo, whom don Bernardo had met during his stay on the East Coast in 1811–1812, was a Spanish officer with a checkered past. He had served in both the Spanish and the British navies during the Peninsular War. Subsequently, don José had been a representative from Santo Domingo to the Spanish Cortes (Parliament) when it convened at Cádiz in 1811. Dismissed from that body, he later entered the United States. There he received funds from Secretary of State James Monroe to foment revolutionary activities in Cuba, but Spanish officials discovered his covert activities and forced him to flee Havana. Upon returning to the United States, Toledo made his way to Natchitoches and became a confederate of William Shaler. The two men combined efforts to slander Gutiérrez and undermine his leadership.[66]

Through publication of two independent newspapers, distributed between Nacogdoches and San Antonio, American volunteers in Texas read allegations of don Bernardo's incompetence and unreasoning independence. *El Mexicano* contained a feature editorial written by Shaler and Toledo in which they demonized Gutiérrez by name, accusing him of the "most frightful calamities." Whatever the impact of this anti-Gutiérrez propaganda, Anglo Americans in San Antonio had good reason to be disaffected with don Bernardo, and additional adherents began to desert in droves, prompting the junta there to dismiss Gutiérrez and replace him with Toledo. On August 1, 1813, the ex-naval officer entered Béxar in a general's uniform, claiming authority from the Spanish Cortes and the U.S. Congress. Three days later, Toledo received the junta's nomination as commander in chief of the Republican Army of the North.[67]

Meanwhile, the implacable Arredondo had recovered from Elizondo's blunder. The commandant general left Laredo on July 26 and moved slowly toward a showdown battle with the republicans. By August 17, Arredondo had arrived at a location south of the Medina River.

In the intervening days, Toledo had marshalled his forces at San Antonio. On August 13 don José received intelligence of the approaching royalist army. Under advice from Colonel Henry Perry, who viewed San Antonio as not ideally defensible, some 1,400 republicans left Béxar for a rendezvous with royalists that would cost the lives of thirteen of every fourteen volunteers (Figure 22).[68]

After the battle of Medina River, Joaquín de Arredondo gave little credit to Indian allies of the republicans, reporting that they were the first to run. Quick to follow the flight of the Native Americans was the cowardly Toledo, who had managed to escape the general carnage. Arredondo was only a bit more complimentary of Anglo Americans. He thought them adept in battle but attributed their fighting qualities to lessons learned from "traitorous Spanish soldiers" who had the benefit of training in the king's army.[69]

The 112 republicans who surrendered at the Medina were quick to experience the wrath of Arredondo. All were summarily shot. On August 20, having captured 215 more republicans along the way and meting out orders for execution of "those deserving death," don Joaquín triumphantly entered Béxar and the killing continued. An additional forty men in San Antonio with real and suspected sympathies for the republican cause paid with their lives. The mothers, wives, and children of those unfortunates were packed into makeshift compounds, where eight of them died of suffocation, and left to wail as shots rang out day after day. Younger and more attractive Bexareñas suffered humiliation, taunts, and ravishment, as well as long hours of labor in royalist barracks, where they converted bushels of corn into tortillas. Mistreatment and exploitation of these unfortunate women ended after fifty-four days, but when finally cast into the streets of Béxar, they were homeless and stripped of all material possessions.[70]

While Arredondo reaped lives at Béxar, Ignacio Elizondo advanced toward Nacogdoches, en route executing a total of seventy-one insurgents, while capturing one hundred prisoners, including "women, with armament, clothing and jewelry." However, don Ignacio failed to reach the East Texas town. At a campsite on the Brazos River, a demented lieutenant, apparently crazed by incessant heat and bloodletting, turned on

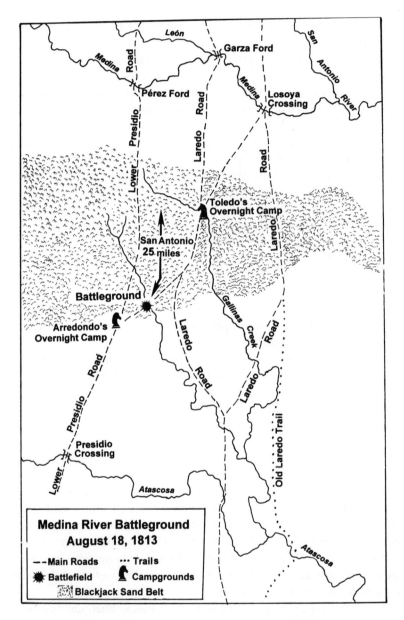

———— FIGURE 22 ————

Map of the Medina River battleground. This map, adapted from an original
drawing by Jack Jackson, depicts the main features of the battleground
and surrounding area. (Cartography by Caroline Castillo Crimm.)

Elizondo's cousin and killed him with a saber. The officer then resisted don Ignacio's efforts to disarm him. In the ensuing scuffle, the lieutenant slashed Elizondo's hand and mortally stabbed him in the lower body cavity. Carried by litter, Ignacio Elizondo died ten days later—most likely of acute peritonitis—and was buried on the banks of the San Marcos River.[71]

In all, Commandant General Joaquín de Arredondo remained in Texas for only a few weeks—just long enough to supervise the retributory slayings and complete his report to the viceroy on the battle of Medina River. As historian Félix D. Almaráz Jr. has remarked, the commandant general's "vengeance on Spanish Texas was swift and hard. Confiscation, detention, and execution were the methods . . . used to restore royalist authority."[72]

Over the next six years, a succession of five interim governors followed the unfortunate Manuel de Salcedo. In 1817 Antonio Martínez began a term that proved to be the last for chief executives of Spanish Texas. Because of events played out in Spain and New Spain, Texas pledged itself to the new Mexican nation in 1821, and on July 19 of that same year the flag of Castile and León was lowered for the last time at San Antonio. Governor Martínez, a conscientious administrator and decent human being, saw the curtain fall on a province where the king's soldiers had "drained the resources of the country, and laid their hands on everything that could sustain life." By don Antonio's own admission, Texas had "advanced at an amazing rate toward ruin and destruction." With Nacogdoches, where Arredondo's officers had exacted additional lives, "nearly expired," it seems certain that Texas in 1821 had a non-Indian population of less than 3,000—fewer than the 3,103 reported in the first census of 1777.[73]

But what of the lives of Gutiérrez and Arredondo after their Texas careers had ended? Having been removed from all authority on August 6, 1813, Bernardo Gutiérrez de Lara left Béxar for Natchitoches. From there he traveled to New Orleans, where he tried unsuccessfully to organize a new liberation effort for Texas. During his stay in the Crescent City, don Bernardo claimed to have fought in the battle of New Orleans with troops under the command of Andrew Jackson. Later, Gutiérrez returned to Natchitoches, where he enlisted in a number of filibustering expeditions, including the James Long ventures of 1819 and 1821.[74]

After the independence of Mexico, Agustín de Iturbide paid tribute to Gutiérrez as a dedicated loyalist, and the former blacksmith returned to Revilla as a hero in 1824. In the next two years, he served as governor of Tamaulipas, as commandant general of the state, and, ironically, as commandant general of the eastern division of the Interior Provinces—the very command held by his archenemy, Joaquín de Arredondo. After resigning as head of the eastern region in 1826, don Bernardo spent the remainder of his life in Tamaulipas, suffering from "the bitterness of poverty, political persecution, and broken health." Recalled to duty only two years before his death, Gutiérrez helped defend his home state from secessionist efforts to create the Republic of the Río Grande. In that engagement, he suffered brief imprisonment by rebels and the looting of his home. Weakened by the experience, Bernardo Gutiérrez de Lara died at Villa Santiago on May 13, 1841, in the home of his daughter, María Eugenia.[75]

Elizabeth Howard West, translator of Gutiérrez's fragmentary diary, has offered a trenchant valedictory on the man: "He was undoubtedly high-tempered; he permitted, if he did not order, cruelty in the treatment of prisoners of war. He was inclined to extremes of judgment. He had limitations, partly inherent, partly due to lack of education and experience; he took himself too seriously. He was capable on occasion of dissimulation." On a positive note, it is well to remember that Bernardo Gutiérrez de Lara had leadership qualities that won him the admiration of many Mexican and Anglo-American leaders. Unable to speak English and without any official papers whatsoever, he presented himself well to the highest officials in the United States government. With only one documented exception—when his forces were under siege at La Bahía—he remained a steadfast advocate of making Texas a part of the new Mexican nation.[76]

After Joaquín de Arredondo left Texas, he headquartered at Monterrey as Spanish commander of the eastern provinces. In that capacity, he crushed an invasion of northeastern New Spain by Francisco Xavier Mina in 1817 by overrunning the insurgent's headquarters at Villa Soto la Marina, the settlement founded in the previous century by José de Escandón. Interestingly, while still serving as commandant general, Arredondo had to pass judgment on Moses Austin's petition to bring three hundred Anglo-American families into Texas. Governor Antonio Martínez had referred this matter to his superior, and after consultation with the Supreme Council of the Eastern Interior Provinces at Monterrey, Arredondo gave his imprimatur on January 17, 1821, insisting that the colonists must comply with the most important condition, that of either being Catholics "or agreeing to become so, before they enter the Spanish territory."[77]

Within months, Agustín de Iturbide's successful formula *(Plan de*

Iguala) for Mexican independence swept Arredondo from power, but not without a last-minute offer from him. On July 3, 1821, with Mexico's separation from Spain a virtual certainty, don Joaquín offered to swear allegiance to the new nation on condition that he retain authority as commandant general. His proposal was vehemently rejected by the citizens of Saltillo, and in the following month, Arredondo fled to San Luis Potosí, where he claimed sanctuary in the Convento del Carmen. Remaining there until December 1821, the former brigadier general slipped out of Mexico through a small port and traveled to Havana on the schooner *Rosita*. Infamous in Texas history as a "butcher," because of his brutal executions of republicans, Joaquín de Arredondo died in Havana in 1837.[78]

Bernardo Gutiérrez de Lara and Joaquín de Arredondo were notable personalities at opposite purposes in Texas' late colonial era. The former was a Mexican patriot who refused to be a willing agent of Anglo-American influence and expansion, which contributed significantly to his removal as president-protector of Texas' First Republic of 1813. The latter remained an essentially pragmatic royalist who concluded that Anglo-American settlers, brought to Texas under restrictive contracts, were far better than the filibustering "rabble" he had killed at the battle of Medina River or the republican traitors at Béxar who had deserved an early grave.

~

COLONIAL WOMEN

Rigors, Responsibilities, and Rights

~

$$I$$n July 1629, near present-day Albuquerque, New Mexico, a delegation of some fifty Jumano Indians arrived at the Franciscan convent of Saint Anthony in old Isleta. The Jumanos, having journeyed a great distance from a land that is now Texas, professed knowledge of a mysterious "Lady in Blue," who had appeared before them out of thin air on many, many occasions. This beautiful young woman had urged the Jumanos to come to New Mexico, where she assured them they would find religious teachers for themselves and their neighbors. The visiting assemblage of natives displayed a rudimentary knowledge of Christianity and when asked who had instructed them replied—the "Woman in Blue." Thus began one of the most persistent and intriguing legends in Texas history. Who was this wraithlike image? To this day, she inspires the Catholic faithful, she challenges the credulity of skeptics, she commands numerous references on the Internet, and she intrigues scholars of lay and religious persuasion alike.[1]

Before the arrival of the Jumanos, the archbishop of New Spain, Francisco Manso y Zúñiga, had written to the religious superior of New Mexico requesting information about the assertions of a Franciscan nun of the Poor Clares Order. The woman in question, although having never left Spain, professed knowledge of Indians on the extreme northern frontier who had not as yet experienced Catholic missionaries in the flesh. She, on the other hand, through the powers of mystical bilocation had been able to transport her spirit among the pagan. Her messages, although delivered in Spanish, were intelligible to the natives in their own tongue. Had the custodian of New Mexico any evidence of such miraculous preaching among his flock?[2]

The "Lady in Blue" of Texas and New Mexico fame was born María

Coronel on April 2, 1602, in the Spanish village of Agreda near the border of Aragón and Navarre. She was the eldest daughter of Francisco Coronel and Catalina of Arana. Baptized on April 11, María would never be physically strong or healthy. At "a very young age," she allegedly had a supernatural vision, and shortly thereafter began to demonstrate unusual piety and remarkable memory. Christian instruction came from her mother, who gave birth to an additional ten children. María later wrote that her parents "made their children pray in constant devotions and had us engage in mental prayer."[3]

At the age of twelve, María Coronel expressed her desire to become a nun and eventually helped convince her mother to turn the family castle into a convent for the Discalced Franciscan Nuns of Immaculate Conception. Both mother and daughter entered the house as novitiates, followed by the commitment of the father, who entered a nearby monastery with the Order of Our Seraphic Father Saint Francis. At that juncture, two of don Francisco's sons were already in residence there. María later wrote that "the Almighty favored our family so much, that all of us were consecrated to him in the religious state."[4]

María Coronel took formal vows on February 2, 1620, when she was not quite eighteen years of age and accepted the religious name María de Jesús. Plagued as always by ill health, the young nun exacerbated her frailness by self-flagellation to the extent of losing a great deal of blood. Ordered by her superiors to halt this dangerous practice, María then engaged in extended fasts limited to bread and water. As one of her admirers has written, "the life of Madre María de Jesús was one continuous act of prayer, penance, and complete self-denial."[5]

The Order of Discalced Nuns, also known as Poor Clares, soon expanded in numbers until the modest Coronel castle could not accommodate them, prompting the cloistered women to move to the convent of the Immaculate Conception in Agreda. At about that time, María de Jesús began to lapse into deep trances, totaling more than five hundred and lasting throughout the 1620s and very early 1630s. On those occasions, she could not be roused, and by her own admission experienced dreams in which her spirit was transported to a distant land where she taught the Gospel to a pagan people. Her alleged miraculous bilocations often took María de Jesús to eastern New Mexico and much of Texas. As historian David J. Weber has observed, those seeking to explain her "behavior rather than in drawing inspiration from it might regard her visions as induced in part by the disease anorexia mirabilis—a 'miraculous' loss of appetite apparently brought on by fasting in search of perfection of the spirit."[6]

As Sister María's trances continued year after year, she described her mystical experiences to her confessor, Father Sebastián Marcilla of Agreda. Marcilla's superiors, in turn, informed the archbishop of New Spain of the nun's revelations. And in May 1628, Archbishop Manso y Zúñiga wrote the religious custodian of New Mexico, requesting any information regarding the young nun's alleged transportations and teachings in northern New Spain. That communication had reached New Mexico shortly before the Jumano delegation had arrived at old Isleta in July 1629.[7]

Prompted by the archbishop's letter, Father Esteban de Perea, then custodian of New Mexico, decided that the timely arrival of the Jumanos warranted the sending of an exploratory party into their land. Guided by a Jumano chieftain, Fathers Juan Salas and Diego López marched some 112 leagues eastward from the Pueblo area. The two padres spent several days in southwest Texas, where they were welcomed by a large band of Indians, who claimed they had been advised of approaching missionaries by the Lady in Blue. Some of the natives bore crosses, and all treated the missionaries with respect.[8]

The assembled Indians described the Lady in Blue as young and beautiful, wearing a brown dress with a rough blue mantle colored like the sky. She had come softly before them like "light at sunset"; she was a kind and gentle person who spoke "sweet" words to them that they could understand; and she taught them to venerate the cross.[9]

When Fathers Salas and López returned to old Isleta, they convinced Fray Alonso de Benavides, a former custodian of New Mexico, that he should go to Mexico City and report on their extraordinary experiences among the Jumanos. From the capital, Benavides then traveled to Spain to seek out the embodied Lady in Blue.[10]

Father Benavides reached Spain in August 1630 and obtained an audience with Fray Bernardino de Siena, the head of the Franciscan Order. The high cleric informed Benavides that he had known about María de Jesús for more than eight years, and that the young nun had become abbess of her convent in Agreda. Father Siena had also received a report from the archbishop of New Mexico, again making reference to Mother María de Agreda. With this information, the former custodian of New Mexico departed for northeastern Spain.[11]

Benavides reached the mother superior's village at the end of April 1631 and went directly to her convent. His eyewitness description of María de Jesús de Agreda bears repeating: The "Abbess of the Convent of the Conception . . . is a woman of about 29 years of age, or a little less, of beautiful face, of white skin but of rosy color and large black eyes. The form of her habit . . . is exactly like our habit, that is, it is of brown sackcloth, very coarse and worn next to the skin . . . and over this brown habit is worn the white sackcloth habit, also coarse, with a scapulary of the same and the cord of Our Father, San Francisco. The cloak is of blue sackcloth, very coarse and the veil is black" [12] (Figure 23).

Remarkably, María de Agreda informed Alonso de Benavides that she recognized him, having been present in spirit when he baptized Piro Indians in New Mexico. She then described a religious companion of Father Alonso in New Mexico, whom she obviously had never seen in person, pointing out the contours and complexion of his face and the fact that although the priest was aged he had no visible gray hairs. Mother María also acknowledged that she had guided Juan de Salas and Diego López on their trek to the land of the Jumanos, and she described the principal Jumano chieftain, whom the Spanish dubbed Capitán Tuerto (Captain Squint Eye), as well as other Indian leaders. When asked by Father Benavides "why it was that . . . [the abbess] had never allowed us to see her when she allowed the Indians to have that privilege, she replied that they had a greater need than we." [13]

Father Benavides closed his interview with María de Jesús by requesting that she verify in writing all that she had told him. She complied, stating, "I declare what it is that has happened in the provinces of New Mexico, Quivira, and Jumanas, and the other nations . . . to whom I was carried by the will of God, and by the hand and the assistance of the Angels, where it happened to me that I saw and did all that I told the Father." Later, in the same document, the abbess remarked that "the events concerning which I have spoken happened to me since the year 1620 and up to this present year of 1631." [14]

By María de Agreda's initial admission, she experienced no further bilocations after 1631. However, in 1634 Alonso de Benavides offered an assessment of the continuing influence of the Lady in Blue on Native Americans. He claimed the conversion of thousands of natives, including many Jumanos who professed "having understood the truth of our Catholic faith since the year of '29." When asked what had motivated them to accept Christianity, the Jumanos had pointed to a portrait of a Franciscan nun, saying "a woman dressed like this passed among us always preaching," but that person, according to the Indians, had a face that was younger. [15]

During the last twenty-two years of her life, the Discalced abbess was an active correspondent with the Spanish king, Philip IV. Enjoying his confidence, María "was an undeniable force in his thinking and decision

La V. M. María de Jesus de Agreda, Predicando á los Chichimecos del Nuebo-méxico. Antt de Czzos.

FIGURE 23

A drawing of María de Agreda. This artwork depicts the Lady in Blue
instructing Indians in the Roman Catholic faith. (Photograph used
with the permission of the Catholic Archives of Texas, Austin.)

making." Believing herself to be obeying a command from God, in those same years she also wrote a controversial work on the life of the Virgin Mary, titled *The Mystical City of God*, which was published posthumously and banned for a time by the papacy.[16]

Late in life, María de Agreda, perhaps tempered by having been the subject of inquisitorial investigation, would cast doubt on some of the events detailed in Father Alonso de Benavides's reports. She asserted that the "visitations" to New Mexico actually ended after 1623, not 1631. She admitted that some of the things related by Fray Alonso actually happened to her, but others "have been exaggerated or misunderstood." In a report to Father Pedro Manero, director general of the Order of Saint Francis in Spain, she wrote: "I was so young when it happened. . . . It seems to me that either it was all the work of my imagination or that God showed me those things by means of abstract images, . . . or perhaps they were shown to me there [in America]. Neither then nor now was, or am, I capable of knowing the way it happened."[17]

María de Jesús died at Agreda on May 24, 1665. Following her death, the bishop of Tarragona in eastern Spain began the process of examining her life and virtues. Pope Clement X on January 28, 1673, signed a decree declaring her worthy of beatification and canonization. Like Father Antonio Margil, she received the title of venerable. Efforts to have the Spanish abbess's cause proceed toward canonization have been actively supported by the Spanish government as recently as the 1970s.[18]

Sainted or not, the legendary Lady in Blue of Texas fame lives on. According to Indian lore, when the blue nun last appeared, she blessed the natives and then slowly went away into the hills. The next morning the area was covered with a blanket of strange flowers that were a deep blue color like her mantle—the first Texas bluebonnets. She has also been credited with creating the first chili recipe, with aiding malaria victims along the Sabine River in the 1840s, and with appearing as an apparition during World War II.[19]

To our knowledge, no European woman, other than those traveling along the Río Grande en route to New Mexico, had set foot within the confines of the modern Lone Star State until the 1680s. In that decade, a number of French women arrived at Fort St. Louis with the ill-fated expedition of René Robert Cavelier, Sieur de La Salle.

Recent discovery of La Salle's ship, *La Belle*, in Matagorda Bay and the recovery of thousands of artifacts in 1996–1997 have shed light on what was to have been a self-sustaining French colony. Founded in early 1685, Fort St. Louis contained perhaps two hundred men, women, and children at the outset. Because the French outpost was off all trade routes and amid a hostile Spanish Sea, otherwise known as the Gulf of Mexico, material culture preserved on *La Belle* includes such articles as wooden combs, shoes, rings, and mirrors that may have been specifically intended for women colonists (Figure 24).[20]

Henri Joutel, principal chronicler of the La Salle expedition, does not specify how many women were among the French pioneers on the Texas coast, but the number of men must have been several times that of women. Overall, the population at Fort St. Louis diminished steadily and rapidly. Some deserted immediately, others died from disease, snakebite, drowning, or Karankawa arrows. La Salle himself was a victim of assassination by his own men in March 1687. At Christmastime in 1688, La Salle's settlement fell victim to a final, brutal attack by Karankawa warriors that resulted in the deaths of the adult colonists. But from the survivors themselves and Henri Joutel's journal, we gain insight into the history of a few women at the doomed French outpost.

Isabelle Planteau of Saint Méry Parish in Paris had married Lucien Talon of the bishopric of Beauvais in Normandy while the two of them resided in Quebec. From their marriage, in about 1671, came three sons and two daughters. The Talons returned to France, arriving there by the time La Salle organized his Gulf voyage of 1684. With one possible exception, these French Canadians were the only sizable family in the company.[21]

When the Talons departed with the La Salle expedition from the port of La Rochelle, Madame Talon was again pregnant and delivered a fourth son, Robert, on the voyage. Thus, a family of eight, with six children ranging in age from a few months to twelve years, arrived in the wilderness that was Texas. And things did not go well for them. The father, according to Joutel, became "lost in the woods" on one of La Salle's expeditions, and the circumstances of his death are not known. Left a widow, Madame Talon found her grief intensified soon after by the death of her elder daughter, Marie-Elizabeth.[22]

Adding to Madame Talon's distress was an unseemly quarrel that developed over the rights of her newborn son, Robert. Gabriel Minime, Sieur Barbier, a lieutenant in the 1684 venture, "used to slip aside from the company with a young maid he had a kindness for." After impregnating the woman, he subsequently married her. Barbier claimed for his offspring the customary privileges granted by the French crown to the first child born in a new colony. Madame Talon countered that her son Robert "though born before our Arrival, ought to be preferred." The matter became temporarily moot when Madame Barbier miscarried and "the dispute was not decided."[23]

FIGURE 24

Artifacts from La Salle's ship, La Belle. These items, including a colander, ladle, and small leather shoe, may have been intended for the use of women at La Salle's Fort St. Louis. (Photograph used with the permission of the Texas Historical Commission.)

On La Salle's third overland expedition, Sieur Barbier was left in charge at Fort St. Louis, in part because he was married and in part because he had suffered a leg injury. When the imperious La Salle departed, he informed Madame Talon that she had to give up ten-year-old Pierre. Her son must join the expedition to the land of the Hasinai Indians, where he would be left to learn their language. The tearful parting of mother and son touched nearly everyone in the colony, and both Talons must have realized that they would never see each other again. Pierre's eleventh birthday fell on March 20, 1687, one day after La Salle's assassination in the wilds of East Texas, and, although not by the commander's design, young Pierre would spend three years among the Hasinais before being freed by Alonso de León in 1690.[24]

Meanwhile, conditions had deteriorated at Fort St. Louis. Those left in Barbier's command included his wife and seven other "Maids." The colony had been deprived of strong leadership, and by May 1687 the settlers were nothing more than a "pathetic band of maimed and misfits, women, and children who clung to a meager existence." But the worst was yet to come. Through the Indian grapevine, the Karankawas learned of La Salle's death and the disunity among his followers that had spawned multiple homicides. The miserable colonists were particularly vulnerable, being duped by the Indians' outward appearances of friendship.[25]

The end came with an attack in late December 1688, accompanied by horrifyingly brutal actions on the part of the Karankawas. Killed outright were two Franciscans priests and Commandant Barbier. The four Talon children, who had already lost their father and older sister and suffered separation from Pierre, saw their mother die by a Karankawa arrow. Initially, Madame Barbier, with a three-month-old infant at her breast, was spared, thanks to the intervention of the Karankawa women, but it was only a brief reprieve. Warriors slew the mother and dashed the baby's head against the trunk of a tree. To their credit, the native women also came to the rescue of the Talon children, protecting and succoring the four of them, as well as Eustache Bréman, who had been taken in by the Talon family.[26]

When Alonso de León arrived at the site of Fort St. Louis in April 1689, he found three corpses, one a woman with an arrow in her back. Moved by the discovery, a member of León's party sat down and drafted by campfire light a rhymed elegy to the colonists who had suffered such a tragic fate:

> O beautiful French maiden fair
> Who pressed sweet roses to your hair
> and with thy snow-white hand
> briefly touched the lily of the land
> and with thy art perfection brought
> Greek ladies now is profile wrought;
> thy needlework made bright
> the miseries of thy plight;
> and now so cold, so dead
> these woods look down upon thy head
> but thou witherest not in vain,
> art seen in death, but not in pain.[27]

By early 1689, only one European female remained in all of Texas. Because of her youth, Marie-Madeleine Talon had been spared the general carnage at Fort St. Louis and was held captive by the Karankawas for approximately eighteen months. When ransomed near Matagorda Bay by Alonso de León, Marie-Madeleine was sixteen and still a virgin. From evidence presented later, the Karankawas had been much taken with the young French maiden, who was "quite pretty," and "greatly desired to abuse [her.]" Only the shrewd intercession of Eustache Bréman saved Marie-Madeleine from violation. The young Frenchman warned the Indians that "if they did violence to her," the "girl's God would make them all die." [28]

Marie-Madeleine and her brothers were taken to Mexico City, where they lived in the viceroy's palace. The Conde de Galve treated them "with great kindness and all sorts of good treatment, regarding them as his household servants and as naturalized citizens." And, when the viceroy and his wife, doña Elvira, returned to Europe in 1697, they took the twenty-two-year-old Frenchwoman with them. Marie-Madeleine subsequently married Pierre Simon of Paris and gave birth to a son in 1699. [29]

After Spaniards withdrew from San Francisco de los Tejas in 1693, Texas was unoccupied by the Spanish for more than two decades, although it was not entirely forgotten or unvisited. The province especially remained on the mind of Father Francisco Hidalgo, who made unfinished work among the Tejas Indians his consuming passion. [30]

Aided by Father Antonio Margil, guardian of the apostolic college of Santa Cruz in Querétaro, and the governor of Coahuila, Franciscan missionary activity in northern New Spain resulted in the founding of Mission San Juan Bautista on January 1, 1700. Situated at modern-day Guerrero, Coahuila, that mission outpost became the "gateway" to Texas. At the nearby presidio of the same name, a single family, the Ramóns, rose to prominence and power. Associated with Presidio San Juan Bautista from its founding date to his death in 1719, was Commandant Diego Ramón. [31]

As earlier noted, when St. Denis and his companions crossed the Río Grande in search of Father Hidalgo in July 1714, the French cavalier and a Spanish maiden named Manuela almost immediately found each other attractive and were soon engaged. It seems likely that St. Denis's intentions to marry Manuela, who had family ties to prominent military and political elites in New Spain, helped him curry favor with the viceroy and establish his bona fides as a would-be Spanish subject. [32]

However, the relationship of St. Denis's fiancée to Commandant Ramón has confounded and confused more than a few modern historians. In several works, doña Manuela is variously referred to as niece, granddaughter, or daughter of the commandant. By 1995, after years of painstaking genealogical research, historian Patricia R. Lemée of Austin,

Texas, has arrived at a positive identification of Manuela's familial ties with the Ramóns.[33]

Manuela was the daughter of Diego Sánchez Navarro y Camacho and Mariana Gomes Mascorro y Garza. Her paternal grandmother was Feliciana Camacho y Botello, a widow who married Commandant Diego Ramón. The commandant then became stepfather and guardian to his wife's minor children, including Manuela's father. Accordingly, doña Manuela, born at Monclova, Coahuila, in 1697, was Diego Ramón's step-granddaughter.[34]

After her marriage to St. Denis in late 1715 or early 1716, the couple was soon separated when the French cavalier left San Juan Bautista in late April 1716 as commissary officer of the Diego Ramón expedition. By then, Manuela had just celebrated her nineteenth birthday and was pregnant. Her complete name after marriage was Manuela Sánchez Navarro y Gomes Mascorro de St. Denis.[35]

The Ramón/St. Denis expedition of 1716 was the first step in Spain's continuous occupation of Texas, a presence that lasted for 105 years. Unlike the Spanish entradas of the late 1680s and early 1690s, the Ramón/St. Denis expedition included female colonists. The first recorded Hispanic women in Texas were María Antonia Longoria, Antonia de la Cerda, Antonia Vidales, Ana María Ximénez de Valdez, María Antonia Ximénez, Juana de San Miguel, and Josefa Sánchez—all married. One single woman, Ana Guerra, entered Texas as its first señorita.[36]

Following the reoccupation of East Texas in 1717–1718, St. Denis fell into disfavor with Spanish authorities in New Spain. Suspicions of his intent to engage in forbidden trade between French Louisiana and New Spain, coupled with a changed political climate occasioned by the death of Louis XIV in 1715, landed the French cavalier in hot water. Imprisoned in Mexico City and separated from Manuela for more than a year, St. Denis finally gained his freedom but was enjoined from ever returning to Texas. Fearing a second imprisonment for ill-tempered remarks made in the capital, on September 5, 1718, he fled toward Natchitoches. Eventually, Spanish authorities permitted Manuela, who had given birth to a second child at San Juan Bautista, to join her husband. Their reunion at Natchitoches could have come as early as 1719 but no later than 1721. Louis Juchereau de St. Denis and Manuela Sánchez Navarro eventually had seven children—two sons and five daughters. When her husband died at Natchitoches in June 1744, doña Manuela was widowed at the age of forty-seven and left with the responsibility of supporting three or four minor children. She continued to live at Natchitoches in the family home until her death on April 16, 1758. Although she never resided in Texas, Manuela is assuredly a high-profile colonial woman of importance to the province. As Patricia R. Lemée has remarked, her marriage to St. Denis "transcended the political complexities of the French and Spanish colonial frontier." That same union gave her "an indirect but intimate influence on cultural interactions from northern New Spain to the French colony of Louisiana for almost half of the eighteenth century."[37]

The eight women who accompanied the Diego Ramón expedition of 1716 were Texas's first Hispanic female residents. These pioneers came as the wives of soldiers, or, in the case of Ana Guerra, soon married one in Texas. However, Spanish officials in Mexico City, especially a judge (*oidor*) of the royal *audiencia* named Juan Manuel de Oliván Rebolledo sought a more permanent hold on the province. Oliván had headed the 1717 investigation of St. Denis in the capital, and when the interrogation of the French cavalier ended on September 18, the *oidor* pondered information gleaned from the Frenchman's declarations of 1715 and the more recent one. His conclusion? St. Denis "had more extensive knowledge of the Province of Texas and adjacent regions than did the Spaniards."[38]

Oliván's response to the French threat was twofold. In late 1717, he recommended the establishment of fortifications at San Francisco de los Tejas, Matagorda Bay, and at a site on the San Antonio River. Each of the military garrisons must be supported by colonies of Spanish and Indian families, who would be subsidized at the rate of three hundred pesos annually. Further inducements would include grants of land for cultivation and stock raising. The *oidor* also recommended that soldiers stationed at the presidios "have the prerequisites of being farmers and married," adding that knowledge of agriculture would lead to improvement of the land grants they received. And, he added, "the ties of matrimony [will cause them] to take root more firmly" and "they will be able to fill their presidios with the children that their wives bear them." As an additional advantage, Oliván believed that married presidials would not "vex" Indian women.[39]

Especially of interest was Oliván's plan to forcibly relocate women and men from the heartland of New Spain to Texas. He proposed that "later, all vagrants and persons of both sexes without a trade found in Mexico [City] and other cities, . . . and any women taken into custody by court action could be sent to these fortifications and colonies." He warned that "those who cannot behave in their native land or in thickly populated districts often change their habits and conduct in distant districts, or in the wilderness." Thus, in Oliván's view, the frontier of New

Spain provided salutary merits for miscreant men and women, while at the same time affording an escape valve that improved the lives of the *gente decente* in the interior.[40]

Oliván's suggestions for peopling Texas with Hispanic families were also responsible for plans adopted by the Council of the Indies in 1719, which included the recruitment of four hundred families from the Canary Islands and the kingdom of Galicia in Spain. But in the meantime, the situation in Texas itself had changed. The background of events leading to the founding of San Antonio in 1718 and Spanish withdrawal from East Texas in 1719 is familiar to our readers. And at this juncture, we are particularly interested in pioneer Hispanic women at Béxar.[41]

The 1718 expedition of Martín de Alarcón, which resulted in the founding of San Antonio, was not intended as a purely military undertaking. True, the primary purpose in setting up Mission San Antonio de Valero and Presidio San Antonio de Béxar was to provide a way station between the Río Grande and the eastern missions, as well as to begin the conversion of natives in the region. But Alarcón also had instructions to recruit civilian families, and he did so. From the very beginning, Villa de Béxar contained a handful of civilian men and their spouses. Those first Bexareños were farmers, muleteers, artisans, and aides to the missionaries.[42]

The Alarcón expedition contained a total of seventy-two persons, including thirty-four soldiers, of whom seven were married with families. It seems reasonable that not all of the seven families remained at Villa de Béxar, for Alarcón continued on to the six missions in East Texas. But any of the husband and wife units residing there would have relocated to San Antonio after the Chicken War of 1719.[43]

Whatever the number of presidial families at Béxar by 1719, it had increased to fifty-four by 1726, but at that same juncture civilian residents totaled only four. The nonmilitary contingent expanded over the next five years to an estimated twenty to twenty-five households. That growth may be explained in part by a relative calm in Indian affairs, which made San Antonio more attractive to frontier families, and by the maturation of soldiers' daughters to marriageable ages. For example, in the early 1720s two offspring of Cristóbal Carabajal and Juana Guerra married soldiers. Overall, eight daughters of the original Bexareños wed and remained in Texas. By 1730, approximately forty married couples made up a portion of the population of San Antonio—this on the eve of momentous changes that were about to affect the total population significantly.[44]

The sudden increase in Hispanic settlers at Béxar fed off two unrelated events, with the first being the more dramatic. In 1731, the arrival of fifty-five Canary Islanders at San Antonio completed the final act in a historical process that had begun with Juan Manuel Oliván's recommendation of 1717 and its endorsement two years later by the Council of the Indies. The ambitious plan to recruit families in Spain and the Canary Islands had lain stillborn for years. Attempts to breathe life into it were frustrated for multiple reasons, including difficulties in recruitment, expense of the enterprise, problems in finding ships bound for the desired ports of New Spain, and inefficiency in the royal bureaucracy. Second, the budget-pinching recommendations of Brigadier General Pedro de Rivera essentially meant closure of the three westernmost missions in East Texas and the relocation of their population to San Antonio. Integrating the displaced East Texans, founding three new missions, accommodating often contentious and pretentious *isleños* (islanders), and defending against a renewed onslaught of Apache attacks placed severe strains on the older Bexareños.[45]

The fifty-five Canary Islanders represented fifteen families, but by the time they had completed the arduous journey across the Atlantic and the trek to Texas, widows headed two of those units. Documents describe María Rodríguez Robayna as having a "good figure . . . long face, fair complexion, black hair and eyebrows." Although only twenty-seven years old, María had six children, ranging from one month to thirteen years of age. The second widow, having an appearance almost identical to the first, was thirty-year-old Mariana Delgado Meleano. She was accompanied by three offspring, ages two to sixteen years. These widows demonstrate an important interpretive point: *Isleño* women were not only wives and mothers but also headed two of the fifteen pioneer families.[46]

The dynamics of how the raw frontier villa that was San Antonio with many divisive elements transformed over time into a viable community have been expertly examined by historian Jesús de la Teja. Within that emerging society one sees the role of pioneer women at Béxar. The vast majority of these Bexareñas were illiterate wives and daughters who represent little more than names in parish and census records. They obviously left no diaries or letters, and learning about their contributions to early Texas history has been difficult but nonetheless doable.

It is our contention that the legal record, consisting of wills, lawsuits, estate settlements, petitions, and legal decisions of magistrates, reveals considerable insight into these "faceless" women. Even unlearned females on the frontier demonstrated an osmotic knowledge of Castilian law, passed down generation after generation from grandmother to mother to daughter. And although San Antonio was blessed by having no lawyers, settlers there still found ways to sue each other. Those cases for the most part were heard by Texas' Spanish governors, who were invariably military men but also served as the chief magistrates of the province.[47]

The persistence of Spanish law in frontier Texas, especially as applied to women's legal rights, is a topic worthy of extended research. Spanish women, as in other countries of medieval and early modern Europe, had inferior status when compared to men. Because of their subordination, women had to be particularly mindful of the expectations of society and conform to those norms of probity; otherwise they faced being branded as outcasts.[48]

It was a peculiar feature of Castilian jurisprudence that almost every possible contingency was covered in the law. This approach gave Spanish magistrates far less latitude than English or Anglo-American judges, for they were almost never required to discern the intent of the malefactor or subsequent interpretations by the courts. The legal rights of women in Spain, and by extension in the Americas, were spelled out in what may seem like excruciating detail and precision. But on a distant frontier like Texas, illiterate and unlearned women overcame many obstacles because their rights were protected by Spanish law, which allowed local magistrates to "exercise their experience, knowledge, and prudence in meting out justice."[49]

Like so many aspects of life in Spain and colonial Spanish America, experiences in the Spanish Reconquest (ca. 720–1492) defined practices from farming to stock raising to the founding of villas and towns. Through the centuries, as the Christian domain crept southward at the expense of Muslim control, men seized land from other men, but women "played indispensable roles as settlers, wives of colonists, mothers of successive generations of defenders, and vital members of the new Hispanic communities." Because life was uncertain and dangerous for men and women alike, the new settlements that grew into villas and towns granted *fueros* (special rights) to women, which guaranteed them property and justice under the law. These same concessions were later incorporated into the statutes of Castile.[50]

To be sure, respectable women on the frontier were encouraged to marry and bear children, but they were also guaranteed protection and privilege under Castilian law. Those considerations did not mean that women had equal status with men, for they did not. And because men did the fighting, women faced the reality of widowhood. Should that occur, widows were expected to honor the memory of their deceased husbands for a year and then remarry. During the interlude, former wives assumed responsibility for children, property, and other family matters. But even women who did not lose husbands were expected to handle the affairs of the household during the absence of their spouses. Such matters were no different in frontier Texas.

Ideally, our treatment of colonial women would follow the lives of representative personalities from cradle to grave. But given the sparseness of existing documentation, that approach is not possible. Early Texas women, of course, first appear in baptismal and marriage records, which tell us little of interest beyond bare names and dates. It is the legal record, to repeat, that humanizes these diverse women and establishes that they too walked the land and breathed the air that once was frontier Texas. Through snippets of information gleaned from litigation, individual women become known to us and add to our knowledge of the role played by their gender in this borderland province. And in looking first at Hispanic, mestizo, mulatta, and Indian women at Béxar, we hope to contribute to the social history of early Texas.[51]

Typically, the role that daughters played in cementing family alliances was crucial. Making a proper marriage for men meant that they might collect a dowry and gain entry to positions of power and influence. Isleños initially monopolized agricultural lands, water rights, and town council positions, but their small numbers made it necessary that they seek marriage partners among the American-born settlers. For example, the six daughters of José Leal and Ana de los Santos, as well as their three sons, married non-isleños. Within three generations, much of San Antonio's population could claim Canary Islander descent, and "no undiluted Isleño stock remained." However, family ties to Canary Islanders often provided a means to achieve higher status for a sizable portion of San Antonio's population.[52]

Aside from marriages serving as a strategic vehicle for social advancement, what did marital status mean for colonial women? Women under Castilian law definitely could own property in their own name. The bride brought dotal (dowry) property into a marriage but retained her separate (paraphernal) holdings. Although the husband exercised managerial control over their joint possessions, there were safeguards against his being a spendthrift, and the wife had to consent to the sale of any material wealth. Furthermore, Castilian law recognized community property rights, meaning that from the moment of matrimony, all assets and liabilities accrued equally to both parties.[53]

The case of María Melián illustrates several of the above points. She and her first husband, Lucas Delgado, were Canary Islanders. Doña María indicated that both she and don Lucas were poor and neither brought any property into the marriage. After Delgado's death, she later wed Juan Leal Goraz and brought "into the power of my husband" one cow. However, by her own testimony, she did not "give him any of the five [cattle] which the king gave me when I came as a settler" to San Fernando de Béxar. This account clearly demonstrates that women could bring dotal property into a marriage, as well as retain paraphernal possessions.[54]

To illustrate the point that a woman's permission was required for her husband to sell property, there is the case of María Alexandra de los Reyes. María's husband, Pedro de Regalado de Treviño, contracted for the sale of a lot with house and improvements to Martín Flores y Valdés. In the document of conveyance, doña María had to renounce the laws "relative to and in favor and defense of women," as well as swearing that she would not "make any claims in opposition to this contract by reason of my marriage, dowry, or . . . hereditary rights." Finally, María stated that she was not "influenced, much less intimidated" by her husband in agreeing to the contract.[55]

Affairs of the family of José de Urrutia reveal a great deal about wives, daughters, and the disposition of property. Urrutia, one of the more famous personalities in the early history of San Antonio, had chosen to live among the Tejas Indians in 1693, rather than withdraw to Coahuila. He later rejoined Spanish society and became presidial commander at Béxar in 1733, a position held until his death in 1740.[56]

During his long life, don José married twice within the church. His first wife, Antonia Ramón, brought no dowry or property into wedlock. The couple had one daughter, also named Antonia. After the death of his first spouse, Urrutia wed Rosa Flores de Valdés, who was also without personal property or dowry. This union produced ten children, four of whom were daughters. Don José's last testament recognizes eleven legitimate children, and they were to "share and share alike" in the majority of his estate.[57]

Because of his position and prominence, the settlement of Captain Urrutia's estate was lengthy and complicated. Consequently, don José's widow, Rosa, and her sons jointly granted power of attorney to Juan de Angulo of Mexico City. That appointment was later revoked, and a new one given to José de Plazas of Boca de Leones. Both men had been empowered to represent these heirs in any claims or other litigation involved in settling the deceased's accounts.[58]

In the year following Urrutia's death, one of his sons, Joaquín, a soldier at the presidio of Béxar, wished to sell his share of a house and lot in Saltillo that formed part of his inheritance. To do so, he had to obtain the permission and consent of his wife, Josefa Hernández. Again we see the necessity of consent from a married woman of property.[59]

Juana de Urrutia, daughter from don José's second marriage, was the widow of Ignacio González and a resident of San Fernando de Béxar. In 1745 she sold her share of an inherited house and lot in Saltillo to her brother Pedro for eighteen pesos. Doña Juana in the following year then disposed of property belonging to her and her deceased husband, which included a lot in San Fernando containing a house and sixteen peach trees. The purchaser was Diego Ramón, who paid five hundred pesos for the property.[60]

To summarize, legal matters relating to José de Urrutia's estate reveal that, subject to the desire of the deceased, legitimate daughters inherited in equal shares with legitimate sons. Widows could grant powers of attorney; a son who inherited property needed his wife's consent in order to make conveyance; and a widow could sell inherited property at her discretion—to those familiar with English and Anglo-American law, these were all unusual powers for women to have.

Another case at Béxar involved Josefa Flores de Valdés, an early resident who had two husbands die intestate. In 1744 doña Josefa granted power of attorney to Francisco de Liñán of Coahuila to collect any money, livestock, water rights, or other valuables owed by debtors to either of her deceased husbands. She also gave Liñán the right to institute legal proceedings and swear oaths in her stead. And she agreed that "for the execution of the foregoing, I bind my person and present and future assets; I empower the justices and judges of His Majesty . . . to compel me to observe and comply with the contents of this power. I renounce . . . [the laws] relative to and in favor of women."[61]

Documents concerning doña Josefa and her business affairs show that women were also involved in transactions involving "human" property, as well as real estate. On October 29, 1743, Señora Valdés sold Governor Justo Boneo y Morales a black slave named Luis, whom she had received from her deceased first husband, Miguel Núñez Morillo. In making the sale, doña Josefa obligated herself as real vendor to guarantee that Luis would belong to Boneo y Morales "for all time." Should, however, the transaction result in default, Josefa pledged to return the sale price of 200 pesos. On that same day, the Bexareña in turn purchased a thirty-three-year-old slave from don Justo for 270 pesos. Thus, a woman could be both vendor and buyer of black slaves.[62]

That women in Spanish colonies had more legal rights and protection than their counterparts in English colonies, or in the early United States, is a given. Equally impressive are the awareness that women of all classes had of those rights and the responsiveness of the legal system to their petitions.

An earlier incident involving the above doña Josefa relates to Antonia Lusgardia Hernández, a free *mulata* residing in San Antonio, and illustrates still another example of a woman's rights, no matter how poor she was, under Spanish law. This case arose in a petition presented to Governor Manuel de Sandoval in 1735. Nine years earlier, Antonia and her daughter moved into the home of Josefa and Miguel Núñez Morillo. While living there, the *mulata* woman gave birth to a son, whom Núñez's wife became attached to and took for baptism as a godchild. However, in the time that Antonia worked in the home, she received no salary and suffered "from lack of clothing and mistreatment." Consequently, she left, taking her children with her.[63]

In her petition to the governor, Antonia claimed that don Miguel had entered her new home, "snatched" her son, and taken him back to the Núñez household. The aggrieved woman declared that the boy, Ignacio, was "the only man I have and the one I hope will eventually support me." She referred to herself as "but a poor, helpless woman whose only protection is a good administration and a good judicial system."[64]

The governor summoned don Miguel and read Antonia's petition to him. Núñez disagreed with the woman's version of events, stating that the *mulata* after the birth of her son had asked doña Josefa to be the godmother "and gave her the said boy." According to don Miguel, Antonia had renounced her rights to the child, and the boy, having left his mother "without being carried or encouraged by anybody," returned of his own volition to the Núñez home.[65]

It appears that the child Ignacio was reunited with his birth mother on orders of Manuel de Sandoval, for in his decision, the governor made reference to a request of don Miguel, namely, that should the *mulata* woman suffer any misfortune in the future, the boy would be returned to the Núñez household for his own protection and "because of the spiritual relationship" of the boy and his godmother, doña Josefa.[66]

If justice was served in the instance of the poor *mulata* mother, the case of an Indian woman unjustly enslaved and passed from master to master until she wound up before Governor Domingo Cabello in the 1780s is even more remarkable. María Gertrudis de la Peña, a native of the region near Camargo, had become the human property of Pedro José de la Peña of Saltillo, who paid fifty pesos to another man for her purchase as a baby and provided a surname for the child. The slave María endured two more changes in masters before arriving at San Fernando, where she petitioned for her freedom.[67]

María's story, as presented in documents submitted to Domingo Cabello, is indeed a sad one. The young Indian, who did not know her exact age or remember her parents, lived in the house of Angel Navarro. María testified that under the name of "Esclava" (Slave) applied to her in the Navarro household, she suffered "many ill-treatments" from the family and especially from don Angel himself. Before her arrival at San Antonio, María stated, she had lived as a daughter with José de la Peña at Saltillo until the age of sixteen, when she became pregnant by her adoptive father. To protect his reputation, Peña sold María to a soldier at Presidio del Río Grande, who also claimed the Indian girl as his daughter, not as slave.[68]

For two years María lived with the presidial until he became angry with her, seized all her clothes, and sold her to Angel Navarro. The new master promised the young woman that he would free her after three years of servitude. María acknowledged that she had agreed to those terms, but "after having experienced the temper and style of the household" of don Angel, she had changed her mind. Asking Cabello for "mercy, justice, and goodwill," María expressed the hope that in San Fernando "there would not be an absence of justice as there had been at the Presidio of Rio Grande."[69]

In his decision, Governor Cabello noted that María Gertrudis was "free by nature" but had nonetheless been sold as property. He declared all transactions involving the woman to be "null, fraudulent, and against all the international laws and that stated by the municipal royal laws of these kingdoms, which greatly favors the freedom of the Indians." Therefore, don Domingo commanded that the young woman be given her freedom and exempted from the obligation of serving Angel Navarro. Cabello, however, recommended that the former slave return to Camargo to join her relatives, if she could locate them, but warned that if she chose to remain in the capital she must live with "orderliness."[70]

Although Spanish law clearly worked to the advantage of María Gertrudis de la Peña, the same legal system that freed her held all females accountable for their behavior. Of particular interest in this vein is a case relating to the adulterous conduct of Rosa Guerra, which ended with the husband, Matías Treviño, being murdered by Rosa's alleged lover, Antonio Tello. This unseemly triangle of love and hate came to light on August 21, 1744, when a mortally wounded Treviño staggered into Mission San Antonio de Valero. Don Matías bled from a single bullet wound and had been severely beaten about the head and shoulders with a gun barrel. The dying man stated that he was attacked by Antonio Tello, while the assailant screamed at him, "Now, you'll see, cuckold."[71]

Treviño claimed that on August 19 a heated argument had erupted in his household. It began with the husband's scolding his wife because he had reason to suspect that she was unfaithful. The wife, Rosa Guerra, allegedly replied in anger, "I promise you that I shall soon be freed from these bothersome vexations. . . . I'll have you killed." Don Matías concluded his deathbed statement by testifying that it was "well known and rumored that the said Tello had illicit relations with [my wife]."[72]

The testimony of a soldier at the Béxar presidio added further justification for the husband's suspicion and anger. While Treviño was away from San Antonio, Tello had built a log house for Rosa and apparently permitted her to live there free of charge. However, according to the presidial, don Antonio was always there. Still another witness deposed that he realized Tello had an ulterior motive for building Rosa's residence, because the two of them were guilty of "objectionable behavior."[73]

Authorities at Béxar arrested Rosa Guerra on the day of her husband's murder, clapped her in shackles, and placed her in custody. In her deposition, Rosa insisted that her husband and the accused had never quarreled, declared that she had paid for the house Tello had constructed, and denied that they had an illicit relationship. In the same testimony, however, the woman admitted that in the recent past she "had been enjoined three times by the alcalde to throw him [Tello] out of her house."[74]

Unfortunately, the documentation relating to this case does not include its final disposition. Tello, who had taken sanctuary in Mission San Antonio de Valero, gave a deposition there and declared his innocence. Three days later, Béxar authorities, with the permission of the prelate, surrounded the mission, but Tello had fled the premises and remained a fugitive. Nevertheless, the fact that the alcalde had placed Rosa under arrest and confined her in fetters illustrates that women had to behave responsibly and morally or face serious consequences.[75]

A second case, occurring almost thirty years later, also involved suspected adultery, and it likewise resulted in murder. That legal proceeding, however, illustrates a different point of law regarding the conduct of women. In April 1772, Juan de Sosa confessed to the murder of Diego Menchaca, a former boarder in the Sosa household. Problems between the two men, who were both soldiers, began when the husband became jealous of Menchaca. Matters only worsened when Menchaca intervened in a domestic quarrel and wounded Sosa for beating his wife, Gertrudis Barrón. The enraged husband then ordered don Diego out of his home and forbade him ever to return there.[76]

Don Juan, however, continued to suspect that his wife and Menchaca were having secret rendezvous, and those suspicions intensified one night when Sosa discovered that Menchaca was not at his assigned post. Try as he might, the increasingly agitated husband could find neither his wife nor the missing sentry. Sosa was about to return to the presidio when he spotted his wife's dog, which always followed her, and realized that she had to be nearby. At about nine o'clock in the evening, Sosa found the couple in another house and entered it. When don Diego tried to eject Sosa from the premises, the infuriated husband struck him three times with his sword.[77]

After the fatal assault, Sosa confessed to the crime but alleged that he had only used the broad side of his blade in the attack and had not intended to kill his wife's lover. In the meantime, doña Gertrudis had "sought protection in the sacred place" of Mission La Purísima Concepción. Luis Antonio Menchaca, presidial captain and magistrate at Béxar, requested permission to have the woman removed from the mission, although "not to be immediately punished or charged with any transgression, but only to protect her" and make sure that those responsible for the murder were properly punished. After the woman was denied sanctuary and arrested, however, the same official decided that the circumstances surrounding the case justified having doña Gertrudis imprisoned "with shackles" in a house "that will meet satisfactory security" until the matter was resolved.[78]

Joaquín de Orendáin, lieutenant at Presidio Béxar and defender of Juan de Sosa, declared that the accused should be freed, because the crime was committed "to save his honor." He emphasized that don Juan had found his wife with the other man in very suspicious circumstances, and proclaimed that "any man has the right to defend his honor, [and] his wife," particularly against anyone "who violently wants to snatch her away."[79]

This case was eventually carried on appeal to Mexico City, where the advocate general of the destitute, acting on behalf of the accused murderer, expressed the opinion that at times there was justification for murder. If a man and woman were found in a secluded place at night, that in itself was "evidence of adultery." And, noted the advocate general, Sosa had already forbidden communication between Menchaca and Gertrudis Barrón. Indeed, don Juan himself was the offended party and was justified in his actions.[80]

In the final disposition of the case, the point was clearly made that a husband, upon discovering his wife in an overt act of adultery or even in circumstances suggesting that immoral act, had the right to kill her lover. In Sosa's case, circumstances did "not [warrant] sufficient proof of infidelity" but served to explain his being so "mad at that moment, blinded by anger, and deeply hurt" that he acted irrationally. Therefore, he should be exculpated. As of May 1773, Sosa's sentence was commuted to time already served. Interestingly, upon his release, Sosa was ordered to pay for twenty-five Masses to be said for the soul of Diego Menchaca, an order that he obeyed, however grudgingly.[81]

The resolution of this case demonstrates that "the unwritten law" of a cuckolded husband's rights, which survived into twentieth-century Texas, was clearly set forth in Castilian law. The precedent dates back to the Siete Partidas of King Alfonso X in the thirteenth century. By those statutes, should a husband find his wife in the act of committing adultery, he had the right to kill the man. He could not, however, kill the wife but must instead hand her over to a judge for punishment.[82]

Because the commission of adultery by a man's wife was a serious offense and an affront to his honor, the husband could appeal to the legal system for assistance in stopping such matters. Antonio Gil Ibarvo in East Texas used this approach in the 1760s when his wife, María Padilla, was publicly carrying on an illicit affair with a soldier named Andrés Chirinos. When measures used by Governor Angel de Martos y Navarette's predecessor had proved ineffective in resolving the issue, Martos arrested Chirinos, whom he accused of scandalous drunkenness and immoral relations with Gil Ibarvo's wife. The soldier was released and reassigned, apparently to La Bahía. Although Chirinos was sternly warned never to return to Los Adaes, the lure of María's attraction was evidently too great. When he reappeared at Los Adaes, he was promptly arrested and again exiled from the capital.[83]

The persistent Chirinos, however, had the incredible "audacity" to return to Los Adaes yet again in 1766. A frustrated Gil Ibarvo again petitioned Governor Martos for a definitive solution to the longtime problem. Don Antonio asked to be spared the continuing shame of public knowledge that "my wife and I were living in a constant state of vexation, anxiety, and discord on account of Andrés Chirinos." Since attempts to exile the offender within Texas had proved ineffective, the cuckolded husband concluded that the only way for him to end "said annoyances" and achieve "matrimonial tranquility" was to send Chirinos permanently to a suitable, distant location or "grant me license to move with my family from this presidio."[84]

The governor decided that removing the offender was preferable to granting the Ibarvo family permission to relocate. That decision was propitious, especially when one considers the role that Antonio Gil Ibarvo would play in the history of East Texas over the following decades. Martos's solution was to sentence Andrés Chirinos to serve the crown without pay for four years at El Morro in Havana, where he received only a subsistence ration. It was hoped that this resolution would allow don Antonio to achieve at least a measure of "matrimonial tranquility," and he did not have to resort to murder as in the case of Juan de Sosa.[85]

The tumultuous story of María Padilla, her husband, and her lover reminds us that although San Antonio was the first major center of Hispanic female population in the province, East Texas also became the home of many families. After the founding of modern Nacogdoches in 1779, the villa grew rapidly and by 1783 had attracted many unsavory elements. Antonio Gil Ibarvo, expressing his concern about those developments, noted that "disorders of all kinds are spreading torrent-like amongst persons of both sexes."[86]

To correct the situation, Gil Ibarvo issued a set of laws, which may have been influenced in part by his own domestic intranquilities. The criminal code, summarized previously in Chapter 9, contains specific punishments for female transgressors. For example, don Antonio detailed punishment for any woman having relations with a married man other than her husband, with repeated offenses drawing increasingly severe penalties. Acting as a "procuress" was likewise a serious and punishable crime. Significantly, any man or woman convicted of adultery was to be "punished with the utmost rigor of the law."[87]

Don Antonio's code, especially harsh as applied to transgressors, nonetheless provided protection for women. The death penalty awaited any man who ravished "a maiden." "Rape in a secluded and deserted place" called for capital punishment, as did committing violence against "a woman living honestly." Likewise, consenting to the prostitution of one's wife or acting as a pimp for any woman carried stiff penalties.[88]

Whatever the efficacy of these Draconian codes, Nacogdoches continued to grow rapidly, reaching a population of 660 by the end of the eighteenth century. Census records dating from 1799 to 1809 afford interesting glimpses into the lives of colonial women on that important frontier in Spanish Texas.

Particularly of interest are the twenty-four women who headed households in 1799. Ranging in age from thirty-four to eighty-five, these widows display tremendous ethnic diversity, including Hispanics, *castas*, Indians, French, and one listed as an "American." The two youngest widows were María Benites and Vicenta Medina. María, a Hispanic native of Los Adaes, had two minor children, ages four and five. Vicenta, a mulatta from Béxar, was the mother of a twelve-year-old son and a thirteen-year-old daughter. The most aged widow was the Hispanic octogenarian Rita Vergara whose sole household companion was an eighteen-year-old grandson.[89]

The ethnic diversity of Nacogdoches, as opposed to the relatively homogeneous Hispanic population of San Antonio, may be seen in documentation dated 1809. Anna Alsop, a native of Pennsylvania, moved with her children to Kentucky, where she married Edmund Quirk. The family then moved to Nacogdoches in 1800. After they became ranchers, the husband deserted the family and became a fugitive for unspecified reasons. The illiterate Anna, who had an unmarried son and daughter, then had to maintain herself "with her labor."[90]

Two illiterate French women residing in Nacogdoches in 1809 were Marie-Madeleine Prudhomme and Marie Rambin. Madame Prudhomme and her husband were married only days before legally migrating to East Texas from Natchitoches around 1800. The couple had four children, with the husband earning a living as a farmer, while the wife was a seamstress. Marie Rambin left Natchitoches with her husband, François Prudhomme, and five children to live in Nacogdoches. In East Texas, Marie gave birth to four additional children, one of whom died. With the death of her farmer husband, Marie Rambin and her children scrambled to make a living. By her own testimony, "the males I have used in the field, and the females [are] making candles and weaving." Madame Rambin acknowledged that she and her husband arrived in Texas without passports, but "were admitted in this place with permission of the Judges."[91]

The adverse circumstances of Madames Prudhomme and Rambin stand in stark contrast to the successes of three Latina ranchers of the late colonial era. In 1779 the top ten cattle owners at Béxar included María Ana Curbelo, who ranked second, and Leonor Delgado, tied for fifth with Félix Menchaca. Doña María Ana, upon the death of her husband in 1778, became the owner of Las Mulas ranch on Cíbolo Creek; doña Leonor, who survived the infamy of bearing an illegitimate child in the 1750s, married Juan José Flores de Abrego and as a widow owned 150 head of cattle by the late 1770s. The signal achievements of these women, however, pale in comparison to those of María del Carmen Calvillo, born at Béxar on July 9, 1756, the eldest of six children of Ygnacio Calvillo and Antonia de Arocha.[92]

Doña María's father acquired the famed Rancho de las Cabras (the Goat Ranch) in present-day Wilson County in the 1790s, following the secularization of Mission San Francisco de la Espada and its lands. By then María del Carmen had married Juan Gavino de la Trinidad Delgado. The couple had two sons and adopted three other children. Don Juan's endorsement of insurgency in the second decade of the 1800s forced him to flee the ranch to escape the purges of Joaquín de Arredondo, and the Gavinos apparently separated at that time. Following the murder of her father at the ranch in April 1814, María del Carmen gained ownership and management of Las Cabras, which dramatically increased in size under the Mexican government in the 1830s. This notable woman died on January 15, 1856, just months short of her hundredth birthday! In her will, María del Carmen Calvillo assured that Rancho de las Cabras would remain in the family by passing ownership of it to two of the adopted children (Figure 25).[93]

The success stories of these Latinas demonstrate that, given the opportunity, their gender could compete on favorable terms with men. In view of their accomplishments and those of earlier women in the colonial period, it is particularly ironic that Jane Long—late on the colonial scene—came to be known as the Mother of Texas.

To be sure, Jane Long was a notable woman and deserves her place in Texas history. The tenth child of Captain William Mackall and Anne Herbert Wilkinson, Jane was born in Maryland on June 23, 1798. At age seventeen, she met and married James Long, shortly after her future husband had fought under Andrew Jackson's command at the battle of New Orleans.[94]

When James Long participated in the 1819 filibustering expedition into Spanish Texas, Jane, then pregnant, reluctantly stayed on U.S. soil with their first child, a toddler named Ann. Shortly after giving birth to a second daughter, Rebecca, Jane hoped to join James in Texas, but health problems exacerbated by "mental anxiety" over her husband's safety forced delays. Leaving both children with her sister in Alexandria, Jane regained her strength and finally reached Nacogdoches in August. Only two months later, she and the other Anglo Americans there had to flee from Spanish troops under the command of Lieutenant Colonel Ignacio Pérez. Upon her return to Louisiana, Jane learned that baby Rebecca had died.[95]

While organizing his second filibustering attempt in 1820, James Long took Jane to Bolivar Peninsula, just east of Galveston Island, where she claimed to have met and dined with Jean Laffite. Later, the Longs returned to the United States to make final preparations for his entry into Texas. When the expedition embarked, Jane vacillated about leaving her only child and eventually could not bear separation from Ann. Delays

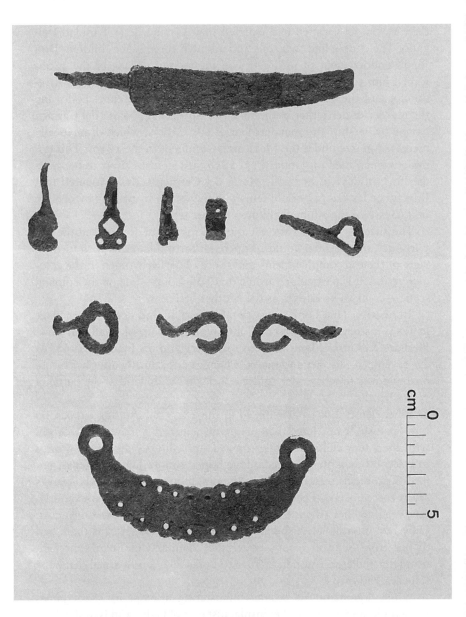

FIGURE 25

Artifacts from Rancho de las Cabras. These metal items include a knife, jingles, rein chain links, and bridge from a bridle bit. (Photograph courtesy of the Center for Archaeological Research, University of Texas at San Antonio.)

kept her from reaching Bolivar until late in the year, some five or six months after James had arrived there. Accompanying Jane was daughter Ann and Kian, a black slave woman.[96]

James Long's filibusters encountered difficulties with supplies, and discontent among the men ran rampant. General Long nonetheless rallied his followers and departed for the interior of Texas in September 1821. Jane, pregnant with their third child, remained behind. James's lengthy absence, owing to his capture by Lieutenant Colonel Ignacio Pérez, caused a general exodus that siphoned off stragglers at Bolivar. But Jane, unaware of her husband's captivity, kept determined faith in him and stubbornly refused to leave. Finally, only she, Ann, and Kian remained.[97]

Left to fend for herself and her dependents, Jane shot birds and fished for food, and she fired a cannon to frighten away menacing Karankawas. The winter of 1821–1822 brought severe cold, and Kian was so ill that Jane had to give birth without assistance. Still, even after learning that James was a prisoner, Jane refused to leave Texas.[98]

Remaining at Bolivar for more than a year, Jane Long kept faith that her husband would secure his freedom and join her. Finally, however, she left for the interior of Texas in March 1822. By that time her new home was part of Mexico. At a place known as Tuscoseta Crossing on the Trinity River, an aged black man built Jane a crude cabin made of scrap lumber and palmetto leaves. And it was there on July 8, 1822, that she learned the sad news of her husband's death in Mexico City.[99]

Initially, Jane Long relocated in San Antonio, but in 1823 she moved to New Orleans and thence to her sister's home in Alexandria, Louisiana. Tragedy, however, continued to befall her, and in the following year, Mary, the daughter she bore on Texas soil, died. Befriended by Ben Milam, who had survived incarceration in Mexico City with James Long and brought news of his last days, Jane, Ann, and Kian moved back to Texas in late 1824.[100]

Jane Long remained in Texas for the rest of her life—through the Mexican period, the Republic, the first era of statehood, and the Confederacy. She died in the reconstructed Lone Star State on December 30, 1880, at the age of eighty-two.[101] Although we view Jane Long with admiration as a notable colonial woman, it is historically unacceptable, given the hundreds of Indian, French, Hispanic, and mixed-ethnic women who preceded her, to accord her the appellation Mother of Texas.

AFTERWORD

These portraits of notable men and women of Spanish Texas reveal persons who are deserving of attention simply for their own life stories. How, for example, can anyone not be moved by an account of the incredible hardships faced by Cabeza de Vaca? Moreover, the biographical approach, in addition to depicting the experiences of individuals on New Spain's northern frontier, also reveals the multiple roles played by key personalities in shaping the early history of Texas. To be sure, the story of Spanish Texas is larger than any single life. But multiple biographies of explorers; missionaries; French Indian agents; Spanish military officials; colonizers and crown agents; a governor, an insurrectionist, and a captain general; and colonial women—which span almost three centuries—add color to the rich tapestry that is Texas history. Collectively, these people remind us of the strengths and weaknesses of early Texans and of identical traits that lie within all of us. We have chosen individuals for their "human" interest and because they made important contributions to the history of the future Lone Star State.

Cabeza de Vaca and Alonso de León, unintentional and intentional explorers, respectively, compiled significant information while reconnoitering Texas in the sixteenth and seventeenth centuries. Cabeza de Vaca's personal growth while living among Native Americans is a significant counterpoint to widely held perceptions of Spanish cruelty to Indians that gave rise to the Black Legend. Also, his *Relación* stands as the first literary contribution to our understanding of Texas and the Southwest. In the case of Alonso de León, one admires his honesty and sympathizes with the rigors of command while he searched for a seemingly invisible French colony, as well as recognizing his role as a military captain in establishing San Francisco de los Tejas, the first Spanish mission in East Texas.

An important religious component of Texas history is nicely illustrated by the lives of María de Agreda, Francisco Hidalgo, and Antonio Margil. Sister María never physically set foot in the New World, yet her alleged bilocations to Texas and New Mexico continue to intrigue both scholars and Roman Catholic faithful. Contrariwise, Father Margil, a self-designated "God's donkey," traveled on foot over much of Central America and to far-off Texas. Declared venerable by the Roman Catholic Church, and at present a candidate for beatification and canonization, Margil left Mission San José in San Antonio as his greatest legacy in Texas. Francisco Hidalgo's charismatic talents as a preacher and his dogged determination in advocating missions for the Hasinais make his life inspiring. Less famous than Margil, Hidalgo is arguably Texas' greatest Franciscan missionary, for he demonstrated an evangelical passion for Texas' native inhabitants that burned brightly for almost three decades.

Linked by business interests and familial ties at Natchitoches, Louis Juchereau de St. Denis and Athanase de Mézières were extraordinary French-Canadian personalities on the Texas scene. Tied to the powerful Ramón family by his marriage to Manuela Sánchez, St. Denis played an important role in bringing a permanent Spanish presence to East Texas that should not be underrated. Athanase de Mézières's rejection by his social-climbing mother and his resultant life among Indians in Canada prepared him for the harsh transitional world of French/Spanish Louisiana. Don Athanase's extraordinary skills as an Indian agent eventually won the confidence of Spanish officials, but in the process he lost financial security and died without being able to provide for his daughters.

Three military officials in the early colonial period played crucial roles in securing and holding Texas for Spain. Financed by the enormous wealth of his silent partner wife, the Marqués de Aguayo performed signal services in the 1720s. Inaugurator of Texas cattle drives and builder of presidios, Aguayo stands as an example of personal sacrifice to a distant monarch. Pedro de Rivera undermined many of Aguayo's accomplishments but ultimately strengthened San Antonio in the process. A "bottom-line" inspector, charged with cost-saving retrenchment— all possible because of increasing accord between Spain and France— Rivera delayed expansion in Texas until the 1740s. At that juncture, Felipe de Rábago, in part because of his outrageous personal conduct, significantly undermined the San Xavier enterprise. Nonetheless, in later life the former rakish commander mended his ways and worked diligently but perhaps unwisely in attempting personal redemption at San Sabá.

Colonizer José de Escandón was an organizer and motivator without peer. A contemporary of the failed enterprises at San Xavier and San Sabá, Escandón broke that pattern with remarkable accomplishments in Nuevo Santander. Don José expended tremendous energy and personal assets, only to die under a legal cloud. The Marqués de Rubí, a crown inspector like Pedro de Rivera, was driven by financial exigencies that overrode personal consideration for the lives of uprooted East Texans. Working to countermand royal directives, colonizer Antonio Gil Ibarvo founded modern Nacogdoches without formal authorization, but his questionable business practices landed him in legal limbo and resulted in banishment from the town that essentially owed its existence to him.

The roles of a governor, an insurrectionist, and a captain general conclude our treatment of notable men. Domingo Cabello, a veteran officer in the Spanish army, reluctantly took the reins of government at San Antonio in 1778. Over the course of an eight-year administration, however, he scored many successes—the most spectacular being a lasting treaty agreement with theretofore indomitable Comanches. In the early nineteenth century, Bernardo Gutiérrez carried Miguel Hidalgo's "Grito de Dolores" northward from New Spain's heartland into Texas. His essentially unwavering commitment to making Texas a part of the emerging Mexican nation is praiseworthy, despite the failure of his efforts. Joaquín de Arredondo, Gutiérrez's adversary, was a vengeful royalist. His brutal executions and repressions, following victory at the Medina River, turned Texas into a ruined province that welcomed escape from Spanish rule.

If we may dare to assess the merits of our own work, the chapter on colonial women ranks as our most satisfying accomplishment. Looking at a few high-profile Latinas and a host of heretofore "faceless" women in colonial Hispanic society—long famous or infamous for its male chauvinism—reveals an unusual degree of legal protection for early Texas women. It is particularly striking that even illiterate females of Indian and mixed ancestry had an ingrained knowledge of their rights and privileges. Provincial magistrates enforced those claims before the bar of justice, as well as demanding that women live responsible lives. Our final chapter, on women, provides welcome balance to traditional accounts of explorers, conquistadors, presidial soldiers, Franciscan missionaries, and governmental officials. Their story adds richness and variety to the great subject that is Texas history.

NOTES

PREFACE

1. "Windows to the Unknown: Cabeza de Vaca's Journey to the Southwest," symposium funded by a National Endowment for the Humanities planning grant; sponsored by the Center for the Study of the Southwest at Southwest Texas State University and the Witte Museum in San Antonio (April 19–21, 1995). For a recent and innovative contribution to route interpretations that argues persuasively against a trans-Texas line of travel, see Donald W. Olson et al., "Piñon Pines and the Route of Cabeza de Vaca," *Southwestern Historical Quarterly* 101 (October 1997): 175–186.

2. See Lewis Hanke, *All Mankind Is One* (De Kalb: Northern Illinois Press, 1974).

3. For an explanation of the Chicken War, see Chapter 5 of this volume.

4. Donald E. Chipman, "The Status of Biography in the Historiography of New Spain," *The Americas* 27 (January 1971): 328.

5. Milton Lomask, *The Biographer's Craft* (New York: Harper and Row, 1986), 2–3.

6. Randolph B. Campbell, "Touchstone Corner," *Touchstone* 14 (1995): Introduction, v.

CHAPTER 1

1. Martin A. Favata and José B. Fernández, *The Account: Alvar Núñez Cabeza de Vaca's "Relación"* (Houston: Arte Público, 1993), 53–54.

2. Ibid., 11–12; Donald E. Chipman, *Nuño de Guzmán and the Province of Pánuco in New Spain, 1518–1533* (Glendale, Calif.: Arthur H. Clark, 1967), 115–116.

3. Morris Bishop, *The Odyssey of Cabeza de Vaca* (New York: Century Company, 1933), 8. The Alvar Núñez portion of Cabeza de Vaca's full name also came from a prominent maternal ancestor who was captain of the fleet of Jerez. The paternal grandfather of Cabeza de Vaca was Pedro de Vera, chief captain in the conquest of the Canary Islands.

4. Ibid., 4.

5. Favata and Fernández, *Account*, 12; John Lynch, *Spain under the Habsburgs* (2 vols.; New York: Oxford University Press, 1964, 1969), 1: 39–41.

6. Bishop, *Odyssey*, 25. Such families as the Mendozas and Guzmáns of Guadalajara, Spain, who had supported Charles, are good examples of those who enjoyed the king's confidence and received appointments in the Indies.

7. Bernal Díaz del Castillo, *Historia verdadera de la conquista de la Nueva España*, Introducción y notas de Joaquín Ramírez de Cabañas (2 vols.; Mexico City: Editorial Porrúa, 1955), 1: capítulo I.

8. Marcus Dods, trans., *The City of God by Saint Augustine* (New York: Modern Library, 1950), 530–532; Donald E. Chipman, *Spanish Texas, 1519–1821* (reprint, Austin: University of Texas Press, 1994), 43.

9. Irving A. Leonard, "Conquerors and Amazons in Mexico," *Hispanic American Historical Review* 24 (November 1944): 561–579; Chipman, *Spanish Texas*, 43.

10. For an excellent summary of the motives of conquistadors, see David J. Weber, *The Spanish Frontier in North America* (New Haven: Yale University Press, 1992), 19–25; for difficulties experienced by Cabeza de Vaca as governor of Asunción, see text below.

11. Hugh Thomas, *Conquest: Montezuma, Cortés, and the Fall of Old Mexico* (New York: Simon and Schuster, 1993), 358–379.

12. Ibid., 585; Chipman, *Spanish Texas*, 28.

13. Chipman, *Spanish Texas*, 28.

14. Favata and Fernández, *Account*, 31.

15. Ibid., 32.

16. Chipman, *Spanish Texas*, 28. For a recent discussion of the location of the Río de las Palmas in the colonial era, see Donald E. Chipman, "Alonso Alvarez de Pineda and the Río de las Palmas: Scholars and the Mislocation of a River." *Southwestern Historical Quarterly* 98 (January 1995): 369–385.

17. Chipman, *Spanish Texas*, 28.

18. Ibid.; Favata and Fernández, *Account*, 49, quotation.

19. Favata and Fernández, *Account*, 53. Later, Narváez's poorly anchored boat was blown into deep water off Matagorda Bay and it presumably sank.

20. Chipman, *Spanish Texas*, 29.

21. Favata and Fernández, *Account*, 55–56, quotation on 55. The Indians occupying Malhado may have been Atakapans. See W. W. Newcomb Jr., *The Indians of Texas: From Prehistoric to Modern Times* (Austin: University of Texas Press, 1984), 59 n. 1.

22. Favata and Fernández, *Account*, 56.

23. Ibid., 57.

24. Chipman, *Spanish Texas*, 29.

25. Favata and Fernández, *Account*, 59–61.

26. Ibid., 62; Rolena Adorno, "The Negotiation of Fear in Cabeza de Vaca's *Naufragios,*" *Representations* 33 (Winter 1991): 173. As Adorno explains it, the Castaways did not become "great shamans because they performed cures but rather that they performed cures because they were perceived to be great shamans."

27. Favata and Fernández, *Account*, 59. For a single eyewitness account of Karankawa cannibalism in the late seventeenth century, see Robert S. Weddle, Mary Christine Morkovsky, and Patricia Galloway, trans. and eds., *Three Primary Documents: La Salle, the Mississippi, and the Gulf* (College Station: Texas A&M University Press, 1987), 271–272.

28. Favata and Fernández, *Account*, 64.

29. Ibid., 64–65.

30. Ibid., 65; Chipman, *Spanish Texas*, 29.

31. Favata and Fernández, *Account*, 65.

32. Donald E. Chipman, "In Search of Cabeza de Vaca's Route across Texas: An Historiographical Survey," *Southwestern Historical Quarterly* 91 (October 1987): 130, 133; Favata and Fernández, *Account*, 65, quotation.

33. Favata and Fernández, *Account*, 65–66.

34. Ibid., 67.

35. Enrique Pupo-Walker, ed., and Frances M. López-Morillas, trans., *Castaways: The Narrative of Alvar Núñez Cabeza de Vaca* (Berkeley: University of California Press, 1993), 55–56.

36. Ibid., 56–58.

37. Favata and Fernández, *Account*, 70–71.

38. Ibid., 71.

39. Basil C. Hedrick and Carroll L. Riley, *The Journey of the Vaca Party: The Account of the Narváez Expedition, 1528–1536, as Related by Gonzalo Fernández de Oviedo y Valdés* (Carbondale: University Museum, Southern Illinois University, 1974), 77, 1st and 2d quotations; Favata and Fernández, *Account,*

71–72, 3d and 4th quotations. Among hunting and gathering groups, male homosexuals were termed *berdaches*.

40. Favata and Fernández, *Account*, 72–73, quotation on 73.

41. Pupo-Walker and López-Morillas, *Castaways*, 64.

42. Ibid.; Hedrick and Riley, *Journey*, 46, quotation.

43. Favata and Fernández, *Account*, 76–78, quotation on 78.

44. Ibid., 78–80, quotations on 80. For an analysis of Cabeza de Vaca as a successful shaman, see Ida Altman and Reginald D. Butler, "The Contact of Cultures: Perspectives on the Quincentenary," *American Historical Review* 99 (April 1994): 489, 489 nn. 27, 31. See also Hedrick and Riley, *Journey*, 62, wherein the Christians are held to be holy and divine men who had come from heaven.

45. Pupo-Walker and López-Morillas, *Castaways*, 73–74. Rolena Adorno makes the important interpretive point that the Indians lost much of their fear of Malacosa because the Castaways "*were not like* [him] . . . as well as by their promise to protect the natives from him." See her "Negotiation of Fear," 175. Italics are hers.

46. T. N. Campbell and T. J. Campbell, *Historic Indians Groups of the Choke Canyon Reservoir and Surrounding Area, Southern Texas* (San Antonio: Center for Archaeological Research, 1981), 65, 1st quotation; Favata and Fernández, *Account*, 85–86, 2d and 3d quotations.

47. Chipman, *Spanish Texas*, 32.

48. Favata and Fernández, *Account*, 97, quotation; Jesse E. Thompson, "Sagittectomy—First Recorded Surgical Procedure in the American Southwest, 1535: The Journey and Ministrations of Alvar Núñez Cabeza de Vaca, *New England Journal of Medicine* 289 (December 27, 1973): 1403–1407. In Spanish nomenclature, "North Sea" referred to the Atlantic Ocean and included the Gulf of Mexico. See Robert S. Weddle, *Spanish Sea: The Gulf of Mexico in North American Discovery, 1500–1685* (College Station: Texas A&M University Press, 1985), 201–202.

49. Chipman, *Spanish Texas*, 32.

50. Ibid. *Más allá* ("farther on") was a Spanish expression for unexplored hinterlands.

51. Ibid., 32–33.

52. Favata and Fernández, *Account*, 105–108, quotation on 105.

53. Ibid., 108, 1st quotation; Jack Lowry, "Remembering Dr. Joe B. Frantz," *Texas Highways* 41 (March 1994): 17, as quoted.

54. Favata and Fernández, *Account*, 110.

55. Hedrick and Riley, *Journey*, 68–70, quotation on 69. Fernández de Oviedo credited the Castaways with bringing permanent peace to the area, but that was not the case. Subsequent revolts in New Galicia claimed the lives of Guzmán's successor as governor and Pedro de Alvarado. See Chipman, *Spanish Texas*, 34–41.

56. Chipman, *Spanish Texas*, 33.

57. Alex D. Krieger, "Un nuevo estudio de la ruta seguida por Cabeza de Vaca

a través de Norte América" (Ph.D. diss., Universidad Autónoma de México, 1955), 229; Chipman, *Spanish Texas*, 33–34.

58. Weber, *Spanish Frontier*, 45–46; Chipman, *Spanish Texas*, 34.

59. Weber, *Spanish Frontier*, 45–49; Chipman, *Spanish Texas*, 34–42.

60. Pupo-Walker and López-Morillas, *Castaways*, xviii–xix; Bishop, *Odyssey*, 167–168.

61. Bishop, *Odyssey*, 191–204.

62. Ibid., 210–212. The New Laws in their entirety could not be enforced in any Spanish province. High officials charged with implementing the unpopular laws were not sent to the Americas until 1544, and even then compliance was years distant. See Clarence H. Haring, *The Spanish Empire in America* (New York: Oxford University Press, 1947), 56–58.

63. Bishop, *Odyssey*, 213–224.

64. David A. Howard, *Conquistador in Chains: Cabeza de Vaca and the Indians of the Americas* (Tuscaloosa: University of Alabama Press, 1997), 198; Bishop, *Odyssey*, 249–290; Favata and Fernández, *Account*, 14.

65. Adorno, "Negotiation of Fear," 186, 1st quotation, as quoted; Samuel Eliot Morison, *The European Discovery of America: The Southern Voyages, A.D. 1492–1616* (New York: Oxford University Press, 1980), 580, 2d quotation.

CHAPTER 2

1. Itinerary of the De León Expedition of 1689, in *Spanish Exploration in the Southwest, 1542–1706*, ed. Herbert E. Bolton (reprint, New York: Barnes and Noble, 1963), 397. Substantial portions of this chapter were published by Donald E. Chipman under the title "Alonso de León: Pathfinder in East Texas, 1686–1690," *East Texas Historical Journal* 33 (Spring 1995): 3–17.

2. Letter of Fray Damián Massanet to Don Carlos de Sigüenza, 1690, in Bolton, *Spanish Exploration*, 362, 1st quotation; Itinerary of the De León Expedition, 398–399, 2d quotation on 398, 3d quotation on 399.

3. Donald E. Chipman, *Spanish Texas, 1519–1821* (reprint, Austin: University of Texas Press, 1994), 41–42.

4. Ibid., 51–53.

5. Ibid., 53; Marc Simmons, *The Last Conquistador: Juan de Oñate and the Settling of the Far Southwest* (Norman: University of Oklahoma Press, 1991), 184.

6. Chipman, *Spanish Texas*, 63–70.

7. Chipman, "Alonso de León," 3.

8. Ibid., 3–4. Alonso de León, the elder, studied Latin, rhetoric, and philosophy under Jesuit instructors at the Real y Máximo Colegio de San Ildefonso de México.

9. Israel Cavazos Garza, ed., *Historia de Nuevo León con noticias sobre Coahuila, Texas y Nuevo México, escrita en el siglo XVII por el Cap. Alonso*

de León, Juan Bautista Chapa y el Gral. Fernando Sánchez de Zamora, 2d ed. (Monterrey: Centro de Estudios Humanísticos, Universidad Autónoma de Nuevo León y Gobierno del Estado, 1961), xviii–xxiii, 3–15.

10. Carlos E. Castañeda, *Our Catholic Heritage in Texas, 1519–1936* (Austin: Von Boeckmann–Jones, 1936–1958), 1:210–211. As noted in Chapter 1 of this volume, the bad reputation of these coastal groups had figured importantly in prompting Cabeza de Vaca and his fellow Castaways to veer inland during their mid-1530s trek toward New Spain.

11. Cavazos Garza, *Historia de Nuevo León,* xxvii, 140. León's marriage to Agustina Cantú produced four sons and two daughters: Alonso, Juan, Santiago, Inés, Mateo, and Juana. See Lilia E. Villanueva de Cavazos, *Testamentos coloniales de Monterrey, 1611–1785* (Monterrey: n.p., 1991), 54.

12. Robert S. Weddle, *The French Thorn: Rival Explorers in the Spanish Sea, 1682–1762* (College Station: Texas A&M University Press, 1991), 45.

13. Ibid., 45–46. León was named interim governor of Nuevo León on December 19, 1682, assumed office at the end of February 1683, and served in that capacity for nine months. See Vito Alessio Robles, *Coahuila y Texas en la época colonial* (Mexico City: Editorial Cultura, 1938), 278 n. 8.

14. Weddle, *French Thorn,* 46, as quoted; Juan Bautista Chapa, *Texas and Northeastern Mexico, 1630–1690,* ed. William C. Foster and trans. Ned F. Brierley (Austin: University of Texas Press, 1997), 112.

15. Chapa, *Texas,* 114; Robert S. Weddle, *Wilderness Manhunt: The Spanish Search for La Salle* (Austin: University of Texas Press, 1973), 64–65.

16. Letter from Ambassador Pedro Ronquillo to the King (August 9, 1686), AGI, México 616.

17. Letter of Fray Damián Massanet, 355.

18. Ibid., 355–356.

19. Alessio Robles, *Coahuila y Texas,* 305–311, quotations on 311.

20. Ibid., 311.

21. Letter of Fray Damián Massanet, 356–357; Weddle, *Wilderness Manhunt,* 138–147; Chapa, *Texas,* 117, quotation.

22. Chapa, *Texas,* 123–124; Itinerary of the De León Expedition, 390.

23. Weddle, *French Thorn,* 72–73. For a detailed treatment of the general route followed by Alonso de León in 1689, see William C. Foster, *Spanish Expeditions into Texas, 1689–1768* (Austin: University of Texas Press, 1995), 16–32.

24. Itinerary of the De León Expedition, 390–391.

25. Ibid., 391–394, quotation on 391; Foster, *Spanish Expeditions,* 20–23; Chapa, *Texas,* 157, 214–215 n. 7.

26. Associated with the expeditions led by León were two others by land and a total of five by sea, all sent in search of La Salle's colony. For details, see Weddle, *Wilderness Manhunt,* 44–158, passim.

27. Itinerary of the De León Expedition, 399–401. Jean Jarry's detailed knowledge of the terrain and physical features of the Matagorda Bay area strongly suggest that he had been a member of La Salle's colony.

28. Ibid., 395–396; Weddle, *French Thorn,* 73. "Hasinai" was the native

name for tribes along valleys of the Neches and Angelina Rivers. "Tejas," a form of greeting among those tribes and even with their amicable but non-Caddoan neighbors, may be translated as "friends" or "allies." Early Spanish expeditions and officials in Mexico City, evidently intrigued by the notion of a "Great Kingdom of the Tejas," established the external practice of using "Tejas" when referring to the "Hasinai." That early spelling is the phonetic equivalent in Castilian Spanish of "Texas," which became the preferred designation. For a thorough discussion of the terms, see Herbert E. Bolton, *The Hasinais: Southern Caddoans as Seen by the Earliest Europeans*, ed. Russell M. Magnaghi (Norman: University of Oklahoma Press, 1987), 53–69.

29. Itinerary of the De León Expedition, 396.

30. Carta de Alonso De León al virrey, dándole cuenta de su jornada a la Bahía del Espíritu Santo, donde hallaron destruída la colonia de los franceses (May 16, 1689), in *Primeras exploraciones y poblamiento de Texas (1686–1694)*, ed. Lino Gómez Canedo (Monterrey: Publicaciones del Instituto Tecnológico y de Estudios Superiores de Monterrey, 1968), 114–115; Weddle, *French Thorn*, 76; Letter of Fray Damián Massanet, 364, quotation.

31. Itinerary of the De León Expedition, 403; Robert S. Weddle, Mary Christine Morkovsky, and Patricia Galloway, trans. and eds., *Three Primary Documents: La Salle, the Mississippi, and the Gulf* (College Station: Texas A&M University Press, 1987), 216. Verification of the smallpox epidemic is lacking. See Weddle, *Wilderness Manhunt*, 195 n. 13.

32. Weddle, *Three Primary Documents*, 237.

33. Itinerary of the De León Expedition, 403.

34. Carta de Alonso De León (May 16, 1689), 114. For treatment of María Jesús de Agreda's alleged bilocations, see Chapter 12 of this volume.

35. Carta de Alonso De León (May 16, 1689), 114–115.

36. William E. Dunn, *Spanish and French Rivalry in the Gulf Region of the United States, 1678–1702: The Beginnings of Texas and Pensacola* (Austin: University of Texas, 1917), 110–111.

37. Chipman, *Spanish Texas*, 248–249.

38. Weddle, *Wilderness Manhunt*, 207.

39. Report of the Fiscal de Hacienda to the Viceroy (November 30, 1716), AMH, Tomo XXVII, 1st quotation; Dunn, *Rivalry*, 116–117; Weddle, *Wilderness Manhunt*, 207–209, 2d quotation on 207.

40. For a biographical treatment of Father Francisco Hidalgo, see Chapter 3 of this volume.

41. Weddle, *French Thorn*, 78. Father Francisco Hidalgo did not accompany the León-Massanet expedition of 1690. See Chapter 3 of this volume.

42. Itinerary of the De León Expedition of 1690, 406–407. See reconstructed route of the De León Expedition of 1690, AGI, Mapas y Planos, México 88. Reproduced in Chipman, *Spanish Texas*, 90.

43. Diary of Alonso de León (1690), AGI, México 617. The fort was allegedly burned by Massanet, but León used the words "we burned the fort" in his entry for April 26. On his first visit to Fort St. Louis in 1689, León had buried

eight French cannon and a swivel gun found at the site. The cannon, in remarkably good shape, were recovered in 1996 and added to artifacts of the La Salle expedition that were salvaged from *La Belle*.

44. Itinerary of the De León Expedition of 1690, 409. Bolton misidentified the San Marcos River, which does not drain into Matagorda Bay.

45. Ibid., 410.

46. Ibid., 411.

47. Ibid., 411–412.

48. Ibid., quotation on 412; Weddle, Morkovsky, and Galloway, *Three Primary Documents*, 215.

49. Itinerary of the De León Expedition of 1690, 414–415. Watermelons were not indigenous to the Americas, but the seeds of European crops were often popular trade items and could be found among Native Americans who farmed lands beyond Spanish control.

50. Diario del general Alonso De León en su entrada a Texas desde Coahuila (March 26 to July 11, 1690) in Gómez Canedo, *Primeras exploraciones*, 144. Atole is gruel made of masa thinned with water.

51. Itinerary of the De León Expedition of 1690, 416.

52. Ibid., 417–418. The site of the first Spanish mission in East Texas has not been confirmed by archaeological evidence. Its likely location was near present-day Augusta. See A. Joachim McGraw, John W. Clark Jr., and Elizabeth A. Robbins, eds., *A Texas Legacy: The Old San Antonio Road and the Caminos Reales* (Austin: Texas State Department of Highways and Public Transportation, 1991), 284. The commemorative site near Weches, Texas, was established in 1936 on the occasion of the centennial of the Texas Republic.

53. Weddle, *Wilderness Manhunt*, 210–211; Weddle, *French Thorn*, 98–100.

54. Gómez Canedo, *Primeras exploraciones*, xviii–xix, quotation on xix. The three priests left in East Texas were Miguel Fontcuberta, Francisco Casañas de Jesús María, and Antonio Bordoy.

55. Weddle, Morkovsky, and Galloway, *Three Primary Documents*, 215; Itinerary of the De León Expedition of 1690, 420–421, quotations; Weddle, *Wilderness Manhunt*, 211–212. The tribal affiliation of the Indians who held the French youths captive has been identified from linguistic data as Karankawan. See Weddle, Morkovsky, and Galloway, *Three Primary Documents*, 239, 288–289.

56. Alonso de León informa al virrey sobre su nueva vista a la Bahía del Espíritu Santo y la fundación de San Francisco de los Tejas (July 14, 1690), in Gómez Canedo, *Primeras exploraciones*, 153–158.

57. Carta del Padre Mazanet al Conde de Galve, informándole sobre su viaje a Texas y exponiendo sus ideas sobre su población e incremento de las misiones (September 1690), in Gómez Canedo, *Primeras exploraciones*, 159–165.

58. Castañeda, *Catholic Heritage*, 1:360–361.

59. Testimony of Efforts to Remove Buoys (January 24, 1691), AGI, México 617. Discovery of a map drawn in 1691 by Manuel Joseph de Cárdenas allowed Bolton to establish the site of Fort St. Louis. See Herbert E. Bolton, "The Location of La Salle's Colony on the Gulf of Mexico," *Mississippi Valley Historical*

Review 2 (September 1915): 165–182. See Map of Manuel Joseph de Cárdenas, 1691, AGI, Mapas y Planos, México 89. Reproduced in Chipman, *Spanish Texas*, 95. Despite Bolton's pioneering work, the location of Fort St. Louis remained a subject of controversy until the eight cannon buried by León in 1689 were unearthed in 1996. For an excellent in situ photograph of these cannon, see William C. Foster, ed., and Johanna S. Warren, trans., *The La Salle Expedition to Texas: The Journal of Henri Joutel, 1684–1687* (Austin: Texas State Historical Association, 1998), 7.

60. Canedo, *Primeras exploraciones*, xxi–xxii; Castañeda, *Catholic Heritage*, 1:362; Weddle, *French Thorn*, 81, quotation. León completed his will on March 13, 1691, and died on March 20. See Villanueva de Cavazos, *Testamentos coloniales*, 56–57.

CHAPTER 3

1. Ross Phares, *Cavalier in the Wilderness: The Story of the Explorer and Trader Louis Juchereau de St. Denis* (Baton Rouge: Louisiana State University Press, 1952), 50.

2. Letter from St. Denis to Francisco Hidalgo (July 20, 1714), CAT.

3. Robert S. Weddle, *The French Thorn: Rival Explorers in the Spanish Sea, 1682–1762* (College Station: Texas A&M University Press, 1991), 193–194, 376 n. 13. Jallot's grandfather was one of the founders of the Hudson's Bay Company.

4. Robert S. Weddle, *San Juan Bautista: Gateway to Spanish Texas* (Austin: University of Texas Press, 1968), 9–10.

5. Hodding Carter, *Doomed Road of Empire: The Spanish Trail of Conquest* (New York: McGraw-Hill, 1963), 34–38. A more detailed treatment of the sack of Veracruz will be found in Chapter 4 of this volume.

6. Juan Domingo Arricivita, *Crónica seráfica y apostólica del colegio de propaganda fide de la Santa Cruz de Querétaro en la Nueva España*, Segunda Parte (Mexico City: Don Felipe de Zúñiga y Ontiveros, 1792), 206.

7. *NHOT*, 2:211–212. Other notable Franciscans who served in Texas were Damián Massanet, Miguel de Fontcuberta, Antonio Bordoy, and Antonio Margil de Jesús.

8. Arricivita, *Crónica seráfica*, 208.

9. Weddle, *San Juan Bautista*, 11.

10. Ibid. For information on Margil's role in founding the missionary college of Zacatecas, see Chapter 4 of this volume.

11. Ibid., 12.

12. Ibid.

13. Ibid., 12–13, quotation on 13.

14. Carlos E. Castañeda, *Our Catholic Heritage in Texas, 1519–1936* (Austin: Von Boeckmann–Jones, 1936–1958), 1:349–350.

15. William C. Foster, *Spanish Expeditions into Texas, 1689–1768* (Austin: University of Texas Press, 1995), 51.

16. Mattie A. Hatcher, trans., "The Expedition of Don Domingo Terán de los Ríos into Texas (1691–1692)," *Preliminary Studies of the Texas Catholic Historical Society* 2 (January 1932): 48.

17. Castañeda, *Catholic Heritage*, 1:362–364.

18. Hatcher, "Expedition of Terán," 55; Weddle, *French Thorn*, 90, as quoted.

19. Weddle, *French Thorn*, 90.

20. Ibid. Father Miguel de Fontcuberta had died of a fever during the previous winter, leaving only two priests to minister to the religious outposts.

21. Ibid.

22. Lino Gómez Canedo, *Primeras exploraciones y poblamiento de Texas (1686–1694)* (Monterrey: Publicaciones del Instituto Tecnológico y de Estudios Superiores de Monterrey, 1968), 188.

23. Ibid., 191–195; Weddle, *French Thorn*, 91.

24. Foster, *Spanish Expeditions*, 69–70.

25. Weddle, *French Thorn*, 93–96. The floods of January 1692 destroyed Mission Santísimo Nombre de María.

26. Ibid., 93, as quoted, 154, 198–199.

27. William C. Foster and Jack Jackson, eds., "The 1693 Expedition of Gregorio de Salinas Varona to Sustain the Missionaries among the Tejas Indians," *Southwestern Historical Quarterly* 97 (October 1993): 265–269.

28. Foster, *Spanish Expeditions*, 86; Castañeda, *Catholic Heritage*, 1:373.

29. Castañeda, *Catholic Heritage*, 1:374–375.

30. Ibid.

31. Donald E. Chipman, *Spanish Texas, 1519–1821* (reprint, Austin: University of Texas Press, 1994), 99.

32. Ibid., 105–106. See Chapter 4 of this volume on Father Margil.

33. Ibid., 106.

34. Ibid.; Isidro Félix de Espinosa, *Crónica de los Colegios de Propaganda Fide de la Nueva España*, ed. Lino Gómez Canedo (Washington, D.C.: Academy of American Franciscan History, 1964), 753; Patricia R. Lemée, "Manuela Sánchez Navarro," *Natchitoches Genealogist* 20 (October 1995): 17.

35. Castañeda, *Catholic Heritage*, 2:22–23; Chipman, *Spanish Texas*, 110; Weddle, *San Juan Bautista*, 92–93. The expedition of 1709 traveled beyond the site of San Antonio and reached the Colorado River.

36. Weddle, *French Thorn*, 124–125; Chipman, *Spanish Texas*, 100–101.

37. Chipman, *Spanish Texas*, 101–103; Weddle, *French Thorn*, 148.

38. NHOT, 5: 755–756; Weddle, *French Thorn*, 164.

39. Jack Jackson, Robert S. Weddle, and Winston De Ville, *Mapping Texas and the Gulf Coast: The Contributions of Saint-Denis, Oliván, and Le Maire* (College Station: Texas A&M University Press, 1990), 4–6; Weddle, *French Thorn*, 173, as quoted.

40. Weddle, *French Thorn*, 174.

41. Ibid., 178.

42. Ibid., 191.

43. Ibid., 191–192.

44. *NHOT*, 5: 755; Jackson, Weddle, and De Ville, *Mapping Texas*, 4–6; Weddle, *French Thorn*, 192.

45. Weddle, *French Thorn*, 192–193.

46. Letter from Diego Ramón to Francisco Hidalgo (July 22, 1714), CAT.

47. Letter from St. Denis to Francisco Hidalgo (July 20, 1714), CAT, quotations; Weddle, *French Thorn*, 194.

48. Lemée, "Manuela Sánchez Navarro," 18; Jackson, Weddle, and De Ville, *Mapping Texas*, 8, 71–72 n. 22. For a more complete treatment of doña Manuela, see Chapter 12 of this volume.

49. Weddle, *French Thorn*, 194, as quoted.

50. Ibid., as quoted.

51. Ibid., 194–195.

52. Chipman, *Spanish Texas*, 111.

53. Weddle, *French Thorn*, 196.

54. Ibid., 196–197.

55. Chipman, *Spanish Texas*, 112; baptized on April 26, 1697, Manuela Sánchez would have been eighteen on her wedding date. See Lemée, "Manuela Sánchez Navarro," 18.

56. Course for the Missions [of Texas] from the Internal Presidios (February 16–July 11, 1716), AMH, Tomo XXVII; Weddle, *French Thorn*, 197. For names of the first Spanish women in Texas, see Chapter 12 of this volume.

57. Course for the Mission [of Texas] from the Internal Presidios (February 16–July 11, 1716), AMH, Tomo XXVII. Herbert E. Bolton placed the mission site on the east bank of the Neches River. See his "Native Tribes about the East Texas Missions, *Quarterly of the Texas State Historical Association* 11 (April 1908): 261–262. The location of this mission and several others has not been confirmed by archaeological evidence.

58. Weddle, *French Thorn*, 199.

59. Chipman, *Spanish Texas*, 115.

60. Weddle, *French Thorn*, 200.

61. Chipman, *Spanish Texas*, 115; Weddle, *French Thorn*, 201.

62. Weddle, *French Thorn*, 202–203.

63. Ibid., 207.

64. Ibid.

65. Weddle, *San Juan Bautista*, 168–171; *NHOT*, 3: 588–589; Robert F. Carter, *The Tarnished Halo: The Story of Padre Francisco Hidalgo* (Chicago: Franciscan Herald Press, 1973), 134.

CHAPTER 4

1. Eduardo Enrique Ríos, *Life of Fray Antonio Margil, O.F.M.*, trans. by Benedict Leutenegger (Washington, D.C.: Academy of American Franciscan History, 1959), 60, as quoted.

2. Ibid., 3, quotation; Peter P. Forrestal, "The Venerable Padre Fray Antonio Margil de Jesús," *Preliminary Studies of the Texas Catholic Historical Society* 2 (April 1932): 6.

3. Isidro Félix de Espinosa, *El peregrino septentrional atlante: delineado en la exemplaríssima vida del Venerable Padre F. Antonio Margil de Jesús* (Mexico City: Joseph Bernardo de Hogal, 1737), 18–19; Forrestal, "Venerable Padre," 6, as quoted.

4. Ríos, *Life of Margil*, 4, 1st quotation, as quoted; Forrestal, "Venerable Padre," 6–7, 2d quotation. Margil called himself "La misma nada" (Nothingness Itself) and believed that total renunciation of self was essential in order to do God's bidding. See Benedict Leutenegger, trans., and Marion A. Habig, ed., *Nothingness Itself: Selected Writings of Ven. Fr. Antonio Margil, 1690–1724* (Chicago: Franciscan Herald Press, 1976), ix.

5. Ríos, *Life of Margil*, 5, as quoted.

6. Ibid.

7. Ibid., 6; Michael B. McCloskey, *The Formative Years of the Missionary College of Santa Cruz of Querétaro, 1683–1733* (Washington, D.C.: Academy of American Franciscan History, 1955), 15–19.

8. McCloskey, *Formative Years*, 19. Llinás's proposal had suggested that the twelve missionaries be headquartered in San Juan del Río, in Córdoba, or in Orizaba, present-day state of Veracruz.

9. Ibid., 28–29. A brief from Innocent XI, dated at Rome on May 8, 1682, gave the pope's sanction to the apostolic college.

10. Isidro Félix de Espinosa, *Crónica de los Colegios de Propaganda Fide de la Nueva España*, ed. Lino Gómez Canedo (Washington, D.C.: Academy of American Franciscan History, 1964), 163. See Chapter 2, n. 7 of this volume.

11. Ibid., 166; Espinosa, *El peregrino*, 39.

12. David F. Marley, *Sack of Veracruz* (Windsor, Ont.: Netherlandic Press, 1993), 11–13; Robert S. Weddle, *Spanish Sea: The Gulf of Mexico in North American Discovery, 1500–1685* (College Station: Texas A&M University Press, 1985), 399.

13. Marley, *Sack of Veracruz*, 29, 59–62.

14. Hodding Carter, *Doomed Road of Empire: The Spanish Trail of Conquest* (New York: McGraw-Hill, 1963), 35–38, quotation on 38; Espinosa, *El peregrino*, 39–40. Captain-general Fernández and his officers, their supplies and water depleted by three months at sea, prudently chose not to engage the nimble pirate fleet in shoal waters with their heavily laden galleons.

15. McCloskey, *Formative Years*, 32–33; Ríos, *Life of Margil*, 12, as quoted.

16. Espinosa, *El peregrino*, 40; Espinosa, *Crónica*, 170.

17. Ríos, *Life of Margil*, 16.

18. Ibid., as quoted.

19. Ibid., 16–17; Espinosa, *Crónica*, 477.

20. Forrestal, "Venerable Padre," 12.

21. Ríos, *Life of Margil*, 38–39.

22. Lewis Hanke, *The Spanish Struggle for Justice in the Conquest of Amer-*

ica (Philadelphia: University of Pennsylvania Press, 1949), 77–81; Ríos, *Life of Margil*, 40–41.

23. Ríos, *Life of Margil*, 46.

24. Ibid., 46–49, quotation on 49.

25. Nancy M. Farriss, *Maya Society under Colonial Rule: The Collective Enterprise of Survival* (Princeton: Princeton University Press, 1984), 18–19, 136; Ríos, *Life of Margil*, 51–56. Farriss argues that survivors of the Lacandón Maya, in actuality, have never been conquered to this day.

26. Ríos, *Life of Margil*, 57.

27. Ibid., 58, as quoted.

28. Espinosa, *El peregrino*, 116.

29. See Espinosa, *Crónica*, 594–595, 595 n. 5 for a version of *El Alabado*, in Spanish. The form of *El Alabado* used by Margil may be found in Leutenegger and Habig, *Nothingness Itself*, 321–322, in English translation. Fray Simón de Hierro, who knew Margil personally, recorded two instances in which Fray Antonio late in life rode a horse and a donkey. See ibid., Appendix 1, 328.

30. Donald E. Chipman, *Spanish Texas, 1519–1821* (reprint, Austin: University of Texas Press, 1994), 106.

31. Ríos, *Life of Margil*, 62.

32. Ibid., 62–63.

33. Ibid., 63.

34. Ibid., 68, as quoted; William H. Oberste, *The Restless Friar: Venerable Fray Antonio Margil de Jesús* (Austin: Von Boeckmann–Jones, 1970), 52. The distance between Querétaro and Oaxaca was 167 leagues, or about 435 miles.

35. Oberste, *Restless Friar*, 53–54.

36. Ríos, *Life of Margil*, 71–73, as quoted on 73.

37. Espinosa, *El peregrino*, 183–185; Ríos, *Life of Margil*, 73–75.

38. Ríos, *Life of Margil*, 76, as quoted.

39. Forrestal, "Venerable Margil," 18–19.

40. Ríos, *Life of Margil*, 92–93. Margil corresponded with Sister Leonor de San José of this convent for a number of years.

41. Ibid., 93, as quoted.

42. Ibid., 95, as quoted.

43. Ibid., 98.

44. Ibid., 98, as quoted.

45. Ibid., 98–99, quotation on 99.

46. Letter from Margil to Huei Tacat and Other Chiefs of Nayarit (May 9, 1711), in Leutenegger and Habig, *Nothingness Itself*, 178.

47. Ríos, *Life of Margil*, 101, as quoted.

48. Margil to the President of the Audiencia of Guadalajara (May 25, 1711), in Leutenegger and Habig, *Nothingness Itself*, 186.

49. Espinosa, *El peregrino*, 258–259; Introduction, Letter from Margil to Madre Leonor de San Joseph (June 21, 1712), in Leutenegger and Habig, *Nothingness Itself*, 45; Oberste, *Restless Friar*, 69, quotation.

50. Introduction, Margil to Fr. Francisco de San Esteban y Andrae (September 15, 1714), in Leutenegger and Habig, *Nothingness Itself*, 207.

51. Espinosa, *Crónica*, xli. Boca de Leones was located at present-day Villadama, Nuevo León.

52. Robert S. Weddle, *San Juan Bautista: Gateway to Spanish Texas* (Austin: University of Texas Press, 1968), 116; William C. Foster, *Spanish Expeditions into Texas, 1689–1768* (Austin: University of Texas Press, 1995), 113–114.

53. Espinosa, *El peregrino*, 278; Foster, *Spanish Expeditions*, 114.

54. Chipman, *Spanish Texas*, 113; Foster, *Spanish Expeditions*, 120.

55. Chipman, *Spanish Texas*, 114.

56. Espinosa, *Crónica*, 724; Chipman, *Spanish Texas*, 114.

57. Foster, *Spanish Expeditions*, 121; Espinosa, *Crónica*, 725–726, quotation on 726.

58. "The Eyes of Father Margil," unpublished paper presented in 1989 by Frances E. Abernethy at Stephen F. Austin State University in Nacogdoches, Texas. *Ojo* in Spanish has many meanings, including a spring (*entrada de agua*).

59. Ríos, *Life of Margil*, 118, 1st quotation, as quoted.

60. Chipman, *Spanish Texas*, 117–118; Jesús F. de la Teja, "Indians, Soldiers, and Canary Islanders: The Making of a Texas Frontier Community," *Locus: An Historical Journal of Regional Perspectives on National Topics* 3 (Fall 1990): 81, 81 n. 2, 84.

61. Carlos E. Castañeda, *Our Catholic Heritage in Texas, 1519–1936* (Austin: Von Boeckmann–Jones, 1936–1958), 2:102–107.

62. Espinosa, *Crónica*, 736–737,

63. Castañeda, *Catholic Heritage*, 2:110.

64. Chipman, *Spanish Texas*, 118–119. For a discussion of the Chicken War, see Chapter 5 of this volume.

65. Ibid. For additional activities of Margil before reaching San Antonio, see Chapter 5 of this volume.

66. Father Margil to Marqués de San Miguel de Aguayo (December 26, 1719) in Leutenegger and Habig, *Nothingness Itself*, 266–271; Castañeda, *Catholic Heritage*, 2:124–130.

67. Castañeda, *Catholic Heritage*, 2:130.

68. Espinosa, *El peregrino*, 292–293.

69. Leutenegger and Habig, *Nothingness Itself*, xviii.

70. Espinosa, *Crónica*, liv; Ríos, *Life of Margil*, 125, as quoted.

71. Ríos, *Life of Margil*, 125–126.

72. Ibid., 126–128.

73. Forrestal, "Venerable Margil," 30–31, 1st quotation; Ríos, *Life of Margil*, 131, 2d quotation.

74. Ríos, *Life of Margil*, 132.

75. Ibid., 134–135.

76. Ibid., 135.

77. Ibid., 135–136, quotation on 136, as quoted.

78. Ibid., 136–137, quotation on 137, as quoted.

79. Leutenegger and Habig, *Nothingness Itself*, xi.
80. Ríos, *Life of Margil*, 96.

CHAPTER 5

1. Robert S. Weddle, *San Juan Bautista: Gateway to Spanish Texas* (Austin: University of Texas Press, 1968), 156.
2. Isidro Félix de Espinosa, *Crónica de los Colegios de Propaganda Fide de la Nueva España*, ed. Lino Gómez Canedo (Washington, D.C.: Academy of American Franciscan History, 1964), 739 n. 7; Donald E. Chipman, *Spanish Texas, 1519–1821* (reprint, Austin: University of Texas Press, 1994), 118. The principal cause of this brief war, which ended in 1720, was Spain's unwillingness to accept the loss of its Italian possessions by terms of the Treaty of Utrecht, 1713–1714.
3. Charles W. Hackett, ed. and trans., *Pichardo's Treatise on the Limits of Louisiana and Texas* (Austin: University of Texas Press, 1931–1946), 1:217, quotation, as quoted.
4. Weddle, *San Juan Bautista*, 156–157.
5. Espinosa, *Crónica*, 738.
6. Weddle, *San Juan Bautista*, 157–158; Espinosa, *Crónica*, 742.
7. Espinosa, *Crónica*, 742.
8. Weddle, *San Juan Bautista*, 158–159; Espinosa, *Crónica*, 742.
9. Carlos E. Castañeda, *Our Catholic Heritage in Texas, 1519–1936* (Austin: Von Boeckmann–Jones, 1936–1958), 2:124–130; Eleanor C. Buckley, "The Aguayo Expedition into Texas and Louisiana, 1719–1722," *Quarterly of the Texas State Historical Association* 15 (July 1911): 19–20. For details of the founding of mission San José by Father Margil, see also Chapter 4 of this volume.
10. Weddle, *San Juan Bautista*, 159.
11. G. Micheal Riley, *Fernando Cortés and the Marquesado in Morelos, 1522–1547* (Albuquerque: University of New Mexico Press, 1973), 29; Ann P. Hollingsworth, "Pedro de Moctezuma and His Descendants, 1521–1718" (Ph.D. diss., University of North Texas, 1980), 85. José Sarmiento de Valladares, Conde de Moctezuma, who served as viceroy of New Spain from 1696 to 1701, inherited the title from his wife, Gerónima de Moctezuma. See Hollingsworth, "Pedro de Moctezuma," 118–119.
12. Frederick C. Chabot, "The Powerful Aguayos" (unpublished paper presented at the Thirty-second Annual Meeting of the Texas State Historical Association, 1929), Austin. See also David B. Adams, "Borderlands Communities in Conflict: Saltillo, San Esteban, and the Struggle for Municipal Autonomy, 1591–1838," *Locus: Regional and Local History of the Americas* 6 (Fall 1993): 39–51.
13. Chabot, "The Powerful Aguayos." Doña Francisca was heiress to the combined fortunes of relatives who were conquerors and pacifiers of a vast re-

gion extending from Durango to Saltillo, the most notable of whom was Francisco de Urdiñola. See Oakah L. Jones Jr., *Nueva Vizcaya: Heartland of the Spanish Frontier* (Albuquerque: University of New Mexico Press, 1988), 75–80.

14. Chabot, "Powerful Aguayos."

15. Ibid.

16. Ibid.

17. Ibid.

18. Letter from the Marqués de San Miguel de Aguayo to the Viceroy (January 12, 1715), AMH, Tomo XXVII.

19. Proposal by the Marqués de San Miguel de Aguayo to the Viceroy (November 9, 1715), AMH, Tomo XVII.

20. Chipman, *Spanish Texas*, 120; Richard G. Santos, trans., *Aguayo Expedition into Texas, 1721* (Austin: Jenkins Publishing, 1981), 19.

21. Charles W. Hackett, "The Marquis of San Miguel de Aguayo and His Recovery of Texas from the French, 1719–1723," *Southwestern Historical Quarterly* 49 (October 1945): 193–214.

22. Robert S. Weddle, *The French Thorn: Rival Explorers in the Spanish Sea, 1682–1762* (College Station: Texas A&M University Press, 1991), 234.

23. Peter P. Forrestal, trans., "Peña's Diary of the Aguayo Expedition," *Preliminary Studies of the Texas Catholic Historical Society* 2 (January 1935): 6; Chipman, *Spanish Texas*, 120; Santos, *Aguayo Expedition*, 23.

24. Chipman, *Spanish Texas*, 121; Hackett, "Marquis de Aguayo," 204.

25. Hackett, "Marquis de Aguayo," 204.

26. Santos, *Aguayo Expedition*, 30.

27. Buckley, "Aguayo Expedition," 32.

28. Forrestal, "Peña's Diary," 20, quotation; Santos, *Aguayo Expedition*, 35; William C. Foster, *Spanish Expeditions into Texas, 1689–1768* (Austin: University of Texas Press, 1995), 151.

29. Santos, *Aguayo Expedition*, 39.

30. Ibid.

31. Ibid., 36.

32. Foster, *Spanish Expeditions*, 151, as quoted.

33. Santos, *Aguayo Expedition*, 41.

34. Foster, *Spanish Expeditions*, 152; Santos, *Aguayo Expedition*, 49.

35. Forrestal, "Peña's Diary"; Foster, *Spanish Expeditions*, 153. For information on the tribes that made up the Ranchería Grande, see *NHOT*, 5:429.

36. Foster, *Spanish Expeditions*, 153.

37. Santos, *Aguayo Expedition*, 55–57.

38. Foster, *Spanish Expeditions*, 154; Santos, *Aguayo Expedition*, 57–58.

39. Santos, *Aguayo Expedition*, 58–59, quotation on 59.

40. Ibid., 61–62.

41. Ibid., 62–65, quotation on 62.

42. Ibid., 66; Buckley, "Aguayo Expedition," 49.

43. Santos, *Aguayo Expedition*, 66–68.

44. Ibid., 68–69.

45. Buckley, "Aguayo Expedition," 51–52.

46. Ibid., 70, 83; Sebastien Le Prestre de Vauban, *A Manual of Siegecraft and Fortification*, trans. George A. Rothrock (Ann Arbor: University of Michigan Press, 1968), x, 121–136.

47. Buckley, "Aguayo Expedition," 53.

48. Chipman, *Spanish Texas*, 123, fig. 16.

49. See *NHOT*, 5:429.

50. Chipman, *Spanish Texas*, 124.

51. Ibid., 124–126.

52. Hackett, "Marquis de Aguayo," 211.

53. Ibid., 211, as quoted; Chipman, *Spanish Texas*, 126.

54. Hackett, "Marquis de Aguayo," 213.

55. Charles W. Hackett, "Visitador Rivera's Criticisms of Aguayo's Work in Texas," *Hispanic American Historical Review* 16 (May 1936): 171–172; Vito Alessio Robles, *Coahuila y Texas en la época colonial* (Mexico City: Editorial Cultura, 1938), 470.

56. Jack Jackson, ed., and William C. Foster, annot., *Imaginary Kingdom: Texas as Seen by the Rivera and Rubí Military Expeditions, 1727 and 1767* (Austin: Texas State Historical Association, 1995), 10; *Diccionario Porrúa de historia, biografía y geografía de México*, 3d ed. (Mexico City: Editorial Porrúa, 1971), 2:1775.

57. Jackson and Foster, *Imaginary Kingdom*, 10–11.

58. Thomas H. Naylor and Charles W. Polzer, comps. and eds., *Pedro de Rivera and the Military Regulations for Northern New Spain, 1724–1729: A Documentary History of His Frontier Inspection and the "Reglamento de 1729"* (Tucson: University of Arizona Press, 1988), 8–10, quotation on 8.

59. Naylor and Polzer, *Pedro de Rivera*, 10; *NHOT*, 1:136–137.

60. Chipman, *Spanish Texas*, 129; Naylor and Polzer, *Pedro de Rivera*, 70–89.

61. Jackson and Foster, *Imaginary Kingdom*, 31 n. 45.

62. Ibid., 58.

63. Naylor and Polzer, *Pedro de Rivera*, 157.

64. Testimony of the Rivera Project (June 2, 1730), AGI, Guadalajara 144, 1st quotation; Naylor and Polzer, *Pedro de Rivera*, 158, 2d quotation.

65. Naylor and Polzer, *Pedro de Rivera*, 158–160, 1st quotation on 159, 2d and 3d quotations on 160.

66. Ibid., 160–161, quotation on 160.

67. Jackson and Foster, *Imaginary Kingdom*, 42.

68. Chipman, *Spanish Texas*, 129–130.

69. Jackson and Foster, *Imaginary Kingdom*, 61; Chipman, *Spanish Texas*, 131, as quoted.

70. Chipman, *Spanish Texas*, 131.

71. Ibid.

72. Ibid.

73. Jesús F. de la Teja, *San Antonio de Béxar: A Community on New Spain's*

Northern Frontier (Albuquerque: University of New Mexico Press, 1995), 31–36; Complaints against Carlos Franquis de Lugo (1737), AGI, Guadalajara 103. The words were *"alcahuetes cornudos cabrones."*

74. Jackson and Foster, *Imaginary Kingdom*, 65, 1st quotation; Weddle, *San Juan Bautista*, 186–195, 2d quotation on 186. For an excellent historiographical assessment of the Rivera Expedition, see Jackson and Foster, *Imaginary Kingdom*, 61–67.

CHAPTER 6

1. Carlos E. Castañeda, *Our Catholic Heritage in Texas, 1519–1936* (Austin: Von Boeckmann–Jones, 1936–1958), 3:329.

2. Ibid., 329–330.

3. Robert S. Weddle, *The San Sabá Mission: Spanish Pivot in Texas* (Austin: University of Texas Press, 1964), 149; Castañeda, *Catholic Heritage*, 3:310.

4. Gary B. Starnes, *The San Gabriel Missions, 1746–1756* (Madrid: Ministry of Foreign Affairs, Government of Spain, 1969), 13–20.

5. Ibid., 31; Castañeda, *Catholic Heritage*, 3:312; Juan Agustín Morfi, *History of Texas, 1673–1779*, trans. and ed. Carlos E. Castañeda (Albuquerque: Quivira Society, 1935), 2:330, quotation.

6. Starnes, *San Gabriel Missions*, 31.

7. Donald E. Chipman, *Spanish Texas, 1519–1821* (reprint, Austin: University of Texas Press, 1994), 154–155.

8. Ibid., 155.

9. Castañeda, *Catholic Heritage*, 3:318–319.

10. Chipman, *Spanish Texas*, 155.

11. Castañeda, *Catholic Heritage*, 3:319.

12. Ibid.

13. Herbert E. Bolton, *Texas in the Middle Eighteenth Century: Studies in Spanish Colonial History and Administration* (Austin: University of Texas Press, 1970), 252.

14. Castañeda, *Catholic Heritage*, 3:320–321, as quoted on 321.

15. Morfi, *History of Texas*, 2:330, quotation; Castañeda, *Catholic Heritage*, 3:326.

16. Statements over Troubles between Captain Felipe de Rábago y Terán and Miguel Pinilla (1752), UTA, Dunn Transcripts.

17. Castañeda, *Catholic Heritage*, 3:326–327.

18. Recommendations of the *auditor de guerra* (March 24, 1752), UTA, Dunn Transcripts; Recommendations of the *fiscal* (March 28, 1752), UTA, Dunn Transcripts. The *auditor de guerra* placed the cost at 20,665 pesos, plus another 6,000 pesos annually to staff the presidio with a captain and fifty soldiers.

19. Recommendations of the *fiscal* (March 28, 1752), UTA, Dunn Transcripts.

20. Statements over Troubles between Captain Felipe de Rábago y Terán and Father Miguel Pinilla (1752), UTA, Dunn Transcripts.

21. Letter from Felipe de Rábago to the Viceroy (May 15, 1752), UTA, Dunn Transcripts.

22. Castañeda, *Catholic Heritage*, 3:328.

23. Ibid., 3:328–329.

24. Statements Concerning Don Felipe de Rábago y Terán, Captain of the Presidio of Santa Rosa del Sacramento in Coahuila (1759), UTA, Dunn Transcripts.

25. Ibid.

26. Investigation by Captain Torbio de Urrutia, Captain of the Presidio of San Antonio de Béxar, into the Deaths of José Ganzabal and Juan José Ceballos (1752), UTA, Dunn Transcripts.

27. Ibid.

28. Statements Concerning Don Felipe de Rábago, Captain of the Presidio of Santa Rosa del Sacramento in Coahuila (1759), UTA, Dunn Transcripts.

29. Letter from Felipe de Rábago to the Viceroy (May 15, 1752), UTA, Dunn Transcripts; Castañeda, *Catholic Heritage*, 3:332.

30. Castañeda, *Catholic Heritage*, 3:332–333.

31. In addition to Manuel Carrillo, the other soldier-suspects were Martín Gutiérrez, Tomás Yruegas, and Juan José Sánchez, alias Marín. See Investigation by Captain Toribio de Urrutia . . . into the Deaths of José Ganzabal and Juan José Ceballos (1752), UTA, Dunn Transcripts; Statements Concerning Don Felipe de Rábago y Terán, Captain of Presidio Santa Rosa del Sacramento in Coahuila (1759), UTA, Dunn Transcripts.

32. Castañeda, *Catholic Heritage*, 3:333–334.

33. Ibid., 3:377–378; Weddle, *San Sabá*, 35.

34. Chipman, *Spanish Texas*, 128, 134–145.

35. William E. Dunn, "Apache Relations in Texas, 1718–1750," *Quarterly of the Texas State Historical Association* 14 (January 1911): 255–262.

36. William E. Dunn, "Missionary Activities among the Eastern Apaches Previous to the Founding of the San Sabá Mission," *Quarterly of the Texas State Historical Association* 15 (January 1912): 196–200.

37. Chipman, *Spanish Texas*, 157–158.

38. Ibid., 158–159.

39. Ibid., 159.

40. Weddle, *San Sabá*, 38–39, quotation on 39.

41. Ibid., 45–46, quotation, as quoted on 46; Chipman, *Spanish Texas*, 159.

42. Weddle, *San Sabá*, 50–53.

43. Ibid., 53–54.

44. Chipman, *Spanish Texas*, 160.

45. Ibid., 160–161.

46. Weddle, *San Sabá*, 63–64.

47. Deposition of Andrés de Villareal, in Lesley B. Simpson, ed., *The San Sabá Papers: A Documentary Account of the Founding and Destruction of the San Sabá Mission* (San Francisco: John Howell-Books, 1959), 68–69.

48. Deposition of Fray Miguel de Molina, in Simpson, *San Sabá Papers*, 85.

49. Ibid., 87–88; Chipman, *Spanish Texas*, 161. The exact location of Mis-

sion Santa Cruz de San Sabá eluded researchers for years. In September 1993, artifacts were unearthed in an alfalfa field outside Menard, and subsequent excavations verified the site. See "Missing Mission Found," *Texas Archeology* 38 (April 1994): 5; and *NHOT*, 5:885.

50. Weddle, *San Sabá*, 86–88.

51. Chipman, *Spanish Texas*, 162–163; Henry E. Allen, "The Parrilla Expedition to the Red River in 1759," *Southwestern Historical Quarterly* 43 (July 1939): 60–61, as quoted on 61.

52. Weddle, *San Sabá*, 123; Allen, "Parrilla Expedition," 68–71; Merits and Services of Diego Ortiz Parrilla (May 3, 1770), AGI, Guadalajara 515, quotation.

53. Statements Concerning Don Felipe de Rábago y Terán, Captain of the Presidio of Santa Rosa del Sacramento in Coahuila (1759), UTA, Dunn Transcripts.

54. Ibid.

55. Castañeda, *Catholic Heritage*, 4: 148; Weddle, *San Sabá*, 148.

56. Proceedings of the *fiscal* (April 20, 1761), AGI, Guadalajara 368, quotations; Papers Relating to Diego Ortiz Parrilla [1760], AGI, Guadalajara 368.

57. Castañeda, *Catholic Heritage*, 4: 41.

58. Review of Presidio San Luis de las Amarillas by Felipe de Rábago (October 12–30, 1760), UTA, Dunn Transcripts; Castañeda, *Catholic Heritage*, 4: 40, 150–151; Statement of Felipe de Rábago on Review of Seventy-seven Men (October 15, 1760), UTA, Dunn Transcripts. Andrés was left at a mission in Monclova.

59. Letter from Felipe de Rábago to Viceroy Marqués de Cruillas (March 2, 1761), UTA, Dunn Transcripts; Castañeda, *Catholic Heritage*, 4: 40.

60. Castañeda, *Catholic Heritage*, 4: 40–41; Chipman, *Spanish Texas*, 176.

61. Morfi, *History of Texas*, 2:394.

62. Chipman, *Spanish Texas*, 177.

63. Ibid.

64. Curtis D. Tunnell and W. W. Newcomb Jr., *A Lipan Apache Mission: San Lorenzo de la Santa Cruz, 1762–1771* (Bulletin 14, Austin: Texas Memorial Muscum, 1969), 3; Weddle, *San Sabá*, 156–158.

65. Chipman, *Spanish Texas*, 177–178.

66. Ibid., 178.

67. Weddle, *San Sabá*, 177–178.

68. Ibid., 180–181.

CHAPTER 7

1. Carlos E. Castañeda, *Our Catholic Heritage in Texas, 1519–1936* (Austin: Von Boeckmann-Jones, 1936–1958), 3:137; Relación de los méritos de José de Escandón, in *Estado general de las fundaciones hechas por D. José de Escandón en la colonia de Nuevo Santander* (Mexico City: Talleres Gráficos de la Nación, 1929, 1930), 2:303.

2. Relación de los méritos, in *Estado general*, 2: 303; Proceedings Related to the Merits and Services of José de Escandón (January 17, 1774), UTA, Hackett Transcripts, quotations.

3. Proceedings Related to José de Escandón (January 17, 1774), UTA, Hackett Transcripts, quotation; Robert S. Weddle, *The French Thorn: Rival Explorers in the Spanish Sea, 1682–1762* (College Station: Texas A&M University Press, 1991), 264.

4. Lawrence F. Hill, *José de Escandón and the Founding of Nuevo Santander: A Study in Spanish Colonization* (Columbus: Ohio State University Press, 1926), 5.

5. Relación de los méritos, in *Estado general*, 2:304.

6. Weddle, *French Thorn*, 258–259, quotation on 259.

7. Ibid., 259–260. Ladrón asked for a percentage of the yield from saline deposits in the area, which he intended to work.

8. Donald E. Chipman, *Spanish Texas, 1519–1821* (reprint, Austin: University of Texas Press, 1994), 166; Weddle, *French Thorn*, 260.

9. Weddle, *French Thorn*, 260; Hill, *José de Escandón*, 57–58.

10. Proceedings Related to José de Escandón (January 17, 1774), UTA, Hackett Transcripts.

11. Relación de los méritos, in *Estado general*, 2:305; Hubert J. Miller, *José de Escandón: Colonizer of Nuevo Santander* (Edinburg, Tex.: New Santander Press, 1980), 5.

12. Copia del acta de matrimonio de Juan J. de Escandón y doña Dominga de Pedrajo (October 5, 1727), in *Estado general*, 2:310; *NHOT*, 2:889.

13. Castañeda, *Catholic Heritage*, 3:137–139, quotation on 137; Hill, *José de Escandón*, 58.

14. Letter from Domingo Valcarcel to Viceroy Agustín Ahumada (March 10, 1746), UTA, Hackett Transcripts, 1st quotation; Order Issued by Viceroy Revilla Gigedo (September 3, 1746), BAT, Reel 3, 2d and 3d quotations. Initially, the San Antonio River in Texas was the proposed northern limit of Nuevo Santander.

15. Castañeda, *Catholic Heritage*, 3:141–142; Hill, *José de Escandón*, 5, 60, 65–66, quotation on 60.

16. Weddle, *French Thorn*, 264; Hill, *José de Escandón*, 59–60.

17. Weddle, *French Thorn*, 265–270; Hill, *José de Escandón*, 60–62. For a discussion of the Río de las Palmas and its confusion with the Río Grande in early colonial times, see Donald E. Chipman, "Alonso Alvarez de Pineda and the Río de las Palmas: Scholars and the Mislocation of a River," *Southwestern Historical Quarterly* 98 (January 1995): 369–385.

18. Weddle, *French Thorn*, 270; Hill, *José de Escandón*, 63.

19. Weddle, *French Thorn*, 271. See *NHOT*, 2:247 for a discussion of the Comecrudo Indians.

20. Weddle, *French Thorn*, 272; Hill, *José de Escandón*, 5.

21. Weddle, *French Thorn*, 272–273; Hill, *José de Escandón*, 63–64.

22. Weddle, *French Thorn*, 273.

23. Ibid.

24. Ibid., 265, 273–274; J. B. Wilkinson, *Laredo and the Rio Grande Frontier* (Austin: Jenkins Publishing, 1975), 16.

25. Weddle, *French Thorn*, 274.

26. Ibid., quotation on 274; Hill, *José de Escandón*, 65–66.

27. Hill, *José de Escandón*, 67–68; Wilkinson, *Laredo*, 17. The Huasteca was a region that bordered the Pánuco River to the west of Tampico.

28. Wilkinson, *Laredo*, 17–18; Hill, *José de Escandón*, 66.

29. Miller, *José de Escandón*, 13–14; Hill, *José de Escandón*, 66.

30. Letter from Domingo Valcarcel to Viceroy Agustín Ahumada (March 10, 1746), UTA, Hackett Transcripts.

31. Weddle, *French Thorn*, 277; Wilkinson, *Laredo*, 19.

32. Weddle, *French Thorn*, 277; Miller, *José de Escandón*, 14.

33. Weddle, *French Thorn*, 277–278; Hill, *José de Escandón*, 73, 75–76.

34. Hill, *José de Escandón*, 77; Weddle, *French Thorn*, 279; Castañeda, *Catholic Heritage*, 3:157–158.

35. Weddle, *French Thorn*, 279–280; Hill, *José de Escandón*, 89–90.

36. Weddle, *French Thorn*, 280; Hill, *José de Escandón*, 78.

37. Weddle, *French Thorn*, 280–281; Miller, *José de Escandón*, 18.

38. Weddle, *French Thorn*, 281, 1st quotation; Informe de José de Escandón (June 13, 1749) in *Estado general*, 2:302, 2d quotation.

39. Hill, *José de Escandón*, 86–87; Miller, *José de Escandón*, 20.

40. Weddle, *French Thorn*, 281; Títulos concedidos por su majestad Fernando VI (October 23, 1749), in *Estado general*, 2:307–309.

41. Hill, *José de Escandón*, 87; Castañeda, *Catholic Heritage*, 3:189–190.

42. Hill, *José de Escandón*, 87–88; Wilkinson, *Laredo*, 21, quotation, as quoted.

43. Wilkinson, *Laredo*, 21–23; Hill, *José de Escandón*, 89, 98–99, 102.

44. Wilkinson, *Laredo*, 24–26; Hill, *José de Escandón*, 100–101.

45. Letter from José de Escandón to Viceroy Revilla Gigedo (August 1, 1750), UTA, Hackett Transcripts; Letter from José de Escandón to Viceroy Revilla Gigedo (September 21, 1750), UTA, Hackett Transcripts, quotation.

46. Report on José de Escandón's Accomplishments by the Marqués de Aranda (October 25, 1755), UTA, Hackett Transcripts.

47. Report from José de Escandón to the Auditor de Guerra (May 6, 1753), UTA, Hackett Transcripts; Auditor's Assessment of Escandón's Report (August 21, 1753), BAT, Reel 4.

48. Reports on Villas Founded by Escandón (1753), UTA, Hackett Transcripts.

49. Ibid.

50. Letter from José de Escandón to Viceroy Revilla Gigedo (December 31, 1753), UTA, Hackett Transcripts; Report from José de Escandón to the Auditor de Guerra (May 6, 1753), UTA, Hackett Transcripts, quotation; Letter from José de Escandón to Viceroy Revilla Gigedo (November 12, 1754), UTA, Hackett Transcripts.

51. Auditor's Assessment of Escandón's Report (August 21, 1753), BAT, Reel 4.

52. Ibid.

53. Ibid.

54. Ibid.

55. Hill, *José de Escandón*, 102, 104–106.

56. Copia de la relación de José de Escandón (August 8, 1755), in *Estado general*, 1:12–45, quotation on 38.

57. Ibid.

58. Ibid., 43–45, quotation on 43. The twenty settlements covered in the August 1755 report were Altamira, Horcasitas, Escandón, Santa Bárbara, Llera, Aguayo, Hoyos, Güemes, Padilla, Capital de Nuevo Santander, Santillana, Soto la Marina, San Fernando, Burgos, Reynosa, Camargo, Mier, Revilla, Dolores, and Real de los Infantes. Also listed was the Hacienda de San Juan. See *Estado general*, 1:12–45.

59. Ibid., quotation on 43.

60. Decreto de Agustín de Ahumada (March 29, 1756), in *Estado General*, 1:3–4, quotation on 3; Instrucciones de Marqués de Amarillas para Tienda de Cuervo y López de la Cámara Alta (March 15, 1757), in *Estado general*, 1:5–10; Weddle, *French Thorn*, 284; Hill, *José de Escandón*, 106–107.

61. Informe del reconocimiento e inspección de la nueva colonia del Seno Mexicano por Tienda de Cuervo (1757), in *Estado general*, 2:3–158, passim.

62. Hill, *José de Escandón*, 107–108; Miller, *José de Escandón*, 27; Carta de José de Escandón al virrey (November 9, 1764), in *Estado general*, 2:202.

63. *Estado general*, Introducción, 1:x, quotations, as quoted.

64. Hill, *José de Escandón*, 108–109; Miller, *José de Escandón*, 27.

65. Miller, *José de Escandón*, 28; Hill, *José de Escandón*, 110–113; Florence Johnson Scott, *Royal Land Grants North of the Rio Grande, 1777–1821* (Rio Grande City, Tex.: La Retama Press, 1969), 12.

66. Miller, *José de Escandón*, 28–31.

67. Ibid., 32.

68. Ibid.; Letter from José de Escandón to the Viceroy (March 1, 1760), UTA, Hackett Transcripts, quotation.

69. Miller, *José de Escandón*, 32–33; Carta de José de Escandón al virrey Marqués de Cruillas (November 9, 1764), in *Estado general*, 2:192–208.

70. Escandón al Marqués de Cruillas (November 9, 1764), in *Estado general*, 2:197–201, 1st quotation on 198, 2d quotation on 200.

71. Ibid., quotation on 202.

72. Miller, *José de Escandón*, 32–33.

73. His Majesty Charles III to Viceroy Marqués de Cruillas (March 11, 1764), UTA, Hackett Transcripts.

74. Report from the *secretaría de cámara* to Viceroy Carlos Francisco de Croix (August 29, 1766), UTA, Hackett Transcripts.

75. Letter from Diego, Bishop of Guadalajara, to Viceroy Carlos Francisco de Croix (November 11, 1766), UTA, Hackett Transcripts. Italics are ours.

76. Miller, *José de Escandón*, 32–33.

77. Legal Proceedings Related to José de Escandón (1769–1773), UTA, Hackett Transcripts; Miller, *José de Escandón*, 33–35.

78. Miller, *José de Escandón*, 34–35; Scott, *Land Grants*, 13–14; Ruby Woolridge, "The Spanish and Mexican Land Grants of Present Day Cameron County" (master's thesis, Texas A&I University, Kingsville, Texas, 1951), 19–20. A third category of land grants, located primarily in Zapata County, consisted of vacant lands that reverted to the crown but were later available for reallocation (1770–1810).

79. Miller, *José de Escandón*, 36.

80. Legal Proceedings Relating to José de Escandón (1769–1773), UTA, Hackett Transcripts.

81. Ibid.

82. Ibid.

83. Ibid.

84. Ibid.

85. Ibid.

86. Ibid.

87. Ibid.

88. Ibid.

89. Ibid. Based on available documentation, Bárbara Resendi's reasons for animosity toward José de Escandón are unclear. Perhaps she believed the count guilty of prosecutable behavior in his Indian policy, but it is noteworthy that gender alone, rather than evidence to the contrary of doña Bárbara's assertions, was used to discredit her.

90. Letter from Charles III to Viceroy Bucareli (January 25, 1773), UTA, Hackett Transcripts; Proceedings Related to José de Escandón (January 17, 1774), UTA, Hackett Transcripts; Statement of Domingo Valcarcel to Viceroy Bucareli (October 10, 1774), UTA, Hackett Transcripts, long quotation.

91. Letter from Charles III to Viceroy Bucareli (January 25, 1773), UTA, Hackett Transcripts.

92. *NHOT*, 4:1074–1075.

93. Miller, *José de Escandón*, 38. The society holds annual conferences directed toward the "Children of Las Porciones."

94. Ibid. The South Texas triangle includes modern-day Starr, Hidalgo, and Cameron Counties.

CHAPTER 8

1. Official Report by De Mézières of the Expedition to Cadodachos (October 29, 1770), BM1, 206, 208–210, quotation on 210. Fort San Luis de Cadodachos (Cadodaquious) was located about 250 miles from Natchitoches on the Red River in present Bowie County, Texas. See Robert S. Weddle, *The French*

Thorn: Rival Explorers in the Spanish Sea, 1682–1762 (College Station: Texas A&M University Press, 1991), 211.

2. Juan Agustín Morfi, *History of Texas, 1673–1779*, trans. and ed. Carlos E. Castañeda (Albuquerque: Quivira Society, 1935), 2:443 n. 17; Julia Vivian, *A Cavalier in Texas* (San Antonio: Naylor Company, 1953), 33, as quoted, 40.

3. Morfi, *History of Texas*, 2:443 n. 17; Robert S. Weddle, *Changing Tides: Twilight and Dawn in the Spanish Sea, 1763–1803* (College Station: Texas A&M University Press, 1995), 10, 11, 15–16, 21. Louis de St. Denis was the son of Louis Juchereau de St. Denis.

4. Herbert E. Bolton, *Texas in the Middle Eighteenth Century: Studies in Spanish Colonial History and Administration* (Austin: University of Texas Press, 1970), 119–120; Weddle, *Changing Tides*, 5–6, 9; Introduction, BM1, 67–68. The Nations of the North included tribes of Caddoan language stock who occupied portions of north central Texas between the Brazos and Red Rivers. The principal tribe, Taovayas, lived on both banks of the Red near present-day Spanish Fort, Texas. See Carol A. Lipscomb, " 'Sorrow Whispers in the Winds': The Republic of Texas's Comanche Indian Policy, 1836–1846" (master's thesis, University of North Texas, 1994), 8.

5. Bolton, *Texas*, 120.

6. Introduction, BM1, 69–73.

7. O'Reilly to De Mézières (September 23, 1769), BM1, 130–131, 1st quotation on 131; Vivian, *Cavalier*, 41; Weddle, *Changing Tides*, 21–22; Lawrence Kinnaird, ed., *Spain in the Mississippi Valley, 1765–1794: Translations of Materials from the Spanish Archives in the Bancroft Library* (Washington, D.C.: U.S. Government Printing Office, 1946–1949), 2:129, 2d quotation. As added incentive to serve Spain loyally, De Mézières's two eldest sons were appointed cadet officers.

8. Vivian, *Cavalier*, 1, 3, 18–19, quotation on 1; Introduction, BM1, 80, 85; Elizabeth S. Mills, "(de) Mézières-Trichel-Grappe: A Study of a Tri-caste Lineage in the Old South," *The Genealogist* 6 (Spring 1985): 34.

9. Violet Wyndham, *Madame de Genlis: A Biography* (London: Andre Deutsch, 1958), 22, 1st quotation; Betje B. Klier, "Théodore Pavie," (unpublished manuscript in possession of the author), 2d quotation. Dr. Klier's information on the early life of Athanase de Mézières is extracted from the *Mémoires* of Madame de Genlis (Paris: Ladvocat, 1825). Mme Genlis was the niece of De Mézières (her mother being the daughter of Madame de la Haye and the half sister of don Athanase); she met her uncle during his stay in Paris.

10. Klier, "Théodore Pavie." In June 1742 the royal edict of banishment was lifted, but De Mézières remained in America. See Mills, "(de) Mézières-Trichel-Grappe," 34. Two of De Mézières's maternal uncles were generals in the French army and may have secured their nephew's military appointment.

11. Vivian, *Cavalier*, 26–27; Introduction, BM1, 83. As noted in Chapter 3 of this volume, Louis Juchereau de St. Denis died in 1744. For an excellent analysis of the interconnectedness of prominent families in Natchitoches and Spanish Texas, see Patricia R. Lemée, "Tios and Tantes: Familial and Political Rela-

tionships of Natchitoches and the Spanish Colonial Frontier," *Southwestern Historical Quarterly* 101 (January 1998): 341–358.

12. Vivian, *Cavalier*, 27, 29, 31–32; Introduction, BM1, 55. The presidio was San Agustín de Ahumada.

13. Mills, "(de) Mézières-Trichel-Grappe," 35–38. Pelagie Fazende's relatives in New Orleans controlled a number of governmental positions in the colony.

14. Introduction, BM1, 83, 86; Kinnaird, *Spain*, 2:129.

15. Introduction, BM1, 87; Vivian, *Cavalier*, 41–42.

16. Introduction, BM1, 88; Vivian, *Cavalier*, 47.

17. Bolton, *Texas*, 120–121; Introduction, BM1, 71–72, 89; Vivian, *Cavalier*, 42.

18. Introduction, BM1, 89; Instructions for the Traders of the Cadaux d'Acquioux and Hiatasses Nations (February 4, 1770), BM1, 148–150.

19. O'Reilly to De Mézières (January 23, 1770), BM1, 134–135, quotation on 135; O'Reilly to De Mézières (January 22, 1770), BM1, 132–134.

20. Introduction, BM1, 91–92; O'Reilly to De Mézières (January 23, 1770), BM1, 136.

21. De Mézières to Unzaga (February 1, 1770), BM1, 140–142, 1st quotation on 140, 2d quotation on 142.

22. Ibid., 142–143; Agreement Made with the Indian Nations in Assembly (April 21, 1770), BM1, 157–158; Vivian, *Cavalier*, 42–43.

23. Agreement Made with the Indian Nations in Assembly (April 21, 1770), BM1, 157–158, 1st quotation on 157, 2d quotation on 158.

24. De Mézières to Unzaga (May 15, 1770), BM1, 161–162; Cecile E. Carter, *Caddo Indians: Where We Come From* (Norman: University of Oklahoma Press, 1995), 183–184.

25. BM1, 162.

26. Ibid., 162–163, quotation on 162; Carter, *Caddo Indians*, 184–185.

27. Unzaga to De Mézières (June 1, 1770), BM1, 171–173, quotation on 173.

28. [José] González to De Mézières (October 30, 1770), BM1, 191–192, quotation on 191; De Mézières to Unzaga (May 20, 1770), BM1, 199–200.

29. De Mézières to Unzaga (May 20, 1770), BM1, 200–202.

30. Unzaga to De Mézières (September 20, 1770), BM1, 203–204.

31. De Mézières to Unzaga (September 27, 1770), BM1, 204–206.

32. Official Report by De Mézières of the Expedition to Cadodachos (October 29, 1770), BM1, 206–208.

33. Ibid., 211–213.

34. Ibid., 213–214, quotation on 213.

35. Ibid., 216–220, 1st quotation on 219, 2d quotation on 218–219, 3d quotation on 218.

36. Unzaga to De Mézières (November 29, 1770), BM1, 232–233.

37. Introduction, BM1, 93; Depositions Relative to the Expedition to Cadodachos (October 30–31, 1770), BM1, 222–230.

38. De Mézières to Unzaga (February 28, 1771), BM1, 238–240.

39. Ibid., 240–241.

40. Unzaga to De Mézières (April 6, 1771), BM1, 247–248, quotation on 248.

41. Barón de Ripperdá to Unzaga (December 31, 1771), BM1, 264.

42. Introduction, BM1, 94; De Mézières to Unzaga (July 3, 1771), BM1, 249–250; Barón de Ripperdá to Unzaga (December 31, 1771), BM1, 264–265; Vivian, *Cavalier*, 50.

43. Barón de Ripperdá to Unzaga (December 31, 1771), BM1, 265–266.

44. Introduction, BM1, 95; Barón de Ripperdá to Unzaga (December 31, 1771), BM1, 268, quotation.

45. Introduction, BM1, 94–95; Kinnaird, *Spain*, 2: 197, quotations; Treaty with the Taovayas (October 27, 1771), BM1, 256–260; Declaration of Gorgoritos, Bidai Chief (December 21, 1771), BM1, 260–262. The treaty with the Taovayas was signed on October 28.

46. Introduction, BM1, 96–97; Barón de Ripperdá to Unzaga (December 31, 1771), BM1, 266–268.

47. Introduction, BM1, 96; Barón de Ripperdá to Unzaga (May 26, 1772), BM1, 273–275, quotation on 275; Bolton, *Texas*, 122.

48. Introduction, BM1, 96; Bolton, *Texas*, 122.

49. Report of De Mézières to Barón de Ripperdá (July 4, 1772), BM1, 297–298, quotation on 297.

50. Barón de Ripperdá to Viceroy Bucareli (July 5, 1772), BM1, 320–321.

51. Vivian, *Cavalier*, 56; De Mézières to Viceroy Bucareli (July 16, 1772), BM1, 311–312; De Mézières to Barón de Ripperdá (July 4, 1772), BM1, 312–314; Barón de Ripperdá to Viceroy Bucareli (July 6, 1772), BM1, 326–327.

52. Viceroy Bucareli to Barón de Ripperdá (September 16, 1772), BM1, 349–351.

53. Vivian, *Cavalier*, 57; Carter, *Caddo Indians*, 191–192.

54. José de la Peña to Unzaga (September 14, 1772), BM2, 13–22, quotation on 16; Vivian, *Cavalier*, 57. There are multiple short letters from de la Peña to Unzaga, all dated September 14.

55. Introduction, BM1, 100; Passport for De Mézières to Go to France (April 23, 1773), BM2, 31–32; Vivian, *Cavalier*, 58.

56. Wyndham, *Madame de Genlis*, 277–278; Klier, "Théodore Pavie."

57. Introduction, BM1, 100, 107–108; Vivian, *Cavalier*, 65–66.

58. Introduction, BM1, 107–108; Weddle, *Changing Tides*, 84–85.

59. Arriaga to Unzaga (May 30, 1774), BM2, 104; De Mézières to Unzaga (December 16, 1774), BM2, 115.

60. De Mézières to Unzaga (September 4, 1774), BM2, 110–111; Unzaga to De Mézières (October 22, 1774), BM2, 113. When carried out in December 1777, the voyage was part of an overall plan for coastal exploration dispatched by Bernardo de Gálvez.

61. Bucareli to Barón de Ripperdá (July 26, 1775), BM2, 79; Bucareli to Barón de Ripperdá (January 17, 1776), BAT, Reel 8.

62. Introduction, BM1, 75–76; Bucareli to Barón de Ripperdá (May 15, 1776), BAT, Reel 8.

63. Vivian, *Cavalier*, 73; De Mézières to Croix (November 15, 1778), BM2, 231–232. The epidemic, which occurred from October to December in 1777, also claimed the lives of Bigotes (Sauto) and Tinhioüen. See Carter, *Caddo Indians*, 207.

64. Vivian, *Cavalier*, 72–73.

65. Weddle, *Changing Tides*, 87–88; Bolton, *Texas*, 124.

66. Barón de Ripperdá to Croix (April 27, 1777), BM2, 123–128.

67. Council of War at Monclova (December 9, 1777), BM2, 147–152, quotation on 148.

68. Council of War at Monclova (December 11, 1777), BM2, 152–163.

69. Ibid., 155, 159–160.

70. Council of War at San Antonio de Béxar (January 5, 1778), 163–169. De Mézières was summoned to Béxar but did not attend the council because of the remoteness of Natchitoches.

71. Ibid., 167–169. The third war council, held in Chihuahua in July 1778, essentially confirmed the recommendations of the earlier councils.

72. De Mézières to the Viceroy (February 20, 1778), BM2, 172, 174–178, 181–182.

73. Ibid., 178–181, 183–185.

74. Ibid., 179–180, 182–183.

75. De Mézières to Croix (March 18, 1778), BM2, 187–189; De Mézières to Croix (March 23, 1778), BM2, 190–191.

76. De Mézières to Croix (April 18, 1778), BM2, 201–203. The Taovaya villages were named San Teodoro and San Bernardo to honor, respectively, Croix and Gálvez.

77. De Mézières to Croix (April 18, 1778), BM2, 201–203.

78. De Mézières to Croix (April 19, 1778), BM2, 207–208.

79. De Mézières to Croix (April 19, 1778) and De Mézières to Croix (April 19, 1778), BM2, 208, 209.

80. De Mézières to Croix (April 19, 1778), BM2, 212–213.

81. De Mézières to Croix (November 15, 1778), BM2, 232–233; Bolton, *Texas*, 432–433.

82. De Mézières to Croix (November 15, 1778), BM2, 232–233, quotation on 233. The destruction and abandonment of Villa Bucareli and the founding of modern Nacogdoches will be addressed in the following chapter on Governor Domingo Cabello y Robles.

83. Croix to De Mézières (September 10, 1778), BM2, 216–217.

84. Croix to Bernardo de Gálvez (September 10, 1778), BM2, 218–219, quotation on 218.

85. Croix to José de Gálvez (September 23, 1778), BM2, 220–221, quotation on 221.

86. Ibid., 222–223, quotation on 223.

87. De Mézières to Bernardo de Gálvez (February 7, 1779), BM2, 239–240; De Mézières to Bernardo de Gálvez (March 17, 1779), BM2, 240. It is possible that De Mézières completed the journey to New Orleans after recovering from this accident.

88. De Mézières to Bernardo de Gálvez (March 17, 1779), BM2, 241; De Mézières to Croix (May 24, 1779), BM2, 254–255.

89. De Mézières to Bernardo de Gálvez (March 17, 1779), BM2, 241; Bernardo de Gálvez to Croix (March 21, 1779), BM2, 243; De Mézières to Bernardo de Gálvez (March 21, 1779), BM2, 244–245; Bernardo de Gálvez to De Mézières (March 22, 1779), BM2, 246.

90. De Mézières to Bernardo de Gálvez (May [?], 1779), BM2, 246; De Mézières to Croix (May 24, 1779), BM2, 254; De Mézières to Croix (August 21, 1779), BM2, 258–260, quotation on 259.

91. De Mézières to Croix (August 21, 1779), BM2, 259; De Mézières to Croix (August 23, 1779), BM2, 260–261.

92. List of Presents Given to Tuacanas and Tancagues (September 13, 1779), BM2, 276–277.

93. Cabello to Croix (June 20, 1779), BAT, Reel 11; Cabello to Croix (August 31, 1779), BAT, Reel 11.

94. Cabello to Croix (October 19, 1779), BAT, Reel 11; Cabello to Croix (October 20, 1779), BAT, Reel 11.

95. Cabello to Croix (October 12, 1779), BAT, Reel 11.

96. De Mézières to Croix (October 7, 1779), BM2, 291–293.

97. Ibid., 294–297.

98. Ibid., 296–298.

99. Ibid., 298–303.

100. Morfi, *History of Texas*, 2:439–440, quotation on 440; De Mézières to Croix (October 13, 1779), BM2, 319–322.

101. Cabello to Croix (November 12, 1779), BAT, Reel 11.

102. Ibid., quotation; Morfi, *History of Texas*, 2:440. A copy of the letter in French is available at the Center for American History, Austin.

103. Cabello to Croix (November 12, 1779), BAT, Reel 11, quotation; Record of the Burial of De Mézières (November 3, 1779), BM2, 327.

104. Croix to Bernardo de Gálvez (January 26, 1780), BM2, 332–333, 1st quotation on 332; Croix to Cabello (December 31, 1779), BAT, Reel 11, 2d and 3d quotations; Croix to José de Gálvez (January 23, 1780), UTA, 4th quotation.

105. Elizabeth A. H. John, "Spanish Relations with the *Indios Bárbaros* on the Northern-most Frontier of New Spain in the Eighteenth Century" (Ph.D. diss., University of Oklahoma, 1957), 126.

106. Louis de Blanc to Esteban Miró (March 30, 1791), in Kinnaird, *Spain*, 2:409.

CHAPTER 9

1. Jack Jackson, ed., and William C. Foster, annot., *Imaginary Kingdom: Texas as Seen by the Rivera and Rubí Military Expeditions, 1727, 1767* (Austin: Texas State Historical Association, 1995), 129. With the arrival of fifty-five Canary Islanders at San Antonio in 1731, Villa de Béxar was renamed San Fernando de Béxar.

2. Ibid., 73–74. The Marquesa de Rubí's title came from her father, José de Antonio Rubí y Bojador, who was viceroy of Mallorca, viceroy of Sardinia, and governor of Antwerp.

3. Ibid., quotation on 74.

4. Donald E. Chipman, *Spanish Texas, 1519–1821* (reprint, Austin: University of Texas Press, 1994), 171–172. France wished to keep the Louisiana territory out of English hands. Spain was obliged to surrender Florida in exchange for Havana, which the English had captured during the war.

5. Ibid., 172.

6. Luis Navarro García, *Don José de Gálvez y la Comandancia General de las Provincias Internas del Norte de Nueva España* (Seville: Escuela de Estudios Hispano-Americanos de Sevilla, 1964), 135. Rubí arrived in New Spain on November 1, 1764. See Janet R. Fireman, *The Spanish Royal Corps of Engineers in the Western Borderlands: Instrument of Bourbon Reform, 1764–1815* (Glendale, Calif.: Arthur H. Clark, 1977), 73.

7. The transfer of Louisiana from France to Spain did not occur immediately, and Spain failed to exercise effective control until 1769.

8. Jackson and Foster, *Imaginary Kingdom*, 78–80.

9. Navarro García, *Don José*, 135; David J. Weber, *The Spanish Frontier in North America* (New Haven: Yale University Press, 1992), 205; Carlos E. Castañeda, *Our Catholic Heritage in Texas, 1519–1936* (Austin: Von Boeckmann–Jones, 1936–1958), 4:222. For examples of inflated prices, see Max L. Moorhead, *The Presidio: Bastion of the Borderlands* (Norman: University of Oklahoma Press, 1975), 57–58.

10. Weber, *Spanish Frontier*, 205.

11. Jackson and Foster, *Imaginary Kingdom*, 75. Urrutia recorded plans of the various presidios and settlements. For Texas presidios, see ibid., Plates 3–7, following 126.

12. See Lawrence Kinnaird, ed. and trans., *The Frontiers of New Spain: Nicolás de Lafora's Description* (Berkeley: Quivira Society, 1958), 44. Rubí's heretofore unknown diary was found in papers acquired in 1989 by the Center for American History at the University of Texas at Austin.

13. Castañeda, *Catholic Heritage*, 4:225.

14. Jackson and Foster, *Imaginary Kingdom*, 93.

15. Weber, *Spanish Frontier*, 207–209.

16. Ibid., 209.

17. Chipman, *Spanish Texas*, 173.

18. Jackson and Foster, *Imaginary Kingdom*, 79, 108–109, quotation on 108.

19. Ibid., 111.

20. Ibid., 114, 1st, 2d, and 3d quotations; Castañeda, *Catholic Heritage*, 4: 192, 4th and 5th quotations, as quoted.

21. Jackson and Foster, *Imaginary Kingdom*, 117–118.

22. Robert H. Thonhoff, *El Fuerte del Cíbolo: Sentinel of the Béxar–La Bahía Ranches* (Austin: Eakin Press, 1992), 39–46. Out of necessity, a military

outpost on the Río de Cíbolo was founded on April 12, 1771, antedating the New Regulations of 1772.

23. Jackson and Foster, *Imaginary Kingdom*, 127, 1st and 2d quotations; Kinnaird, *Frontiers of New Spain*, 166, 3d quotation. The comments of Rubí and Lafora are perhaps overstated. When Gaspar José de Solís visited this mission in June 1768, the administrative books of the mission recorded "twelve baptisms, eight burials, and five marriages." See Margaret K. Kress, trans., "Diary of a Visit of Inspection of the Texas Missions Made by Fray Gaspar José de Solís in the Year 1767–1768," *Southwestern Historical Quarterly* 35 (July 1931): 69.

24. Jackson and Foster, *Imaginary Kingdom*, 128, 1st and 2d quotations; Kinnaird, *Frontiers of New Spain*, 166.

25. Jackson and Foster, *Imaginary Kingdom*, 129.

26. Ibid., 129–130, quotations on 129.

27. Ibid., 130. The Spanish captain general of Louisiana was Antonio de Ulloa, but the colony was not under firm Spanish control until the arrival of Alejando O'Reilly in 1769.

28. Ibid., 133.

29. Ibid., 134.

30. Ibid., 135–141, quotations; Kinnaird, *Frontiers of New Spain*, 178. Rubí, as did Lafora, also reported on mission Nuestra Señora del Rosario, located about five miles west of the Espíritu Santo mission. The engineer counted "seventy-one baptized persons and thirty savages, many more having escaped to live at liberty with their relatives."

31. Jackson and Foster, *Imaginary Kingdom*, 142–145, quotation on 145. In a rare example of interjecting personal matters into his diary, Rubí noted that the three *familia* members "were resentful" of their near-drowning.

32. Ibid., 145–157; *NHOT*, 5:705; Moorhead, *The Presidio*, 57 n. 26. Although Rubí's recommendations would involve twenty-four presidios, he did not inspect a recently established garrison at Julimes in Nueva Vizcaya.

33. Elizabeth A. H. John, *Storms Brewed in Other Men's Worlds: The Confrontation of Indians, Spanish, and French in the Southwest, 1540–1795* (College Station: Texas A&M University Press, 1975), 439.

34. Chipman, *Spanish Texas*, 181.

35. John, *Storms*, 439.

36. Chipman, *Spanish Texas*, 181. In all, Rubí's proposal for seventeen presidios reduced the total, exclusive of Nuevo Santander and Baja California, by seven, representing an annual saving to the crown of 79,928 pesos. See Moorhead, *The Presidio*, 50–60.

37. Chipman, *Spanish Texas*, 181.

38. Jackson and Foster, *Imaginary Kingdom*, 179–182, quotations throughout.

39. Moorhead, *The Presidio*, 60–61; John, *Storms*, 441. Father José de Calahorra y Sáenz of the Nacogdoches mission had earlier proposed such an Indian policy. See John, *Storms*, 302.

40. Jackson and Foster, *Imaginary Kingdom*, 181.

41. Ibid., 227; Castañeda, *Catholic Heritage*, 4:257–258. In Article 16 of his *dictamen*, Rubí considered the "advantages" of "total extermination" but immediately followed that suggestion with an alternative, which was to reduce the Lipans so completely in strength that they could no longer cause mischief or practice their "constant fickleness." See Jackson and Foster, *Imaginary Kingdom*, 181–182.

42. *NHOT*, 5: 705.

43. Ibid.; Jackson and Foster, *Imaginary Kingdom*, 223–225.

44. Moorhead, *The Presidio*, 59, 64–65. Moorhead argues that presidios La Bahía del Espíritu Santo, San Juan Bautista, and Janos were appropriately located.

45. Jackson and Foster, *Imaginary Kingdom*, 210, 220–221, quotation on 210; Kinnaird, *Frontiers of New Spain*, ix. For a thorough assessment of the Rubí recommendations, as well as historiographical interpretations of them, see Jackson and Foster, idem, 209–228.

46. Navarro García, *José de Gálvez*, 143. Gálvez arrived in New Spain on August 25, 1765.

47. Sidney B. Brinckerhoff and Odie B. Faulk, *Lancers for the King: A Study of the Frontier Military System of Northern New Spain, with a Translation of the Royal Regulations of 1772* (Phoenix: Arizona Historical Foundation, 1965), 37. The Interior Provinces included Nueva Vizcaya, Sonora, Sinaloa, California, New Mexico, Coahuila, Texas, Nuevo León, and Nuevo Santander. For a nicely crafted small book on Oconor, see Mark Santiago, *The Red Captain: The Life of Hugo O'Conor, Commandant Inspector of the Interior Provinces of New Spain* (Tucson: Arizona Historical Society, 1994).

48. Brinckerhoff and Faulk, *Lancers*, 61.

49. Castañeda, *Catholic Heritage*, 4:294.

50. Ibid., 294–295. Oconor's orders reached Ripperdá on May 18, 1773.

51. Ibid., 295.

52. Ibid., 296, quotation, as quoted.

53. Ibid., 296. Variant spellings for Ibarvo include Ibarbo and Ybarbo. In Spanish, *lobonillo* may be translated as "wart," "mole," or "wen."

54. "Captain Antonio Gil Ybarbo of Nacogdoches," unpublished manuscript in the Robert Bruce Blake Research Collection, UTA, vol. 45. Hereafter cited as Blake Collection. For speculation that Gil Ibarvo's parents did not arrive via New Orleans, see Francis E. Abernethy, "The Y'Barbo Legend in Early Spanish Settlement," *East Texas Historical Journal* 25 (Fall 1987): 41–42.

55. "Gil Ybarbo," Blake Collection, vol. 45. For marital difficulties of the Gil Ibarvos, see Chapter 12 of this volume.

56. Ibid.

57. Ibid.

58. Copy of a communication from Hugo Oconor to Viceroy Bucareli (April 5, 1776), in Letter from Ramón de Castro to Juan Cortés (January 10, 1792), Blake Collection, vol. 53.

59. "Gil Ybarbo," Blake Collection, vol. 45; Oakah L. Jones Jr., *Los Paisanos: Spanish Settlers on the Northern Frontier of New Spain* (Norman: University of Oklahoma Press, 1996), 45.

60. Chipman, *Spanish Texas*, 186; Jones, *Los Paisanos*, 45.

61. Herbert E. Bolton, "The Spanish Abandonment and Re-occupation of East Texas, 1773–1779," *Quarterly of the Texas State Historical Association* 9 (October 1905): 86–87.

62. Ibid.

63. Ibid., 87–88; Petition from Gil Ibarvo et al., to Barón de Ripperdá (October 4, 1773), Blake Collection, vol. 45, quotations. The number of petitioners is often given as seventy-five, but a copy of the petition lists seventy-eight names.

64. "Gil Ibarvo," Blake Collection, vol. 45; F. Todd Smith, *The Caddo Indians: Tribes at the Convergence of Empires, 1542–1854* (College Station: Texas A&M University Press, 1995), 73. The Hainai were one of eight tribes in the Hasinai Confederation.

65. Petition from Gil Ibarvo to Hugo Oconor (January 8, 1774), Blake Collection, vol. 44; "Gil Ibarbo," Blake Collection, vol. 45. Bucareli's favorable impression of Texita, whom he found "intelligent and capable," may have helped influence the viceroy's favorable decision. See Smith, *Caddo Indians*, 73, as quoted.

66. "Gil Ibarbo," Blake Collection, vol. 45.

67. Ibid.

68. Letter from Gil Ibarvo to Viceroy Bucareli (May 10, 1774), Blake Collection, vol. 44; Father José de la Garza's Affidavit on the Character and Service of Gil Ibarvo (November 14, 1787), BAT, Reel 17.

69. "Gil Ibarbo," Blake Collection, vol. 45.

70. Ibid.; Letter from Pedro de Nava to the Governor of Texas (October 15, 1796), BA, Reel 26; Copy of Proceedings Concerning Gil Ibarvo's Commission as Judge of Contraband Cases (April 20, 1780), BA, Reel 13.

71. Castañeda, *Catholic Heritage*, 4:334–337.

72. The Old Stone Fort on the Stephen F. Austin State University campus is not located where it was originally built, and much of the structure contains newly cut rock.

73. Letter from Ramón de Castro to Juan Cortés (January 10, 1792), Blake Collection, vol. 53; Letter from Ramón de Castro to Manuel Muñoz (December 27, 1791), BA, Reel 21. Gil Ibarvo may have kept his title as magistrate. The 1792 census of Nacogdoches lists Antonio Gil Ibarvo as a Spanish judge. See Census of Nacogdoches (December 31, 1792), Blake Collection, vol. 18.

74. A Criminal Code for Nacogdoches (1783), Blake Collection, vol. 45.

75. Ibid.

76. Peña had many aliases, including "The Little Braggart," and "Sky-blue Breeches."

77. Letter from Gil Ibarvo to Governor Rafael Martínez Pacheco (July 15, 1789), Blake Collection, vol. 52; "Gil Ibarbo," Blake Collection, vol. 45.

78. "Gil Ibarbo," Blake Collection, vol. 45.

79. Letter from Gil Ibarvo to Governor Rafael Martínez Pacheco (July 15, 1789), Blake Collection, vol. 52; "Gil Ibarbo," Blake Collection, vol. 45, quotation.

80. "Gil Ibarbo," Blake Collection, vol. 45.

81. Ibid.

82. Letter from Gil Ibarvo to Manuel Muñoz (March 22, 1791), Blake Collection, vol. 52; Petition from Gil Ibarvo to the Viceroy (March 22, 1791), Blake Collection, vol. 52.

83. Antonio Gil Ibarvo's Request for Documents Relating to Contraband Charges Against Him (September 30–October 15, 1795), BA, Reel 25; Letter from Pedro de Nava to the Governor of Texas (November 29, 1796), BA, Reel 26.

84. Letter from José Miguel del Moral to Governor Elguézabal (October 14, 1799), BA, Reel 29.

85. *NHOT*, 3:812. Gil Ibarvo was buried in the old Spanish cemetery in Nacogdoches, a site that is presently covered by the Nacogdoches County Courthouse.

86. Father José de la Garza's Affidavit on the Character and Service of Gil Ibarvo (November 14, 1787), BAT, Reel 17.

CHAPTER 10

1. Alfred B. Thomas, trans. and ed., *Teodoro de Croix and the Northern Frontier of New Spain, 1776–1783* (Norman: University of Oklahoma Press, 1941), 27–35; Order of Barón de Ripperdá Prohibiting Celebrations of the Arrival of Teodoro de Croix (December 31, 1777), BAT, Reel 9; Report of Teodoro de Croix to José de Gálvez (October 30, 1781), AGI, Guadalajara 253, quotation. Croix later praised Texas for its rich land, abundant rivers, and mineral deposits.

2. Merits and Services of Domingo Cabello (June 30, 1779), UTA, Dunn Transcripts.

3. Ibid. This conflict began in the Americas in 1739 as the result of a maiming incident at sea, involving Spaniards and a British subject, that came to be derisively known as the "War of Jenkins' Ear."

4. Ibid.

5. Ibid.

6. Ibid.

7. Ibid.

8. Ibid.

9. Robert S. Weddle, *Changing Tides: Twilight and Dawn in the Spanish Sea, 1763–1803* (College Station: Texas A&M University Press, 1995), 152.

10. Ibid.

11. Letter from Bernardo de Gálvez to José de Gálvez (January 25, 1779) in Lawrence Kinnaird, ed., *Spain in the Mississippi Valley, 1765–1794: Transla-*

tions of Materials from the Spanish Archives in the Bancroft Library (Washington, D.C.: U.S. Government Printing Office, 1946–1949), 1:325, 1st quotation; Weddle, *Changing Tides*, 153, 2d quotation, as quoted.

12. Weddle, *Changing Tides*, 154.

13. Account of the Capture of a Spanish Schooner by Indians at the Bay of Espíritu Santo (March 20, 1779), in Kinnaird, *Spain*, 1:332; Weddle, *Changing Tides*, 154–155.

14. Account of the Capture, in Kinnaird, *Spain*, 1:332; Weddle, *Changing Tides*, 154–155.

15. Account of the Capture, in Kinnaird, *Spain*, 1:333.

16. Ibid., 333–334; Weddle, *Changing Tides*, 156–157.

17. Donald E. Chipman, *Spanish Texas, 1519–1821* (reprint, Austin: University of Texas Press, 1994), 192.

18. Athanase de Mézières to Teodoro de Croix (October 7, 1779), BM2, 298–303, 1st quotation on 303, 2nd quotation on 302; Weddle, *Changing Tides*, 158–160.

19. Introduction, BM1, 32; Weddle, *Changing Tides*, 160–161.

20. Domingo Cabello to Esteban Miró (September 21, 1783), in Kinnaird, *Spain*, 2:86–87; Weddle, *Changing Tides*, 161–162, quotation on 161, as quoted.

21. Carlos E. Castañeda, *Our Catholic Heritage in Texas, 1519–1936* (Austin: Von Boeckmann–Jones, 1936–1958), 4:329.

22. Ibid., 320.

23. Ibid., 329–330.

24. Herbert E. Bolton, *Texas in the Middle Eighteenth Century: Studies in Spanish Colonial History and Administration* (Austin: University of Texas Press, 1970), 435, quotation, as quoted.

25. Castañeda, *Catholic Heritage*, 4:332, as quoted.

26. Ibid., 332–334. Domingo Cabello attributed the abandonment of Villa Bucareli to the flood of February 14, but it is clear that the main exodus occurred almost a month earlier. See Herbert E. Bolton, "The Spanish Abandonment and Re-occupation of East Texas, 1773–1779," *Quarterly of the Texas State Historical Association* 9 (October 1905): 131 n. 3.

27. Bolton, *Texas*, 437–439.

28. Ibid., 442–443.

29. Castañeda, *Catholic Heritage*, 4:337–338.

30. Bolton, *Texas*, 441–442.

31. Castañeda, *Catholic Heritage*, 4:340. Nacogdoches remained poorly defended throughout Cabello's governorship. In early 1784, don Domingo reported that the town had no muskets, pistols, swords, or lances. See General Status of Armaments, Province of Texas (January 31, 1784), BAT, Reel 14.

32. Castañeda, *Catholic Heritage*, 4:340–341.

33. Ibid., 341–343.

34. Bolton, "Spanish Abandonment," 134–136.

35. Light T. Cummins, *Spanish Observers and the American Revolution,*

1775–1783 (Baton Rouge: Louisiana State University Press, 1991), 113–114; Chipman, *Spanish Texas*, 192.

36. Croix's Report of 1781, in Thomas, *Teodoro de Croix*, 75, quotation; Chipman, *Spanish Texas*, 198; Odie B. Faulk, *The Last Years of Spanish Texas, 1778–1821* (The Hague: Mouton, 1964), 63.

37. Croix's Report of 1781, in Thomas, *Teodoro de Croix*, 74, quotation; Chipman, *Spanish Texas*, 198.

38. Thomas W. Kavanagh, *Comanche Political History: An Ethnohistorical Perspective, 1706–1875* (Lincoln: University of Nebraska Press, 1996), 95, quotation; Stanley Noyes, *Los Comanches: The Horse People, 1751–1845* (Albuquerque: University of New Mexico Press, 1993), 148.

39. Kavanagh, *Comanche*, 95.

40. Ibid.

41. Noyes, *Los Comanches*, 148–149.

42. Letter from Domingo Cabello to Felipe de Neve (August 19, 1784), BAT, Reel 15; Kavanagh, *Comanche*, 96.

43. Cabello's Report of Gifts to Friendly Nations of the North (June 17, 1785), BAT, Reel 15; Kavanagh, *Comanche*, 96–97; Elizabeth A. H. John, ed., and Adán Benavides, trans., "Inside the Comanchería, 1785: The Diary of Pedro Vial and Francisco Xavier Chaves," *Southwestern Historical Quarterly* 98 (July 1994): 28.

44. Kavanagh, *Comanche*, 98; John and Benavides, "Inside the Comanchería," 36–37. "Captain Iron Shirt" wore a chain mail upper garment, which he claimed to have taken from an Apache chief; "Captain Shaved Head" had no hair on one side and very long hair on the other.

45. John and Benavides, "Inside the Comanchería," 39.

46. Ibid.

47. Ibid., 40.

48. Kavanagh, *Comanche*, 99.

49. Ibid., as quoted.

50. Letter from Domingo Cabello to José Antonio Rengel (October 3, 1785), BAT, Reel 15; Kavanagh, *Comanche*, 100, as quoted.

51. Letter from Domingo Cabello to José Antonio Rengel (October 3, 1785), BAT, Reel 15, quotation; Faulk, *Last Years*, 65.

52. Letter from Domingo Cabello to José Antonio Rengel Reporting on Gifts for Indians (May 20, 1785), BAT, Reel 15; Faulk, *Last Years*, 65–66; Chipman, *Spanish Texas*, 198–199.

53. F. Todd Smith, *The Caddo Indians: Tribes at the Convergence of Empires, 1542–1854* (College Station: Texas A&M University Press, 1995), 79. In August 1779, Cabello had deliberately plied visiting Hasinais with gifts and escorted them out of San Antonio just hours before a delegation of six hundred Lipan Apaches arrived there.

54. Ibid.

55. Ibid., 80–81; Letter from Domingo Cabello to Felipe de Neve (July 15, 1784), BAT, Reel 15, quotation.

56. Smith, *Caddo Indians*, 81, as quoted.

57. Chipman, *Spanish Texas*, 207.

58. Noel M. Loomis, and Abraham P. Nasatir, *Pedro Vial and the Roads to Santa Fe* (Norman: University of Oklahoma Press, 1967), 268.

59. Chipman, *Spanish Texas*, 208. For treatment of continued efforts to discover the most direct path between San Antonio and Santa Fe, see 208–209.

60. Domingo Cabello to Teodoro de Croix (June 20, 1779), BAT, Reel 11.

61. Ibid. The clear implication here is that Ripperdá's "former businesses" were illegal.

62. Domingo Cabello to Commandant General Croix (October 19, 1779), BAT, Reel 11.

63. Odie B. Faulk, "Texas during the Administration of Governor Domingo Cabello y Robles, 1778–1786" (master's thesis, Texas Technological College, 1960), 117–118, 1st quotation on 117, as quoted, 2d quotation on 118.

64. Ibid., 124–125, quotation on 125, as quoted. Charles R. Cutter in *The Legal Culture of Northern New Spain, 1700–1810* (Albuquerque: University of New Mexico Press, 1995), 132, has documented such utterances in Texas and elsewhere on the northern frontier.

65. Letter from José Antonio Rengel Appointing Domingo Cabello as Interim Governor of Nueva Vizcaya (April 16, 1785), BAT, Reel 15; Letter from José Antonio Rengel Notifying Domingo Cabello of His Appointment to Cuba (February 9, 1786), BAT, Reel 16.

66. Chipman, *Spanish Texas*, 180, 289–290 n. 29. Martínez Pacheco was ultimately cleared of all charges, and blame was placed on Governor Angel de Martos and Marcos Ruiz. See Weddle, *Changing Tides*, 298 n. 24.

67. Faulk, *Last Years*, 85.

68. Ibid.

69. Chipman, *Spanish Texas*, 203.

70. John R. Alden, *The American Revolution, 1775–1783* (New York: Harper and Row, 1954), 190–191; Jack Jackson, *Los Mesteños: Spanish Ranching in Texas, 1721–1821* (College Station: Texas A&M University Press, 1986), 341.

71. Chipman, *Spanish Texas*, 204–205. On occasion, cattle had been driven from Texas to Coahuila in earlier times.

72. Jackson, *Los Mesteños*, 341.

73. Ibid.

74. Letter from Domingo Cabello to Teodoro de Croix (June 18, 1779), BA; Jackson, *Los Mesteños*, 341–342.

75. Jackson, *Los Mesteños*, 156–157.

76. Ibid., 156–157.

77. Ibid., 157. Italics are ours.

78. Letter from Commandant General Pedro de Nava to Governor Manuel Muñoz (March 17, 1797), BA. At the time of his declared innocence, Cabello held the rank of field marshal.

79. Faulk, "Texas," 127, as quoted.

80. Athanase de Mézières to Teodoro de Croix (October 13, 1779), BM2, 319.

81. Faulk, "Texas," 127, as quoted.

CHAPTER 11

1. Mattie A. Hatcher, trans., "Joaquín de Arredondo's Report of the Battle of the Medina, August 18, 1813," *Quarterly of the Texas State Historical Association* 11 (January 1908): 221, 229, quotation on 229; *NHOT*, 4:601.

2. Ted Schwarz, *Forgotten Battlefield of the First Texas Revolution: The Battle of the Medina, August 18, 1813*, ed. and annot. Robert H. Thonhoff (Austin: Eakin Press, 1985), 82, 89, 102; *NHOT*, 4:601–602. The exact number of republican dead cannot be determined. Arredondo's estimate was one thousand "*más que menos.*"

3. Stanley Noyes, *Los Comanches: The Horse People, 1751–1845* (Albuquerque: University of New Mexico Press, 1993), 156, 1st and 3d quotations; Elizabeth A. H. John, *Storms Brewed in Other Men's Worlds: The Confrontation of Indians, Spanish, and French in the Southwest, 1540–1795* (College Station: Texas A&M University Press, 1975), 722, 2d quotation.

4. Appointment of Manuel de Salcedo as Governor of Texas (March 13, 1807), AGI, Guadalajara 302; *NHOT*, 2:323–324. Salcedo was appointed governor at the age of thirty-one.

5. *NHOT*, 5:363–364.

6. Carlos E. Castañeda, *Our Catholic Heritage in Texas, 1519–1936* (Austin: Von Boeckmann–Jones, 1936–1958). "The Passing of the Missions, 1762–1782" is the subtitle of volume 4. Italics are ours.

7. Maurine T. Wilson and Jack Jackson, *Philip Nolan and Texas: Expeditions to the Unknown Land, 1791–1801* (Waco: Texian Press, 1987), 73.

8. Donald E. Chipman, *Spanish Texas, 1519–1821* (reprint, Austin: University of Texas Press, 1994), 215.

9. Ibid., 217. This conflict is more commonly known in Great Britain and the United States as the Peninsular War.

10. Ibid.

11. Michael C. Meyer and William L. Sherman, *The Course of Mexican History*, 5th ed. (New York: Oxford University Press, 1995), 281, quotation; Chipman, *Spanish Texas*, 217.

12. Luis Castillo Ledón, *Hidalgo: La vida del héroe* (Mexico City: Talleres Gráficos de la Nación, 1948–1949), 1:111–114.

13. Chipman, *Spanish Texas*, 223; *NHOT*, 5:188–189. For publication of Pichardo's massive compilation, see Charles W. Hackett, ed. and trans., *Pichardo's Treatise on the Limits of Louisiana and Texas* (Austin: University of Texas Press, 1931–1946).

14. Chipman, *Spanish Texas*, 223–224.

15. Ibid.

16. Odie B. Faulk, *The Last Years of Spanish Texas, 1778–1821* (The Hague: Mouton, 1964), 124–125, as quoted.

17. Chipman, *Spanish Texas*, 224–225; Faulk, *Last Years*, 125, quotation.

18. Nettie Lee Benson, ed. and trans., "A Governor's Report on Texas in 1809," *Southwestern Historical Quarterly* 71 (April 1968): 605–611, quotation on 610.

19. Ibid., 611.

20. Ibid.

21. Ibid., 612–613.

22. Félix D. Almaráz Jr., *Tragic Cavalier: Governor Manuel Salcedo of Texas, 1803–1813* (Austin: University of Texas Press, 1971), 54–64, quotation on 55. The deputy commandant general was Bernardo Bonavía.

23. Ibid., 64, 96. Mariano Jiménez was a major caudillo among the insurrectionists.

24. Ibid., 99–114.

25. Ibid., 114–115.

26. Ibid., 116–117.

27. J. Villasana Haggard, "The Counter-Revolution of Béxar, 1811," *Southwestern Historical Quarterly* 43 (October 1939): 224–225; Almaráz, *Tragic Cavalier*, 118.

28. *NHOT*, 3:576.

29. Almaráz, *Tragic Cavalier*, 118–121; Haggard, "Counter-Revolution of Béxar," 225–227.

30. Haggard, "Counter-Revolution of Béxar," 231–232; Chipman, *Spanish Texas*, 233. For an excellent account of the trial and execution of Father Hidalgo and his *criollo* officers, see Félix D. Almaráz Jr., "Texas Governor Manuel Salcedo and the Court-martial of Padre Miguel Hidalgo, 1810–1811," *Southwestern Historical Quarterly* 99 (April 1996): 458–464.

31. Chipman, *Spanish Texas*, 233; Almaráz, *Tragic Cavalier*, 124.

32. Lorenzo de la Garza, *Dos hermanos héroes* (Mexico City: Editorial Cultura, 1939), 11. It was a custom in the Gutiérrez family to name all males José, but sons were consistently referred to by their second given name. Don Bernardo and doña María followed that tradition by naming all five of their sons José.

33. Castañeda, *Catholic Heritage*, 6:2.

34. Ibid., 2–3.

35. Garza, *Dos hermanos*, 12; Julia K. Garrett, *Green Flag over Texas: A Story of the Last Years of Spain in Texas* (New York: Cordova Press, 1939), 35, quotation.

36. Haggard, "Counter-revolution of Béxar," 233–234; Chipman, *Spanish Texas*, 234.

37. Elizabeth Howard West, trans. and ed., "Diary of José Bernardo Gutiérrez de Lara, 1811–1812, I," *American Historical Review* 34 (October 1928): 58; J. B. Gutiérrez de Lara to the Mexican Congress (August 1, 1815), *The Papers of Mirabeau Buonaparte Lamar* (reprint, Austin: A. C. Baldwin and Sons, 1973), 1:7–8, 1st quotation on 7, 2d quotation on 8; *NHOT*, 4:616–617;

Kathryn Garrett, "The First Constitution of Texas, April 17, 1813," *Southwestern Historical Quarterly* 40 (April 1937): 293, 3d quotation.

38. Garza, *Dos hermanos*, 35–36, as quoted.

39. Ibid., 34–40; Elizabeth Howard West, "Diary of José Bernardo Gutiérrez de Lara, 1811–1812, II," *American Historical Review* 34 (January 1929): 289; Chipman, *Spanish Texas*, 234.

40. Richard W. Gronet offers evidence that correspondence between William Shaler and Secretary of State James Monroe substantiates that the special agent was following "a broadly based series of instructions from his superiors in Washington." See his "The United States and the Invasion of Texas," *The Americas* 25 (January 1969): 281, 285–286.

41. Ibid., 292–293, quotation on 293; Chipman, *Spanish Texas*, 235.

42. Gronet, "United States," 284, as quoted.

43. Garrett, *Green Flag*, 167; Chipman, *Spanish Texas*, 235; Garrett, "First Constitution," 299.

44. Harry M. Henderson, "The Magee-Gutiérrez Expedition," *Southwestern Historical Quarterly* 55 (July 1951): 49; Chipman, *Spanish Texas*, 235.

45. Almaráz, *Tragic Cavalier*, 169.

46. Castañeda, *Catholic Heritage*, 6:97–98.

47. Ibid., 98.

48. Ibid.

49. Almaráz, *Tragic Cavalier*, 171; Harris G. Warren, *The Sword Was Their Passport: A History of American Filibustering in the Mexican Revolution* (Baton Rouge: Louisiana State University Press, 1943), 50.

50. Castañeda, *Catholic Heritage*, 6:100, 100 n. 32.

51. Ibid., 101, as quoted.

52. Ibid., 102–103.

53. Garrett, "First Constitution," 301–303, 305, quotation on 305. For a translation of the First Constitution of Texas, see idem, 305–308.

54. Bernardo de Gutiérrez to the Citizens of Béxar (April 22, 1813), UTA, Operations of War, Hackett Transcripts, 1st quotation; Proclamation of Bernardo de Gutiérrez [April 22, 1813], UTA, Operations of War, Hackett Transcripts.

55. Garrett, "First Constitution," 301–302.

56. Castañeda, *Catholic Heritage*, 6:104, as quoted.

57. A biographical dictionary and an encyclopedia entry both list Arredondo's birth year as 1778. See José María Miquel i Vergés, *Diccionario de insurgentes* (Mexico City: Editorial Porrúa, 1969), 50, and *Enciclopedia de México* (Mexico City: Secretaría de Educación Pública, 1987–1988), 1:601. The date 1768 appearing in *NHOT*, 1:255, would appear to be in error. Spaniards typically became military cadets in their pre- or early teens, not in their late teens.

58. Letter from Joaquín de Arredondo to Viceroy Venegas (January 5, 1812), UTA, Operations of War, Hackett Transcripts; Forwarded Copy of Ordinance Appointing Arredondo as Commandant General of the Eastern Provinces (June 3, 1813), AMM; Castañeda, *Catholic Heritage*, 6:104–106. In his letter

to the viceroy, Arredondo boasted of having achieved "total peacefulness and tranquility" in his province.

59. Joaquín de Arredondo to Viceroy Calleja (March 30, 1813), UTA, Operations of War, Hackett Transcripts; Castañeda, *Catholic Heritage*, 6:104–105. Arredondo consistently referred to insurrectionists as *chusma* (rabble). His coarse language prefaced Gutiérrez's name with such adjectives as "perfidious," "iniquitous," or "ridiculous," reserving "vile" for Anglo Americans.

60. Díaz de Bustamante to Joaquín de Arredondo (March 30, 1813), UTA, Operations of War, Hackett Transcripts. Italics are ours.

61. Castañeda, *Catholic Heritage*, 6:105, 1st quotation; Díaz de Bustamante to Joaquín de Arredondo (April 8, 1813), UTA, Operations of War, Hackett Transcripts; Garza, *Dos hermanos*, 20, 2d quotation.

62. Castañeda, *Catholic Heritage*, 6:106. Dissent among Anglo Americans in San Antonio had apparently been spurred on by secret communications from William Shaler.

63. Letter from Joaquín de Arredondo to Viceroy Félix María Calleja (June 7, 1813), UTA, Operations of War, Hackett Transcripts; Report of Ignacio Elizondo to Joaquín de Arredondo (June 18, 1813), UTA, Operations of War, Hackett Transcripts; Castañeda, *Catholic Heritage*, 6:107.

64. Letter from Ignacio Elizondo to Joaquín de Arredondo (June 23, 1813), UTA, Operations of War, Hackett Transcripts; Letter from Joaquín de Arredondo to Viceroy Félix María Calleja (June 25, 1813), UTA, Operations of War, Hackett Transcripts; Castañeda, *Catholic Heritage*, 6:107–108.

65. Castañeda, *Catholic Heritage*, 6:108.

66. NHOT, 6:519.

67. Gronet, "United States," 301–302, quotation on 302; NHOT, 6:519.

68. Castañeda, *Catholic Heritage*, 6:113–114; NHOT, 6:519.

69. Hatcher, "Arredondo's Report," 226, quotation; Chipman, *Spanish Texas*, 237. Toledo later received a pardon from King Ferdinand VII and became a career Spanish diplomat, holding posts in Switzerland and Italy. He died in Paris in 1858. See NHOT, 6:519.

70. Hatcher, "Arredondo's Report," 233; Schwarz, *Forgotten Battlefield*, 108–110.

71. Letter from Ignacio Elizondo to Joaquín de Arredondo (September 2, 1813), UTA, Operations of War, Hackett Transcripts; Letter from Ignacio Elizondo to Joaquín de Arredondo (September 12, 1813), Robert Bruce Blake Research Collection, UTA, vol. 46, quotation; Letter from Joaquín de Arredondo to Ignacio Elizondo (September 12, 1813), UTA, Operations of War, Hackett Transcripts.

72. Almaráz, *Tragic Cavalier*, 180.

73. Félix D. Almaráz Jr., *Governor Antonio Martínez and Mexican Independence in Texas: An Orderly Transition* (reprint, San Antonio: Bexar County Historical Commission, 1979), 9–11; David J. Weber, *The Mexican Frontier, 1821–1846: The American Southwest under Mexico* (Albuquerque: University of New Mexico Press, 1982), 4, 10, 1st and 2d quotations, as quoted, 3d quota-

tion; Chipman, *Spanish Texas*, 240–241; Alicia V. Tjarks, "Comparative Demographic Analysis of Texas, 1777–1793," *Southwestern Historical Quarterly* 77 (January 1974): 305. When Stephen F. Austin passed through Nacogdoches in July 1821, he counted only one church and seven houses among the town's ruins. See "Journal of Stephen F. Austin on His First Trip to Texas, 1821," *Quarterly of the Texas State Historical Association* 7 (April 1904): 289. Weber estimates the non-Indian population of Texas in 1821 at about 2,500.

74. *NHOT*, 3:392–393.

75. Garza, *Dos hermanos*, 204; West, "Diary," 61, quotation; *Diccionario Porrúa de historia, biografía y geografía de México* (5th ed.; 3 vols.; Mexico City: Editorial Porrúa, 1986), 2: 1357.

76. West, "Diary I," 62.

77. Chipman, *Spanish Texas*, 238–239; Castañeda, *Catholic Heritage*, 6:189, quotation, as quoted. At Natchitoches on July 1, 1821, Stephen F. Austin made specific reference to Arredondo's concession to his father. See Eugene C. Barker, ed., *Annual Report of the American Historical Association, 1919: The Austin Papers* (Washington, D.C.: Government Printing Office, 1924, 1928), 1, part 1, 399.

78. Miquel i Vergés, *Diccionario*, 50; Vito Alessio Robles, *Coahuila y Texas en la época colonial* (Mexico City: Editorial Cultura, 1938), 664. Francisco Xavier Mina was a former Spanish patriot who had fought Napoleon's armies in the Peninsular War until his capture by the French in 1810. After repatriation, Mina became a sworn enemy of Ferdinand VII. He was executed by firing squad in Mexico on November 11, 1817.

CHAPTER 12

1. Donald E. Chipman, *Spanish Texas, 1519–1821* (reprint, Austin: University of Texas Press, 1994), 61.

2. Ibid.

3. *NHOT*, 1:56; Carlos E. Castañeda, "The Woman in Blue," *The Age of Mary: An Exclusively Marian Magazine* (January–February 1958): 28; "María's Report to Father Manero," in Clark Colahan, *The Visions of Sor María de Agreda: Writing Knowledge and Power* (Tucson: University of Arizona Press, 1994), 115, quotations. Colahan presents strong evidence that María had Jewish ancestry, which may account for the family's extreme and overt manifestations of Christian piety—intended to deflect suspicion of Judaizing. According to Castañeda, only four of the eleven Coronel children reached maturity.

4. Joseph Mary Madden, "A Brief Biography of Venerable Mary of Agreda," *Age of Mary* (January–February 1958): 91–92; Cuthbert Gumbinger, "The Tercentenary of Mother Agreda's *Mystical City of God*," *Age of Mary* (January–February 1958): 16, quotation, as quoted. Sources are not in agreement as to whether María became a nun of her own volition or because of her mother's initiative. See, for example, T. D. Kendrick, *Mary of Agreda: The Life*

and Legend of a Spanish Nun (London: Routledge and Kegan Paul, 1967), 6, and Colahan, *Visions*, 9.

5. Madden, "Brief Biography," 92–94, 98, quotation on 98.

6. *NHOT*, 1:56; Chipman, *Spanish Texas*, 61; David J. Weber, *The Spanish Frontier in North America* (New Haven: Yale University Press, 1992), 100. As Weber notes, modern-day manifestations of anorexia mirabilis are known as anorexia nervosa.

7. *NHOT*, 1:56.

8. Chipman, *Spanish Texas*, 61; Castañeda, "Woman in Blue," 25.

9. Castañeda, "Woman in Blue," 22–24.

10. William H. Donahue, "Mary of Agreda and the Southwest United States," *Age of Mary* (January–February 1958): 37.

11. Alonso de Benavides's Letter from Spain, 1631, *Age of Mary* (January–February 1958): 126–127.

12. Ibid., 126.

13. Ibid., 127.

14. Letter of Venerable María de Agreda, 1631, *Age of Mary* (January–February 1958): 127–128.

15. Memorial of Father Alonso de Benavides Regarding the Conversions of New Mexico (February 12, 1634), CAT.

16. *NHOT*, 1:56; Colahan, *Visions*, 14, quotation; Gumbinger, "Tercentenary," 16–17; John S. Sabo, "An Apology for *The Mystical City of God*," *Age of Mary* (January–February 1958): 1. Between 1643 and 1665, more than six hundred letters passed between María de Agreda and Philip IV.

17. Kendrick, *Mary of Agreda*, 42; Colahan, *Visions*, 94, 97; "Report to Father Manero," 120, quotations.

18. Gumbinger, "Tercentenary," 16; Simon J. Draugelis, "Moral Crucifixion of *The Mystical City of God*, in *Age of Mary* (January–February 1958): 41; Colahan, *Visions*, 1–2.

19. *NHOT*, 1:56; Castañeda, "Woman in Blue," 28; Francis E. Abernethy, ed., *Legendary Ladies of Texas* (Denton: University of North Texas Press, 1994), 13.

20. Robert S. Weddle, *The French Thorn: Rival Explorers in the Spanish Sea, 1682–1762* (College Station: Texas A&M University Press, 1991), 27; invited visitation by Chipman to the Texas A&M Conservation Research Lab (June 3, 1997), College Station, Texas. These items have not been conclusively determined to be gender-specific.

21. Robert S. Weddle, Mary Christine Morkovsky, and Patricia Galloway, trans. and eds., *Three Primary Documents: La Salle, the Mississippi, and the Gulf* (College Station: Texas A&M University Press, 1987), 210. The paymaster of the company had a young son and presumably a wife who accompanied him.

22. Ibid., 211.

23. Henri Joutel, *Joutel's Journal of La Salle's Last Voyage* (reprint, Chicago: Caxton Club, 1896), 72, 76–77, 1st quotation on 72, 2d and 3d quotations on 77; William C. Foster, ed., and Johanna S. Warren, trans., *The La Salle Expedi-*

tion to Texas: The Journey of Henri Joutel, 1684–1687 (Austin: Texas State Historical Association, 1998), 142–143; Weddle, *French Thorn*, 35. The issue of firstborn rights may have resurfaced at the time of Madame Barbier's second pregnancy. See Weddle, Morkovsky, and Galloway, *Three Primary Documents*, 211.

24. Weddle, *French Thorn*, 35; Weddle, Morkovsky, and Galloway, *Three Primary Documents*, 211.

25. Weddle, *French Thorn*, 39, 71, quotation on 39; Joutel, *Journal*, 77.

26. Weddle, Morkovsky, and Galloway, *Three Primary Documents*, 237–238.

27. Presented here is the middle stanza of the poem, which eulogizes the woman. For the complete text, translated by Robert S. Weddle, see his *Wilderness Manhunt: The Spanish Search for La Salle* (Austin: University of Texas Press, 1973), 187–188. An alternate (unrhymed) translation appears in Juan Bautista Chapa, *Texas and Northeastern Mexico, 1630–1690*, ed. William C. Foster and trans. Ned F. Brierley (Austin: University of Texas Press, 1997), 134–135.

28. Weddle, Morkovsky, and Galloway, *Three Primary Documents*, 252.

29. Ibid., 247–248, quotation on 247; Weddle, *French Thorn*, 217–218, 221. Marie-Madeleine may have returned to Canada, where her son married in 1719. See Weddle, Morkovsky, and Galloway, *Three Primary Documents*, 223.

30. Chipman, *Spanish Texas*, 105.

31. Ibid., 105–106; Robert S. Weddle, *San Juan Bautista: Gateway to Spanish Texas* (Austin: University of Texas Press, 1968), 28.

32. *NHOT*, 5:756.

33. For imprecision in the relationship of Manuela to the Ramóns, see, for example, Chipman, *Spanish Texas*, 105; T. R. Fehrenbach, *Lone Star: A History of Texas and Texans* (New York: Collier Books, 1968), 42; and Ross Phares, *Cavalier in the Wilderness: The Story of the Explorer and Trader Louis Juchereau de St. Denis* (Baton Rouge: Louisiana State University Press, 1952), 85.

34. Patricia R. Lemée, "Manuela Sánchez Navarro," *Natchitoches Genealogist* 20 (October 1995): 18. Manuela was baptized on April 26, 1697.

35. Ibid.

36. Course for the Missions [of Texas] from the Internal Presidios (February 16–July 11, 1716), AMH, Tomo XVII.

37. *NHOT*, 5:756; Lemée, "Manuel Sánchez Navarro," 19–20.

38. Weddle, *French Thorn*, 202.

39. J. Villasana Haggard, trans., "Spain's Indian Policy in Texas," *Southwestern Historical Quarterly* 44 (October 1940): 241.

40. Ibid., 242.

41. Chipman, *Spanish Texas*, 135.

42. Jesús F. de la Teja, "Indians, Soldiers, and Canary Islanders: The Making of a Texas Frontier Community," *Locus: An Historical Journal of Regional Perspectives on National Topics* 3 (Fall 1990): 84.

43. Jesús F. de la Teja, "Forgotten Founders: The Military Settlers of Eighteenth-Century San Antonio de Béxar," in *Tejano Origins in Eighteenth-Cen-*

tury San Antonio, eds. Gerald E. Poyo and Gilberto M. Hinojosa (Austin: University of Texas Press, 1991), 31.

44. Ibid., 32.

45. Chipman, *Spanish Texas*, 130–133, 135–138.

46. Testimonio de las diligencias hechas por el señor factor Don Manuel Angel de Villegas Puente para el despacho y aviso de las familias que . . . pasan apoblar a la provincia de los Texas (1730–1734), UTA, photostats from original documents in the possession of Mr. Louis Lenz, Lake Charles, Louisiana.

47. For judicial procedure without representation by formal counsel, see Joseph W. McKnight, "Law without Lawyers on the Hispano-Mexican Frontier," *West Texas Historical Association Year Book* 66 (1990): 51–65.

48. See Jean A. Stuntz, "The Persistence of Castilian Law in Frontier Texas: The Legal Status of Women" (Master's thesis, University of North Texas, 1996), for a study in progress.

49. Charles R. Cutter, *The Legal Culture of Northern New Spain, 1700– 1810* (Albuquerque: University of New Mexico Press, 1995), 34, quotation. With regard to the profusion of Spanish laws relating to the Indies, by 1635 the crown had issued some 400,000 royal *cédulas*. See Clarence H. Haring, *The Spanish Empire in America* (New York: Oxford University Press, 1947), 113.

50. Stuntz, "Persistence," 3–5; Heath Dillard, *Daughters of the Reconquest: Women in Castilian Town Society, 1100–1300* (Cambridge: Cambridge University Press, 1984), 12, 16–17, quotation on 12.

51. See De la Teja, "Indians," 84–85.

52. Jesús F. de la Teja, *San Antonio de Béxar: A Community on New Spain's Northern Frontier* (Albuquerque: University of New Mexico Press, 1995), 24– 25, quotation on 25.

53. Stuntz, "Persistence," 19; Joseph W. McKnight, *The Spanish Elements in Modern Texas Law* (Dallas: n.p., 1989), 8.

54. Last will and testament of María Melián (December 3, 1740), BAT, Reel 2. The Spanish crown provided Canary Islanders with several inducements to relocate in Texas, including livestock.

55. Contract of Sale of Lot by Pedro de Regalado (June 25, 1745), BAT, Reel 2. For a similar illustration, see Contract of Sale of Land by Joseph Padrón (October 17, 1740), BAT, Reel 2.

56. Chipman, *Spanish Texas*, 106, 138.

57. Last Will and Testament of José de Urrutia (July 4, 1740), BAT, Reel 2. Antonia Ramón was the daughter of Commandant Diego Ramón of San Juan Bautista.

58. Power of Attorney from Rosa Flores de Valdés to José de Plaza (August 27, 1745), BAT, Reel 2.

59. Contract of Sale of House and Lot by Joaquín de Urrutia (November 16, 1741), BAT, Reel 2.

60. Contract of Sale of House and Lot by Juana de Urrutia (March 15, 1745), BAT, Reel 2; Contract of Sale of House and Lot by Juana de Urrutia (April 30, 1746), BAT, Reel 2.

61. Power of Attorney from María Josefa de Valdés to Francisco de Liñán (April 21, 1744), BAT, Reel 2.

62. Contract of Sale of a Negro Slave by María Josefa Flores de Valdés (October 29, 1743), BAT, Reel 2; Contract of Sale of a Negro Slave by Lieutenant Colonel Justo Boneo y Morales (October 29, 1743), BAT, Reel 2.

63. Petition of Antonia Lusgardia Hernández to Governor Manuel de Sandoval (August 9, 1735), BAT, Reel 2.

64. Ibid.

65. Decree of Governor Manuel de Sandoval [August 1735], BAT, Reel 2.

66. Ibid.

67. Writ from María Gertrudis de la Peña to Governor Domingo Cabello [January 25, 1785], BAT, Reel 6; Testimony of María Gertrudis de la Peña (February 7, 1785), BAT, Reel 6.

68. Writ from María Gertrudis de la Peña to Governor Domingo Cabello [January 25, 1785], BAT, Reel 6; Testimony of María Gertrudis de la Peña (February 7, 1785), BAT, Reel 6.

69. Writ from María Gertrudis de la Peña to Governor Domingo Cabello [January 25, 1785], BAT, Reel 6; Testimony of María Gertrudis de la Peña (February 7, 1785), BAT, Reel 6, 1st and 2d quotations from "Writ," 3d quotation from "Testimony." María's testimony indicates that in the more remote outposts of New Spain, justice was not always served as it was in a provincial capital.

70. Order Issued by Governor Domingo Cabello (March 3, 1785), BAT, Reel 6.

71. Testimony of Francisco Joseph de Arocha (August 21, 1744), BAT, Reel 3; Deposition of Matías Treviño (August 21, 1744), BAT, Reel 3. Castilian laws with respect to punishing women culpable of adultery were broadened in the Americas to apply equally to mestizas. See *Recopilación de leyes de los reynos de las Indias* (Madrid: Consejo de la Hispanidad, 1943), Ley 4, Título 8, Libro 7.

72. Deposition of Matías Treviño (August 21, 1744), BAT, Reel 3.

73. Deposition of Jerónimo Flores (August 21, 1744), BAT, Reel 3; Deposition of Joseph de la Garza (August 21, 1744), BAT, Reel 3.

74. Statement of Notary Public Joseph de Arocha (August 21, 1744), BAT, Reel 3; Deposition of Rosa Guerra (August 21, 1744), BAT, Reel 3.

75. Deposition of Antonio Tello (August 21, 1744), BAT, Reel 3; Statement by Alberto López de Aguado [August 24, 1744], BAT, Reel 3.

76. Confession of Juan de Sosa (April 23, 1772), BAT, Reel 7; Testimony of Gertrudis Barrón (April 25, 1772), BAT, Reel 7.

77. Confession of Juan de Sosa (April 23, 1772), BAT, Reel 7; Defense of Juan de Sosa by Joaquín de Orendáin (May 19, 1772), BAT, Reel 7.

78. Confession of Juan de Sosa (April 23, 1772), BAT, Reel 7; Summons Issued for Gertrudis Barrón (April 23, 1772), BAT, Reel 7, 1st quotation; Summons to Priest of Mission Concepción to Deliver Gertrudis Barrón (April 24, 1772), BAT, Reel 7, 2d quotation; Order for Arrest of Gertrudis Barrón (April 25, 1772), BAT, Reel 7, 3d quotation.

79. Defense of Juan de Sosa by Joaquín de Orendáin (May 19, 1772), Reel 7.

80. Opinion of Joseph Fernández de Córdoba on Behalf of Juan de Sosa (January 27, 1773), BAT, Reel 7.

81. Summation of Proceedings by Domingo de Valcarcel (February 25, 1773), BAT, Reel 7, quotations; Order by Governor Barón de Ripperdá for Release of Juan de Sosa (May 24, 1773), BAT, Reel 7.

82. Samuel P. Scott, trans., *Las siete partidas* (Chicago: Commerce Clearing House, 1931), Part 7, Title 17, Law 13; Title 14, Part 3, Law 12; Stuntz, "Persistence," 34–35. Despite these long-standing guidelines of Castilian jurisprudence, an official in Mexico City opined that Juan de Sosa would have been justified in killing his wife also.

83. Investigation by Governor Angel Martos (January 20, 1763), BAT, Reel 4; Petition from Gil Ibarvo to Governor Angel Martos (July 2, 1766), BAT, Reel 4.

84. Petition from Gil Ibarvo to Governor Angel Martos (July 2, 1766), BAT, Reel 4.

85. Decree of Governor Angel Martos (July 12, 1766), BAT, Reel 4.

86. Criminal Code for Nacogdoches (1783), Robert Bruce Blake Research Collection, vol. 45, UTA.

87. Ibid.

88. Ibid.

89. Census of Nacogdoches (December 31, 1799), Robert Bruce Blake Research Collection, vol. 18, UTA. The census lists a total of 208 families, of which widows headed 24 (11.5 percent).

90. Sworn Statement of Anna Alsop (August 16, 1809), Robert Bruce Blake Research Collection, Supplement, vol. 6, UTA.

91. Sworn Statement of Marie-Madeleine Prudhomme (August 1, 1809) and Sworn Statement of Marie Rambin (July 27, 1809), Robert Bruce Blake Research Collection, Supplement, vol. 6, UTA.

92. De la Teja, *San Antonio*, 23, 115, 145; *NHOT*, 1:912.

93. *NHOT*, 1:912; *NHOT*, 5:435. Rancho de las Cabras is a State Historic Site near Floresville.

94. Anne A. Brindley, "Jane Long," *Southwestern Historical Quarterly* 56 (October 1952): 211–212, 214, 219; *NHOT*, 5:150.

95. *NHOT*, 4:274; Brindley, "Jane Long," 211–212, 214–219; *NHOT*, 5:150.

96. Brindley, "Jane Long," 220–223.

97. *NHOT*, 5:150; Brindley, "Jane Long," 224–225; *NHOT*, 4:278.

98. Brindley, "Jane Long," 225–228.

99. Ibid., 229–230; *NHOT*, 4:273. The circumstances surrounding James Long's death are uncertain. He was perhaps the victim of an accidental shooting by a Mexican sentry on April 8, 1822, or, if the suspicions of Benjamin Rush Milam were correct, deliberately murdered on orders of José Félix Trespalacios. See *NHOT*, 4:717–717.

100. Brindley, "Jane Long," 231–235.

101. *NHOT*, 4:275.

BIBLIOGRAPHY

ARCHIVAL MATERIALS

Archival materials utilized in the preparation of this book are preserved in the collections listed below. Unpublished Spanish-language reports, letters, proceedings, and the like are appropriately cited in the notes with their titles translated into English.

Archivo General de Indias, Seville (cited as AGI)
Archivo del Ministerio de Hacienda, Madrid (cited as AMH)
Archivo Municipal de Múzquiz, Múzquiz (Coahuila) (cited as AMM)
Béxar Archives, Austin (cited as BA)
Béxar Archives Translations, Denton (cited as BAT)
Catholic Archives of Texas, Austin (cited as CAT)
Robert Bruce Blake Research Collection, 75 vols. (1958–1959), Barker Texas
    History Center/Center for American History, Austin
Robert Bruce Blake Research Collection, Supplement, 18 vols. (1969–1970),
    Barker Texas History Center/Center for American History, Austin
University of Texas Archives (Barker Texas History Center/Center for American
    History), Austin (cited as UTA)

PUBLISHED MATERIALS

This bibliography contains only works that are cited in the notes section.

Books

Abernethy, Francis E., ed. *Legendary Ladies of Texas.* Denton: University of
    North Texas Press, 1994.

Alden, John R. *The American Revolution, 1775–1783.* New York: Harper and Row, 1954.

Alessio Robles, Vito. *Coahuila y Texas en la época colonial.* Mexico City: Editorial Cultura, 1938.

Almaráz, Félix D., Jr. *Governor Antonio Martínez and Mexican Independence in Texas: An Orderly Transition.* Reprint. San Antonio: Bexar County Historical Commission, 1979.

————. *Tragic Cavalier: Governor Manuel Salcedo of Texas, 1803–1813.* Austin: University of Texas Press, 1971.

Arricivita, Juan Domingo. *Crónica seráfica y apostólica del colegio de propaganda fide de la Santa Cruz de Querétaro en la Nueva España.* Part 2. Mexico City: Don Felipe de Zúñiga y Ontiveros, 1792.

Barker, Eugene C., ed. *Annual Report of the American Historical Association, 1919: The Austin Papers.* 2 vols. Washington, D.C.: Government Printing Office, 1924, 1928.

Bishop, Morris. *The Odyssey of Cabeza de Vaca.* New York: Century Company, 1933.

Bolton, Herbert E. *The Hasinais: Southern Caddoans as Seen by the Earliest Europeans.* Edited by Russell M. Magnaghi. Norman: University of Oklahoma Press, 1987.

————. *Texas in the Middle Eighteenth Century: Studies in Spanish Colonial History and Administration.* Austin: University of Texas Press, 1970.

————, ed. and trans. *Athanase de Mézières and the Louisiana-Texas Frontier, 1768–1780.* 2 vols. Cleveland: Arthur H. Clark, 1914.

————, ed. *Spanish Exploration in the Southwest, 1542–1706.* Reprint. New York: Barnes and Noble, 1963.

Brinckerhoff, Sidney B., and Odie B. Faulk. *Lancers for the King: A Study of the Frontier Military System of Northern New Spain, with a Translation of the Royal Regulations of 1772.* Phoenix: Arizona Historical Foundation, 1965.

Campbell, T. N., and T. J. Campbell. *Historic Indian Groups of the Choke Canyon Reservoir and Surrounding Area, Southern Texas.* San Antonio: Center for Archaeological Research, 1981.

Carter, Cecile E. *Caddo Indians: Where We Come From.* Norman: University of Oklahoma Press, 1995.

Carter, Hodding. *Doomed Road of Empire: The Spanish Trail of Conquest.* New York: McGraw-Hill, 1963.

Carter, Robert F. *The Tarnished Halo: The Story of Padre Francisco Hidalgo.* Chicago: Franciscan Herald Press, 1973.

Castañeda, Carlos E. *Our Catholic Heritage in Texas, 1519–1936.* 7 vols. Austin: Von Boeckmann-Jones, 1936–1958.

Castillo Ledón, Luis. *Hidalgo: La vida del héroe.* 2 vols. Mexico City: Talleres Gráficos de la Nación, 1948–1949.

Cavazos Garza, Israel, ed. *Historia de Nuevo León con noticias sobre Coahuila, Texas y Nuevo México, escrita en el siglo XVII por el Cap. Alonso de León,*

Juan Bautista Chapa y el Gral. Fernando Sánchez de Zamora. 2d ed., Monterrey: Centro de Estudios Humanísticos, Universidad Autónoma de Nuevo León y Gobierno del Estado, 1961.

Chapa, Juan Bautista. *Texas and Northeastern Mexico, 1630–1690*. Edited by William C. Foster and translated by Ned F. Brierley. Austin: University of Texas Press, 1997.

Chipman, Donald E. *Nuño de Guzmán and the Province of Pánuco in New Spain, 1518–1533*. Glendale, Calif.: Arthur H. Clark, 1967.

————. *Spanish Texas, 1519–1821*. Reprint. Austin: University of Texas Press, 1994.

Colahan, Clark. *The Visions of Sor María de Agreda: Writing Knowledge and Power*. Tucson: University of Arizona Press, 1994.

Cummins, Light T. *Spanish Observers and the American Revolution, 1775–1783*. Baton Rouge: Louisiana State University Press, 1991.

Cutter, Charles R. *The Legal Culture of Northern New Spain, 1700–1810*. Albuquerque: University of New Mexico Press, 1995.

De la Teja, Jesús F. *San Antonio de Béxar: A Community on New Spain's Northern Frontier*. Albuquerque: University of New Mexico Press, 1995.

Díaz del Castillo, Bernal. *Historia verdadera de la conquista de la Nueva España*. Introducción y notas de Joaquín Ramírez de Cabañas. 2 vols. Mexico City: Editorial Porrúa, 1955.

Diccionario Porrúa de historia, biografía, y geografía de México. 3d ed., 2 vols. Mexico City: Editorial Porrúa, 1971.

Diccionario Porrúa de historia, biografía, y geografía de México. 5th ed., 3 vols. Mexico City: Editorial Porrúa, 1986.

Dillard, Heath. *Daughters of the Reconquest: Women in Castilian Town Society, 1100–1300*. Cambridge: Cambridge University Press, 1984.

Dods, Marcus, trans. *"The City of God" by Saint Augustine*. New York: Modern Library, 1950.

Dunn, William E. *Spanish and French Rivalry in the Gulf Region of the United States, 1678–1702: Beginnings of Texas and Pensacola*. Austin: University of Texas, 1917.

Enciclopedia de México. 14 vols. Mexico City: Secretaría de Educación Pública, 1987–1988.

Espinosa, Isidro Félix de. *Crónica de los Colegios de Propaganda Fide de la Nueva España*. Edited by Lino Gómez Canedo. Washington, D.C.: Academy of American Franciscan History, 1964.

————. *El peregrino septentrional atlante: Delineado en la exemplaríssima vida del Venerable Padre F. Antonio Margil de Jesús*. Mexico City: Joseph Bernardo de Hogal, 1737.

Estado general de las fundaciones hechas por D. José de Escandón en la colonia de Nuevo Santander. 2 vols. Mexico City: Talleres Gráficos de la Nación, 1929, 1930.

Farriss, Nancy M. *Maya Society under Colonial Rule: The Collective Enterprise of Survival*. Princeton: Princeton University Press, 1984.

Faulk, Odie. B. *The Last Years of Spanish Texas, 1778–1821*. The Hague: Mouton, 1964.

Favata, Martin A., and José B. Fernández. *The Account: Alvar Núñez Cabeza de Vaca's "Relación."* Houston: Arte Público, 1993.

Fehrenbach, T. R. *Lone Star: A History of Texas and Texans*. New York: Collier Books, 1968.

Fireman, Janet R. *The Spanish Royal Corps of Engineers in the Western Borderlands: Instrument of Bourbon Reform, 1764–1815*. Glendale, Calif.: Arthur H. Clark, 1977.

Foster, William C. *Spanish Expeditions into Texas, 1689–1768*. Austin: University of Texas Press, 1995.

Foster, William C., ed., and Johanna S. Warren. *The La Salle Expedition to Texas: The Journal of Henri Joutel, 1684–1687*. Austin: Texas State Historical Association, 1998.

Garrett, Julia K. *Green Flag over Texas: A Story of the Last Years of Spain in Texas*. New York: Cordova Press, 1939.

Garza, Lorenzo de la. *Dos hermanos héroes*. Mexico City: Editorial Cultura, 1939.

Gómez Canedo, Lino, ed. *Primeras exploraciones y poblamiento de Texas (1686–1694)*. Monterrey: Publicaciones del Instituto Tecnológico y de Estudios Superiores de Monterrey, 1968.

Hackett, Charles W., ed. and trans. *Pichardo's Treatise on the Limits of Louisiana and Texas*. 4 vols. Austin: University of Texas Press, 1931–1946.

Hanke, Lewis. *All Mankind Is One: A Study of the Disputation between Bartolomé de Las Casas and Juan Ginés de Sepúlveda in 1550 on the Intellectual and Religious Capacity of the American Indians*. De Kalb: Northern Illinois University Press, 1974.

———. *The Spanish Struggle for Justice in the Conquest of America*. Philadelphia: University of Pennsylvania Press, 1949.

Haring, Clarence H. *The Spanish Empire in America*. New York: Oxford University Press, 1947.

Hedrick, Basil C., and Carroll L. Riley. *The Journey of the Vaca Party: The Account of the Narváez Expedition, 1528–1536, as Related by Gonzalo Fernández de Oviedo y Valdés* (Carbondale: University Museum, Southern Illinois University, 1974.

Hill, Lawrence F. *José de Escandón and the Founding of Nuevo Santander: A Study in Spanish Colonization*. Columbus: Ohio State University Press, 1926.

Howard, David A. *Conquistador in Chains: Cabeza de Vaca and the Indians of the Americas*. Tuscaloosa: University of Alabama Press, 1997.

Jackson, Jack. *Los Mesteños: Spanish Ranching in Texas, 1721–1821*. College Station: Texas A&M University Press, 1986.

———, Robert S. Weddle, and Winston De Ville. *Mapping Texas and the Gulf Coast: The Contributions of Saint-Denis, Oliván, and Le Maire*. College Station: Texas A&M University Press, 1990.

Jackson, Jack, ed., and William C. Foster, annot. *Imaginary Kingdom: Texas as*

Seen by the Rivera and Rubí Military Expeditions, 1727 and 1767. Austin: Texas State Historical Association, 1995.

John, Elizabeth A. H. *Storms Brewed in Other Men's Worlds: The Confrontation of Indians, Spanish, and French in the Southwest, 1540–1795.* College Station: Texas A&M University Press, 1975.

Jones, Oakah L., Jr. *Los Paisanos: Spanish Settlers on the Northern Frontier of New Spain.* Norman: University of Oklahoma Press, 1996.

———. *Nueva Vizcaya: Heartland of the Spanish Frontier.* Albuquerque: University of New Mexico Press, 1988.

Joutel, Henri. *Joutel's Journal of La Salle's Last Voyage.* Reprint. Chicago: Caxton Club, 1896.

Kavanagh, Thomas W. *Comanche Political History: An Ethnohistorical Perspective, 1706–1875.* Lincoln: University of Nebraska Press, 1996.

Kendrick, T. D. *Mary of Agreda: The Life and Legend of a Spanish Nun.* London: Routledge and Kegan Paul, 1967.

Kinnaird, Lawrence, ed. and trans. *The Frontiers of New Spain: Nicolás de Lafora's Description.* Berkeley: Quivira Society, 1958.

———, ed. *Spain in the Mississippi Valley, 1765–1794: Translations of Materials from the Spanish Archives in the Bancroft Library.* 3 vols. Washington, D.C.: U.S. Government Printing Office, 1946–1949.

Leutenegger, Benedict, trans., and Marion A. Habig, ed. *Nothingness Itself: Selected Writings of Ven. Fr. Antonio Margil, 1690–1724.* Chicago: Franciscan Herald Press, 1976.

Lomask, Milton. *The Biographer's Craft.* New York: Harper and Row, 1986.

Loomis, Noel M., and Abraham P. Nasatir. *Pedro Vial and the Roads to Santa Fe.* Norman: University of Oklahoma Press, 1967.

Lynch, John. *Spain under the Habsburgs.* 2 vols. New York: Oxford University Press, 1964, 1969.

Marley, David F. *Sack of Veracruz.* Windsor, Ont.: Netherlandic Press, 1993.

McCloskey, Michael B. *The Formative Years of the Missionary College of Santa Cruz of Querétaro, 1683–1733.* Washington, D.C.: Academy of American Franciscan History, 1955.

McGraw, A. Joachim, John W. Clark Jr., and Elizabeth A. Robbins, eds. *A Texas Legacy: The Old San Antonio Road and the Caminos Reales.* Austin: Texas State Department of Highways and Public Transportation, 1991.

McKnight, Joseph W. *The Spanish Elements in Modern Texas Law.* Dallas: n.p., 1989.

Meyer, Michael C., and William L. Sherman. *The Course of Mexican History.* 5th ed. New York: Oxford University Press, 1995.

Miller, Hubert J. *José de Escandón: Colonizer of Nuevo Santander.* Edinburg, Tex.: New Santander Press, 1980.

Miquel i Vergés, José María. *Diccionario de insurgentes.* Mexico City: Editorial Porrúa, 1969.

Moorhead, Max L. *The Presidio: Bastion of the Borderlands.* Norman: University of Oklahoma Press, 1975.

Morfi, Juan Agustín. *History of Texas, 1673–1779*. Translated and edited by Carlos E. Castañeda. 2 vols. Albuquerque: Quivira Society, 1935.

Morison, Samuel Eliot. *The European Discovery of America: The Southern Voyages, A.D. 1492–1616*. New York: Oxford University Press, 1980.

Navarro García, Luis. *Don José de Gálvez y la Comandancia General de las Provincias Internas del Norte de Nueva España*. Seville: Escuela de Estudios Hispano-Americanos de Sevilla, 1964.

Naylor, Thomas H., and Charles W. Polzer, comps. and eds. *Pedro de Rivera and the Military Regulations for Northern New Spain, 1724–1729: A Documentary History of His Frontier Inspection and the "Reglamento de 1729."* Tucson: University of Arizona Press, 1988.

Newcomb, W. W., Jr. *The Indians of Texas: From Prehistoric to Modern Times*. Austin: University of Texas Press, 1984.

Noyes, Stanley. *Los Comanches: The Horse People, 1751–1845*. Albuquerque: University of New Mexico Press, 1993.

Oberste, William H. *The Restless Friar: Venerable Fray Antonio Margil de Jesús*. Austin: Von Boeckmann–Jones, 1970.

The Papers of Mirabeau Buonaparte Lamar. Reprint. 5 vols. Austin: A. C. Baldwin and Sons, 1973.

Phares, Ross. *Cavalier in the Wilderness: The Story of the Explorer and Trader Louis Juchereau de St. Denis*. Baton Rouge: Louisiana State University Press, 1952.

Pupo-Walker, Enrique, ed., and Frances M. López-Morillas, trans. *Castaways: The Narrative of Alvar Núñez Cabeza de Vaca*. Berkeley: University of California Press, 1993.

Recopilación de leyes de los reynos de las Indias. 3 vols. Madrid: Consejo de la Hispanidad, 1943.

Riley, G. Micheal. *Fernando Cortés and the Marquesado in Morelos, 1522–1547*. Albuquerque: University of New Mexico Press, 1973.

Ríos, Eduardo Enrique. *Life of Fray Antonio Margil, O.F.M.* Translated by Benedict Leutenegger. Washington, D.C.: Academy of American Franciscan History, 1959.

Santiago, Mark. *The Red Captain: The Life of Hugo O'Conor, Commandant Inspector of the Interior Provinces of New Spain*. Tucson: Arizona Historical Society, 1994.

Santos, Richard G., trans. *Aguayo Expedition into Texas, 1721*. Austin: Jenkins Publishing, 1981.

Schwarz, Ted. *Forgotten Battlefield of the First Texas Revolution: The Battle of the Medina, August 18, 1813*. Edited and annotated by Robert H. Thonhoff. Austin: Eakin Press, 1985.

Scott, Florence Johnson. *Royal Land Grants North of the Rio Grande, 1777–1821*. Rio Grande City, Tex.: La Retama Press, 1969.

Scott, Samuel P., trans. *Las siete partidas*. Chicago: Commerce Clearing House, 1931.

Simmons, Marc. *The Last Conquistador: Juan de Oñate and the Settling of the Far Southwest*. Norman: University of Oklahoma Press, 1991.

Simpson, Lesley B., ed. *The San Sabá Papers: A Documentary Account of the Founding and Destruction of the San Sabá Mission*. San Francisco: John Howell-Books, 1959.

Smith, F. Todd. *The Caddo Indians: Tribes at the Convergence of Empires, 1542–1854*. College Station: Texas A&M University Press, 1995.

Starnes, Gary B. *The San Gabriel Missions, 1746–1756*. Madrid: Ministry of Foreign Affairs, Government of Spain, 1969.

Thomas, Alfred B., trans. and ed. *Teodoro de Croix and the Northern Frontier of New Spain, 1776–1783*. Norman: University of Oklahoma Press, 1941.

Thomas, Hugh. *Conquest: Montezuma, Cortés, and the Fall of Old Mexico*. New York: Simon and Schuster, 1993.

Thonhoff, Robert H. *El Fuerte del Cíbolo: Sentinel of the Béxar–La Bahía Ranches*. Austin: Eakin Press, 1992.

Tunnell, Curtis D., and W. W. Newcomb Jr. *A Lipan Apache Mission: San Lorenzo de la Santa Cruz, 1762–1771*. Bulletin 14. Austin: Texas Memorial Museum, 1969.

Tyler, Ron, et al., eds. *The New Handbook of Texas*. 6 vols. Austin: Texas State Historical Association, 1996.

Vauban, Sebastien Le Prestre de. *A Manual of Siegecraft and Fortification*. Translated by George A. Rothrock. Ann Arbor: University of Michigan Press, 1968.

Villanueva de Cavazos, Lilia E. *Testamentos coloniales de Monterrey, 1611–1785*. Monterrey: n.p., 1991.

Vivian, Julia. *A Cavalier in Texas*. San Antonio: Naylor Company, 1953.

Warren, Harris G. *The Sword Was Their Passport: A History of American Filibustering in the Mexican Revolution*. Baton Rouge: Louisiana State University Press, 1943.

Weber, David J. *The Mexican Frontier, 1821–1846: The American Southwest under Mexico*. Albuquerque: University of New Mexico Press, 1982.

———. *The Spanish Frontier in North America*. New Haven: Yale University Press, 1992.

Weddle, Robert S. *Changing Tides: Twilight and Dawn in the Spanish Sea, 1763–1803*. College Station: Texas A&M University Press, 1995.

———. *The French Thorn: Rival Explorers in the Spanish Sea, 1682–1762*. College Station: Texas A&M University Press, 1991.

———. *San Juan Bautista: Gateway to Spanish Texas*. Austin: University of Texas Press, 1968.

———. *The San Sabá Mission: Spanish Pivot in Texas*. Austin: University of Texas Press, 1964.

———. *Spanish Sea: The Gulf of Mexico in North American Discovery, 1500–1685*. College Station: Texas A&M University Press, 1985.

———. *Wilderness Manhunt: The Spanish Search for La Salle*. Austin: University of Texas Press, 1973.

Weddle, Robert S., Mary Christine Morkovsky, and Patricia Galloway, trans. and eds. *Three Primary Documents: La Salle, the Mississippi, and the Gulf*. College Station: Texas A&M University Press, 1987.

Wilkinson, J. B. *Laredo and the Rio Grande Frontier*. Austin: Jenkins Publishing, 1975.

Wilson, Maurine T., and Jack Jackson. *Philip Nolan and Texas: Expeditions to the Unknown Land, 1791–1801*. Waco: Texian Press, 1987.

Wyndham, Violet. *Madame de Genlis: A Biography*. London: Andre Deutsch, 1958.

ARTICLES AND BOOK CHAPTERS

Abernethy, Francis E. "The Y'Barbo Legend in Early Spanish Settlement." *East Texas Historical Journal* 25 (Fall 1987): 39–43.

Adams, David B. "Borderlands Communities in Conflict: Saltillo, San Esteban, and the Struggle for Municipal Autonomy, 1591–1838." *Locus: Regional and Local History of the Americas* 6 (Fall 1993): 39–51.

Adorno, Rolena. "The Negotiation of Fear in Cabeza de Vaca's *Naufragios*." *Representations* 33 (Winter 1991): 163–199.

Allen, Henry E. "The Parrilla Expedition to the Red River in 1759." *Southwestern Historical Quarterly* 43 (July 1939): 53–71.

Almaráz, Félix D., Jr. "Texas Governor Manuel Salcedo and the Court-martial of Padre Miguel Hidalgo, 1810–1811." *Southwestern Historical Quarterly* 99 (April 1996): 435–464.

Altman, Ida, and Reginald D. Butler. "The Contact of Cultures: Perspectives on the Quincentenary." *American Historical Review* 99 (April 1994): 479–503.

Benson, Nettie Lee, ed. and trans. "A Governor's Report on Texas in 1809." *Southwestern Historical Quarterly* 71 (April 1968): 603–615.

Bolton, Herbert E. "The Location of La Salle's Colony on the Gulf of Mexico." *Mississippi Valley Historical Review* 2 (September 1915): 165–182.

———. "Native Tribes about the East Texas Missions." *Quarterly of the Texas State Historical Association* 11 (April 1908): 249–276.

———. "The Spanish Abandonment and Re-occupation of East Texas, 1773–1779." *Quarterly of the Texas State Historical Association* 9 (October 1905): 67–137.

Brindley, Anne A. "Jane Long." *Southwestern Historical Quarterly* 56 (October 1952): 211–238.

Buckley, Eleanor C. "The Aguayo Expedition into Texas and Louisiana, 1719–1722." *Quarterly of the Texas State Historical Association* 15 (July 1911): 1–65.

Campbell, Randolph B. "Touchstone Corner." *Touchstone* 14 (1995): iv–vii.

Castañeda, Carlos E. "The Woman in Blue." *The Age of Mary: An Exclusively Marian Magazine* (January–February 1958): 22–29.

Chipman, Donald E. "Alonso Alvarez de Pineda and the Río de las Palmas: Scholars and the Mislocation of a River." *Southwestern Historical Quarterly* 98 (January 1995): 369–385.

———. "Alonso de León: Pathfinder in East Texas, 1686–1690." *East Texas Historical Journal* 33 (Spring 1995): 3–17.

———. "In Search of Cabeza de Vaca's Route across Texas: An Historiographical Survey." *Southwestern Historical Quarterly* 91 (October 1987): 127–148.

———. "The Status of Biography in the Historiography of New Spain." *The Americas* 27 (January 1971): 327–339.

De la Teja, Jesús F. "Forgotten Founders: The Military Settlers of Eighteenth-Century San Antonio de Béxar." In *Tejano Origins in Eighteenth-Century San Antonio.* Edited by Gerald E. Poyo and Gilberto M. Hinojosa. Austin: University of Texas Press, 1991.

———. "Indians, Soldiers, and Canary Islanders: The Making of a Texas Frontier Community." *Locus: An Historical Journal of Regional Perspectives on National Topics* 3 (Fall 1990): 81–96.

Donahue, William H. "Mary of Agreda and the Southwest United States." *The Age of Mary: An Exclusively Marian Magazine* (January–February 1958): 35–39.

Draugelis, Simon J. "Moral Crucifixion of *The Mystical City of God.*" *The Age of Mary: An Exclusively Marian Magazine* (January–February 1958): 41–60.

Dunn, William E. "Apache Relations in Texas, 1718–1750." *Quarterly of the Texas State Historical Association* 14 (January 1911): 198–274.

———. "Missionary Activities among the Eastern Apaches Previous to the Founding of the San Sabá Mission." *Quarterly of the Texas State Historical Association* 15 (January 1912): 186–200.

Forrestal, Peter P., trans. "Peña's Diary of the Aguayo Expedition." *Preliminary Studies of the Catholic Historical Society* 2 (January 1935): 5–34.

———. "The Venerable Padre Fray Antonio Margil de Jesús." *Preliminary Studies of the Texas Catholic Historical Society* 2 (April 1932): 5–34.

Foster, William C., and Jack Jackson, eds. "The 1693 Expedition of Gregorio de Salinas Varona to Sustain the Missionaries among the Tejas Indians." *Southwestern Historical Quarterly* 97 (October 1993): 264–311.

Garrett, Kathryn. "The First Constitution of Texas, April 17, 1813." *Southwestern Historical Quarterly* 40 (April 1937): 290–308.

Gronet, Richard W. "The United States and the Invasion of Texas." *The Americas* 25 (January 1969): 281–306.

Gumbinger, Cuthbert. "The Tercentenary of Mother Agreda's *Mystical City of God.*" *The Age of Mary: An Exclusively Marian Magazine* (January–February 1958): 16–21.

Hackett, Charles W. "The Marquis of San Miguel de Aguayo and His Recovery of Texas from the French, 1719–1723." *Southwestern Historical Quarterly* 49 (October 1945): 193–214.

———. "Visitador Rivera's Criticisms of Aguayo's Work in Texas." *Hispanic American Historical Review* 16 (May 1936): 162–172.

Haggard, J. Villasana. "The Counter-Revolution of Béxar, 1811." *Southwestern Historical Quarterly* 43 (October 1939): 222–235.

———, trans. "Spain's Indian Policy in Texas." *Southwestern Historical Quarterly* 44 (October 1940): 232–244.

Hatcher, Mattie A., trans. "The Expedition of Don Domingo Terán de los Ríos into Texas (1691–1692)." *Preliminary Studies of the Texas Catholic Historical Society* 2 (January 1932): 3–67.

———, trans. "Joaquín de Arredondo's Report on the Battle of the Medina, August 18, 1813." *Quarterly of the Texas State Historical Association* 11 (January 1908): 220–236.

Henderson, Harry M. "The Magee-Gutiérrez Expedition." *Southwestern Historical Quarterly* 55 (July 1951): 43–61.

Itinerary of the De León Expedition of 1689. In *Spanish Exploration in the Southwest, 1542–1706,* edited by Herbert E. Bolton. Reprint. New York: Barnes and Noble, 1963.

John, Elizabeth A. H., ed., and Adán Benavides Jr., trans. "Inside the Comanchería, 1785: The Diary of Pedro Vial and Francisco Xavier Chaves." *Southwestern Historical Quarterly* 98 (July 1994): 27–56.

"Journal of Stephen F. Austin on His First Trip to Texas, 1821." *Quarterly of the Texas State Historical Association* 7 (April 1904): 286–307.

Kress, Margaret K., trans. "Diary of a Visit of Inspection of the Texas Missions Made by Fray Gaspar José de Solís in the Year 1767–1768." *Southwestern Historical Quarterly* 35 (July 1931): 28–76.

Lemée, Patricia R. "Manuela Sánchez Navarro." *Natchitoches Genealogist* 20 (October 1995): 17–21.

———. "Tios and Tantes: Familial and Political Relationships of Natchitoches and the Spanish Colonial Frontier. *Southwestern Historical Quarterly* 101 (January 1998): 341–358.

Leonard, Irving A. "Conquerors and Amazons in Mexico." *Hispanic American Historical Review* 24 (November 1944): 561–579.

"Letter of Fray Damián Massanet to Don Carlos de Sigüenza, 1690." In *Spanish Exploration in the Southwest, 1542–1706,* edited by Herbert E. Bolton. Reprint. New York: Barnes and Noble, 1963.

Lowry, Jack. "Remembering Dr. Joe B. Frantz." *Texas Highways* 41 (March 1994): 16–17.

Madden, Joseph Mary. "A Brief Biography of Venerable Mary of Agreda." *The Age of Mary: An Exclusively Marian Magazine* (January–February 1958): 91–98.

McKnight, Joseph W. "Law without Lawyers on the Hispano-Mexican Frontier." *West Texas Historical Association Year Book* 66 (1990): 51–65.

Mills, Elizabeth S. "(de) Mézières-Trichel-Grappe: A Study of a Tri-caste Lineage in the Old South." *The Genealogist* 6 (Spring 1985): 4–84.

"Missing Mission Found." *Texas Archeology* 38 (April 1994): 5.

Olson, Donald W., et al. "Piñon Pines and the Route of Cabeza de Vaca." *Southwestern Historical Quarterly* 101 (October 1997): 175–186.

Sabo, John S. "An Apology for *The Mystical City of God.*" *The Age of Mary: An Exclusively Marian Magazine* (January–February 1958): 1–4.

Thompson, Jesse E. "Sagittectomy—First Recorded Surgical Procedure in the American Southwest, 1535: The Journey and Ministrations of Alvar Núñez

Cabeza de Vaca." *New England Journal of Medicine* 289 (December 27, 1973): 1403–1407.

Tjarks, Alicia V. "Comparative Demographic Analysis of Texas, 1777–1793." *Southwestern Historical Quarterly* 77 (January 1974): 291–338.

West, Elizabeth Howard, trans. and ed. "Diary of José Bernardo Gutiérrez de Lara, 1811–1812, I, II." *American Historical Review* 34 (October 1928): 55–77; 34 (January 1929): 281–294.

THESES, DISSERTATIONS, AND UNPUBLISHED WORKS

Abernethy, Francis E. "The Eyes of Father Margil." Unpublished paper presented in 1989 at Stephen F. Austin State University, Nacogdoches, Texas.

Chabot, Frederick C. "The Powerful Aguayos." Unpublished paper presented in 1929 at the Thirty-second Annual Meeting of the Texas State Historical Association, Austin.

Faulk, Odie B. "Texas during the Administration of Governor Domingo Cabello y Robles, 1778–1786." Master's thesis, Texas Technological College, 1960.

Hollingsworth, Ann P. "Pedro de Moctezuma and His Descendants, 1521–1718." Ph.D. diss., University of North Texas, 1980.

John, Elizabeth A. H. "Spanish Relations with the *Indios Bárbaros* on the Northern-most Frontier of New Spain in the Eighteenth Century." Ph.D. diss., University of Oklahoma, 1957.

Klier, Betje B. "Théodore Pavie." Unpublished manuscript in possession of the author.

Krieger, Alex D. "Un nuevo estudio de la ruta seguida por Cabeza de Vaca a través de Norte América." Ph.D. diss., Universidad Nacional Autónoma de México, 1955.

Lipscomb, Carol A. "'Sorrow Whispers in the Winds': The Republic of Texas's Comanche Indian Policy, 1836–1846." Master's thesis, University of North Texas, 1994.

Stuntz, Jean A. "The Persistence of Castilian Law in Frontier Texas: The Legal Status of Women." Master's thesis, University of North Texas, 1996.

Woolridge, Ruby. "The Spanish and Mexican Land Grants of Present Day Cameron County." Master's thesis. Texas A&I University, Kingsville, 1951.

INDEX